THE BOOK OF *Ballet*

THE BOOK OF

Genevieve Guillot and Germaine Prudhommeau / Trans. Katherine Carson

PRENTICE-HALL, INC., ENGLEWOOD CLIFFS, NEW JERSEY

A SPECTRUM BOOK

Ballet

Library of Congress Cataloging in Publication Data

Prudhommeau, Germaine.
    The book of ballet.

    (A Spectrum book)
    Translation of Grammaire de la danse classique.
    Edition of 1969 by G. Prudhommeau and G. Guillot.
    Includes bibliographical references and index.
    1. Ballet.   2. Ballet dancing.   I. Guillot,
Genevieve, joint author.   II. Title
GV1787.P7513   792.8'2   75-35930
ISBN 0-13-079905-X

COVER PHOTO:
Veronica Tennant as *Sleeping Beauty*;
National Ballet of Canada   (Photo by Jack Mitchell)

THE BOOK OF BALLET

Genevieve Guillot and Germaine Prudhommeau

A SPECTRUM BOOK

10 9 8 7 6 5 4 3 2 1

Printed in the United States of America

Prentice-Hall International, Inc., *London*
Prentice-Hall of Australia Pty. Limited, *Sydney*
Prentice-Hall of Canada, Ltd., *Toronto*
Prentice-Hall of India Private Limited, *New Delhi*
Prentice-Hall of Japan, Inc., *Tokyo*
Prentice-Hall of South-East Asia Private Limited, *Singapore*

Contents

INTRODUCTION   1

| **THE ELEMENTS**   7

Placement of the Foot, 8
The *Dehôrs,* 10.
Fundamental Positions, 11.
Positions of the Body, 17.
Positions of the Arms, 18.
Positions of the Head, 20.
Derivative Positions, 23.
Complex Poses, 32.

2 **THE STEPS A TERRE**   43

Nontraveling Steps, 46.
Traveling Steps, 59.
Les Pliés, 82.

3 **THE LEAPS**   93

Simple Movements, 95.
Batterie à Croisements, 131.
Batterie de Choc, 139

4 **THE TURNS**   147

Tours à terre sur Deux Pieds, 149.
Tours à Terre sur Un Pied, 156.
Tours à Terre Relevés sur Un Pied, 162.
Tours Sautés, 176.

5 **ACROBATICS**   189

6 **THE ARMS**   195

Arm Positions, 213.
Ports de Bras, 221.
Mouvements de Bras, 225.
The Hands, 240.
Mimicry, 245.

7 **EXECUTION**   251

The *Adagio,* 252.
Les Enchâinements, 288.
Series, 300.

8 **THE DANCING LESSON**   309

Lesson for Female Dancers, 313.
Lesson for Male Dancers, 356.
Lesson for Beginning Girls, 366.
Lesson for Beginning Boys, 381.
The First Dance Lesson, 390.

INDEX   400

Introduction

1

The dance is an eternal and universal art. Hardly a people exists that does not practice it in one or another of its forms. As far back as we can go in time we find it in varying states of development, and held in varying degrees of esteem, but always present.

Out of a slow elaboration over the centuries there has issued one of the purest and most beautiful forms: the classical dance.

It is not the accomplishment of one person, nor of one culture, nor of a single period. It is the result of a long evolution that, little by little, has selected those movements that are most in accord with its ideal.

2

Before establishing the grammar of the classical dance, we shall attempt to define the dance itself.

First of all, it is *movement:* it is the result of a succession of poses in time. It exists only at the very moment of its creation and leaves behind no material trace. This impossibility of leaving tangible proof of its existence may explain why the dance has been refused the place it deserved.

3

Which elements distinguish choreographic movements from all others?

They are governed by rules: they must be in *harmony* with the aesthetic of the time and place of their execution.

4

These harmonious movements are coordinated by an element related to time: *rhythm,* of whose cadence the variations are practically infinite.

5

There are harmonious and rhythmic movements that are stimulated by an outside agent: the rotation of the earth causes circles to be described around the stars about which the planets revolve in masterly rings—so perfectly harmonious that they can be defined by mathematical formulae and according to a rhythm that, albeit quite slow, is nonetheless of great regularity.

Electrical impulses provoke muscular contractions with which one might obtain movements similar to those of the dance.

We could multiply these examples, but we would be dealing only with pseudo-dances. In order for there to be a true dance, the movement must result from the *will* of the subject.

6

However, all voluntary, harmonious, and rhythmic movements do not constitute a dance: an antelope moving through a progression of leaps voluntarily executes movements that are graceful and rhythmic. But this is not a dance; it is running.

A sower wearing a sack slung over his left shoulder plunges his right hand into it then describes a broad semi-circle as he tosses the seed into the air. The dancer assuming his position at the barre makes exactly the same gesture. What then is the criterion?

It is that the sower has no concern for the beauty of his movement nor for its rhythm; he tries to scatter his seed over the widest possible area with the least effort. It is only by accident that his gesture has taken this aesthetic form and this rhythm.

The dancer, by contrast, pursues no material end; his movement exists only as a function of itself—it is its own goal.

It is the result of the movement that counts—it is its execution. An athlete who does a scissors-leap aims at reaching as high an elevation as possible. He employs this movement because he judges it to be the most suitable for realizing his plan. If another movement seemed to him preferable, he would use it. Thus it is that in athletics we have seen the scissors-leap yield to the *rouleau.* Whatever movement is involved, the thing that is necessary is to leap high.

The dancer who executes a *temps de flèche* makes about the same movement as the athlete who makes a leap. But he will not sacrifice his movement in order to gain a few centimeters. For him it is the *temps de fléche* that counts, not height, even though he may achieve the highest possible leap.

If the dance movement has no other end than itself, it may, on the other hand, serve to translate a feeling. A circle of *piqués* may express intense joy, distraction, or deep despair, but it is above all a circle of *piqués*. It is a little like a brick, which may be used to build a house or a wall or a bridge: that will be its use—not its purpose nor its cause. Similarly, the dance movement is not caused by the variation in which it is used: it already exists. The variation is its use, not its purpose.

7

In sum, we may give as a definition of the dance: deliberate, harmonious, rhythmic movements that are their own reason for being.

8

We have said that the dance is formed from a succession of poses constituting *moments of movement.*

These moments do not all have the same importance nor the same role at the heart of the movement. Two of them actually establish the movement. Two others are particular circumstances within the first two.

9

The essential moments are the principal stages of the movement, of which they somehow form the framework. Take for example a simple dance step such as the *battement à la seconde*. It includes two essential moments: the fifth and the second *à la hauteur*.

Two essential moments constitute the minimum possible for the execution of a movement: passage from one pose to another.

If the foot then returns to close in fifth, we shall have for the ensemble three essential moments: fifth, second *à la hauteur*, fifth.

The ensemble of the essential moments of a movement is both necessary and sufficient to define it.

For a given dance step, the number of essential moments is generally not very large.

10

Among the essential moments are the secondary or intermediate moments. There is no limit to their number because the smaller one considers an interval of time, the more of them one finds. Essential moments and secondary moments make up the movement.

11

The role of the secondary moments is usually unimportant. But certain ones of them are formed by a particularly harmonious combination of lines. These are the aesthetic moments.

The aesthetic moment plays a very large role in the dance. It is especially sought for the immobile poses when, at the beginning or end of a variation, there is not the rapidness of movement that requires certain positions for the sake of balance.

12

Finally, in certain steps there is a characteristic moment: this is an essential moment whose combination of lines is found in no other step. It is sufficient in itself for identifying this step. It is very valuable for those who study the reproduction of the movement. For example: the characteristic moment of an *entrechat* (Fig. 49).

13

We have defined the word "dance" and seen the moments of the movement. We shall now move on into the systematic study of the steps of the classical dance by establishing a logical order progressing from the simplest to the most complex and by seeking out the fundamental components of each family of steps.

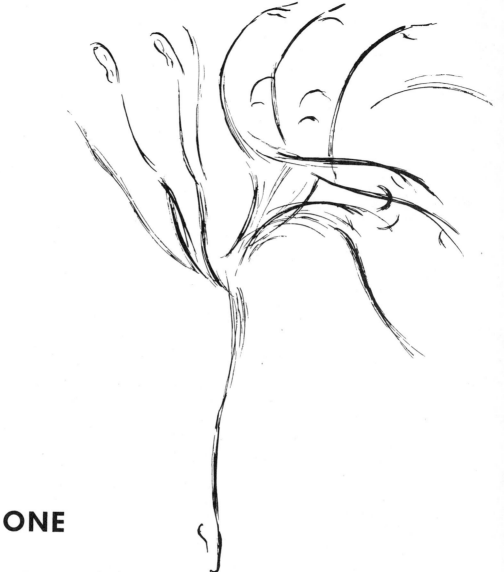

ONE

The Elements

14

The dance, as we said in the Introduction, is a succession of movements produced by the *enchaînement*, or serial arrangement, of poses formed by the combining of positions of the various parts of the human body.

We shall begin by studying the positions that the component parts of the human body can assume: the legs, the trunk or torso, the arms, and the head; the feet are studied with the legs, the hands with the arms. Afterward, we shall analyze two complex poses that form an entity and are used as such in dance steps.

First, we must define two fundamental notions: the *assiette du pied* and the *dehors*.

PLACEMENT OF THE FOOT*

15

The manner in which the foot rests on the floor is known as the **assiette du pied**. Three *assiettes* are recognized, distinguishable one from another by the portion of the foot that is in contact with the floor.

- *A plat*: The entire sole of the foot rests on the floor.
- *Sur la demi-pointe*: The joints of the toes rest on the floor.
- *Sur la pointe*: The tips of several toes (three, generally) rest on the floor.

8   *Assiette du pied.

The fourth *assiette du pied*, in which the heel alone rests on the floor, does not exist in pure classical dance but is used in *danses de caractère*, or folk dances.

16

The **assiette à plat** is very common. It is the largest polygon of support the foot can provide. Normal for a dancer at rest, it is the starting position for dance steps and occurs frequently in the course of the dance.

17

The **demi-pointe** (Fig. 1a) represents a lightening of the preceding *assiette*. The classical dance, in its quest for an effect of lightness, has a tendency to reduce contact with the floor. Often employed in the seventeenth and eighteenth centuries, the *demi-pointe* has now been supplanted by the *pointe* among female dancers, but continues to be utilized by male dancers, as well as in exercises and in the course of certain steps.

Figure 1. a, *demi-pointe*
b, oblique *pointe*
c, classical *pointe*
d, neoclassical *pointe*

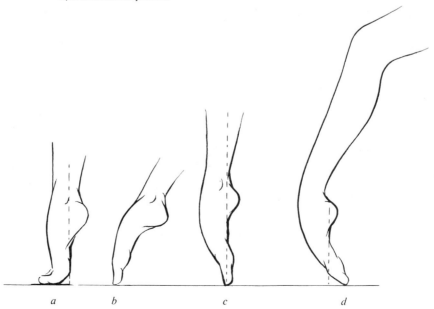

a   b   c   d

18

The **pointe** (Fig. 1c) has the least possible amount of surface contact. A recent acquisition of our classical dance, it seems to have originated from a dual effort: to achieve a feeling of lightness by reducing the polygon of support and to eliminate angles. Notice, in fact, that in the *demi-pointe,* especially when it is very high (Fig. 1a), the toes form a right angle with the instep. Being of a linear, and not an angular aesthetic nature, classical dance tends to do away with all angles and replace them with supple lines.

When the foot rises on the toe, it no longer presents an angle.

Tradition attributes the discovery of *pointes* to Marie Taglioni (1804-1884) in about 1826; other dancers—Avdotia Istomina (1799-1848) and Amalia Brugnoli (who danced in Vienna in 1823), etc.—probably also rose *sur les pointes* during the same period or a little earlier. It is entirely possible that the normal tendency of the classical dance toward the *pointe* may have brought about its discovery simultaneously in several locations.

Oblique at first (Fig. 1b), as is evidenced by the padding in the slippers of the period, the *pointe* rose progressively until it became completely vertical. It is impossible to remain on a *pointe* that is oblique; the dancer would immediately pitch forward and fall. Only the vertical *pointe* permits sufficient force for rising, standing, leaping, etc.

Dancing on the tips of the toes is now inseparable from the idea we have come to have of the classical female dancer.

The neoclassical reform carries *pointes* still farther and has the toes resting on the toenails (Fig. 1d).

THE DEHORS*

19

One of the essential principles of the classical dance is the **dehors**, or turn-out.

The inner side of the leg and the foot must be presented to the spectator; that is, the leg must rotate 90 degrees outwardly from its normal position.

The position of the leg *en dehors* is contrary to nature. It necessitates constant training from a very early age and laborious exercises to force it.

10   *Literally, outside; *en dehors* means going outward from the body.

If the leg is raised to the side in a normal position, the hip rises at the same time, producing an ungraceful hump. If, on the contrary, the leg is *en dehors*, the hip is lowered and the line of the body is perfect.

If the leg is kept in this position while descending, the dancer will have assumed, once the foot has been placed, a position that we shall define later as a *seconde en dehors*.

20

Starting from the second position, the *dehors* is imposed progressively upon all the positions, becoming more and more rigorous. It is now such an integral part of the classical dance that we have been able to reintroduce the normal positions in association with the neoclassical, and even as a part of it, into the contemporary dance vocabulary.

The classical dance is not alone in imposing the *dehors* upon its performers: certain Middle and Far Eastern dances make constant use of it, in particular those of India, Cambodia, China, and Japan.

FUNDAMENTAL POSITIONS

21

We have already used the term "position" repeatedly in a general sense, because it can be applied to any part of the body.

In the classical dance the word means: "a placement of the legs with both feet resting on the floor (*à plat*)." To describe this we shall use the expression **basic position**.

There are five of these basic positions; they form the foundation not only of the dance but of all movements of the legs.

The strictness of the law of the *dehors* in the classical dance led the neoclassics to add two more positions, bringing the total to seven. But the latter two are merely "normal" variations of basic positions already known.

We are going to study each of the five basic positions in detail.

22

In the **first position** (Fig. 2), the heels are touching. The position is "normal" if the feet are in contact from heel to toe; it becomes more and more *en dehors* as the feet are opened out, until the *dehors* is reached, when the feet are in a straight line.

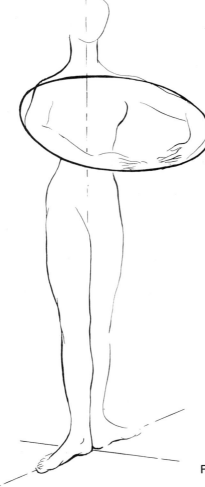

Figure 2. First position

23

The neoclassics call the first "normal" position, "**sixth position**," reserving the name of "first" for the position *en dehors*.

24

The **second position** (Fig. 3) is a common one. It is a well-balanced position, with the feet spread apart laterally, to each side, to augment

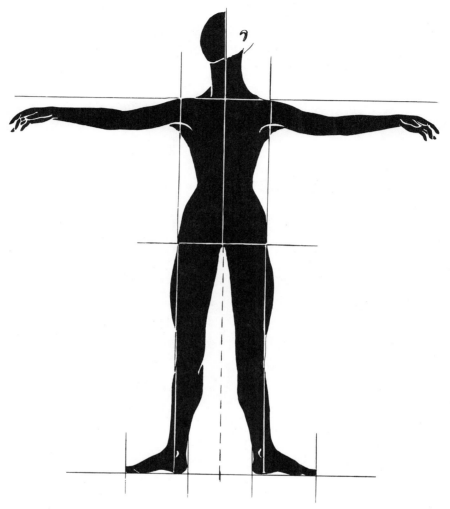

Figure 3. Second position

the polygon of support. The wider they are spread apart, the more easily they are placed *en dehors*. The classical rule sets the separation at the length of one foot.

25

In the **third position** (Fig. 4), the heel of one foot is placed at the middle of the other foot. It is intermediate between first and fifth position. For this reason it has been almost totally abandoned today in

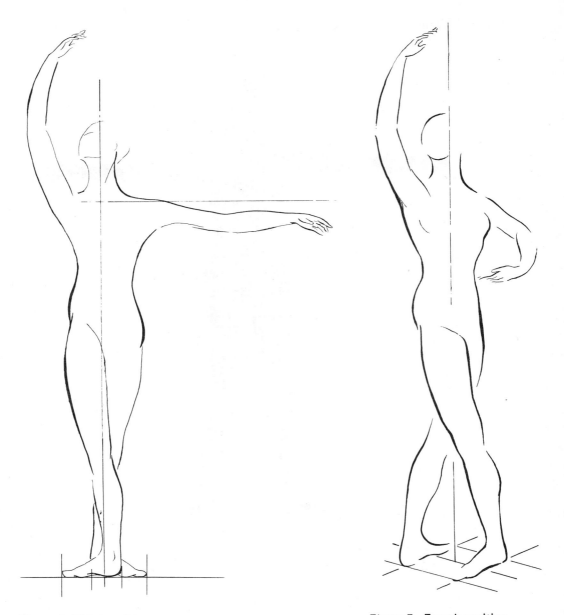

Figure 4. Third position

Figure 5. Fourth position

favor of the fifth. It is not a natural position, and the crossing of the feet reduces the balance.

This position is useful, however, in exercises for beginners who might not be able to achieve the fifth position correctly.

26

The **fourth position** (Fig. 5) is natural and balanced. It is based on the same principle as the second: the separation of the feet. But while in the second position this separation was lateral, in the fourth it is forward, which assures a still firmer footing. In the classical dance it often serves as a preparation for turns and at the end of circular movements that are too rapid to be finished in fifth position. As in the second position, the separation must be the length of a foot.

27

The neoclassics have given the name of **seventh position** to the fourth "normal" one, but they rarely take it *à plat* and generally rise in this position on the toes, which are almost always curved, until they rest on the toenails (Fig. 1d).

28

There are two intermediate positions, the **quatrième ouverte** (open) and the **quatrième croisée** (crossed). The first of these is intermediate between the second and fourth. The *quatrième croisée* is taken with legs crossed, as the name indicates, but without the thighs touching.

29

The **fifth position** (Fig. 6), with the toes of each foot against the heel of the other, is a forced position. Used constantly today in the classical dance, it is the starting position for almost all steps.

30

The **position de départ** (starting position) of a natural movement is the first position. In gymnastics, for example, one starts out "heels together, toes apart." The *dehors*, which at an early date became a rule of the classical dance, has the tips of the toes completely separated. The two feet are on the same line, forming a long, narrow, rectangular polygon of support. Balance is therefore difficult.

By crossing the feet in third position, we achieve a better balance; this was the *position de départ* for classical steps until the nineteenth century.

The concern among dancers to emulate and to outstrip one another has led to a progressive tightening of the third position into the fifth, which has become the contemporary *position de départ* (Fig. 7).

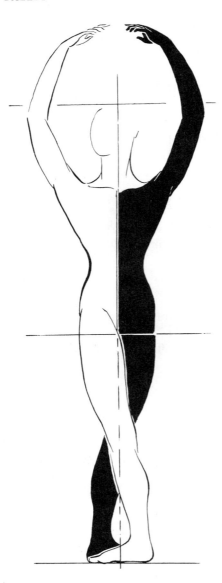

Figure 6. Fifth position

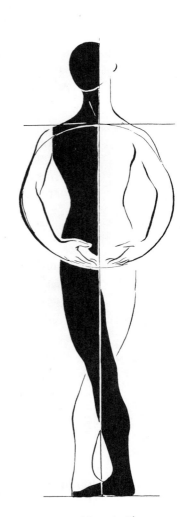

Figure 7. *Position de départ*

It may be noted that at the end of the nineteenth century, although all the manuals specified that dance steps were to begin in the fifth position, the first photographs show scarcely any position but the third.

POSITIONS OF THE BODY

31

The **corps de face** (body facing forward) is the most common position in human life. It is used just as frequently in the dance.

32

The **épaulé** (literally, "shouldered") is the second position of the body. It is produced by twisting the trunk on the hips in a direction that, in principle, makes a right angle with the legs. Actually, there are intermediate stages all the way from 0 to 90 degrees. In the pure classical dance, the body is always rotated toward the rear leg. But folk dances and the modern vocabulary also make use of an *épaulé* that is directed toward the front leg.

33

The **corps penché de côté** (body leaning sideways) is a less usual position. It is very difficult to execute. Seldom used on the stage, it is only employed in certain subtle turns (*pirouettes à deux*) when the male dancer intercepts the female dancer by grasping her by the waist.

The *penché de côté* may accompany the *épaulé* in certain folk dances.

34

The **corps penché en avant** (body leaning forward) is often employed. We use it in bows and with certain steps.

It should be noted that there are two kinds of *penché en avant*. The first, which is never very accentuated, is produced by curving the spinal column above the pelvis, which remains vertical; only the thoracic cage is bent. This is what is familiarly known as the *dos rond* (rounded back).

The second *penché en avant*, which can actually bring the trunk the full length of the legs, with the head down, is achieved by bending at the hips. Only the legs remain vertical; the trunk pivots as one unit.

These two types of *penché* are generally used in combination.

35

The **corps penché en arrière** (body leaning backwards) or *cambré* (arched) has become a movement of grace and difficulty in the classical dance. It is used more frequently than one might suppose. Normally, it is found at the end of certain *pirouettes* in the very classical ballets such as *Swan Lake* (choreography by M. Petipa and L. Ivanoff), in folkloric variations such as *Petrouchka* (choreography by Fokine), and in modern choreographies such as *Miracle in the Gorbals* (choreography by R. Helpmann).

36

The **ensellé**, which we shall group with the positions of the body (although, strictly speaking, it is not one of them), is attained by making the back hollow and thrusting the hips forward. Highly regarded in certain countries (e.g., in Africa, and among the comic characters of the ancient Greek stage), this position is formally forbidden in the classical dance (Fig. 103).

POSITIONS OF THE ARMS

37

The classical dance defines five positions of the arms, at times chosen arbitrarily, in addition to a position for rest or for starting.

38

Position de départ: arms low in front of the body, slightly raised and barely touching the dancer's skirt, palms in the air, thumbs turned inward, fingers supple. The two arms trace an ellipse (Fig. 7).

This is used as a starting position for most steps, particularly for those opening in fifth position. It is also the rest position—the one that can be assumed when the dancer is not moving.

39

First position (Fig. 2): arms extended forward horizontally. This position is reached from the preceding one by raising the arms until the hands are at the level of the chest; the hands are kept carefully curved. The shoulders must remain low.

The first step is rarely used for its own sake, but it serves as an intermediate stage in numerous *ports de bras* (movements of the arms).

40

Second position (Fig. 3): arms to the sides, horizontally; elbows raised, slightly bent; hands extending from the arms, palms forward, bent slightly inward, below shoulder level.

This position accompanies quite naturally the second position of the legs and certain movements developing from a second position.

41

Third position (Fig. 4): one arm vertical, slightly bent; the other as in second position.

The upraised arm forms a sort of frame around the head. The hand is in a vertical plane slightly in front of the body. Holding the head erect, the dancer can just see the tips of his fingers when he raises his eyes as much as possible.

This arm position is also called *bras d'attitude* because it normally accompanies the posture known as *attitude* (§ 82).

42

Fourth position (Fig. 5): one arm vertical, the other bent in front of the body.

The vertical arm is held as in third position.

The arm in front of the body is in a position much like that of first position, but a little more bent. The hand must not extend beyond the middle of the chest.

43

Fifth position, or *bras en couronne* (arms in a circle) (Fig. 6): the two arms, raised vertically, frame the head slightly in front of the plane of the face (§ 516); the hands are not completely joined.

44

The classical vocabulary recognizes only these positions, but for the convenience of this study, we shall define a **sixth position**, to which we shall refer each time it is used—which is quite often: one arm is laterally horizontal (as in second position); the other is curved toward the front of the body, the hand reaching as far as the middle of the chest, as in fourth position (Fig. 8).

Figure 8. Sixth position of the arms

POSITIONS OF THE HEAD

45

In the classical dance, the positions are seldom used in their pure form. The head is almost always in a moment of transition, which results in a combination of positions.

In this section we shall define only the fundamental positions; the movements accompanying the dance steps will be described with the steps themselves.

46

The **tête de face** (face toward the front) is normal in daily life. In the classical dance it is taken with the shoulders low and the chin slightly raised in such a way as to define clearly the line of the neck.

It was highly regarded in the seventeenth century for the *entrées*—the initial entrances—of the ballets.

47

The **profil** (profile) is achieved by turning the head to the right or to the left.

Most often a partial profile is used. The complete profile is found in folk dances (*Prince Igor*, choreography by Fokine) or when certain artistic or aesthetic effects are sought, as in *Symphonie Concertante* (choreography by M. Descombey).

At the present time the profile is frequently used for numerous steps.

48

The **tête penchée de côté** (head bent sideways) is practically never used in pure classical dance. It may serve to arouse, in the spectator, certain special impressions: awkwardness, in *Petrouchka* (choreography by Fokine); the marionnette, in *Guignol et Pandore* (choreography by S. Lifar); coquetry, in *La Korrigane*, (choreography by L. Mérante); and the like.

49

The **tête penchée en avant** (head bent forward) has various uses.

In pure classical dance, it serves as a starting position for numerous movements, or even to accentuate the position that will follow—usually a *tête de face* or a profile.

It can express a vareity of things:

• *The curtsy* (whether to the audience or to another personage): Sylvia before Diane, in the third act of *Sylvia* (choreography after L. Mérante);

• *Shame*: *Guignol et Pandore*;

• *Tears*: Swanilda teased by Franz, in the first act of *Coppélia* (choreography after Saint-Léon);

• *Fear*: Snow-White before the hunter, in the second tableau of the first act of *Blanche-Neige* (choreography by Lifar);

• *Humility*: Giselle before the queen of the Wilis, in the second act of *Giselle* (choreography after J. Perrot and J. Coralli);

• *The dancer's bow* (Fig. 9); and the like.

Figure 9

50

The **tête penchée en avant** can be combined with the **profil**.

This position is found frequently at the beginning of an adagio or of a romantic variation. It, too, can express a variety of sentiments.

51

The **tête penchée en arrière** (head bent backward), which is utilized in a certain number of exercises involving a *cambré* (arch), is seldom used on the stage. It can, however, be found at the end of turns concluding with the partner's back to the audience, in a *cambré* (the adagio from *Mirages*, choreography by Lifar), and with certain special expressions— for example, Helen's variation, gazing at herself in the looking-glass (ballet from *Faust*, choreography by A. Aveline).

22

52

The **tête de profil penchée en arrière** (head in profile bent backward) is found at the conclusion of certain steps. Infrequently used in the ballet, it is found occasionally in stylized dances: the warriors in *Créatures de Prométhée* (choreography by Lifar), the Greek dances in *Daphnis et Chloé* (choreography by Fokine), and the like.

DERIVATIVE POSITIONS

53

In the basic positions we have already studied, both feet remain flat on the floor. The *derivative positions* are those in which only one foot is flat. The other foot can be either *sur la demi-pointe* or in the air. The free leg—that is, the one that does not support the weight of the body—can be held straight or bent, at a fairly good height.

Demi-positions (half-positions) are those in which the free foot touches the floor; **positions dérivées** (derivative positions) are those in which the leg in the air is held straight; **raccourcis** are those in which the leg in the air is bent.

It should be stressed that we are speaking of positions—that is, of elements making up the poses whose combinations (*enchaînment*) produce movement. It is possible for these positions to be taken by a character who is not in motion, but they will occur most often when an action is in progress.

54

The **demi-première** (Fig. 12b): one foot is flat; the other, *sur la pointe*, is placed laterally against the heel of the first. In classical dance, this seldom-used position uses the *dehors* to bring the sole of the foot that is *sur la pointe* alongside the other leg.

By extension, the term *demi-première* is used to designate any position in which the toe of one foot is brought alongside the other, which itself remains *à plat*. By "alongside" we mean in a lateral radius the length of the foot.

55

The **demi-seconde** is much more popular than the *demi-première*. It is a movement in which one foot is *à la pointe* (Fig. 10). It is an essential moment in a great number of steps.

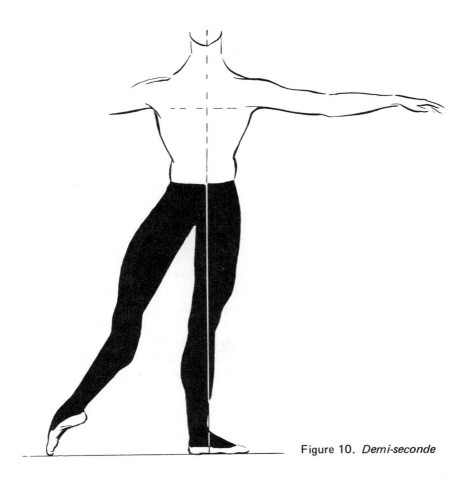

Figure 10. *Demi-seconde*

56

The **demi-troisième** is used a great deal. One of the feet is *à la pointe* before or behind the middle of the other foot, which remains flat.

In practice, we shall consider as *demi-troisième* every position in which one foot is placed *à la pointe* immediately behind or in front of the other foot, which remains *à plat* (Fig. 12c).

In the classical ballets, the female dancers at rest on the stage often adopt this position. For this reason, it is the demi-position most frequently used when the dancer is immobile. Aside from this, it is also the essential moment in, for example, the step known as *bourrée*.

57

The **demi-quatrième** (Fig. 11) is the most frequently used of the demi-positions. It is a position in which one foot is *sur la pointe*, either forward (*devant*) or backward (*derrière*); rarely employed when the dancer is immobile, this position is the essential moment of a very large number of steps—*dégagés en quatrième, marche, départ de détournés*, and the like.

58

The **demi-cinquième**: one foot is *à la pointe* against the toe of the other foot, which is flat, *en dehors*, either before or behind it. By extension, we shall designate as *demi-cinquième* those demi-positions in which one foot is *à la pointe* before or behind the other foot, which is *croisé*

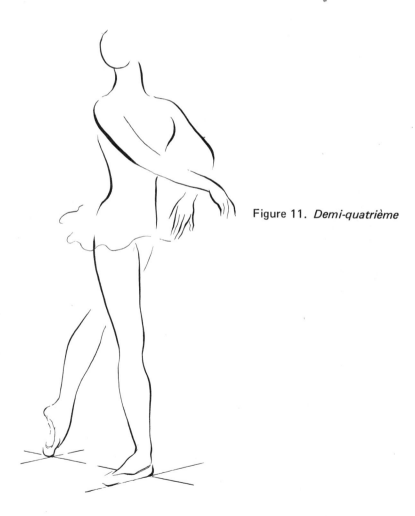

Figure 11. *Demi-quatrième*

(crossed)—that is, when the foot is *en dehors* and past the middle of the foot which is *à la pointe* or when the foot is *en dedans* and past the middle of the other foot (Fig. 12a).

59

After these demi-positions, we shall study the derivative positions that are properly so-called—that is, those in which one leg is raised outstretched. The names of these positions correspond to the general directions implied by the names of the basic positions. Specifically, these are: *seconde*, for everything lateral; *quatrième*, for everything forward or backward. Added to these are the complementary directions of the *quatrième ouverte* (Fig. 14c) and the *quatrième croisé* (Fig. 14a), corresponding to the basic positions of that name (§ 28).

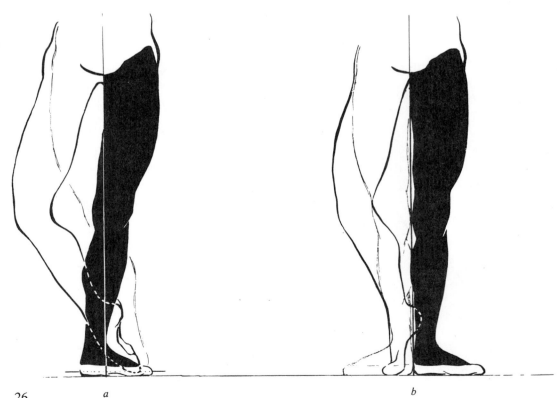

a   *b*

60

When the line passing horizontally through the free foot (the foot in the air) intercepts the supporting leg at mid-calf or below that point, the position is said to be **à la demi-hauteur** (at half-height). All derivative positions can be taken *à la demi-hauteur* (Fig. 13b).

61

When the line passing horizontally through the free foot intercepts the supporting leg at a point above the mid-calf, the position is said to be **à la hauteur**. Normally this will be a horizontal position (Fig. 13c).

The present tendency is to raise the free leg as high as possible, forming an obtuse angle—sometimes quite wide (more than 135 degrees)—with the supporting leg.

Positions *à la hauteur* are more difficult to sustain than those *à la demi-hauteur*.

Figure 12. a, *demi-cinquième*
b, *demi-première*
c, *demi-troisième*

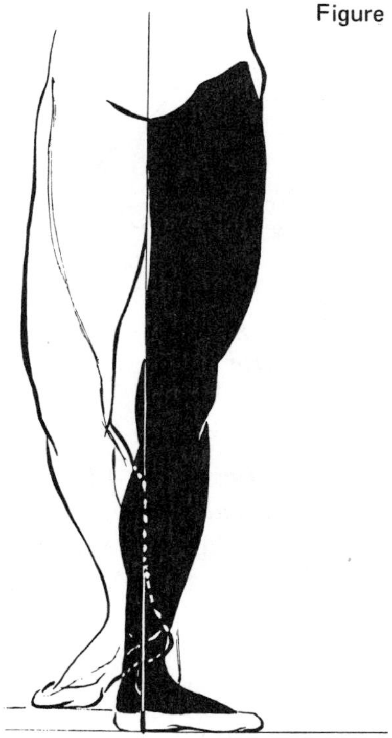

c

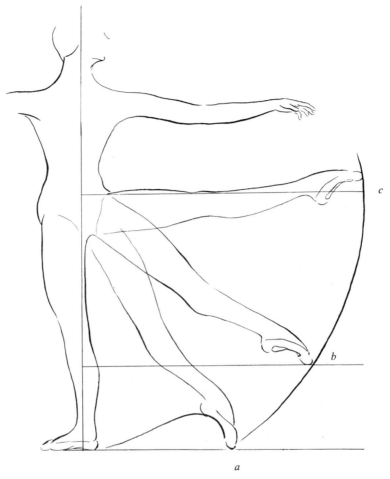

Figure 13. a, *demi-seconde*
          b, *seconde à la demi-hauteur*
          c, *seconde à la hauteur*

62

The **derivative second positions** (Fig. 13b and c) are executed with a leg outstretched laterally *à la hauteur* or *à demi-hauteur*. They serve as the essential moments in a considerable number of steps: *battements* (§ 112), *grands ronds de jambe* (§ 126), *développés* (§ 129), *fouettés* (§ 130), and the like.

63

The **derivative fourth positions** are divided into two groups: the *quatrième devant* (forward fourth) (Fig. 14b) and the *quatrième derrière* (backward fourth).

With a fourth *croisée* (Fig. 14a), the arms are generally placed in third position (§ 41), the raised arm corresponding to the supporting leg. The body is *épaulé* (twisted forward) toward the free leg, and the head is turned to the side in the direction of the free leg.

For a *quatrième ouverte* (open fourth), the positions of the body and the arms are much the same, but the direction changes with relation to the audience, and the head is turned toward the side of the supporting leg (Fig. 14c).

Figure 14. *Quatrième devant à la hauteur*
        a, *croisée*
        b, *normale*
        c, *ouverte*

a

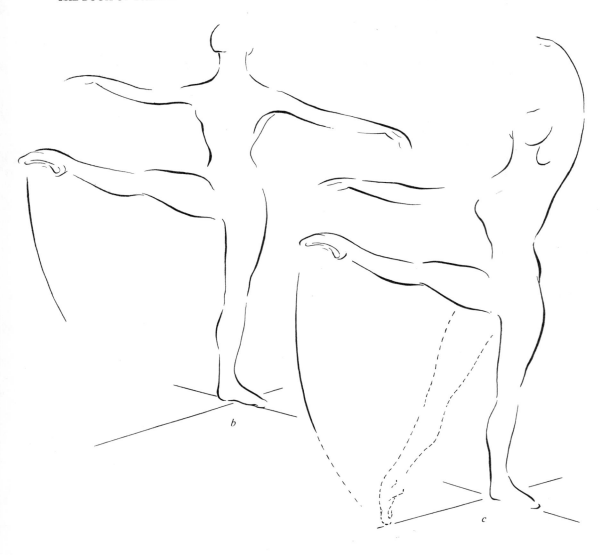

A *quatrième ouverte* in which the *épaulement* ("shouldering") is directed toward the supporting leg, with the arm corresponding to the free leg lifted, is a *quatrième effacée* (Fig. 15), sometimes incorrectly called a *seconde effacée*.

The *quatrième derrière ouverte* is intermediate between the *quatrième derrière* and the second.

Figure 15. *Quatrième effacée*

These are the derivative positions most often employed. They may be used when the dancer is in repose and are the essential moments in an even greater number of steps than are the derivative seconds.

64

A derivative position with the leg bent in the air is a **raccourci** ("shortening").

Raccourcis are characterized as *quatrième devant, à la seconde* (Fig. 16), and *quatrième derrière*, according to the direction of the leg.

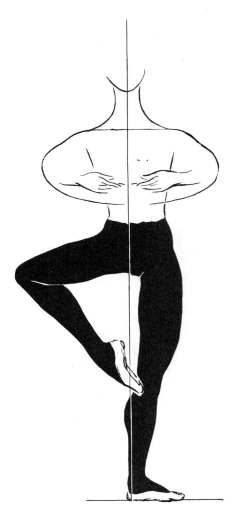

Figure 16. *Raccourci à la seconde*

This is a position that is as much used for its own sake as for when it is the essential moment in numerous steps.

Certain schools say *attitude devant* for *raccourci en quatrième devant*.

COMPLEX POSES

65

Thus far we have studied those positions that are concerned with only one element of the body. To these the classical dance adds **complex** poses formed by combining positions of the various parts of the body. Their names reflect the leg positions involved.

66

Although the terms *quatrième derrière à la hauteur* and *raccourci en quatrième derrière* are not altogether uncommon, it is absolutely impossible to establish a definition that would differentiate them from the terms *arabesque* and *attitude*.

67

The **arabesque** is a pose in which one leg is raised outstretched straight behind the body, and one arm is extended forward.

68

We distinguish **four classical arabesques**, according to whether the arm extended forward corresponds to the leg raised backward, and whether the raised leg is on the side toward the audience or away from it.

In reality there are only two different poses. There seem to be four simply because each can be seen by the spectator from two sides. In a round theatre, only two *arabesques* can be distinguished.

69

Arabesque ouverte: the leg on the side toward the audience is raised outstretched *au quatrième derrière* (behind the body); the supporting leg is taut; the body faces front, slightly *épaulé* (shoulder twisted forward) toward the leg in the air and leans forward very slightly; the head faces forward, leaning slightly backward, with the attention directed toward the forward hand; the arm on the side of the supporting leg is stretched forward horizontally, the palm facing down; the other arm is extended backward. The two arms form a straight line that rises slightly to the front (Fig. 17).

It should be recalled that because the classical dance is of a linear nature, angles are to be avoided (including the straight line, which is actually a straight angle). Therefore, when we speak of an extended arm it does not mean that the arm is perfectly straight.

70

Arabesque ouverte à bras croisé: same position for the legs; the body faces forward; the head is in almost the same position, slightly turned

Figure 17. *Arabesque ouverte*

toward the forward hand; the arms have the same symmetry as in the
preceding position, but the forward arm is on the same side as the
raised leg (Fig. 18).

71

Arabesque croisée: the supporting leg is on the side toward the
audience. The positions are exactly the same as for the open *arabesque*,
except that the head is turned a little more to the side of the forward
arm.

72

Arabesque croisée à bras ouvert: same position for the legs; the body
faces forward, with the head in the same position; the arm on the side
of the raised leg is in front, the other arm is a little less toward the rear
than in the other three arabesques.

Figure 18. *Arabesque ouverte à bras croisés*

73

The terms *arabesque ouverte* and *arabesque croisée* are part of a language that is current in classical dance; the expressions *arabesque ouverte à bras croisé* and *arabesque croisée à bras ouvert* are not in use, but they are the only logical terms in which to define these positions.

74

We have not stipulated the height to which the rear leg is raised. Classical doctrine in the nineteenth century and at the beginning of the twentieth held that it should be horizontal, making a 90-degree angle with the supporting leg. In 1931, Antonine Meunier[1] wrote: "In the

[1] Antonine Meunier: *La Danse classique* (Ecole francaise). Firmin Didot, 1931.

arabesque one of the legs is extended perpendicular to the floor, the other leg is raised *en quatriéme derriére* [leg outstretched behind the body], at the height of the hip."

But by virtue of the constant tendency to excel or surpass, the leg is now raised higher and higher. In 1949, Serge Lifar wrote in his *Traité de Danse académique*: "The whole weight of the body rests on one leg, the other is extended backward, quite straight at the knee, with an opening of at least 90 degrees."[2]

Finally, in 1950, Lycette Darsonval wrote, in some documents later to be elaborated upon in the *Dictionnaire d'Esthétique,* that the free leg must be "raised to the maximum behind the body."

In less than twenty years we see a clearly marked difference.

If the free leg is raised *à la demi-hauteur*, we will have a **demi-arabesque**.

75

In the different types of *arabesques*, variations can be introduced by **modifying the position of the arms**. Most often it is with the open arabesque that these modifications are found. The most frequently used variations are as follows: both arms extended forward, one a little higher than the other; both arms raised, wide apart, palms forward; the forward arm bent back in front of the body; and the like.

A particular search for expression may lead choreographers to create arm positions that are quite varied: in the second act of *Giselle*, Giselle makes an *arabesque* with her hands clasped in a gesture of prayer.

76

The knee of the supporting leg can be bent (**plier**) in different types of *arabesques*, occasionally with a special significance: for example, *Istar* (choreography by Lifar).

77

The body can be **penché en avant** (leaning forward). The rear leg then rises in such a way that the line formed by the leg, the trunk, the head, and eventually the arm, is capable of holding its shape, while at the same time rocking on the horizontal axis of the hips.

[2] Serge Lifar: *Traité de Danse académique*. Bordas, 1949, p. 82.

78

The neoclassical technique has been enriched by two new *arabesques*, which are obtained by a shifting of the axis[3] and which can only be executed with a partner or with the aid of props. In practice they are done only *sur la pointe*.

In the **arabesque étirée** (drawn-out *arabesque*), the supporting leg is obliquely behind the body. The free leg rises very high, almost *en grand écart* (widely separated, as in a split).

This *arabesque* is much used in the contemporary ballets (*Pas de Dieux*, choreography by Gene Kelly; *La Symphonie Concertante*, choreography by Michel Descombey).

79

The **arabesque poussée** ("pushed") is obtained by shifting the axis forward. Most often the female dancer in this position is held at the waist by her partner. The angle of the two legs is reduced to less than 90 degrees because of the slant of the supporting leg.

This arabesque is used less frequently than the preceding ones.

80

Very little is known of the **historical origin** of the word *arabesque* as it concerns the dance. From the writings of Carlo Blasis, at the beginning of the nineteenth century, it would indeed appear that the term hand not yet acquired its present meaning:

Arabesque ornaments, in painting, are ornaments composed of plants, bushes, slender branches and flowers, with which painters enrich compartments, panels, friezes, etc. In architecture, they are leaf-work, stalks with which pediments and copying are often embellished. The taste for these ornaments comes to us from the Moors and Arabs, whose name they have retained.

Dancing masters also introduced this term in their art to express picturesque groups composed of male and female dancers, intertwined in a thousand different ways by means of garlands, rings, hoops surrounded with flowers and occasionally antique rustic instruments which they hold in their hands. These attitudes—enchanting and thus diversified—recall for us those delicious bacchanales one sees on ancient bas-reliefs, and by their airy lightness, their variety, their charm and the numerous contrasts they successively present, they have somehow made the word *arabesque* natural and proper to the dance. I can flatter myself for having been the first to have given the precise explanation for this expression as it is applied to our art, an

---

[3] *See* Serge Lifar: *Traité de Danse académique*. Bordas, 1949.

explanation without which this word would seem a mockery of the one employed originally by painters and architects, and which used to belong to them exclusively."[4]

Thus, at the beginning of the nineteenth century, the word *arabesque* was popularly used in the dance in a linear sense: it designated either the sinuous movements of dancers performing the *farandole* or artistic groupings. This meaning is borrowed directly from the vocabulary of the plastic arts, as Blassis himself states.

One might suppose that as certain of these lines were followed by dancers taking the pose that later would be called *arabesque*, the term passed from the whole to the part, through a shift of meaning, examples of which are not unusual in linguistics.

81

Attitude is a pose in which one leg is raised *au raccourci en quatrième derrière*—the knee bent behind the body, with the body held straight. We distinguish two classical *attitudes*.

82

In *attitude ouverte* (Fig. 19b), the leg on the side nearer the audience is raised behind the body, with the hip horizontal to the trunk and the lower part of the leg bent backward on the same horizontal plane, forming a 90-degree angle with the hip, the toe firmly outstretched. The body is facing front, with the head more or less in profile on the side of the raised arm and looking slightly backward. The arms are in third position (§ 41), with the raised arm on the side of the raised leg.

83

For **attitude croisée**, the supporting leg is on the side nearer the audience (Fig. 19a). Only the position of the head is different: it can be in profile toward the horizontal arm so that the dancer can face the audience.

84

Certain schools, the Russian in particular, do not bend the working knee as much. The angle formed by the hip and the bottom of the leg is then obtuse (Fig. 19c).

[4] Cited by Serge Lifar: *Traité de Danse académique*, p. 76.

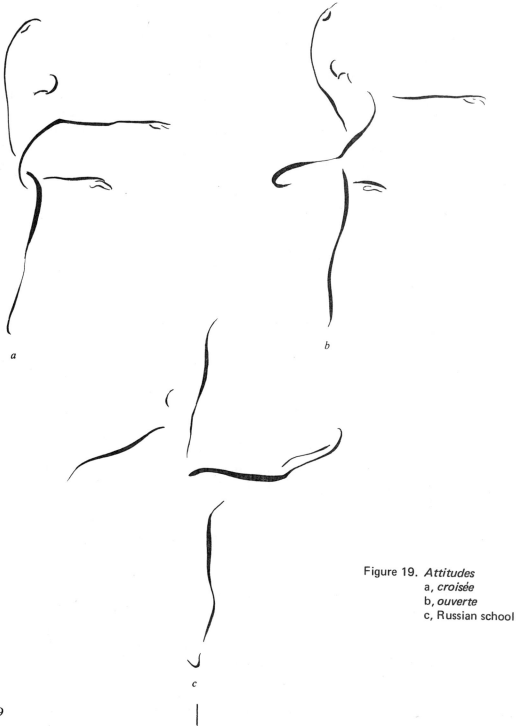

Figure 19. *Attitudes*
a, *croisée*
b, *ouverte*
c, Russian school

85

There are only a few classical **variations** on *attitude*. These are obtained solely by varying the arm positions.

One can find, for example: the reversal of the position of the arms, the raised arm corresponding to the supporting leg; this pose will be found most especially before turns *en dedans* (in a direction leading toward the dancer's body). The arms in fourth position (§ 42), the raised arm corresponding to the raised leg; this pose is used in ballets in the style of the eighteenth century. The hands on the hips, as in the first act of *Coppélia* (choreography after Saint-Léon), and the like.

86

One could define a **demi-attitude** in which the hip of the free leg would be lower than the horizontal plane. The term is not in common use; the pose occurs in certain folk dances: the *Danses polovtsiennes du Prince Igor* (Fokine).*

87

As in the *arabesque*, the supporting leg can be bent in different *attitudes*.

By shifting the center of balance, *attitudes étirées* ("drawn-out") or *poussées* ("pushed") can also be formed in the neoclassical ballets.

88

Classical tradition has it that the pose was invented by Carlo Blasis, after the *Mercury* of Giovanni da Bologna (1534-1608). It may be that Blasis introduced it into the classical vocabulary, but it was well known before that, since the Greeks, for example, used it a great deal two thousand years ago in forms quite akin to our own.

89

The **quatrième effacée** (set-back fourth) is executed with one leg raised forward in the *quatrième ouverte* position; the body is *épaulé* on the side of the supporting leg; the arms are in third (§ 41), with the raised arm a little more open and the forearm and hand turned slightly more to the back; the head is in profile on the side of the raised arm, leaning a little toward the back (Fig. 14).

*Ed. note: Parenthesized names from this point on will indicate the choreographer.

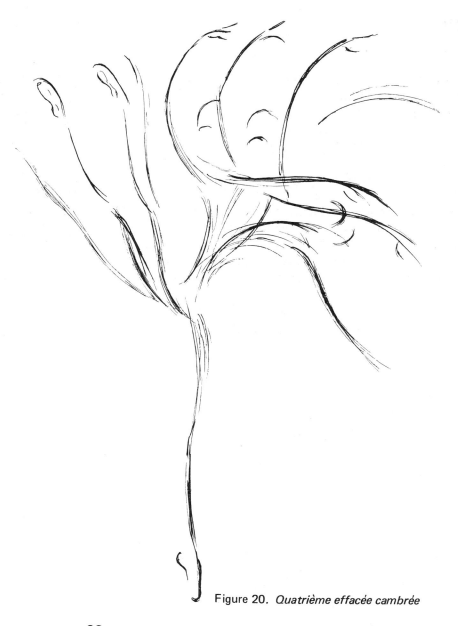

Figure 20. *Quatrième effacée cambrée*

90

The **quatrième effacée cambrée** (set-back fourth, arched) is formed from the preceding position by reversing the arms (Fig. 20) and arching the body. The head is in profile on the side of the raised arm and is looking very slightly backward.

    This pose is often taken before a traveling step such as a *marche* (walk) or a *couru* (running step).

91

In his *Traité de Danse académique*,[5] Lifar describes the **écarté en arrière** (extended position toward the back), in which one leg is raised *à la hauteur* in an intermediate position between the second position and the *quatrième derrière*; the body is *épaulé* toward the raised leg; the arms are in third, the raised arm corresponding to the working leg; and the head is in profile toward the supporting leg.

Yvette Chauvire designates *écarté à la seconde* as a pose in which the leg is vertical in second, with the body leaning slightly to the side of the supporting leg. The arms may be in third (§ 41), fourth (§ 42), or fifth (§ 43) position. The vertical arm in the first two cases corresponds to the working leg. The head may have the same position as with an *attitude* (§ 82) or the position diametrically opposed to it: somewhat in profile toward the supporting leg, looking slightly forward.

[5] Chapter VIII, § 34.

TWO

The Steps à Terre

92

With the elements we have just defined in Chapter One, we can obtain a very wide variety of poses and an infinite number of pose sequences or dance steps. We shall now try to give an idea of their complexity. We shall bypass the *dehors* (movements leading away from the dancer's body) and, consequently, the *dedans* (movements leading toward the dancer's body). Nor shall we concern ourselves with the more complex positions: for example, the *corps épaulé penché en avant* (body twisted forward). We shall take up only the classical positions of the arms. Thus, from the outset we are considerably reducing the number of possibilities.

We merely envisage the possible combinations of the positions defined. There are five basic positions of the legs, three of which can be taken with either right or left foot forward, which makes a total of eight positions. For the trunk and the head, out of the five positions, two can be taken to the right or to the left, bringing the total to seven positions. Of the five arm positions, two are asymmetrical, which brings the total to seven positions.

All the accepted derivative positions, of which there are six, may be taken with the right or the left leg, bringing the total to twelve. Finally, the three *raccourcis*, in similar fashion, yield six positions. To sum up:

- Positions of the legs: 26
- Positions of the trunk: 7
- Positions of the arms: 7
- Positions of the head: 7

93

These 47 positions can be combined in 13,284 different ways. Because each of them can be taken *à plat*, *sur la demi-pointe*, or *sur la pointe*, this gives 39,852 possibilities.

This number is considerable: a dancer who might successively take the 39,852 different **poses**, allowing two seconds for each (which is clearly not enough), would require almost a whole day (exactly 22 hours, 8 minutes, 24 seconds) to pass them in review.

94

We are concerned here only with complex poses, of the type that photographs can show us.

If we pass on to **movement**, we very quickly reach astronomical figures. Movement is actually achieved by the passage from one complex pose to another, these being the essential movements. A movement includes a minimum of two essential moments. These can be combined in 1,588,181,904 different manners—more than a billion and a half. We see right away that it is impossible to enumerate the theoretical steps of the dance.

The dancer who might pass in five seconds from one pose to another would need 250 years to execute all these simple movements.

95

In practice, very few of the steps are actually used. In the first place, certain combinations are physically incompatible; other violate the laws of balance; still others have been eliminated for aesthetic reasons. In a word, a large number remain out of use. But there is still a vast field for innovators.

All the great contemporary choreographers (Lifar, Maurice Béjart, Michel Descombey, Roland Petit, etc.) are adding new terms to the existing vocabulary.

Consider moreover the extraordinary variety of dances that, like the Hindu dance, call attention to movements of the eyes, the fingers, and so forth.

96

We shall group the dance steps in three categories: **les pas à terre** (steps executed on the ground), **les sauts** (leaps), and **les tours** (turns). We shall designate as *pas à terre* those in which the legs never leave the ground at the same time. These are subdivided into two categories: those in which at least one foot remains immobile on the ground and those in which both feet move. We shall call the first of these "nontraveling steps" and the second "traveling steps." We shall devote a separate section to *pliés* (a *plié* is a bending of the knees while both feet are on the ground).

NONTRAVELING STEPS

97

In the nontraveling steps (*pas à terre sans parcourir*) the **weight of the body** rests on one leg alone, the one whose foot remains immobile on the ground. Because the other leg is free, it can maneuver either stretched or bent, on the ground or in the air. The supporting leg can only be bent.

At the end of a step the body weight may shift from one leg to the other or be equally distributed between the two. This is not possible during a step because one cannot, without leaping, move the leg supporting the weight of the body.

98

In the classical dance the **position de depart** is the fifth. In our explanations we shall give the starting position as the fifth, with the right foot forward.

99

The most elementary nontraveling step is obtained by the **shifting of the center of balance** in the basic position. The trunk weight, supported by two legs (that is, the weight of the body being equally divided between them), passes to one leg alone. This shifting of the center of balance can be accentuated by lifting the foot that has become free *sur la demi-pointe*. This very elementary movement can be executed in second or in fourth position. It produces an on-the-spot balance.

100

Next we come to the **passage from one position to another.** Let us consider first, third, and fifth as one and the same *position de depart*.

We shall thus have the passage to the second or to the fourth, or from the second to the fourth and vice versa.

This passage is made with the foot flat on the ground. If both legs remain outstretched, the weight of the body at the end of the step is divided between the two legs, and there is a shift in the center of balance. If the supporting leg bends, it can sustain the weight of the whole body and there is no shift. These movements constitute not so much a dance step as the preparation for a step.

101

Chutes (falls) **in position** are formed by passing from one position to another while bringing the weight of the body quickly onto the working leg as soon as it becomes immobile.

102

Thus far we have studied passages from position to position with the feet flat. The passage from a position to a half-position constitutes the first true dance step: the **dégagé** (literally, disengaged). *Dégagés* are done without shifting the center of balance; the weight of the body remains constantly on the same leg; and both legs remain outstretched.

In the classical *dégagé*, the toe of the working foot must remain in contact with the ground during its movement.

Because the body is not moving, the spacing of the demi-position is limited to the distance the toe of the extended leg can reach.

103

The **dégagés à la seconde** (Fig. 21) are executed as follows: the dancer, who is in fifth position, makes one of his legs glide (*glisser*) laterally, keeping the toe in contact with the ground, until a *demi-seconde* is obtained (§ 55).

This *dégagé* can be achieved as well with the forward as with the rear foot.

104

Most often the *dégagé* is completed by a **fermeture** (closing) that brings the foot back into fifth position with a movement that is the reverse of the preceding one.

The closing may bring forward the foot that was there initially; in this case, we say that the *dégagé* does not change feet.

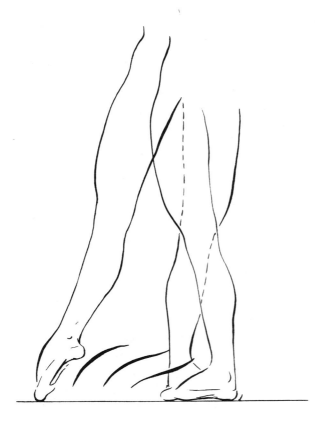

Figure 21. *Dégagé à la seconde*

If a *dégagé* begun by the forward foot changes feet, we call it a *dégagé en remontant* (*dégagé* ascending).

If a *dégagé* begun by the rear foot changes feet, we call it a *dégagé en descendant* (*dégagé* descending).

It is obvious that one cannot make several *dégagés en descendent* or *en remontant* with the same foot; *dégagés en descendent* or *en remontant* are made in sequence with alternating feet.

105

The terms **en descendent** and **en remontant** are generally applied to traveling steps. They indicate respectively a forward or backward direction.[1]

For the *dégagés* these expressions are only justified when the dancer executes a series of alternating *dégagés* with changes of feet.

[1] Theatre stages were, until recent years, constructed on a slant toward the audience, hence the use of these terms. The rehearsal halls, the *foyer de la danse*, and the stage of the *Théâtre national de l'Opéra* are thus built on an incline.

Each step causes him to advance or draw back a distance equal to the span of his foot.

Actually, in the case of the descending *dégagé* begun with right foot forward, at the end of the first step the left foot is moved forward and, serving as a support, permits the right foot to pass in front of its turn, and so on.

106

Dégagés can be done as an exercise, starting with first position.

In folk ballets and in certain modern forms, we find **dégagés avec jambe libre pliée** (*dégagés* with the working leg bent), accompanied by a shift in the center of balance—for example, *Entre deux Rondes* (Lifar).

107

The **dégagé en quatrième devant** is executed according to the general rule for *dégagés*. It is the forward foot that passes to the *demi-quatrième* (§ 57). The closing brings it back to its initial position.

108

We shall conclude with **dégagés en quatrième derrière**, executed like *dégagés en quatrième devant*, with the difference that it is the rear foot that moves.

109

The *dégagé* can also be performed in **quatrième croisée, quatrième ouverte**, and so on.

110

In the nontraveling steps performed *à terre* that we have seen thus far, the working leg moved off the ground either just barely or not at all. We shall now concern ourselves with the steps in which it is raised freely.

We shall begin with the **battements** (literally, "beatings"). There are many of these; their principle is the passage of one leg from the starting position to an accepted derivative position, with the trunk remaining immobile.

We shall first study simple *battements* that comprise three essential moments: starting position, derivative position, starting position.

111

Battements are said to be **à la hauteur** when the derivative position is *à la hauteur* (§ 61); if the derivative position is *à la demi-hauteur* (§ 60), we speak of *battements à la demi-hauteur*.

All battements can be performed *à la demi-hauteur* or *à la hauteur*. We shall not insist further on this fact nor shall we return to it; it will be sufficient to attach the terms *demi-hauteur* and *hauteur* to the names of the different types of *battements*.

112

Battements à la seconde are made by bringing the extended leg into second position at *hauteur* or *demi-hauteur*. The leg brought into the derivative position does not remain there but falls back into the starting position.

In the classical dance, with the fifth starting position, we find the same categories for *battements à la seconde* as for the *dégagés à la seconde*:

- *Battements à la seconde* with no change of feet;
- *Battements à la seconde en descendant;*
- *Battements à la seconde en remontant.*

We can also use first position (§ 22) as a starting or as an ending position.

113

Battements en quatrième devant bring the extended leg into *quatrième devant, hauteur* or *demi-hauteur*.

With fifth as the starting position, the forward leg is raised and returns to a closed position in front. These *battements* involve no change of feet.

They can be performed very high and may bring the working leg almost to a vertical position.

114

Battements en quatrième derrière bring the leg into *quatrième derrière, hauteur* or *demi-hauteur*.

The rear leg is raised and returns to a closed position in back.

The leg can hardly be raised above the horizontal if the trunk remains forward as it should be.

A **temps de cuisse** (leg movement) is the reverse of a *battement en quatrième derrière*—that is, a step in which the leg in *quatrième derrière à la hauteur* descends in fifth and rises in *quatrième derrière à la hauteur*. In general it is done in *quatrième derrière ouverte*.

115

Simple *battements* are easily executed. They are one of the basic exercises of the classical dance as of gymnastics. They constitute an element that can be combined with a very large number of complex steps.

116

Similarly, **battements can be done starting from other basic positions.** After those in fifth, it is the *battements* starting from first position that are executed most often; for beginners, it is *battements* in third.

Battements may also be done with the supporting leg *tendue* or *pliée* (outstretched or bent); they may be done *à plat, sur la demi-pointe,* or *sur la pointe*; they may be finished or begun with *pointes à terre en demi-quatrième* (§ 57) or *en demi-seconde* (§ 55).

Battements can be related to *développés* (§ 129) and *fouettés* (§ 130) when they are executed in very rapid rhythm. These are then considered as *battements* with a bending of the working leg.

117

We shall next study *battements* that necessitate the passage of the leg through several accepted derivative positions.

Battements en cloche (bell) have the following successive essential moments:

- *Position de départ*;
- *Quatrième devant à la hauteur*;
- First position;
- *Quatrième derrière à la hauteur*;
- First position;
- *Quatrième devant à la hauteur*;
- First position;
- *Quatrième derrière à la hauteur*; and so on.

The step concludes with a closing into starting position. The leg, passing constantly from *quatrième devant* to *quatrième derrière* by way of first position, imitates in its movement a bell ringing in full peal, whence the name of the step.

These *battements* are generally done in very rapid rhythm.

The *battement* is more an exercise than a true dance step.

118

Before studying the *battements arrondis* (rounded), let us define the terms *dehors* and *dedans* as applied, no longer to a position—as studied in the second section of Chapter One (the *dedans* being the opposite of the *dehors*)—but to a movement.

The **dehors** is made up of the series *quatrième devant—seconde—quatrième derrière*; that is, a clockwise direction.

The **dedans** is made up of the series *quatrième derrière—seconde—quatriéme devant;* in other words, a counterclockwise direction.

119

The **battements arrondis** leading outward and inward (*dehors* and *dedans*) are performed by proceeding from the *position de départ* through the passage of the extended leg to the accepted derivative positions in the order indicated above (§ 118), with either a return to the starting position or, if one is doing a series of *battements arrondis*, passage into first.

They may be done at *demi-hauteur* when all the derivative positions are at *demi-hauteur*, at *hauteur* if they are at *hauteur*. In this case, the second position will always be a little higher than the fourths. In general, the two fourths are at *demi-hauteur*, the second is at *hauteur*.

The leg does not come to a stop at any position; the foot describes a circle on an oblique plane, whence the name of the step. It is related to the *ronds de jambe*, which we shall study in paragraphs 122 to 127.

120

Battements sur le cou-de-pied (on the instep) are a variation on the simple *battement*: the dancer, in fifth position, slightly raises the working foot, bringing it up an inch or so from the ground, the heel against the other leg, just above the ankle.

The knee of the working leg is bent. It is extended for the execution of the *battement*.

Battements on the instep can be done in all positions, with the supporting leg either bent or straight. In second position, the free heel closes before or behind the supporting leg. In *quatrième derrière,* it closes behind.

These *battements* are sometimes also known as **frappés.**

121

Petits battements sur le cou-de-pied cause the heel of the working foot to pass before and behind the ankle of the supporting leg. The toe is slightly lowered and is turned decidedly outward. The upper leg must not move; the heel remains in contact with the other leg. These *battements* are done to an extremely rapid beat. They serve as preparation for *entrechats.*

Petits battements on the instep can also be made tapping one foot always in front of the other.

122

Ronds de jambe are so called because they cause the working foot to describe a circle (two semicircles in perpendicular planes for the *grands ronds de jambe à la hauteur*).

123

We shall begin with **ronds de jambe à terre.** These are done either *en dehors* or *en dedans,* according to the order indicated (§ 118) (Fig. 22).

They start out with a *dégagé en quatrième devant* when they lead outward, and in a *dégagé en quatrième derrière* when they lead inward. The foot passes next into second, then into the other fourth before closing in starting position. If the movement is then to be repeated several times, the dancer passes into first position.

During the whole *rond de jambe,* the free toe remains in contact with the ground, on which it glides while describing a semicircle. The heel comes to rest only at the passage into first or at the closing. Both knees remain unbent.

124

Ronds de jambe à terre pliés are executed like the preceding ones, but the supporting leg is bent during the whole movement, except at the start and at the passage into first position, as well as at the closing.

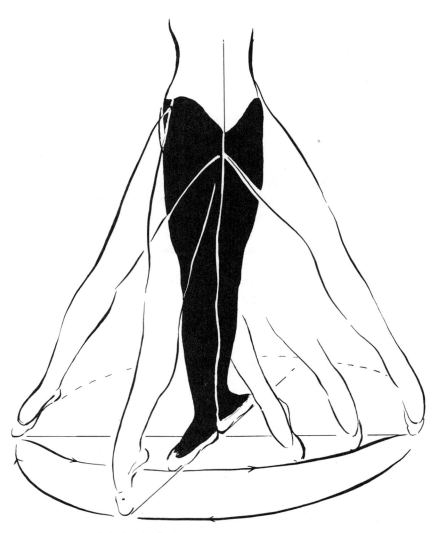

Figure 22. *Rond de jambe à terre*

125

Ronds de jambe soutenus (sustained) are those in which the leg remains in the air throughout the whole movement.

126

Grands ronds de jambe soutenus (Fig. 23) are executed either *en dehors* or *en dedans* (§ 118), with one leg constantly *à la hauteur*, the latter describing, between the two fourth positions, a horizontal semicircle passing through *seconde à la hauteur*. The movement begins with a *battement en quatrième à la hauteur* without closing, or a *développé*. In order to pass from one fourth to the other at the end of the movement, the knee is bent, the upper leg remaining *à la hauteur*; the leg passes *au raccourci* into second position, then is stretched anew, forward and backward, to do another *rond de jambe* in the same direction. During this passage the foot describes a semicircle in a vertical plane.

127

Petits ronds de jambe soutenus à la seconde are executed starting from the *raccourci à la seconde* (§ 64). The upper leg remains immobile; the

Figure 23. *Grand rond-de-jambe soutenu*

lower leg forms a cone whose top is the knee, the toe of the foot describing a horizontal circle.

If the foot turns in a clockwise direction, the small *ronds de jambe* is *en dehors*; if it moves counterclockwise, it is *en dedans*.

128

Petits ronds de jambe soutenus en quatrième devant are executed in the same manner, but starting from the *raccourci en quatrième devant* (§ 64). They are done *en dedans* or *en dehors*. At the present time they are used, *en dehors*, in the music hall; this is one of the characteristic elements of the French cancan.

129

With the **développés** we take up another category of step. Its essential moments are as follows: *position de départ, raccourci*, derivative position *à la hauteur* corresponding to the *raccourci*.

Développés can be performed in second position, *quatrième devant,* or *quatrième derrière*. There is no closing when the *développé* is done directly in sequence with another step; otherwise, the leg returns to the starting position in a closing with a simple *battement*.

130

Fouettés, the opposite of *développés*, have as their essential moments the following: *position de départ*, derivative position *à la hauteur,* corresponding *raccourci*. Like *développés, fouettés* are executed in second position, *quatrième devant*, or *quatrième derrière*.

In the classical dance the *fouetté à la seconde* is currently employed in place of the closing with a *battement à la seconde* (§ 112). *Fouettés en quatrième devant* serve as a transition when one wishes to move from a *quatrième devant à la hauteur* to an *arabesque* taken on the same leg. The *fouetté en quatrième derrière* is used to pass from an *arabesque* to a *développé en quatrième devant*. The term *fouetté* is not generally used in the two latter cases.

131

The **flic-flac** does not belong to the classical repertory, but to that of folk dances; it allows adaptations, however, that permit it to be executed in classical fashion.

The dancer in normal first position (§ 22) raises one leg *au raccourci en quatrième derrière*, inconspicuously brushes the foot on the ground to bring it into *quatrième devant à la demi-hauteur*, then brushes it once more to bring it *au raccourci en quatrième derrière*. It is these two *frottements* (brushings) that have given their name to the step.

132

The **flic-flac tombé** ("fallen flic-flac") begins with a *flic-flac*. When the leg has returned *au raccourci*, it brushes the ground to pass into *quatrième devant à la demi-hauteur*, but this time to an open position, at a 45-degree angle to the preceding *quatrième devant*. At the same time the body turns toward the moving leg. The forward foot is placed *en quatrième ouverte* with a bending of the knee.

133

The **pas de cheval** (horse's step) commences from fifth or from normal first position. The dancer lifts his foot (there is no rule specifying whether it should be the forward or the rear one); does a *développé en quatrième devant, en quatrième ouverte,* or in second, *à la demi-hauteur*; places the toe *à terre* and closes while brushing it on the ground. A step sequence can be made from several of these. They can also be done *sur les pointes*.

They serve most often to translate the movement of an animal stamping on the ground with his hoof: the doe in the first act of the *Chevalier et la Damoiselle* (Lifar), the horse in *Idylle* (Georges Skibine).

134

The **gigue** begins in **demi-cinquième** (half-fifth) (§ 58) and consists of the rapid passage from one *demi-cinquième* to the other.

The trunk is inclined sideways, toward the foot that is à plat. The arms are crossed in front of the chest, hands flat. The head turns slightly to the side toward which the body is leaning.

135

The step we are now about to describe is of **Slavic** origin but has found a place in the folk dances of the classical ballet.

The dancer, in normal first position (§ 22), poises one foot *sur la pointe* in second position, the knee bent and decidedly *en dedans*; the knee of the supporting leg also bends a little. He then poises the same foot in the same place but on the heel, toe in the air, knee straight, with the leg *en dehors*; the knee of the supporting leg bends a bit more. The leg can then be either closed or brought *au raccourci en quatrième devant,* not *en dehors,* so as to stamp the foot forcibly in place.

As the foot is poised *sur la pointe,* the arm on the side of the working leg is bent laterally, the shoulder pushed foward, the hand on the hip; the other arm is raised to place the hand behind the head. The body is *épaulé* toward the supporting leg; the head faces front. As the foot is poised on the heel, the *épaulé* is toward the working leg, with the other shoulder moving back; the head remains face forward. The movement of the trunk follows that of the leg.

The head may move slightly, following the movement of the body. Although this movement is of Slavic origin, it may be executed by beginning from a fifth position; it is thus found in classical ballets, for example: the *gigue* in the second act of *Coppélia* (Saint-Léon).

136

Piétinements ("stampings") form a whole group of steps that, without being strictly classical, have, however, found a place in the ballet.

They are of varied origin. Certain ones belong to the Slavic repertory, others to the Spanish, and still others to the modern ballet.

137

The **piétinement à plat** ("flat-footed stamping") is one of the most primitive steps. It consists of raising each foot alternately and bringing it down *à plat* in the same place. It is generally done in normal first position (§ 22).

It is found especially in ballets of Russian character.

138

The **piétinement espagnol** is also performed from a normal first position: one foot is poised *sur la demi-pointe,* in its place, then brought down *à plat,* the heel striking with force; the heel of the other foot does the same. The rhythm of these "stampings" may be quite varied.

These *piétinements* are found in all ballets of Spanish character.

139

The **piétinement non saccadé** (literally, "non-jerky stamping") consists of making each foot move alternately from *à plat* to *sur la pointe* and vice versa, in normal first position.

It is a step used in ballets in the modern style: the Phlegmatic, in *The Four Temperaments* (Georges Balanchine).

It may serve to represent marching: Guignol as prisoner, in *Guignol and Pandora* (Lifar).

140

The same *piétinement en quatrième normale* (§ 27) depicts the flight of Esmeralda, in *Notre-Dame de Paris* (Roland Petit).

TRAVELING STEPS

141

Having seen the nontraveling steps, we shall now consider the traveling steps (*pas à terre avec parcours*)—that is, those in which both legs move about but never leave the ground at the same time.

In general, one single step usually terminates in a location other than the point of departure. A combination or series of steps may bring the dancer back to where he started after a longer and shorter circuit.

142

The most elementary of the traveling steps is the **marche**. This is composed of a succession of descents *en quatrième devant*. In the normal *marche*, the forward leg supports the weight of the body when the rear leg leaves the ground; the knee bends and the rear leg moves forward and comes to rest on the heel, while the weight of the body passes between the two legs then onto the forward leg, since the former supporting leg—now become the rear—is raised *sur la pointe*.

143

The dancer adapts the normal *marche* in different ways. When it is of no particular importance—for example, the one used by a dancer coming into place—it is executed like a normal *marche*, but on the **demi-pointe**. That is, the foot reaches the ground via the toe instead of the heel.

144

The **marche à reculons** (backward walk) is more rare. At present it is found mostly in certain very special cases: fear, for example.

145

Another adaptation of the normal *marche* is executed in the following manner: the rear leg is raised *sur la pointe* and moves forward while brushing on the floor; starting in first position, the whole foot remains *à plat* until *en quatrième position devant*. It is only when this leg has concluded its movement that the other leg passes *sur la pointe*. Thus, during half the movement both feet remain *à plat*. Most inelegant when it is done with the legs stiff, if becomes artistic when accompanied by a flexing of the knees during the passage into first position. The *marche* with both feet *à plat* is currently used as a parade march by the British Army.

146

This step is sometimes called *coupé*, but the same word also serves to designate a very different step that we shall see in the leaps. At other times it is called *passé*. This name must be more especially reserved for another leaping step. Finally, the term **"passer la jambe devant"** ("to bring the leg foward") is currently used. It is a rather curious example of a step whose only proper terminology uses a verb instead of the corresponding noun.

147

Variations of the *marche* may be obtained by the passage of the working leg through derivative positions. One of these *marches*, which is well-known, is the goose-step of the German Army, in which the leg passes *en quatrième devant à la hauteur*. This march is heavy and inelegant, whereas the *marche* of the dancers, male and female, in the procession of the corps de ballet of the Opera, based on the same principle but with elevation only *à la demi-hauteur en quatrième devant*, is quite elegant indeed. The reason why the same step executed in two different cases produces totally opposite aesthetic impressions is that in the first, the movement is gross, jerky, and breaks the lines; while in the second it is supple, very smoothly joined, and harmonious.

148

Instead of rising in the *quatrième devant* derivative position, the leg may move **au raccourci**. This type of *marche*, frequently employed nowadays in gymnastics, is little used in the dance.

149

There are also *marches* in which the working leg is raised *en quatrième derrière* position before moving forward. This type is used quite frequently in the classical dance with *piqués sur la pointe*.

The passage to **attitude**, which is rare, is performed with feet *à plat* in the ballet *La Mort du Cygne* (music by F. Chopin, choreography by Lifar).

150

Very close to the *marche* are the **pas de bourrée courus**, or simply the *courus*, which are executed in classical dance *sur la pointe* by women and *sur la demi-pointe* by men. With this mode of traveling, the same foot always remains forward; starting from fifth position *sur pointes* or *demi-pointes*, right foot forward, the right foot moves in *quatrième devant* always *sur la pointe* or *demi-pointe*, then the left foot returns to its place behind the right. In general this step is executed very rapidly, except in certain special cases with individual nuances: the death of Phèdre in *Phèdre*, by Jean Cocteau (music by Georges Auric, choreography by Lifar). It may be done forward, backward, or to the side, the foot moving then in second position instead of the fourth. This is a popular method of traveling in a ballet.

These *courus* can also be done in sixth or in normal first position (§ 22).

In this case, each foot moves alternately *en quatrième devant*.

151

Again very closely akin to the *marche* are the **emboités** ("encased" or "locked" steps), which are executed primarily by women and *sur la pointe*. Starting from fifth, *sur les pointes*, the foot pointed straight ahead, the left foot moves in second, scarcely at *demi-hauteur*, and comes to rest immediately in front of the right foot, which then performs the same movement. The dancer advances very little using this step.

152

The **chassé** ("chased" step) is one whose coordinated character is more prominent than that of the various types of *marche* studied above. The step is executed as follows: the dancer, in fifth position, raises the rear leg slightly *en quatrième derrière*, then brings it back to the ground, while the other leg slides into *quatrième devant*; at this moment the rear foot must be in exactly the place originally occupied by the forward foot. This step owes its name to the fact that the foot that drops back seems to push the other forward. It must not be performed by jumping; the feet slide on the ground.

153

Chassés ouverts or **croisés** may be done, according to whether the forward leg moves *en quatrième ouverte* or *quatrième croisé* (§ 28), with *épaulement* toward the rear or the forward leg.

With the *chassé ouvert,* the arms are to the side, but not so far as second position (§ 40). With the *chassé croisé,* the arm on the side of the rear leg is bent in front of the body, the other arm in second position (§ 44).

154

The *chassé* need not necessarily be taken from a fifth position. It may **start with a quatrième derrière**, either *à terre* or *à la demi-hauteur*. But in general this latter position is seldom used because it is not easily adapted to the *chassé*, which is rather a confined step.

155

Chassés en remontant (ascending) may be done while slightly raising the forward leg in fourth position, as the other leg glides *en quatrième derrière*.

This step is not in common use in the classical dance.

156

We now take up a series of dance steps adapted from the *marche*, but which retain only some very vague connections with it: the **glissades** (glides). Thus far we have seen only steps that move foward, rarely those to the rear. The *glissades* permit movement forward, backward, or to the side.

157

The classical vocabulary utilizes most of all the **glissades in second position**, that move to the side. They are of two types.

158

The **glissade en descendent** is executed from a fifth position—*demi-plié* (half-bending). The rear foot advances into second position and immediately descends *à plat*; the weight of the body shifts to this leg, which bends. The other foot proceeds to close foward, gliding on the ground. Both legs are straightened again.

The body faces forward. The head is in profile on the side toward which the dancer is moving. The arms are in sixth position (§ 44); the one that is bent is on the side toward which the dancer is going.

159

The **glissade en remontant** is executed in exactly the same manner except that it is the forward foot that goes into second position, with the other foot firm, behind it, according to the technique just explained.

160

In the classical dance, *glissades* are extremely frequent. They may be employed alone (a succession of *glissades* giving a continuous movement to the side) or in combination with other steps.

There are many of these combinations (which we shall discuss later in paragraphs 747 to 752) that have acquired such a unity that they themselves almost amount to steps, such as the *glissade assemblée*. In these cases, the legs are not straightened again at the end of the *glissade,* the *demi-plié* providing the impulse for what follows.

161

One **variation on the glissade in second position** consists of a combination of the two preceding steps: the rear foot moves into second position and the other foot advances to close in back; the first foot takes off again in second position, and the other foot returns to close in front. The shifting is always effected to the side and in the same direction, but each foot in turn takes its place in front. This variation is used, for example, in *Giselle* (Coralli and Perrot), at the beginning of the first act, in the *pas de deux* of Giselle and Albert.

In this case the *glissades* are referred to as *glissades devant* and *glissades derrière*.

With a series of these *glissades*, the dancer may always keep the same arm position (§ 44) or reverse the position with each *glissade*, with the bent arm on the side of the leg that closes in front. The trunk

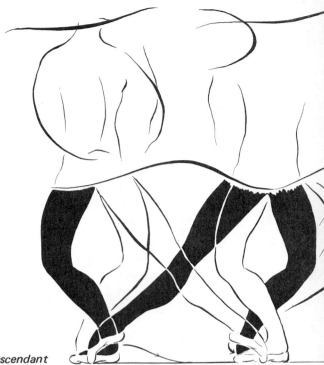

Figure 24. *Glissade en descendant*

is *épaulé* toward the arm extended to the side; the head turns toward the arm that is curved in.

162

If the classical dance especially favors these two types of *glissade*, the Spanish dance prefers a third: the *glissade en quatrième derrière*. The principle is always the same: the rear leg moves toward its place, falling in *en quatrième derrière*, and the other leg advances to close forward while gliding. In the Spanish dance this movement is accompanied by a balancing of the hips.

This *glissade* has found a place in the academic vocabulary, but it is found essentially in ballets of a Spanish character (*El Amor brujo, Bolero, The Three-Cornered Hat*, and the like).

163

The **glissade en quatrième devant**, which is executed according to the general principle of *glissades* but by releasing the forward foot and closing behind with the other foot, is very rare. It is found expecially in ballets in eighteenth-century style: *Castor and Pollux* (Nicholas Guerra).

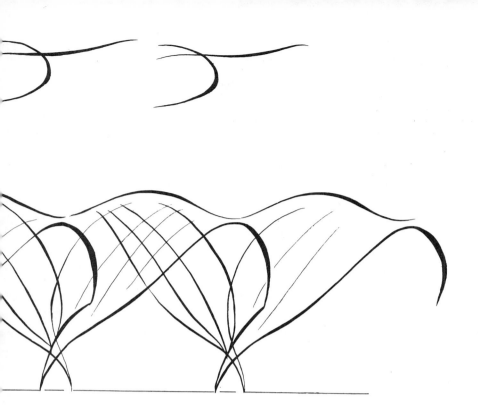

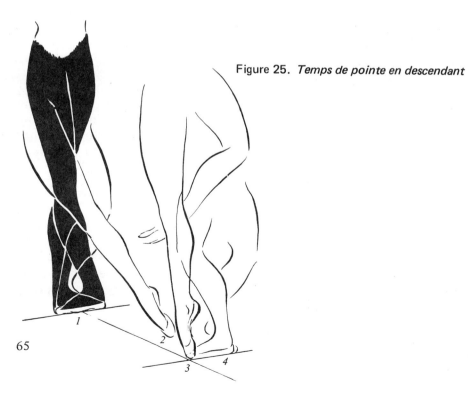

Figure 25. *Temps de pointe en descendant*

65

164

Still in the family of the linear movements are the *temps de pointe,* also called *piquées,* which, although they have a special choreographic value of their own, remain very close to the *marche.*

They are of several types, the common principle being a succession of *raccourcis* always executed by the same leg, with the supporting leg stepping directly *sur la pointe* at the beginning of each step and descending *à plat* at the end. The classical dance recognizes two types of *temps de pointe:* descending and ascending.

165

Temps de pointe en descendent: the dancer, in fifth position, right foot forward, bends the left knee while releasing the other leg and raising it slightly, then steps directly *sur la pique*—that is, *sur la pointe* or *demi-pointe*—his right foot *en quatrième devant,* and raises his left leg *au raccourci en quatrième derrière.* He then rests his left foot immediately behind the right, which simultaneously descends from its *pointe.* The knees, which are slightly bent, are straightened again for this closing (Fig. 25).

Several *piqués* can be done in succession by releasing the right foot at the moment when the left is coming into place.

The dancer may also conclude the step by resting the right foot *à plat*—that is to say, by descending from its *pointe*, thus keeping the working leg *au raccourci.*

166

The action of placing one foot *sur la pointe* while shifting the weight of the body onto it is called **piquer**, hence the name *piqués* sometimes given to this series of steps.

167

Temps de pointe en remontant: the dancer, in fifth position, right foot forward, places his left foot *sur la pointe en quatrième derrière* and brings his right leg *au raccourci en quatrième devant,* then rests his right foot immediately in front of the left and closes in fifth or simultaneously releases the left leg *au raccourci en quatrième derrière* before straightening it again to resume the step; or else he descends from his left *pointe*, keeping the right leg free *au raccourci.*

168

In both cases the shifting is always effected in the same direction: forward for the *temps de pointe en descendant,* backward for *en remontant.*

The step may be performed **ouvert** or **croisé**. For the *temps de pointe en descendent, croisé,* if the right foot is forward, movement is oblique toward the left; for the *ouvert,* if the right foot is forward, it is oblique toward the right. The *temps de pointe en remontant* are executed almost exclusively *ouverts,* with movement oblique toward the left if the right foot is forward. (The directions of movement for the *ouvert* and the *croisé* are automatically reversed when it is a question of steps that advance or draw back.)

169

The *temps de pointe piqués* do not change feet, but a **variation** reveals their close relationship to the *marche.*

En descendent, the leg moves *en demi-arabesque* instead of from the *raccourci en quatrième derrière,* the supporting foot comes down from the *pointe* and settles *à plat,* while the working leg comes to *piquer sur la pointe* in front of the other, which is then raised *en demi-arabesque,* and so forth.

En remontant, the movement is the same, but the leg is raised *en quatrième devant à la demi-hauteur* and makes a *piqué* behind the supporting leg.

The variation can also be done *en descendant* with a *raccourci en quatrième derrière* in place of the *demi-arabesque.*

170

Besides these classical types, there is a third, the **temps de pointe in second position**, which is executed with a movement to the side and uses the *raccourci in second.*

171

In addition to the *temps de pointe,* which in general imply a succession of *piqués,* one can have **piqués isolés** (isolated) in any derivative position whatever.

172

The term *temps de pointe* also designates another step that is very different from the preceding one, as much in its execution as in its principle. We have already seen in § 146 that the terms *coupé* and *passé* have two very different meanings. It so happens that in the dance several different steps have the same name and, conversely, a single step may have several names. This art has barely begun to be studied in a rational fashion. It is transmitted chiefly through oral tradition, and the technical terms undergo many transformations according to the schools that employ them. One may judge just how far this practice may lead if one is aware that the French terms are commonly used all over the world and consequently by persons for whom such words as *chassé* or *glissade* have no semantic value.

173

The second type of *temps de pointe* is a **relevé sur les deux pointes** (rising on the toes). It is rarely employed for its own sake. It may serve:

- As a starting position for a step performed *sur les pointes*: *emboîtés* at the beginning of the pizzicato section of *Sylvia* (L. Mérante);
- As an *élan* (impulse) for a leap: *entrechat* No. 6 (§ 340 and 753), *tour en l'air* (turn in the air) (§ 461 and 753), and the like.
- As a brief pause at the end of a variation (solo).

174

We have just used the term **relevé**; it is the second manner of rising *sur les pointes*, the first being the *piqué* (§ 166). One can also rise *sur les pointes* in all the basic positions (§ 22 to 29) and their derivatives (§ 53 to 64).

This second manner is much more difficult to execute than the first. It requires a long period of training (at the ballet school of the Théâtre national de l'Opéra there is a minimum of two years before students are allowed to rise *sur les pointes*) and considerable muscular force, as well as a very firm Achilles tendon.

175

There is a third way of reaching the *pointe*: by **leaping up (sautant)**. We shall study this manner at greater length in the sections devoted to the leap (§ 249, 254, 258, 260, 267, 279, 283, 298, 465).

176

The **relevé sur les deux pointes** is not limited to the fifth position (§ 173). It may be done *in all the basic positions.*

In first position (§ 22), it is intended especially for class use to exercise the instep and to develop sufficient strength for rising on the toes.

In normal first (or sixth) position (§ 23), we find numerous *relevés sur pointes* or *demi-pointes* in the neoclassical or modern ballets: *Icare* (Lifar).

In second position (§ 24) and in classical fourth position (§ 26), it is an exercise, a transition step, a preparation, or a step with a value of its own in the ballet.

In normal fourth (or seventh) position (§ 27), the *relevé sur les deux pointes* is frequent in the neoclassical or modern ballets, where it may conclude in a position with knees bent (*pliés*) and toes *outrepassées* (overextended): the does in the first act of the *Chevalier et la Damoiselle* (Lifar).

177

Relevés in derivative positions are done in all the positions *à la hauteur* or *à la demi-hauteur en attitude* and *en arabesque*. They constitute a daily exercise for the class. These different *relevés* have their place in the ballet, whether in the midst of the variations or in the *adagios* with a partner.

They are a very important element in the classical vocabulary, and there is hardly a variation (solo) in which examples of them are not found.

178

Relevés en raccourci (§ 64) are, like the preceding one, frequently used in all the positions.

They also serve as a class exercise, as a transition step, or as a step with its own value in the ballet. They may be donè in series, in class, or on the stage.

179

Battements (§ 110 to 116) may be taken *relevés sur la pointe* in all positions (Fig. 26). They are done in this manner in class at the barre and in the center of the floor. In the ballet, examples of them may be

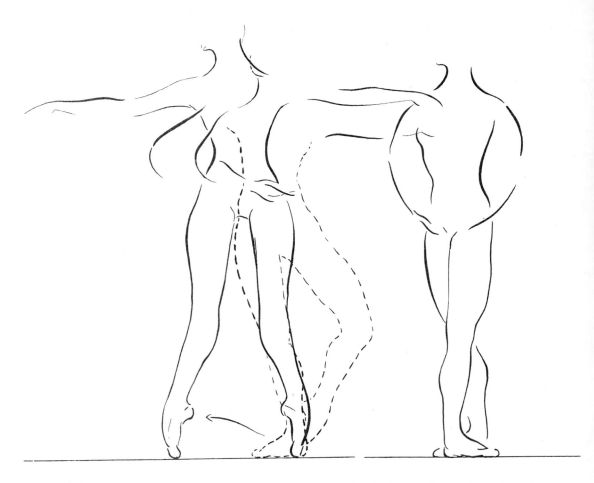

found in numerous variations and in classical, neoclassical, and modern ensembles.

180

The **battement arrondi** (§ 119) is taken *relevé sur la pointe*, especially as a class exercise. Examples of it may, however, be found on the stage, especially in the *adagios* with a partner.

181

The **petits battements sur le cou-de-pied** (§ 121) may be taken *relevés sur la pointe* when they are executed with a partner: *adagio* from the second act of *Lac des Cygnes* (M. Petipa and L. Ivanoff).

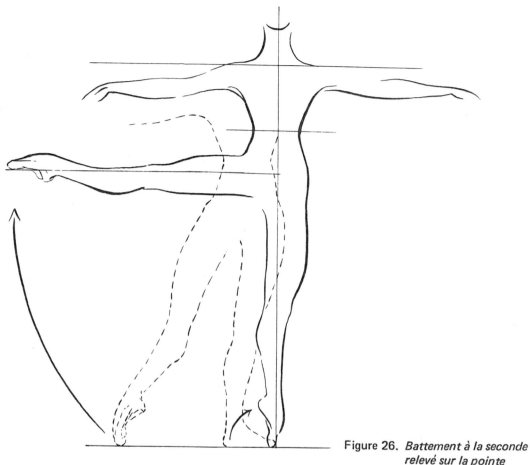

Figure 26. *Battement à la seconde relevé sur la pointe*

182

The **ronds de jambe** (§ 122 to 128) in their various techniques may be done *relevés sur la pointe*.

Grands ronds de jambe soutenus (§ 126) will be found *relevés* in *adagios* with a partner.

Petits ronds de jambe soutenus (§ 127) *relevés* are often found on the stage, either alone, as in the beginning of Odette's variation in the second act of *Lac des Cygnes,* or in combination with other steps, for example, a *glissade* (§ 748).

183

The **développé** (§ 129) **relevé** is quite common in the ballets: the Courtesans in the ballet from *Faust* (A. Aveline).

This step is done especially *en quatrième devant*, generally open, but occasionally with the following combination: a *développé en quatrième croisée*, a *développé en quatrième ouverte*; or by a series of *développés* in a diagonal, followed by *fouettés* (§ 130) in which the working leg does not rest on the ground.

The *développé relevé* may be done in varying tempos, very rapidly or very slowly, especially with a partner.

184

The **fouetté relevé** (§ 130) is a little less frequent than the preceding examples. It is done as an exercise and is also found in a few ballets: for example, by the ants in *Le Festin de l'Araignée* (Aveline).

185

Different choreographic adaptations of the *marche* (§ 147, 148, and 149) may be done **relevées sur la pointe**, at the time the leg passes into the derivative position.

A *marche* with *relevés* is found in the funeral march of the Mayfly in *Le Festin de l'Araignée* (Aveline).

186

There is a *relevé* step that is very close kin to the *passés-cabrioles* (§ 256): the **passé-relevé**. The technique is exactly the same, but the leap is replaced by a *relevé* on the left *pointe*.

It is a balanced step that is done in class and widely used on the stage.

187

In the *passé* (§ 313), the leap may also be replaced by a *relevé*, the technique remaining the same.

This step serves most often as preparation for turns or for other *relevés*. One might call this step a **passé sur pointe**.

188

We come to the last step that is still related to the *marche*, this owing to its shifting always in the same direction. It is the **pas de basque**, a very complex step that constitutes a veritable choreographic entity.

It is of two types: the *pas de basque en descendent* and the *pas de basque en remontant*.

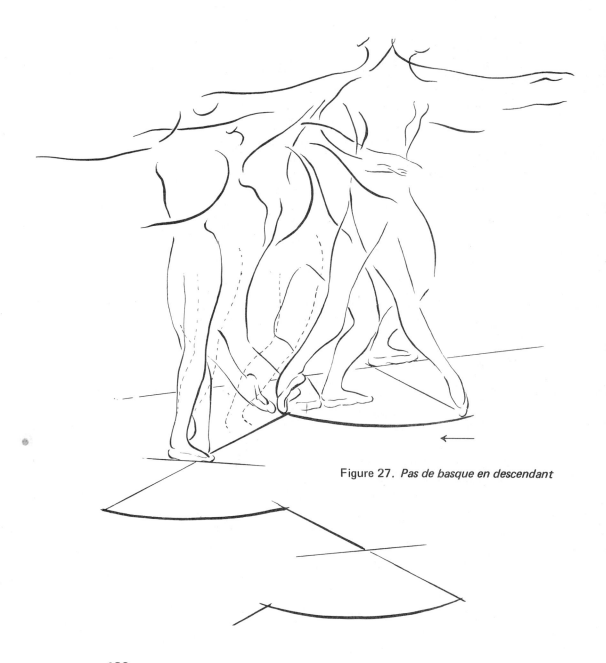

Figure 27. *Pas de basque en descendant*

189

The **pas de basque en descendant** is executed as follows (Fig. 27): the dancer, in fifth position, right foot forward, slightly bends both knees, then extends the right foot while shifting it into *quatrième devant*, barely off the ground; this foot describes the arc of a circle before coming to a rest *à plat en quatriéme ouverte;*[2] at this precise moment the left foot commences its movement, which causes it to pass *à plat* into first position, both knees a little bent; it continues to shift *en quatrième devant*, is placed *à plat*, while the knees are straightened once more and the right foot is raised *sur la pointe* and proceeds to glide on the ground to close in *cinquième derrière*.

The *pas de basque* is accompanied by an arm movement that is in harmony with it. The arms begin in sixth position (§ 44), with the curved arm on the side of the forward leg; they open into second position, following the movement of the right foot; then the left arm descends low in front and ascends bent in front of the body, following the movement of the left leg. The sixth position is maintained for the last *temps* (single movement) of the step.

The body remains mostly face forward, but is slightly *épaulé* toward the side of the extended arm. The change in the *épaulement* is done at the moment of the *quatrième ouverte*.

190

The **pas de basque en remontant** is quite different from the preceding one. The dancer, in fifth position, right foot forward, brings his left foot into second position (§ 103), and effects a *jeté* downward (§ 266); the right leg, *au raccourci en quatrième derrière*, barely raised, is then placed *en quatrième derrière croisée*, as far back as possible; the left leg closes *en cinquième devant* by gliding on the ground, and the knees are straightened out.

As with the *pas de basque en descendent,* the *pas de basque en remontant* is accompanied by a particular arm movement.

The arms are in second position (§ 40) during the shift into second (*dégagé à la seconde*) (§ 103). During the *jeté* upward, the arm on the side of the leg making the *jeté* is curved in front of the body and opens into second position during the *glissade*, with a slight movement of the wrist.

The *épaulement* follows the movement of the leg making the *jeté*.

The movement of the head is quite close to that accompanying the *pas de basque en descendant*, with a slight leaning forward at the moment of the *jeté*.

The step we have described is traditionally called the *pas de basque en remontant*, although it would be logical to reserve that term

---

[2]The exaggeration of the *dehors* leads certain dancing masters to have the foot placed in second position instead of *en quatrième ouverte*.

for a step whose technique is the opposite of the *pas de basque en descendant*.

191

We have definitely concluded the steps that are more or less related to the *marche*. The last series of steps we shall consider, the **pas de bourrée**, does not require any strictly regulated direction of movements. There are several types of *bourrée*: simple, *dessous* (downward), *dessus* (upward), upward and downward, *bateau* (boat), and so on.

192

Pas de bourrée simple: the dancer, in fifth position, right foot forward, bends the right leg while shifting the left foot into second position (§ 103) lifted slightly off the ground, then brings it on *pointe* to immediately behind the right foot in *demi-cinquième* (§ 58) (Fig. 28). The right foot is released into second and is also brought onto *pointe*. The left foot then proceeds to close in fifth in front of the right foot, which comes back down *à plat*. The dancer is ready to start out again from the other foot.

This isolated step causes a slight shift toward the right; the following step will produce the same shift to the left.

Normally a series of these steps should result in neither an advance nor a retreat.

193

We have described the *pas de bourrée* executed *sur la pointe* but it may also be done *sur demi-pointe*. This is true for all the other types of *pas de bourrée* we are about to describe.

When several *pas de bourrée* are combined in a phrase, one may also close without coming down from the *pointe*.

194

The *pas de bourrée simple* is very widely used. It is one of the basic steps of the classical dance and one of the first the student learns. It often serves for the changing of feet: when a dancer has completed one step and wishes to have another foot forward in order to perform the following step, he does a *pas de bourrée*. Certain preparations for turns are made with a *pas de bourrée* (§ 426). Because the step has a choreographic value of its own, it is found in series in the ballet: variation of the doll, in the second act of *Coppélia* (Saint-Léon).

Numerous folk dances include the *pas de bourrée*; it is found, for example, in the modern Greek *kalamatianos*, in Spain, in the Basque country, and the like.

195

The *pas de bourrée* is accompanied by a well-defined **arm movement**.

From starting position (§ 38), the arms open into second position (§ 40) (Fig. 28) after passing through first position (§ 39) with the *dégagé*. In the last *temps* (single movement), they come down again into starting position.

When several *pas de bourrée* are joined in a phrase, in the last *temps* the arm on the side of the rear leg bends in front of the body in sixth position (§ 44) (Fig. 28) and the opening of the arms into second takes place in the second *temps*, when the feet are also in second position.

Figure 28. *Pas de bourrée*

During the *pas de bourrée*, the body remains face forward.

In an isolated *pas de bourrée*, the head is in profile on the side of the leg that moves into second.

When several *pas de bourrée* are combined, the head is turned in profile to the side of the curved arm (Fig. 28).

196

The **pas de bourrée dessous** or *en remontant* is also in three *temps*.

The dancer, in fifth position, right foot forward, bends the left leg while shifting the right foot into second position (§ 103) lifted very slightly off the ground, then makes a *pointe* immediately behind the left foot *en demi-cinquième* (§ 58); the left foot is shifted into second and also rises *sur la pointe*. The right foot next comes to close in fifth behind the left foot, which comes back down *à plat*. The dancer is then ready to start out again with the other foot.

This step causes a slight shift to the left when begun with the right foot, and vice versa, and results in a slight backward movement.

197

The **pas de bourrée dessus** is executed according to the principle of the *pas de bourrée*. The dancer, in fifth position, right foot forward, shifts his left foot into second and then points it behind the right, which in its turn is brought *sur la pointe* in second; the left foot closes in fifth in front of the right, which comes back down *à plat*.

This step causes a shift to the right. The dancer, now ready to start out again with his right foot, will move toward the left in order to return to the level of his starting point. The step results in a slight advance.

198

The **pas de bourrée dessus et dessous** is a combination of the preceding elements: the dancer, in fifth position, right foot forward, shifts the left foot into second at *demi-hauteur* and brings it *sur la pointe* immediately in front of the right foot *en demi-cinquième*; the right foot moves into second *sur la pointe* and the left foot closes in fifth behind the right foot, which comes down again *à plat*. This constitutes the first part of the step; the dancer is once again in fifth position with the right foot forward. He then shifts his right foot into second position at *demi-hauteur* and brings it *sur la pointe* immediately behind the left foot; the left foot shifts into second *sur la pointe* and the right foot returns to close in fifth in front of the left foot, which comes back down *à plat*.

A series of these steps always leads the dancer back to the same place with the same foot forward: the first part of the step causes an oblique forward shift toward the right, the second part an oblique backward shift toward the left, leading the dancer back exactly to the place he started from. Thus, if the dancer has the right foot forward, the shifting is done from back to front and from front to back on an oblique line from left to right. If the left foot is in front, the oblique line will go from right to left.

199

The **pas de bourrée bateau** (boat) is distinguished by its manner of execution. The dancer, in fifth position, right foot forward, shifts the left foot *en quatrième derrière ouverte*, while *en plié*, and brings it *sur la pointe* behind the right foot in *demi-cinquième*; the right foot is brought *sur la pointe en quatrième ouverte* and the left foot is brought into place *à plat*, immediately behind the right, which shifts into *quatrième ouverte à la demi-hauteur*. This constitutes the first part of the step. The right foot is brought *sur la pointe* in front of the left, which in its turn makes a *pointe en quatrième derrière ouverte*; then the right foot comes to rest *à plat* in front of the left foot, which shifts into *quatrième derrière à la demi-hauteur*.

A series of these steps always leads the dancer back to the same place, with the same foot forward. The shift is made from front to back on an oblique line whose angle with the horizontal is more open than for the *pas de bourrée dessus et dessous*.

200

Whereas for the *pas de bourrée dessous, dessus,* and *dessus*-and-*dessous* the positions of the arms, the trunk, and the head were the same as for the *bourrée simple*, the *pas de bourrée bateau* is accompanied by arm positions peculiar to itself.

During the first part of the step the arms rise in first position (§ 39), then open into second (§ 40). During the second part of the step the arms remain in second, and only the hands are turned toward the rear.

When several *pas de bourrée* are joined together, the arms do not come back down in starting position at the end of the step. They remain in second, and only the hands are turned to the front during the first part of the step and to the rear during the second.

The body, gently *epaulé* toward the rear leg, leans slightly backward during the first part of the step and slightly forward during the second.

The head is in profile on the side of the rear leg; it follows the movement of the body.

201

The last type is the **pas de bourrée double**. This is executed in exactly the same length of time as a *pas de bourrée simple* (§ 192); it therefore implies a much more rapid movement of the legs. It involves no change of feet. There are two kinds of *pas de bourrée double*: *en descendant* and *en remontant*.

202

For the **pas de bourrée double en descendant**, the dancer, in fifth position, right foot forward, bends his left foot and shifts it into second position *à la demi-hauteur*, then brings it *sur la pointe* in front of the right foot, which is in turn brought *sur la pointe* in second, but almost against the left foot; the left foot returns *sur la pointe* behind the right foot, which comes to rest *à plat*, crossing in front, and the left foot shifts into second position at *demi-hauteur*.

Masters of the classical dance generally say that the step is done *dessus-dessous* because the left foot comes *sur la pointe* first in front of the other foot (upward), then behind it (downward).

The arms remain in sixth position (§ 44), with the curved arm on the side of the leg that shifts.

The body, practically face front and bent forward very slightly, and the head, in profile to the side of the curved arm, do not move during the execution of the step.

203

The **pas de bourrée double en remontant** is exactly the reverse of the preceding step. The dancer, in fifth position, right foot forward, shifts his right foot into second *à la demi-hauteur* and brings it *sur la pointe* behind the left foot, which is in its turn brought *sur la pointe* in second, but almost against the right foot; the right foot is brought *sur la pointe* in front of the left, which comes to rest *à plat* while crossing behind, and the right foot is shifted into second at *demi-hauteur*.

The positions of the arms, the trunk, and the head are a mirror image of the preceding ones.

204

These *pas de bourrée*, which are done *sur la pointe*, except for the last movement, and are very rapid, were particularly suited to the expression of the Italian style of the late nineteenth century. They are now relatively little-used.

205

The **pas de bourrée courus** are thus misnamed, because their technique has nothing in common with the execution of the *pas de bourrée*. They were described in paragraph 150.

206

In addition to these steps, which are limited to a purely classical range, there are **isolated steps** of diverse origins that have found a place in the classical ballet, certain of them since the nineteenth century.

207

The **pas de gigue** begins with a *petit rond de jambe soutenu* in second position *en dedans* (§ 127) executed with the rear leg; the supporting foot rises *sur la demi-pointe*. The working foot comes to rest *à plat* in front of the supporting foot, still *sur la demi-pointe*, which forms a *demi-cinquième* (§ 58). Next, the dancer executes a *gigue* (§ 134) with two *changements en demi-cinquième* and begins anew with the other foot.

This step has been used since *Coppélia* (1870) in the *gigue* in the second act (Saint-Léon).

The same step is found in dances of sailors and sailors' wives, either with the arms in the position of the *gigue* (§ 134) or with the hand shading the eyes in the position of a lookout or with both hands making the gesture of pulling on a rope to hoist a sail, and so on. For example, the departure of the sailor's in the first tableau of the *Noces Fantastiques* (Lifar), the dance of the *Sailor* (Jean Guelis), and the like.

208

The **marche espagnole** is based on the same principle as the *piétinement* (§ 138), but instead of coming *sur la pointe* in first position, the foot comes *sur la pointe* in *quatrième devant*.

This *marche* is employed in ballets in the Spanish style: for example, the variation of the third Duclinea of the *Chevalier Errant* (Lifar).

209

The **polonaise** is a dance of folk origin that was first introduced as such in certain ballets such as the third act of *Lac des Cygnes* (Petipa and Ivanoff); it has since been used in purely classical ballets such as *Suite de Danses* (Yvan Clustine).

The *polonaise* is a *marche* in which, in the first movement (*temps*) and afterwards in all three movements, the leg is raised *en quatrième devant à la demi-hauteur*, while the supporting leg is bent, before being placed *en quatrième devant*.

The strong movement of the classical *polonaise* is the reverse of that of the *polonaise* of folklore.

210

The *valse* is considered to be essentially a turning dance, but the **temps de valse** can be executed either with or without turning. There are two forms.

In the first, the dancer, in fifth or first position, places a foot *en quatrième ouvert à plat*. He brings his other foot back to the side of the first, raises both feet *sur la demi-pointe*, then rests them *à plat*. He begins again with the other foot.

In the second form, which has only one classical version, in the second movement the foot is placed *sur la demi-pointe* in front of the other one, which is slightly raised and then brought to rest in the same place.

The arms, the trunk, and the head sway gently, following the movements of the legs.

211

The **pas de polka piquée** is performed starting from a normal first position (§ 23), but may be executed in classical fashion starting from the fifth. One foot is *développé* in order to come to rest *en quatrième devant* and the other is placed near it and a little to the rear; the first is raised, then brought to rest slightly forward. The rear foot is lifted to begin the whole step anew.

This polka step may also be done *sur la demi-pointe* or *sur la pointe*. The most popular form of the polka step is done with a slight leap in the first movement.

LES PLIES *

212

The **pliés** belong most often to the nontraveling steps and rarely to the traveling steps, but they still remain in the category of steps executed *à terre,* even when they serve as a starting or stopping point for movements involving leaps or turns.

As their name indicates, they are based on the flexing of one or both knees.

213

Pliés have an essential place in classical dance, aside from their own importance: they are indispensable before *relevés*, *sauts* (leaps), and a certain number of *tours*; and also after sauts and certain *tours*, as well as in the course of the execution of numerous steps.

They act as a veritable spring and must, as a consequence, be done with great suppleness, without abruptness. The impulse furnished by the *plié* must be reflected throughout the whole body.

Pliés are executed either in complete form (with maximum bending of the knee or knees) or in *demi-plié* (with moderate bending) (Fig. 29). For the spring (*élan*), *demi-pliés* are always used.

214

Pliés in the basic positions are executed by a simultaneous flexing of both knees.

In classical dance, the *pliés* in the uneven positions—first, third, and fifth—are executed *à fond* (with a deep bend) while raising the heels from the ground. *Pliés* in the even positions—second and

*Literally, "bendings."

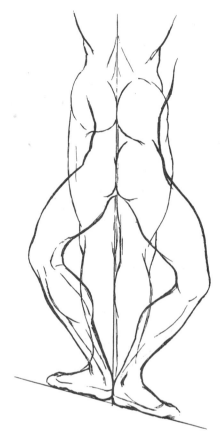

Figure 29. *Demi-plié en première*

fourth—are done only partially while keeping the feet *à plat*. But actually, *pliés* in fourth position are done while raising the heels, and in certain modern ballets the heels are also raised in second position.

In all the classical *pliés*, the legs must remain *en dehors*.

On the whole, *pliés* are used more as exercises or as elements of a step than for their own sake in ballets.

215

Pliés in first position are primarily a class exercise (Fig. 29).

They are found on the stage in a few steps using first position, for example, *soubresauts* (sudden bounds or leaps) in first position: *Etudes* (Harald Lander).

216

Pliés in third position are very rare, inasmuch as this position is itself very little used and practically never on the stage. These *pliés* will only be found therefore as a class exercise.

217

Pliés in fifth position are by far the most frequently employed of the *pliés* in uneven-numbered positions. They are found as a limbering-up exercise in class, executed at the barre, or in the middle of the floor during the *adagio*.

They form a part of a great number of steps. They serve as an impulse for the *relevés*, the *sauts,* and *tours* and are found at the end of certain *sauts* and *tours*—generally speaking, the ones that end in fifth position. This is because one cannot alight from a leap without bending the knees, and when a turn or series of turns is rapid, one needs a *plié* to recover his balance.

218

Pliés in second position are used as a class exercise.

They are rarely used for their own sake on the stage, although one is done by Œnone, in *Phèdre* (Lifar).

They are used as a beginning for certain *sauts* starting from second position: *Daphnis and Chloé* (George Skibine), and for the *tours relevés à la seconde* (§ 441). They are found at the end of *sauts* as *échappés* (§ 299).

219

Pliés in fourth position (Fig. 30) serve as a class exercise.

They are seldom employed as preparation for *sauts*: *Etudes* (Lander), but are very frequently used to prepare for *tours relevés* on one foot *en dehors* or *en dedans* (§ 426, 427).

They generally conclude rapid *tours* and especially series of *tours* when the narrow polygon of support of the fifth position would not be sufficient for the recovery of a satisfactory balance.

220

Pliés en demi-positions—that is, with one foot *à plat* the other *sur la pointe*, and both knees bent—must not be confused with the *pliés pointe à terre* (toe on the ground), which we shall take up later.

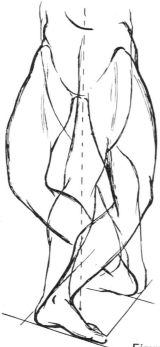

Figure 30. *Demi-plié en quatrième*

They are rather infrequent. A few examples are found, in second position or in *quatrième ouverte*, in *Entre Deux Rondes* (Lifar).

The *plié en demi-cinquième* is utilized in *révérences* (bows or curtsies), particularly in the little *révérence* of the pupils of the Ecole de Danse [de la Théâtre nationale de l'Opéra].

It is found also at the start of certain steps executed on a diagonal.

221

Unequal pliés—that is, those in which the knees are bent unequally but without causing a foot to be raised *sur la pointe*—do not exist in classical dance. A few examples can be found in the Spanish dance and in the modern ballets: *Le Sacre du Printemps* (Maurice Béjart).

222

Pliés in derivative positions, like *pliés* in basic positions, have a triple function: classwork, use for their own sake in ballets, and as the end or as an essential moment (§ 9) of a step.

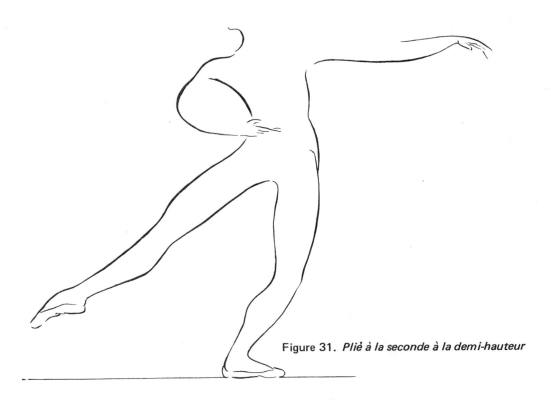

Figure 31. *Plié à la seconde à la demi-hauteur*

Pliés can be done in all the derivative positions, but in general we are only concerned with *demi-pliés*.

223

Pliés à la demi-hauteur, *en quatrième devant*, in second position (Fig. 31), or *en quatrième derrière*, are very frequently used in exercises at the barre. They prepare for the *relevés* (§ 174).

They are found at the beginning of certain *sauts*—for example, all the *assemblées* (§ 288 to 297); at the beginning of *tours sautés* (leaping turns)—for example, *soubresauts tournés* in derivative position (§ 464); at the end of *sauts*—for example, the *sissonnes* (§ 278 to 283) or *tours sautés*, such as the *pas de bourrée jeté* (§ 475). They represent the essential moments of a great number of steps—for example, the *pas de bourrée* (§ 191 to 198).

224

The **pliés à la hauteur** *en quatrième devant*, second, and *quatrième derrière* are a very difficult exercise in *adagio*.

Onstage, *pliés* are used especially in *arabesques* (§ 76)—for example, in the second act of *Giselle* (Coralli and Perrot).

They may be the essential moment in certain steps, but less often than the *pliés à la demi-hauteur*.

225

The **pliés en raccourci** are the most frequently used of the *pliés* in deviative positions.

They occupy an important place in limbering-up exercises, and they are the essential moment of a very large number of steps. In particular, many *sauts* begin or end with a *plié en raccourci*, among them the *jetés* (§ 265 to 270), the *saut de chat* (§ 276), the *gargouillade* (§ 277), the *coupé sauté* (§ 314), and the like. Certain turns also involve *pliés en raccourci*: the *tours relevés* taken directly on one foot (§ 446), the *fouettés* (§ 455), and so on, as well as *tours sautés* such as the *petits jetés en tournant* (§ 467), the *sauts de chat en tournant* (§ 472), and the like. Generally speaking, the *plié en raccourci* is a component of all steps involving a *relevé sur la pointe* or a *saut* with the working leg *au raccourci*.

226

In the **pliés pointe à terre**, one leg is extended, toe on the ground, *en quatrième devant*, in second position (Fig. 32), or *en quatrième derrière*; the other leg, which gives support, has the foot *à plat* and the knee bent.

The difference between this position and the *plié* in demi-position (§ 220) is that in the latter case both knees are bent, whereas for the *plié pointe à terre* only the knee of the supporting leg is bent.

It is an exercise that is used often, particularly at the barre, with *dégagés* (§ 102), during *adagios*, and so on.

These *pliés* may be used onstage: the *plié pointe à terre en quatrième devant* gives a form of *révérence*.

The *pliée pointe à terre* in second position is accompanied by certain *ports de bras,* and so on.

227

In the **fondu**, the supporting leg is deeply bent and the other leg is *en quatrième derrière*, the foot placed *à plat*. Both feet are thus quite far apart. Usually it involves a *quatrième croisée* (Fig. 33).

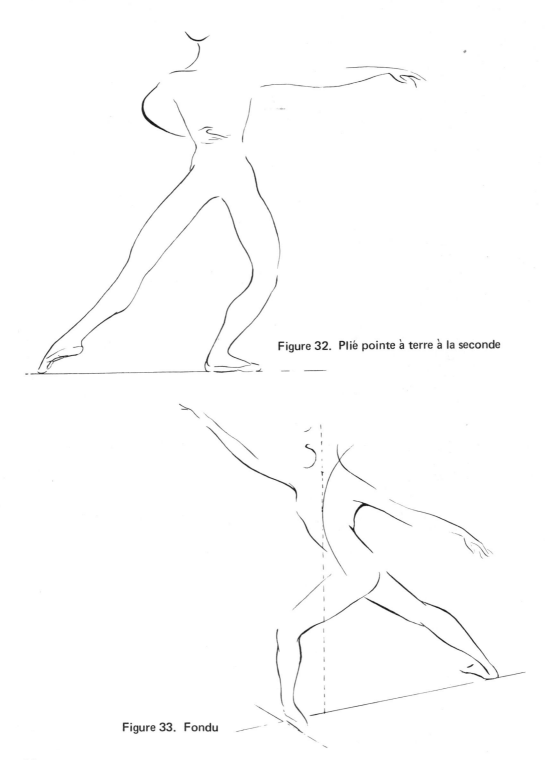

Figure 32. Plié pointe à terre à la seconde

Figure 33. Fondu

In gymnastics this posture is called a split.

In *fondu*, various types of *ports de bras* are used (§ 584). These are at present very widely practiced in class during the *adagio*, but they may also be found on the stage: *Etudes* (Lander).

⌣

228

The family of **agenouillements** (kneelings) includes essentially two types: on both knees or on one alone, with, for the latter case, a very great number of variations according to the position of the other leg.

In Western cultures, the influence of the Christian religion has tended to give kneeling the meaning of adoration or humility.

This influence has had its effect on the ballet, but kneeling may also be found that has no significance other than aesthetic.

229

Kneeling on both knees (*l'agenouillement à deux genoux*) may be done without bending at the hips.

We find it with a religious meaning in the church scene from *Notre-Dame de Paris* (Petit). In this same ballet, Quasimodo, humiliated, is found several times on both knees.

The two bearers of incense in the first act of *Aïda* (Aveline) kneel down on both knees, transferring this sense of religious meaning to ancient Egypt.

In *Le Sacre du Printemps* (Béjart), at the beginning, the men move forward on both knees.

Chloé is on bended knees in the second tableau of *Daphnis et Chloé* (Skibine) to pleads with the pirates.

Moving in this position is more unusual. A *marche* executed on both knees may be noted, however, during the duel of the Red Knight, in the second act of the *Chevalier et la Damoiselle* (Lifar).

On the whole, we are dealing with a less aesthetic posture, one employed either with a precise significance or in certain forms of the modern ballet.

230

If, while kneeling on both knees, the dancer bends at the hips, he obtain a **position assise sur les talons** (seated position on the heels).

This is a posture of repose, in which one may remain. It is, for example, the customary manner in which the Japanese sit.

Among ourselves it is found most often with a significance similar to one of those in the preceding paragraph and is employed frequently along with the simple kneeling on both knees—for example, in the church scene of *Notre-Dame de Paris*, or at the opening of *Sacre du Printemps*; or in character dances: the Egyptian women in *Alexandre le Grand* (Lifar).

231

Kneeling on one knee *(l'agenouillement sur un genou)* is much more frequent than on both.

Its most elementary form is kneeling with the working leg *au raccourci en quatrième devant*. It is the position of genuflexion, that of the knights at their dubbing, that of the cadets of Saint-Cyr at the baptism of promotion, and the like.

In the dance, the posture is found in this form in certain modern ballets such as *Notre-Dame de Paris*, and even in the classical ballets: the pages and knights in the first act of the *Chevalier et la Damoiselle*.

Taken *en dehors*, this position is frequently used in the classical dance at the end of steps or of variations or for poses, for example: two *tours en l'air* ending on the knee in *Pas de Trois* (Balanchine); two *tours sur pointe* ending on the knee in *Grand Pas classique* (Gsovsky). Serenade from *Suite en Blanc* (Lifar); in the second act of the *Moulin enchanté* (David Lichine); at the end of a variation, as with the four cygnets in the second act of *Lac des Cygnes* (Petipa and Ivanoff); in a pose, as the four little rats around the pedestal in *Suite de Danses* (Clustine).

232

L'agenouillement sur un genou au raccourci in second position or **en quatrième derrière** is very rare. It is used only in character ballets, expecially those in Oriental style: *Siang-Sin* (Léo Staats).

233

L'agenouillement sur un genou with the other leg extended *en quatrième devant*, in second position, or *en quatrième derrière* is much more in use than the preceding fashions.

En quatrième devant, assis sur le talon, is the typical posture of the swan: in *Le Cygne* (Fokine), in *La Mort du Cygne* (Lifar), *Le Lac des Cygnes,* and even of birds in general: *L'Oiseau bleu* (Petipa), *L'Oiseau de Feu* (Fokine). In this case, the trunk is tilted forward, resting on the leg, and the arms are stretched out in front with the hands crossed and the head between the arms, as under the wings.

En quatrième devant the dancer may have the pose of an archer drawing a bow: the huntresses in *Sylvia* (Lucien Mérante).

In second position, rare examples of it are found in the ballets: the dance of the Soldiers in the first act of *La Damnation de Faust* (Béjart); most often it is a final pose used in certain groups: *La Symphonie Fantastique* (Léonide Massine), or at the close of variations: *Boléro* (Lifar).

En quatrième derrière it is a final position: variation of the Young Man in *Mirages* (Lifar), of the one who drags himself along before dying: *Icare* (Lifar).

234

The positions **on all fours** (*à quatres pattes*) can be taken on the hands and feet with knees bent: the men in *Le Sacre du Printemps* (Béjart); less frequently, with the knees straight: *Prélude à l'Après-Midi d'un Faune* (Lifar), *La Symphonie concertante* (Descombey). The knees may also be resting on the ground: death of the Spider in *Le Festin de l'Aragnée* (Aveline), variation of the Young Girl in the *La Symphonie concertante*, the animal of the scene in the fields in *La Symphonie fantastique*.

235

The **marche à quatre pattes** may be done on the hands and feet: Œnone in *Phèdre* (Lifar), the drunken Orion in the second act of *Sylvia* (Mérante). It is the customary mode of traveling for fauns and satyrs: first act of *Sylvia, Prélude à l'Après-Midi d'un Faune,* first tableau of *Pas de Dieux* (Kelly).

It may be done on the hands and knees: the evil spirits in *L'Appel de la Montagne* (Serge Peretti).

Finally, it may be found performed on the knees and the forearms—it is a mode of traveling for characters who drag themselves on the ground: the Witches in the second tableau of *L'Oiseau de Feu* (Fokine), the infernal guests at the Sabbath in *La Symphonie fantastique*, and so on.

236

In certain cases **déplacement** (moving from one place to another) may cause the character to pass through different positions in succession: forms of *marches à quatres pattes*, rolling on the ground, and the like.

For example, the pirates seized with terror in the second tableau of *Daphnis et Chloé* (Skibine), the demons of Hades in *Lucifer* (Lifar).

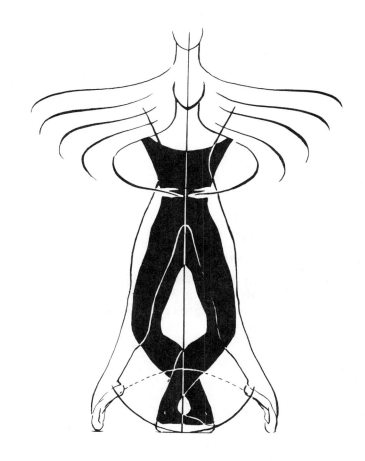

THREE

The Leaps

237

In all the steps we have studied thus far, the dancer has moved around without his feet leaving the ground at the same time; that is, without his jumping. We are now going to see him move no longer on a surface, but in a space of three dimensions.

238

The **saut** (leap) is an element of the dance that presents very special characteristics. It may be very primitive: it is found among peoples as underdeveloped as the aborigines of Australia (dance of the kangaroo), and it goes back to prehistoric times (the leap of the deer executed by the Sorcerer of the grotto of the three brothers, in *les Pyrénées*). But certain forms of civilization systematically refuse it: in Indonesia, Polynesia, and so forth. Elsewhere, it is permitted to men but forbidden to women: Japan, certain parts of Greece, and so on. Where it does exist, there is sometimes reluctance to perform it: on Greek vases, dancers are rarely depicted in the air. Even if their position corresponds to a moment in which they are in the air, they have one or both feet on the ground.

It seems that there is about it some sort of taboo or religious prohibition: that man is destined to live on earth and he must not try to separate himself from it. An idea found in all the myths and legends the world over is that of the fall of the man who wants to fly.

239

In classical dance, the *saut* has a great importance—it answers man's desire to become lighter. A very great variety of forms, some of them complex, have developed, and contemporary choreographers continue to add new terms to them.

We shall classify the *sauts* according to the logic of their technique as follows: *temps simples* (simple movements) and *batterie* (beats), with this latter category divided into *batterie à croisements* (beats with crossings) and *batterie de choc* (beats with impact).

Dancing masters distinguish between *petite* and *grande batterie*. We shall indicate in passing whether the steps fall into one or the other category.

The turning leaps will be discussed in Chapter Four, in the fourth section.

SIMPLE MOVEMENTS*

240

The most elementary form of the *saut* is the **soubresaut**, popularly known as **saut à pieds joints** (leap with feet together). It is the movement of elevation produced by a forceful straightening of the knees without any modification of posture.

It is a natural leap, very elementary, that is also done outside the dance.

241

In its natural form, the *saut à pieds joints* combines most often the ascending movement with a **progression**, almost always toward the front. The choreographic *soubresaut*, by contrast, is executed in place.

However, *soubresauts* may be deliberately choreographed to be performed while moving from one place to another—for example, in the second act of *Giselle* (Coralli and Perrot).

242

In teaching classical dance, the term *soubresaut* is reserved for the *soubresaut* in fifth position (§ 249).

We shall apply it to the other *sauts* in the same category—that is, those in which the *position de départ*, maintained throughout the *saut*, is the same as the position for alighting. There are *soubresauts* in all the basic and derivative positions.

*Temps simples.

243

The **soubresaut in first normal position** is used in classical ballets with a comical or grotesque character. With the restoration of the normal positions to the contemporary vocabulary, the *soubresaut* in first position is becoming popular: *Notre-Dame de Paris* (Petit), *Renard* (Béjart), and the like.

244

The **soubresaut in classical first position**, which is very arduous if executed perfectly, because it involves a very narrow polygon of support and therefore delicate state of balance, seems however to be held in high regard by contemporary choreographers. It is found, for example, in: *Etudes* (Lander), *Sarabande* (Attilio Labis).

245

The **soubresaut in normal second position** figures in numerous primitive dances; it is used in the character forms of the ballet, where it gives an impression of force, clumsiness, and of intense contact with the ground. It may be found in the contemporary ballets, but only rarely: *Le Sacre du Printemps*.

246

The **soubresaut in classical second position** is a class exercise. It may be found in the ballets, but often as a connecting or intermediate step—for example, after an *échappé* (§ 299). It is found for its own sake in a few ballets of modern choreography: with the soldiers in the first act of *La Damnation de Faust*.

247

The **soubresaut in third position** is practically never used in normal position.

Many **soubresauts** in fifth position (§ 249) are executed in an incomplete manner and are completed in classical third position. However, to conform to custom, we shall employ the term *soubresaut in fifth*.

248

The **soubresaut in fourth position**, in its normal form, exists in primitive dances but not to the extent of the *soubresaut* in second (§ 245). It is rarely used in the ballet.

In its classical form it is rare. Like the *soubresaut* in second position (§ 245), it is an intermediate or connecting step.

249

The **soubresaut in fifth position** is a frequent class exercise, but it is also found on the stage, either for its own sake or as a connecting step.

Employed for its own sake, and independently, the *soubresaut* in fifth permits considerable elevation.

In series it may give an impression of surging (rebounding) or of flight: the second act of *Giselle*.

Soubresauts in fifth may be executed *sur la pointe*: the variation of the two female dancers of the *pas de trois* of *Divertissement* (Petipa); occasionally with a comic character: the mother-in-law of *Guignol et Pandore* (Lifar).

As a transition step, the *soubresaut* in fifth is often employed; most often it serves as an impulse for a greater leap: *tour en l'air* (§ 461), for example. It is also found before certain turns taken in fifth position.

250

The **saut de l'ange** (angel's leap) is a *soubresaut* in fifth but with a postural modification while in the air: the trunk is arched and the legs are bent slightly toward the rear; the arms are in third position (§ 41) and the head is in profile toward the side of the raised arm and leaning gently backward.

The *saut de l'ange* is a difficult leap, almost exclusively masculine, and is employed only for its own sake: masculine variation from *L'Oiseau bleu* (Petipa).

251

After the *soubresauts* in basic positions, we shall consider the **soubresauts in derivative position**, and first those with the working leg extended.

In accordance with the rule for *soubresauts*, these are done without any postural modification. They may not achieve much elevation because the muscles of one leg alone must support the whole weight of the body. The movement begins and ends with a *plié*.

252

The **soubresaut en quatrième devant à 1 demi-hauteur** is performed as an exercise.

It is employed as a transition step.

The *soubresaut en quatrième devant à la demi-hauteur* is found in the *cabriole devant* (§ 255) when it is *non battue* (when the calves are not "beaten" together).

253

The **soubresaut in second position** is rare. It is done as an exercise *à la demi-hauteur* and is found *à la hauteur* or *demi-hauteur* in the *glissade cabriole* in second (§ 255) *non battue* (Fig. 34).

254

The **soubresaut en quatrième derrière** is done more frequently than the two preceding ones. It is found *à la demi-hauteur*, done alternately with each leg, at the entrance of the children's mazurka in *Suite de Danses* (Clustine).

It also forms part of the *cabriole en quatrième derrière, non battue*.

Soubresauts that are slightly raised in *arabesque* are found in advancing series: the Wilis crossing each other in "tiroirs"[1] in the second act of *Giselle*; in withdrawing series: variation of Swanilda, at the beginning of the Slavic theme in the first act of *Coppélia* (Saint-Léon). They may also be done *sur la pointe*: the Rubis, first movement of the *Crystal Palace* (Balanchine).

255

A **cabriole non battue** consists of the half of a *battement* that carries the working leg to the desired derivative position, *à la hauteur* or *demi-hauteur*; of a *soubresaut* in this derivative position; and of a closing that leads the working leg back to the ground.

It is preceded by a step acting as an impulse: *passé* (§ 313) for the *cabriole en quatrième devant*; *glissade* (§ 158) for the various other types of *cabriole*, and the like.

256

There is a **passé-cabriole** with postural modication during the *saut* (Fig. 35).

The dancer, in fifth position, right foot forward, makes a *passé* (§

---

[1]Two lines of dancers who cross each other, overlapping, are called *tiroirs* (drawers).

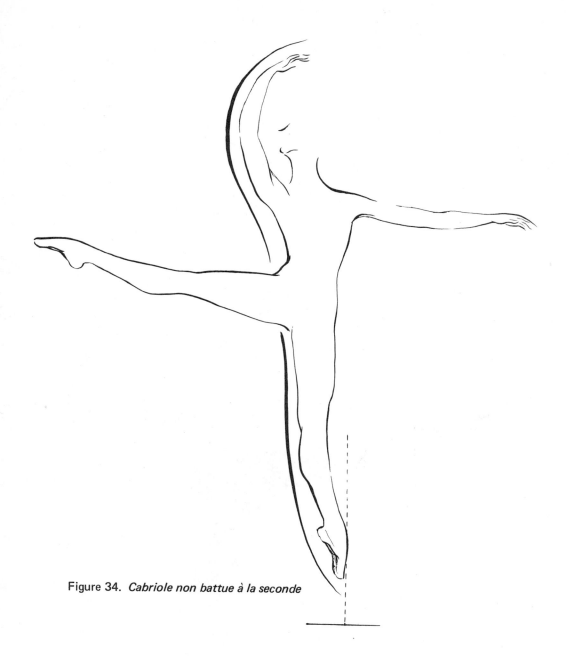

Figure 34. *Cabriole non battue à la seconde*

313) *en quatrième croisée*, raises the right leg in *quatrième devant ouverte à la hauteur*, leaps, and, when he has attained the height of the trajectory, returns, while keeping the leg in the same place, which causes it to move into *quatrième derrière à la hauteur*. The arms, beginning with *position de départ* (§ 38), rise in first position (§ 39) and open toward second (§ 40) but come to a stop before reaching that

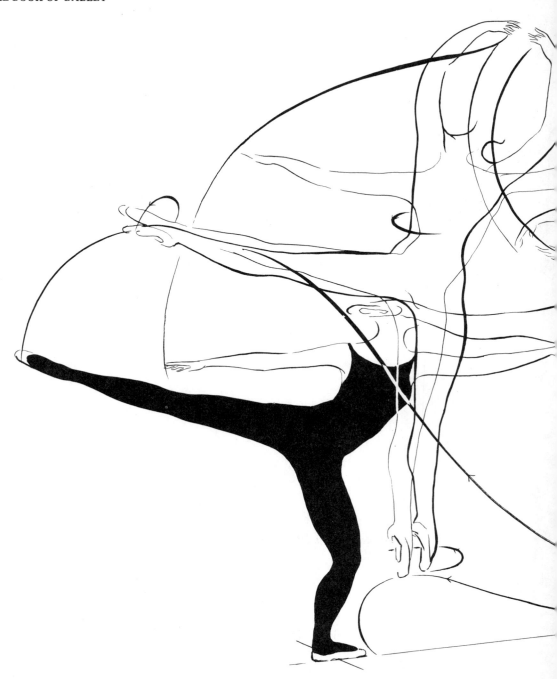

Figure 35. *Passé-cabriole non battu*

position. In the *passé*, the arms come back down at the sides to the starting position. They rise *en couronne* (in a circle) (§ 43) at the same time that the leg is rising *en quatrième devant*. They open and take their place *en arabesque* (§ 69) with the turning of the body.

The *passé* may be replaced by a *petit coupé sauté* (§ 314). In this case, the *cabriole* tends rather to be done *à la demi-hauteur* because the push-off is less strong.

The *cabrioles battues* will be discussed in paragraphs 362 to 371; the *pas de bourrée-cabriole en tournant*, in paragraph 478.

257

Soubresauts en raccourci are much more frequent than those in a derivative position with the working leg outstretched. While they occur in nonchoreographic forms, they are also employed in ballets, *à plat* or *sur la pointe*.

258

Soubresauts en raccourci en quatrième devant done with each leg alternately are the steps of the children's *ronde* (round dance). An adaptation of this is found in certain ballets—for example, with the little peasant girls in the first act of *Lac des Cygnes* (Bourmeister).

Taken with one foot *à plat*, they give a comical or grostesque note: the clown in the first act of *Lac des Cygnes* (Bourmeister); but done *sur la pointe*, in series, it is a purely classical step: the diagonal of the variation in the first act of *Giselle*.

Finally, isolated *soubresauts* are found here and there in ballets—for example, the shuttlecocks of *Jeux d'Enfants* (Aveline).

259

Soubresauts en raccourci in second position are quite rare: they are found in variations of a very definite character: athletes in *Phèdre* (Lifar), Chinese in *Casse-Noisette* (Petipa).

260

On the other hand, **soubresauts en raccourci en quatrième derrière** or *en attitude* are very frequently used.

In everyday life, they are used, for example, in the game of hopscotch.

This usage has been adapted choreographically in *Grandeur*

Nature, a ballet from *L'Age heureux*, created for television by Michel Descombey.

Like the *soubresauts en quatrième devant*, they may give a comical impression: Polichinelle in *Salade* (Lifar).

Isolated *soubresauts sur la pointe* are found in the classical ballets—for example, in *Suite en Blanc* (Lifar), *Etudes* (Lander), and the like.

261

The series of steps that we are now about to consider has no name. These *sauts* have a characteristic in common with *soubresauts*: they begin and end in the same position, either basic or derivative.

But there is a postural modification during the moment in the air. It is actually to this category that the *passé-cabriole* that we studied in paragraph 256 should be related.

262

Among the classical forms of these **sauts executed on both feet** we have the one that is accompanied by an *écart* (split-type separation) of the two legs outstretched in second position. It begins and ends in fifth. The same *saut* is found in Russian folk dances, for example, and starts from a first normal position.

We have, with the same type of *écart*, one leg positioned *en quatrième devant à la hauteur* and the other *en quatrième derrière*.

The two legs may also be bent, with the feet staying joined together. This step is very frequently used in dances of buffoons.

Less frequently, this type of *saut* is taken starting from a second or from a fourth position.

263

With one leg free, the *saut* begins and ends on the same foot. The working leg may pass through several derviative positions. For example, a *grand rond de jambe soutenu à la hauteur* (§ 126): variation of Cléopâtre from the ballet of *Faust* (Aveline).

The leg may be outstretched or bent, and it may or may not return to its initial position. Because the possibilities are very numerous, we shall not undertake to analyze all of them.

Male dancers often do a *battement en cloche* (§ 117) or a passage from *quatrième devant* to *quatrième derrière* by way of the *raccourci* in second position while in the air: *Arcades* (Labis).

〰️⌣〰️

264

After the family of *soubresauts*, we shall study that of the *jetés*. It is divided into two groups: the *petits jetés* and the *grands jetés*.

The principle of the *jeté* is to leap from one leg and alight on the other.

265

We shall begin with the group of **petits jetés**. These have as their principle the passage from a *raccourci* with one leg to the corresponding *raccourci* with the other leg.

The trunk is inclined in the direction of the movement.

266

The **petit jetée en descendant** or **petit jeté dessous** is performed starting from a fifth position, right foot forward. The left leg moves into second barely *à la demi-hauteur*, while gliding on the floor as the right leg bends. The dancer leaps, his supporting foot projecting him into the air, and falls back on the left foot, which comes to rest in front of the spot the right foot had occupied, while the right leg is placed *au raccourci* to the rear. The dancer is ready to begin again with the other foot (Fig. 36).

In class the *petits jetés* are often done in series.

On the stage there are also series of *petits jetés*: *Soir de Fête* (Léo Staats); or isolated *petits jetés* as transition steps; or after another step with which it is combined: *glissade-jeté* (§ 750), and so on.

267

Petits jetés en descendant can also be executed **without shifting into second position** by bringing the leg forward immediately. In this case they are more rapid and very compact, are seldom used except in series, and can be executed *sur la pointe*. The trunk is distinctly bent forward.

They are found *à plat* in the variation of the four cygnets in the second act of *Lac des Cygnes* (Petipa and Ivanoff), *sur la pointe* on repeated occasions by Juliette in *Roméo et Juliette* (Lavrovski).

Figure 36. *Petit jeté en descendant*

268

We all know and use these *jetés*: it is the **race** (*course*); when we run, we leap from one leg to the other while bending the free leg backward and our body forward. The only difference between the *course* and the *petits jetés* is that the former aims at obtaining the greatest speed possible, while the latter, being essentially aesthetic, demands supple movements—easy, precise, legs *en dehors*, toes taut. In the *course,* the leg is thrust forward and placed well beyond fourth position; in the *petits jetés*, it is placed in such a way that if the other foot had not been lifted, it would have closed *en cinquième devant*.

The *course* is modified for the classical ballet. It is found, for example, in Albert's flight in the second act of *Giselle* (Coralli and Perrot); executed by the athletes of *Phèdre* (Lifar), the students of *Jeux d'Enfants* (Aveline), the pirates of *Daphnis et Chloé* (Skibine), and the like.

269

Petits jetés en remontant or **petits jetés dessus** are the reverse of the *en descendant*. The dancer, in fifth position, right foot forward, moves his right leg into second position barely *à la demi-hauteur*, while bending his left leg; he then leaps and alights on the right foot, which is brought to rest behind the spot the left foot had occupied, while the left leg is positioned in front *au raccourci*. He is ready to depart again from the other foot.

This *petit jeté* has uses very much akin to those of the preceding one.

It can also be done without the move into second position, but it is almost never executed except *sur la pointe*.

270

Petits jetés in second position are done by passing from a *raccourci* in second with the right leg to a *raccourci* in second with the left leg, and so forth. In this step, the dancer remains in one place, and the trunk remains straight.

These *jetés* are unknown in the classical dance, but they are found in character dances: variation of the Chinese in *Casse-Noisette* (Petipa), dance of the Tarasque in *Santons* (Aveline).

They are used very frequently in certain regions, in particular in the sacred dances of the Lamas of Tibet.

271

The **jeté pointé** is composed of a *petit jeté dessous* (§ 266) in which the working leg, instead of remaining *au raccourci*, shifts *pointe à terre* (toe to the ground) into second position.

272

The **grand jeté** (Fig. 37) is executed with the knees straight.

This is one of the most athletic *sauts* of the classical dance; in it the dancer tries to cover the greatest possible distance, horizontally and vertically; consequently, this step is preceded by others that provide the momentum.

However, for greater clarity we shall explain it commencing from the fifth position. Let us assume, then, that the dancer is as usual in fifth, right foot forward: he lifts the right leg *en quatrième devant à la hauteur* and, while executing this movement, with a violent spring of the left leg he projects himself as far forward and as high as possible; the left leg rises *en quatrième derrière à la hauteur*, and the step is completed by landing on the right leg.

When it is preceded by a *temps d'élan* (movement of impulse), the *grand jeté* begins when the forward leg rises *en quatrième à la hauteur*.

These leaps allow memorable performances: in *Zadig* (Lifar), A. Kalioujny leapt over a high stage more than a foot and a half high on which dancers were seated, thus realizing a leap over four and a half feet in height and more than nine feet long. In *Le Spectre de la Rose* (Fokine), Nijinsky appeared to fly through the window while doing a *grand jeté*. When the step is perfectly executed, both legs are horizontally in the air in a split (§ 489).

To produce its maximum effect, the *grand jeté* must be executed in profile to the audience so that the elevation of the leap and the separation of the legs can be better appreciated.

273

The first **essential moment** is the departure, when the forward leg rises *en quatrième devant*. The second essential moment is the one in midair. It is a characteristic moment; its representation alone permits identification of the step. Both legs are outstretched, one in front, the other behind, and the trunk is positioned between the two legs, the head and shoulders sustained to assist the elevation.

Toward the end of this moment, the body is borne on the forward leg to prepare for the descent. The third essential moment is the resumption of contact with the ground; the forward leg is placed first *sur la demi-pointe*, then *à plat*, while the knee is bent and then straightened again to serve as a spring to lessen the impact of the landing, which otherwise would be very great; the rear leg then descends from *quatrième derrière* to find its place.

274

The term *grand jeté* is sometimes incorrectly applied to very high *petits jetés*. Generally speaking, we have come to say *petits jetés* for small leaps and *grands jetés* for very high leaps, without taking into account the mechanics of the step.

Figure 37. *Pas tombé, posé, grand jeté*

275

The **grand jeté may be terminated in attitude**. But this version is used less frequently. It is found in the choreographies of Bournonville. It may be noted that the leg that is bent in *attitude* forms, with the trunk, a less aerodynamic ensemble than that of the leg that is extended.

276

The **saut de chat** (cat's leap) (Fig. 38) appears as a variation on the *petits jetés* in second position. Actually, it begins in the same fashion: the dancer, in fifth position, right foot forward, raises his left leg *au raccourci* while bending the right leg; he leaps while bringing the right

leg also *au raccourci* in second, and alights on his left leg, which is bent. But instead of resuming the movement in the opposite direction, he closes the right foot *en cinquième devant* and extends it again. He may resume the step with the same leg.

This movement, when always done with the same foot, produces a shift to the side.

The classical rule dictates that the *saut de chat* begin with the rear foot.

The *saut de chat* possesses a characteristic moment: that in midair when the dancer has both legs *au raccourci* in second position.

It is a step that is much used in the ballet: variation of the four cygnets in the second act of *Lac des Cygnes* (Petipa and Ivanoff).

277

The **gargouillade** is very close to the *saut de chat*. The dancer, in fifth position, right foot forward, executes with his right leg a *petit rond de jambe soutenu* (sustained) *en dehors en quatrième devant* (§ 128), then a *saut de chat* taken directly by the right leg.

The only difference is in the *petit rond de jambe*. It may be

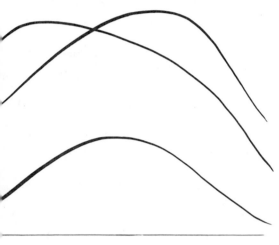

Figure 38. *Saut de chat*

observed that this *saut de chat* is taken with the forward foot, whereas normally it is executed with the rear foot.

The *gargouillade* is done less frequently in the ballet than the *saut de chat*, but it is found in some very classical variations: the fiancée in the divertissement of the opera *Roméo et Juliette* (Aveline).

278

After the family of *jetés* we shall consider that of the **sissonnes**. All *sissonnes* begin with a *soubresaut* in first or fifth position, but when the dancer has reached the height of this vertical trajectory, he places one of his legs in a derivative position and alights on the other leg.

We shall distinguish three types of *sissonne* executed with the legs outstretched and three types of *sissonne en raccourci*; each type may include variants.

279

The **sissonne en descendant** is executed as follows: the dancer, in fifth position, right foot forward, leaps vertically, his feet together; at the height of the trajectory he raises the left leg *en quatrième derrière* and alights on the right foot, a little in front of his *point de départ*; the left leg then closes *en cinquième derrière*.

The dancer may then start afresh with the same foot. A succession of *sissonnes en descendant* causes a forward progression. The trunk is inclined slightly forward in the direction in which he is going. The leap may vary in height and the dancer may lift his leg *en quatrième derrière à la hauteur* or *demi-hauteur*.

The higher the leap, the higher the leg is raised, and the less quickly the dancer will execute the movement. The time of execution may vary from the *simple* to the *double*.

The leg is most often *en quatrième ouverte*, with the body *épaulé* toward the rear leg; the arms rise laterally into second and return to the starting position, following the movement of the leg.

In a series of *sissonnes* the arms rise and descend laterally to the rhythm of the movement of the leg that is being lifted.

This *sissonne* may be done with a falling back *sur une pointe* after a very shallow leap.

At the present time this step is often used, as much by male as by female dancers. The men leap very high, keep their legs together very precisely during the first *temps*, and rise *en quatrième derrière à la hauteur*; some of them bring up the forward leg also *à la demi-hauteur*. They do the step slowly, striving to remain as long as possible in the air.

Women may execute the step in two fashions: slowly, while lifting the leg *en quatrième derrière à la hauteur*; or very quickly, while raising the leg only *à la demi-hauteur*. In the first case, the step should give the impression of lightness, of insubstantiality.

For this reason it is found in the ballet of the *Sylphides* (Fokine) and in the second act of *Giselle* (Coralli and Perrot).

In the second case, it is a step brilliantly employed in character dances: variation of Djali in the first act of the *Deux Pigeons* (Aveline).

In neither case do the women keep their legs close together long; they raise one *en quatrième derrière* almost immediately after having left the ground.

280

A **variant on the sissonne en descendant** consists of raising the forward leg *en quatrième derrière* instead of the rear leg.

This variation produces much less forward progression than the standard *sissonne*. It is executed with each leg alternately, in a crossed position.

281

The **sissonne en remontant** begins as do the preceding ones, but the dancer, having started out from fifth position, right foot forward, raises the right leg *en quatrième devant ouverte à la hauteur* or *demi-hauteur* when he reaches the height of his trajectory. He alights on the left leg, a little behind his *point de départ*. The right leg comes up to close in fifth, and the dancer is ready to start out anew with the same foot.

A succession of *sissonnes en remontant* effects a rearward progression. The body leans gently toward the rear—that is, in the direction toward which the dancer is going.

Sissonnes may be executed alternately *en remontant* and *en descendant*, but this suggests a very ungainly balancing of the body. It is, therefore, done only with very small *sissonnes* in which the body is not leaning but rather follows, with slight *épaulements*, the movement of the leg. The head turns to the side of the leg that is being raised.

The arm movements are the same as for the *sissonne en descendant* (§ 279). The arms may also remain in third position (§ 41), with the raised arm on the side of the supporting leg.

282

The various observations made about the execution of the *sissonne en descendant* apply as well to the *sissonne en remontant*.

The *sissonne en remontant* is used less often in the ballets than the *sissonne en descendant*.

283

The last type of *sissonne* is the **sissonne in second position** (Fig. 39).

The principle is the same: departure in *soubresaut*; at the height of the vertical trajectory one of the legs rises in second position *à la hauteur* or *demi-hauteur*; the dancer falls back on the other leg; the first leg returns to close in fifth. In general, if the dancer begins in fifth position, right foot forward, it is the left leg that rises in second and closes *en cinquième devant*.

The body is inclined gently to the right. Because this step implies a slight sideways progression to the right, we find once again the principle common to *sissonnes*: the body leans to the side toward

Figure 39. *Sissonne à la seconde*

which the dancer is going—that is, in the direction opposite to the leg being raised.

The dancer may also raise the leg from the front and close it from either the rear or the front, or raise the leg from the rear and close from the rear.

This step may be done *sur la pointe*.

Certain *sissonnes* combine with other steps to form an ensemble—for example, *sissonne-posé-assemblée* (§ 773), which is also called *sissonne double*.

284

The **sissonnes en raccourci** are rarely known by this name. However, they do exist. Certain ones are used especially as a class exercise. Others are found in ballets.

285

The **sissonne en raccourci en quatrième devant** is done as an exercise, occasionally combined with *assemblées*.

One of its variations is used on the stage: the leg *au raccourci* does a *développé* (§ 129) *en quatrième devant*. The arm on the side opposite the leg is extended forward parallel to it, as if the hand were caressing the leg.

This step is done in a crossed position (*croisé*). It is found, for example, in the Mazurka of *Suite de Danses* (Clustine).

There is a special form of *sissonne en raccourci en quatrième devant*. It is the one a dancer executes in a *pas de deux* when, having started out in fifth position, she leaps, supported by her partner, who sets her down most often *sur une pointe*, with the other leg *au raccourci en quatrième devant*.

286

The **sissonne en raccourci in second position** is most often done *en descendant* with the rear foot, which rises and closes *devant*; or *en remontant* with the forward foot, which rises and closes *derrière*. This is an exercise.

287

The **sissonne en raccourci en quatrième derrière** is performed as an exercise.

En attitude, it is a step found in ballets often before a *relevé sur la pointe en attitude*.

288

The principle of the *assemblées* is the exact opposite of that of the *sissonnes*: one leg is in the air; the dancer leaps and alights on the two feet together. There are as many types of *assemblée* as of *sissonne*. But the variations are less numerous and the step is used less frequently onstage, because the *sissonne*, which terminates on one foot, produces an effect of lightness, whereas the *assemblée*, bringing both feet to the ground at the same time, has a heavier appearance.

289

The **assemblées in second position** are by far the most frequently employed. *Assemblées* are characterized as *devant* or *derrière* according to whether the leg in the air closes in front of or behind the other one. They are done with or without changing feet.

Figure 40. *Assemblée devant* with change of feet

290

Assemblée devant with change of feet (Fig. 40): the dancer, in fifth position, left foot forward, does a *battement*, sliding his foot on the ground before lifting it; he brings his right leg up *à la demi-hauteur* or *hauteur* and simultaneously bends his left leg. He leaps by straightening this leg and alights in fifth, right foot forward.

291

Assemblée derrière with change of feet: the dancer, in fifth position, right foot forward, lifts his right leg in second position, leaps, and alights in fifth, left foot forward.

These two *assemblées* are those most often used. In class they are performed in series, alternately with each leg, descending with the forward *assemblées*, then ascending with the *assemblées derrière*.

They combine with other steps—for example: *glissade-assemblée* (§ 751), *assemblée-changement de pied*, and so on.

292

The **assemblées without change of feet** are done toward the front when the dancer, in fifth position, right foot forward, lifts his right leg in second and alights in fifth, right foot forward; they are done toward the back when it is the left foot that is raised.

These *assemblées* are used less often, they are not done in series, and they are, above all, transition steps. Generally speaking, the *assemblées* serve to return to the ground, more choreographically than a simple closing, a leg that a preceding step may have left in the air.

293

Assemblées en quatrième devant are done according to the same principle, with the forward leg raised in fourth position *à la hauteur* or *demi-hauteur* and closing forward.

This step, not *en dehors*, is used very frequently in peasant dances.

In classical dance, *passés-assemblées en quatrième effacée* (§ 89) on the diagonal are often done in series.

294

The **assemblée en quatrième derrière** is seldom used for its own sake; it is a transition step.

295

Assemblées en raccourci are seldom used. They are found mainly as exercises after *sissonnes en raccourci* (§ 284 to 287) and as transition steps. They are not generally called *assemblées*.

296

There is an unnamed *saut* whose technique is akin to that of the *assemblées*: the dancer, with one leg in the air, **leaps and alights in second or in fourth position**.

These steps are known from popular or folkloric forms of the dance, but they have found a place in the ballet. In second position, they figure in the sabre dance from *Siang-Sing* (Staats). In fourth, they serve as preparation for turns. They are very widely used in the modern ballet.

297

In all the *assemblées*, care must be taken to make the strong movement (*temps*) well defined at the height of the trajectory; otherwise the step tends to be ruined.

An *assemblée en quatrième devant* is often done with both legs brought together at the height of the trajectory. This step is a preparation for the *batterie*.

298

We now take up a new family of *sauts*, less important than the preceding ones: the *échappés*.

The principle of these *sauts* is the passage from fifth position to a basic even-numbered position. At present the *échappé* is done in two different fashions:

- *Sur la pointe* or *demi-pointe*, the *saut* is very weak—just sufficient to permit movement of both feet at the same time but not aiming at any effect of elevation. Both legs are straight on alighting.

- When the dancer alights with feet *à plat*, he can leap quite high and alight with knees bent. Male dancers try to keep the two legs close together as long as possible in midair.

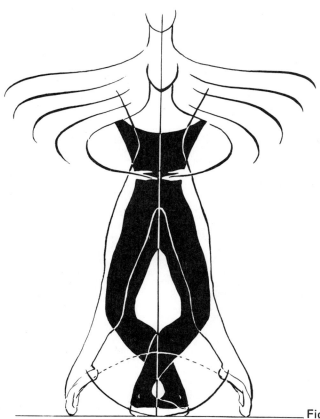

Figure 41. *Echappé sur pointes*

299

The **échappé in second position** is the most popular. The dancer, in fifth position, right foot forward, does a *plié*, leaps, and alights in second position.

For an *échappé sur la pointe*, the two *pointes* are about two feet apart for small, rapid, connected *échappés* and about two-and-a-half feet apart if one pauses on the *échappé* (Fig. 41).

For the *échappé sauté*, the position achieved is a classical second (§ 24). Care must be taken not to separate the legs too much unless the choreography requires it for a particular reason. Male dancers make a greater separation than do women (Fig. 42).

The legs must remain close together until the height of the trajectory, since the accent is on this moment.

The movement of both legs must always be perfectly symmetrical.

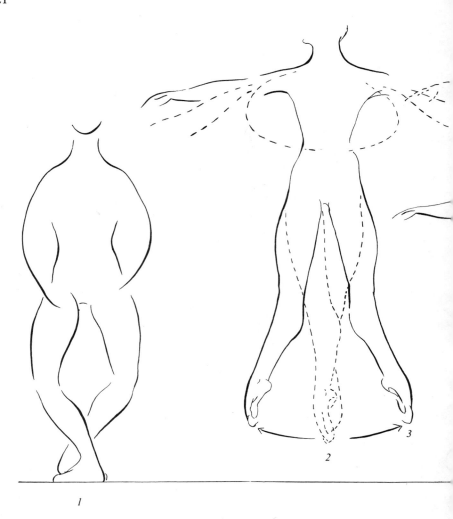

1

2

3

300

To **close the échappé**, the dancer leaps once again and brings his legs into fifth position. This second *saut* is always less elevated than the first because the position in second, with legs spread apart, renders the spring more difficult.

The *échappé* may be closed without changing feet—that is, with the right foot forward if the step began with the right foot forward. It may also be closed with a change of feet—that is, with the left foot forward if the step began with the right foot forward.

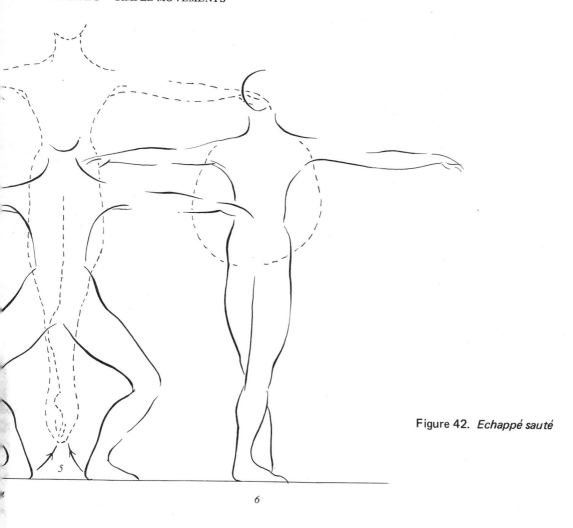

Figure 42. *Echappé sauté*

Even more than for the *échappé* proper, care must be taken to accent the height of the trajectory and not to flatten out the landing (*retombée*).

301

The **uses** of the *échappé* in second position vary according to the manner in which it is executed.

When it is done *sur la pointe*, it may serve as an introduction to a turn (§ 429).

121

It may also have a value of its own when it is executed, *sur la pointe*, but that is uniquely for female dancers.

The *échappé à plat* is employed alone or in combination with other steps. It is a movement used especially by male dancers.

302

The **échappé in fourth position** is done almost like the *échappé* in second. The dancer, in fifth position, right foot forward, leaps and alights in fourth, right foot forward. To close his *échappé*, the dancer has to execute the reverse movement: leap from fourth to alight in fifth.

The *échappé* in fourth position involves no change of feet.

303

The **uses** of this step are somewhat different from those of the *échappé* in second. We find, especially for female dancers, that the *échappé sur les deux pointes* with knees unbent has an aesthetic value of its own.

In general, it is done *croisé*.

The *échappé à plat* serves as preparation for *tours en dehors* or *en dedans* (§ 426, 427), *en attitude, en arabesque*, and the like.

A few examples of *échappés à plat* for their own sake may be found in the modern ballets.

304

The **arm movements** accompany the movement of the legs.

For the *échappés* in second position *sur les pointes*, the arms open to the sides at the same time that the legs do and close with them. The head is turned to the side of the leg that is in front at the beginning and returns to face front at the closing. If the *échappés* are in series and rapid, the arms rise only *à la demi-hauteur*.

For the *échappés à plat*, the arms rise freely into second position (§ 40) or *en couronne* (§ 43), with the *échappés* lifted very high. In this case, they come back down in second position for the landing.

With the *échappés* in fourth position, the arms may follow the movement of the legs in reverse: the arm on the side of the rear leg is extended forward half-horizontally; the other arm is extended backward or to the side in the same way. The head is turned to the side of the forward arm.

When the *echappé* is in preparation for turns, the arms are placed in sixth position (§ 44).

〜〰〜

305

After these large groups of sauts, we shall now see some *sauts isolés*.

Certain of these might be integrated into a more important group; others are unique in their genre. Several of them are closely related to sports.

306

The **saut du faon** (leap of the fawn) is not known by this name in classical dance but rather in figure skating.

It begins like a *grand jeté*, but in midair the forward leg bends back *au raccourci en quatrième devant*, then is extended once again for the fall.

This step is very difficult and demands great elevation. It is a male dancer's step.

It may sometimes be embellished with a *petit rond de jambe au raccourci en quatrième devant* (§ 128) as in *Theme and Variations* (Balanchine).

307

The **temps de flèche** (arrow movement) is still another movement that occurs both in the dance and in gymnastics. It is the so-called "American leap" or "scissors leap."

While in midair, each outstretched leg executes, in turn, a *battement en quatrième devant* (§ 113).

In the classical dance, the dancer, in fifth position, right foot forward, does a *plié* and raises his right leg *en quatrième devant à la hauteur* following a parallel trajectory, while the right leg comes back down passing through *quatrième ouverte*. The step closes in fifth, left foot forward, thus changing feet.

There is a tendency to do the *temps de flèche* by lifting the legs directly *en quatrième devant* as in folk dances, but the beauty of the step is a result of the passages into *quatrième croisée*, fourth position, *quatrième ouverte* with the right leg, and vice versa for the left leg, with the leg describing a semicircle in front during its *battement* (Fig. 43).

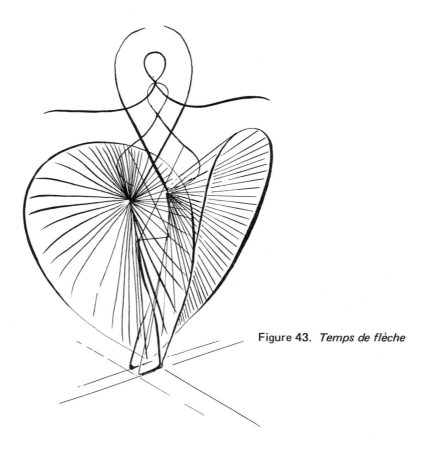

Figure 43. *Temps de flèche*

The left leg is raised at the moment when the right leg passes from *quatrième croisée* into fourth position, and the right foot is placed when the left leg arrives *à la quatrième croisée*.

The arms, having left the *position de départ*, rise *en couronne* (§ 43) while passing through first position (§ 39), then come back down while passing through second (§ 40).

This step, with its very pretty effect, figures in some classical variations, of which one of the best known is the *manège* (a circular series of turns—literally, "merry-go-round") in the Slavic style from the first act of *Coppélia* (Saint-Léon). Very often the step is preceded by a *coupé* (§ 314), which serves as an impulse. The body leans forward, to right itself in the *temps de flèche*.

In gymnastics, the athlete leaps as he lifts his leg, and the separation of the *battement* between the right and the left is much less. In classical dance, the moment that separates the passage of the two legs at the height of their trajectory is equal to half the total time employed in performing the step. In gymnastics, there is only about a quarter or a third of the time.

The *temps de flèche* possesses a characteristic moment: the one in which both legs are in the air.

308

The *temps de flèche*, which we have just discussed, is performed toward the front. It may also be executed **toward the rear**. This much more difficult step exists, but it is rare. It is used especially in acrobatics, but it is also found in certain modern choreographies: dance of the soul of Marguerite in the second act of *La Damnation de Faust* (Béjart).

309

The **ballonné**, as opposed to the two preceding steps, is employed uniquely in the dance. The dancer, in fifth position, right foot forward, bends both knees and slides the right foot on the ground to bring it into *quatrième devant à la hauteur* in *effacée* position (§ 89); he leaps while bending the right leg *au raccourci quatrième devant* (§ 64) and alights on the left foot. This step does not end in fifth, but with one leg *au raccourci*.

If several *ballonnés* are strung together, the right leg is placed *en quatrième devant*, and the left slides to close behind in fifth. The step may then be repeated. It is done on a diagonal.

The arms are in third position (§ 41), with the raised arm on the side of the working leg.

Ballonnés are often combined with the *pas de basque* (§ 189), which effects a change of feet: three *ballonnés*, a *pas de basque* in the children's mazurka from *Suite de Danses* (Clustine).

310

The *ballonnés* may also be done **in second position,** according to the same technique; the arms are in sixth position (§ 44), with the arm that is curved on the side of the working leg.

In the *raccourci*, the *pointe* may be placed either in front or in back of the knee of the supporting leg. Two types of *ballonnés* may be strung together without resting the working leg on the ground. We then refer to *ballonnés devant and ballonnés derrière.*

This is, above all, an exercise step.

311

The **saut de basque** has a technique that, on the whole, is that of the *pas de basque* (§ 189), but in the first *temps* the working leg does a sort of *jeté*, while describing substantially the same movement as for the *pas de basque*; at the end of this movement the supporting leg is placed *au raccourci devant*.

312

The **ballotté** begins in fifth position, right foot forward. The dancer bends the left leg while bringing it *au raccourci derrière*, then jumps onto it while doing a *développé* with the right leg *en quatrième ouverte à la hauteur*.

He bends back the right leg *au raccourci,* jumps onto it, and does a *développé* with the left leg *en quatrième ouverte derrière*.

In general, the arms move from one sixth position (§ 44) to the other, with the arm that is bent on the side opposite the leg doing the *développé*.

A beautiful example of this step is found in the first act of *Giselle* (Coralli and Perrot).

313

The **passé**: the dancer, in fifth position, right foot forward, executes a petite *sissonne en descendant*. But instead of closing the left leg *en cinquième derrière*, he moves it forward in fourth through the intermediary of the first position and may raise the rear foot *sur la demi-pointe*. This step does not terminate in fifth position: it is the preparation for another *pas, saut,* or *tour,* for which it serves as an impulse. It ends in fourth when it precedes a *tour, en demi-quatrième* (§ 57) when it precedes a *saut.*

314

The **coupé sauté** is in a sense an isolated *petit jeté*. The dancer, his left leg in the air *en raccourci* in second position, *en quatrième derrière, en arabeque,* or *en demi-arabesque,* leaps onto that leg while bringing the right leg *au raccourci*. The *saut* is, in general, very small, and the right leg does not rise very much and is ready to execute another step.

The essential role of this *coupé* is to permit the dancer who finds himself supported on one leg to free it in order to do another step.

315

The **pas tombé** commences in fifth position, right foot forward. The dancer raises the left leg *en quatrième ouverte derrière à la demi-*

hauteur while gently bending the right leg, then leaps while bringing the left leg forward; the foot is placed in front of the right leg, which moves immediately forward to find its place *en quatrième ouverte* while the knee bends; the final position is a *fondu* (§ 227).

The body is bent forward, *épaulé* toward the rear leg.

This is, above all, a transition step that combines with numerous other steps.

316

The **chassé sauté** has a technique akin to that of the *chassé* described in paragraph 152. But when the leg is lifted *en quatrième derrière à la demi-hauteur*, the other leg bends, then straightens to bring about the *saut*, while the raised leg comes back down for a *chassé* in fourth position in front of the other leg.

These *chassés* may have low or high *sauts*. Diagonals may be composed of *chassés sautés*: variation of the Prince in *Divertissement*, extract from *La Belle au Bois dormant* (Petipa).

The arms are in sixth position (§ 44), with the arm that is bent on the side of the rear leg; less frequently they are in second position (§ 40).

The *chassés* may be performed *ouverts* or *croisés*

317

Chassés sautés may be executed **in second or en quatrième derrière**. Those of the latter type are practically never used in classical dance, but they are a part of the vocabulary of the modern dance.

318

The **demi-contretemps** begins like a *sissonne en raccourci* (§ 285) with the rear foot; it ends by having the leg move forward *au raccourci* and placing it in fourth position.

This step has no importance of its own; it combines with other steps, often the *sautés*, to form classical sequences.

319

The **contretemps** is a *demi-contretemps* with the leg held straight. We have already described this step in paragraph 313 under the name of *passé*.

The term *contretemps* is rarely employed.

320

To do a **failli devant**, the dancer, in fifth position, right foot forward, slides it along the ground while moving *à la demi-hauteur en quatrième effacée*; he then leaps with an *assemblé*.

The *saut* is very small; the whole of the step is, moreover, quick, as if sketched.

The arms are in sixth position (§ 44), with the arm that is bent on the side of the working leg.

The *failli* can also be executed to the rear according to the same technique.

This is a step with no value of its own; it is used solely to begin or to prepare for (by supplying the impulse for) another step: *saut* or *tour*.

321

The quantity of **transition steps** (*pas de liaison*) just noted that have no intrinsic value may be somewhat surprising.

But it is characteristic of the dance that nothing be left to chance. Although in athletics only the essential movements are considered, those supplying an impulse being most often racing steps, in the dance no detail is neglected; the accessory steps themselves are invested with a theatrical manner, and it is a characteristic of their execution that the perfection of the artist is recognized.

322

A certain number of *sauts* unknown to the pure classical vocabulary are currently present in character dances, in particular in the **danse russe** (Russian dancing).

They were introduced into the classical repertoire especially by the Ballets Russes of Diaghilev.

They occupy a place in such works as *Petrouchka*, the *Danses Polovtsiennes* from *Prince Igor, Shéhérazade*, The *Trépak* from the *Casse-Noisette,* and so on.

323

One of the simplest consists of crouching in first position, then rising while spreading the feet in second position by an *échappé sur les talons* (on the heels). The jump is not emphasized but provides only what is needed to allow movement from the first position into the second.

This step is very frequently used in Russian folklore, particularly in the dances of the Ukraine and the Caucasus.

324

The **marteaux** are, in the opinion of many, the very symbol of the Russian dance. They are performed in a crouching position, with the dancer extending his legs forward alternately while jumping.

The *saut* is very slight, just enough so that the leg extended forward can bend back under the body while the other one is being outstretched. This movement is repeated a great number of times in sequence. In general, it is performed only by men.

325

There are **marteaux in second position** rather than *en quatrième devant*. The principle is exactly the same, but the legs are extended toward the side instead of toward the front.

This type has proved to be easier and less widely used in modern times.

Occasionally it is seen performed by children.

326

Another typically Russian step is the **saut de carpe** (leap of the carp). The dancer jumps, feet together, sending his legs backward to the side with the knees bent; he inclines his body to the side and touches his heels with his hand while in midair. This is a very difficult leap, requiring both elevation and speed simultaneously. It is executed from alternating sides with, between times, a *soubresaut* in first position, accompanied by a clapping of the hands; it may also be executed simultaneously on both sides, with the lower part of the legs spreading a little so that each hand touches the heel on its side: the Young Maiden of the *Danses Polovtsiennes* from *Prince Igor* (Fokine).

327

Less typically Russian are the **coups de pieds**, because they are also found among such widely dispersed peoples as black Africans and the Australian aborigines. They also exist, however, in present-day Russian dancing.

Their principle is to bring both feet, or one alone, into contact with the buttocks in the course of a leap.

328

The **coups de deux pieds** consist of jumping and striking the lower back with both feet at the same time and alighting on both feet. They require the performer to achieve a very high elevation. They are more frequent in Russia and are very rare elsewhere.

This step includes a characteristic moment, the one in which both feet are in contact with the buttocks.

329

The **coups d'un pied** are *petits jetés dessus* (§ 266) in which one foot strikes the lower part of the back.

They are very frequent in all primitive dances but are rarely found elsewhere.

330

We shall now consider a typically Russian step that is very complex and difficult. The dancer has the right leg bent, the left outstretched in second position on the ground, and both hands on the ground. He moves his left leg *en quatrième devant*, raising the hands one after the other; then, continuing the turn, he causes that leg to move under the right leg and finally brings it to its first position. He does this a great number of times in succession and so rapidly that the observer fancies he sees the leg turning around the body. We find an adaptation of this step in the Trépak of the ballet *Casse-Noisette* (choreography after Ivanoff, modified by J.-J. Etchevery).

There is no name for this step.

331

The **temps de bottes** begins in a normal first position (§ 23). The dancer raises a leg to the side, in normal second *à la demi-hauteur*, while bending the supporting leg. He leaps, bringing the working leg close to the other. This supporting leg rests with a sideways movement to the side of the free leg. The free leg is placed in normal second position, and the other leg returns to be placed against it in normal first.

This step might be likened to a *balloneé* (§ 310) not executed *en dehors* and with the working leg brought to ankle level instead of knee level.

The arms are half-horizontal to the sides, palms down, at the moment of landing. They descend low in front, then open again immediately.

This step was introduced very early into the classical vocabulary; it has been found in the Mazurka from *Coppélia* (Saint-Lèon) since 1870.

BATTERIE A CROISEMENTS*

332

The **batterie** (beating step) consists of the *croisement* (crossing) or striking (*choc*) of the legs in midair in the course of a *saut*. Strikings or crossings may be single or multiple. All *sauts battus* (jumps that include beats) are elaborations of simple *sauts*. On the other hand, not all *sauts simples* are *battus*. The present tendency is to include beats in jumps as often as possible. Male dancers in particular do so as often as they can.

The *grands jetés*, the *sauts de chat*, and the isolated steps (*temps de flèche, ballonné, passé, coupé*, and *pas tombé*) are about the only ones that bypass the *batterie.*

Female dancers, even though they must be able to execute a certain number of *pas battus* (beating steps), nevertheless reserve the right to do *sauts simples.*

333

We shall now study the **batterie à croisement**. All the steps in this category belong to the large family of **entrechats**. The term is, however, especially reserved for *entrechats* of the *soubresaut* type, which we shall discuss first. All of these *sauts* must be executed with the knees straight while in midair, and the legs remaining well *en dehors.*

334

The **entrechats, as such, are numbered** in classical dance from three to eight. We recognize *entrechats* 1 and 2 under another name, however. At the present time, the constant effort to excel and surpass could lead to the performance of *entrechats* through 10.

Although certain questions arise concerning the numbering of these steps, we shall propose in principle that the uneven-numbered *entrechats* begin with a *croisement devant* of the forward foot and the even-numbered *entrechats*, with a *croisement derrière.*

The *entrechats* are labeled according to the number of broken lines described by each foot while in midair (Figs. 43 through 48).

335

Entrechat 1 is the *soubresaut* in fifth position (§ 249). The term *entrechat 1* is absolutely never used; we mention it only to complete

*Literally, "beats with crossings."

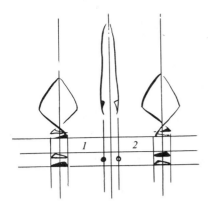

Figure 44

the series. In practice, however, since the foot does not describe a broken line, one might argue that the *soubresaut* should rather be called *entrechat 0.*

336

Entrechat 2 is called *changement de pied* (change of foot). The dancer, in fifth position, right foot forward, bends the knees, jumps, and alights in fifth with the left foot forward (Fig. 44).

337

Entrechat 3 is the first to bear the name of *entrechat.* The dancer, in fifth position, right foot forward, does a *plié*, jumps, crosses the right foot more pronouncedly in front, and alights in fifth with the left foot in front (Fig. 45).

338

Entrechat 4. The dancer, in fifth position, right foot forward, does a *plié*, jumps, moves into fifth with the left foot forward, and alights in fifth with the right foot forward (Fig. 46).

339

Entrechat 5. The dancer, in fifth position, right foot forward, does a *plié*, jumps, crosses the right foot more pronouncedly in front, moves into fifth with the left foot forward, and alights in fifth with the right foot forward (Fig. 47).

340

Entrechat 6. The dancer, in fifth position, right foot forward, does a *plié*, jumps, moves into fifth with the left foot forward, then into fifth with the right foot forward, and alights in fifth with the left foot forward (Fig. 48).

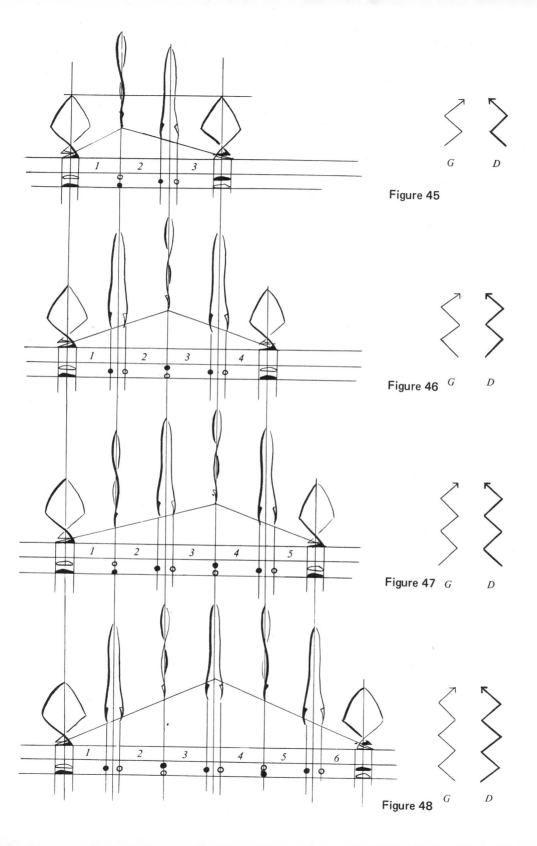

Figure 45

Figure 46

Figure 47

Figure 48

341

Entrechat 7. The dancer, in fifth position, right foot forward, does a *plié*, jumps while crossing the right foot more pronouncedly in front, moves into fifth with the left foot forward, then into fifth with the right foot forward, and alights in fifth with the left foot forward.

The term *entrechat 7* is generally applied to another step, which we shall describe later (§ 348), but logically it should be applied uniquely to the one we have just described.

342

Entrechat 8. The dancer, in fifth position, right foot forward, does a *plié*, jumps, passes successively into fifth with the left foot forward, into fifth with the right forward, into fifth with the left foot forward, and then alights in fifth with the right foot forward.

With *entrechat 8* the series of classical *entrechats* is concluded. These are the only ones that are now possible for female dancers; they never go beyond *entrechat 6* on the stage. The leading male dancers are about the only ones to execute the *entrechats 8* on the stage.

343

Entrechat 10. The dancer, in fifth position, right foot forward, jumps and moves successively into fifth with the left foot forward, right foot forward, left forward, and right forward, and then closes in fifth with the left foot forward.

This *entrechat* is very rare. It is virtually never executed on the stage, and only excellent dancers do it as an exercise. Nijinsky is said to have achieved it.

344

Theoretically, one can define an *entrechat* of any number whatever. In practice, it does not appear that *entrechats* of a number higher than those described have ever been executed.

However, with the support of a partner or with other support, *entrechats* up to a very high number will be found in the ballet—for example: when a dancer lifts his partner and she crosses and uncrosses her legs in midair, a movement very widely used in *adagios*; or, as in the first tableau of *Petrouchka* (Fokine), when the dancers are held up by a support, they do *entrechats* as long as they please.

345

On the whole, the uneven-numbered *entrechat* is always more difficult to achieve than the *entrechat* of the next higher even number: *entrechat 3* is more difficult than *entrechat* 4; *entrechat 5,* more difficult than *entrechat 6; entrechat 7,* much more difficult than *entrechat 8.*

It will thus be understood why *entrechat 7* as we have described it is almost never employed, its difficulty being greater than that of *entrechat 8,* which marks the present limit of possibilities of *entrechats* on the stage.

In general, *entrechats* 3 and 4 are classed in the *petite batterie,* the others in the *grande batterie.*

346

Entrechats 3 and 6 possess two distinct values. The first is the same as that of the other *entrechats,* the intrinsic value of the movement of elevation made brilliant by the rapid crossing and uncrossing of the feet.

But beyond that, these *entrechats* that begin with the right foot forward and end with the left foot forward may serve for changing feet. When the dancer has finished a step in fifth and needs to have the other foot forward in order to do the following step, the choreographer may have him execute an *entrechat 3* or an *entrechat 6.*

We find here the same idea that was present at the creation of the springing steps (*pas d'élan*), which we studied in the preceding sections: in classical dance, not even the most elementary details are left up to chance. The simple fact of having to move the left foot forward instead of the right foot results in the execution of a step that is already very difficult in itself.

347

We pointed out in § 341 the uncertainty about the definition of *entrechat 7.* Generally speaking, the nomenclature of the *entrechats* has given rise to—and continues to give rise to—numerous polemics. There is great confusion about the use of certain terms, and their meanings vary from one school to another. For example, we have not mentioned the **Royal** because it was not called for in our numerical succession. But according to the schools, this word designates *entrechat 3* (§ 337), *entrechat 5* (§ 339), or even *entrechat 4* (§ 338).

Historically it seems probable that it might apply to *entrechat 5*, because *entrechat 3* and *entrechat 4* were already in existence. The young Louis XIV, a great lover of the dance, used to participate in the ballets. It appears that someone, perhaps in a courtly gesture, may have wanted to flatter the king by attributing to him a manner of doing *entrechat 4* that was more brilliant than that of the other gentlemen, by crossing first in front.

However that may be, in the face of the controversies we have adopted a logical terminology based on the traditional vocabulary of the Opéra.

Thus it is that we have proposed that all the *entrechats* as such begin and end on both feet; that in the even-numbered *entrechats* the forward foot crosses first to the rear; and that in the uneven-numbered *entrechats* it crosses to the front (§ 334).

348

On the basis of the same principles, we shall define the *entrechats* beginning or ending on one foot, and we shall name them as follows—**entrechats volés** (flying): those in which the dancer, having started out in fifth, alights on one foot, generally on the one that would have been in front; the working leg remains *en quatrième devant*.

In principle, all the *entrechats* can be *volés*; in practice, only *entrechats* 3, 4, 5, and 6 are so executed. It is *entrechat 6 volé* that certain dancing masters call *entrechat 7*.

349

The **entrechats de volée** are taken in flight—that is, starting with one leg in the air. Often this leg happens to be *en quatrième devant*, occasionally in second position.

It is *entrechat 5* in particular that is done in this manner. The *entrechats de volée* are almost always preceded by a step that gives them momentum—for example, a *glissade* (§ 158) or a *passé* (§ 313).

350

The *entrechat* possessed a **characteristic moment,** the one when the two feet are crossed in the air. It is theoretically the same for all *entrechats,* but in practice the uneven-numbered *entrechats* present a more distinctive crossing than do the even-numbered: in the uneven-numbered ones, the two feet cross beyond each other; in the even-numbered ones, they remain one in front of the other (Fig. 49).

Figure 49. Characteristic moment of the
even-numbered *entrechat*

A *batterie* is all the more brilliant when the crossing is more accentuated and consequently executed more rapidly. But for the individual, the difference in the degree of crossing lies in the difference between the even- and uneven-numbered *entrechats*.

351

The **brisés** are a form of *entrechat 4 de volée*. These *glissades en descendant battues* (§ 158) are executed on a diagonal. The dancer, in fifth position, right foot forward, moves his left leg into second *à la demi-hauteur*, jumps, and executes an *entrechat 4 de volée*; his left leg passes in front of the right, and he alights in fifth, right foot forward.

This step produces a sideways progression toward the left—that is, to the side of the leg that is in back when the step begins. It involves no change of feet, and the dancer may execute a whole series of *brisés*, one after another.

The body turns and leans gently to the side toward which the dancer is going. The arms are in sixth position, with the curved arm on the side toward which the dancer is going.

352

Brisés volés de volée are executed alternately *devant* and *derrière*.

The dancer, in fifth position, right foot forward, does a *plié* while moving his left leg *en quatrième derrière à la demi-hauteur*; he leaps, crosses his left leg in front of the right, and alights in a *plié* on the left foot, with the right leg *en quatrième croisée devant à la demi-hauteur*. This is the first part of the step. He leaps again immediately, crossing the left leg in front of the right, and alights on the right; he then does a *plié* with his left leg *en quatrième derrière à la demi-hauteur ouverte*. This is the second part of the step. The dancer may start again by stringing together a series of these steps.

The body leans forward during the first part of the step and backward during the second. The head is turned to the side of the leg that is in the air. The arms are generally in second position, but asymmetrical, one of the arms being half-horizontal, the other half-vertical (§ 532). The arm that is lower is on the side of the supporting leg.

The *brisé de volée*, a brilliant but difficult step, is used particularly in masculine variations, and especially in codas: for example, in the *pas de deux* of *L'Oiseau bleu*, taken from *La Belle au bois dormant* (Petipa).

353

The **échappé battu** is an *entrechat 3* or *5* completed with the legs spread apart in second position.

The *échappé battu 3* is executed as follows: the dancer, in fifth position, right foot forward, does a *plié*, leaps, crosses the right foot more pronouncedly in front of the left and falls back in second, then does a *plié*.

To close the step, the dancer does a *plié*, leaps, brings his legs together in fifth, right foot forward, and alights in fifth, left foot forward.

In general, the two movements are joined, and the dancer does not straighten his legs between them.

For the *échappé battu 5*, the dancer, in fifth position, right foot forward, does a *plié*, leaps, crosses his right foot more pronouncedly in front of the left, then moves into fifth with the left foot forward, then the right foot forward, and alights in second position, knees bent.

To close, he leaps, moves into fifth with the left foot forward, then right foot forward, and alights in fifth, left foot forward.

354

Echappés could also be executed **with the other types of entrechat**—for example, the 4th or the 6th—by applying the following principle: for the opening, the dancer executes his *entrechat* normally, then alights in second position; for the closing of an *échappé battu 4* begun with the right foot forward, the dancer would leap, move into fifth with the left foot forward, and alight in fifth with the right foot forward; for an *échappé battu 6* begun with right foot forward, he would close while leaping, then move into fifth with the right foot forward, then left foot forward, before alighting in fifth with the right foot forward.

These two steps are not in common use at the present time.

355

The majority of these beating steps that we have just seen are *pas à terre* or *sauts simples*, complicated by the *batterie*; *entrechats* are *soubresauts battus*; the *entrechats* volés are *sissonnes battues*; the *entrechats de volée* are *assemblées battues*; the *brisé* is a *glissade battue*.

356

Generally speaking, *les pas battus à croisements* are brilliant and, since the introduction of the Italian style at the end of the nineteenth century, have been very much in favor. Male and female dancers practice them, but the men leap higher and execute beats from higher elevations than do the women.

BATTERIE DE CHOC*

357

Having examined the *pas de batterie à croisements*, we are now going to discuss the **batterie de choc** (beating steps with striking). In the steps of this type, the legs strike one against the other in midair. In general,

*Literally, "beats with impact."

there is only one impact (*choc*). Occasionally the male dancers strike their legs one against the other before alighting.

There are two main types of steps executed with *batterie de choc*: the *petits jetés* and the *cabrioles*.

358

The **petits jetés dessous** (downward) are done in the following manner: the dancer, in fifth position with right foot forward, raises his left leg into second position *à la demi-hauteur*, sliding the left foot while the right knee bends; the left knee bends in its turn, bringing the foot behind the calf of the right leg; immediately the dancer jumps, striking the left shinbone with the right calf; the left foot moves forward and rests *à terre*, with the knee bent, in front of the space that had been occupied by the right foot; the right leg is *au raccourci en quatrième derrière* against the other leg.

The dancer may start afresh with the other foot without closing in fifth position.

The moment of impact between the two legs is the characteristic moment.

359

The **petits jetés dessus** (upward) are done according to the same technique as those *dessous,* but the dancer, in fifth position with the right foot forward, lifts the right leg into second, and it is the right foot that will be in front of the left calf. During the *saut,* after the right calf has struck the left shinbone, the right foot rests *à terre* behind the place the left foot had occupied, with the left foot *au raccourci en quatrième devant*.

The dancer may start anew with the other foot without closing in fifth.

360

For some unknown reason the term **jeté battu** has been very popular with persons more or less unacquainted with the dance. Generally it is the only technical term they know, although occasionally they add to it that of *entrechat*. Numerous authors have used it in novels without knowing its exact significance. This step is, however, neither one of the most simple nor one of the most complicated, and while it is not rare, many other steps are used more often.

<hr>

361

The word **cabriole** is one of the rare dance terms whose etymology is certain and very old. It comes from the Latin word *capra,* meaning *goat.* The *cabriole* represents the leap of a goat. In current language it means a *leap,* but a more or less fantastic leap. The *Petit Larousse illustré* says: "an agile leap that is made while turning oneself around." Let us point out right away that the word has never had this meaning in the technical vocabulary. Most modern dictionaries give about the same definition. The dictionary of Maurice Lachâtre, published in 1881, gives a definition that seems to us more accurate: "Leap, nimble and agile caper. . . . Choreography: generic name for all leaps and especially for those where the legs beat against one another: the *entrechats* are *cabrioles.*"

We shall return to the second part of this definition, but let us first consider the general meaning.

According to the dictionary (except for the last one cited), the meaning of the word might correspond either to dangerous *sauts* or to *tours en l'air* (§ 461). But these steps are a very difficult type, never executed by the uninitiated. One might question the need for a word to designate anything so rare. It is often said that children do *cabrioles* and that, therefore, they involve neither dangerous *sauts* nor *tours en l'air.* Often the word is applied to *soubresauts en raccourci en quatrième devant* alternately with each leg (§ 258), the step of children's circle games. Sometimes it also signifies *soubresauts* in first position (§ 243), commonly called *sauts à pieds joints.* Finally, it may mean a somersault (*culbute*) (§ 495).

As far as the choreographic sense of the word is concerned, we have an observation to make. It had at first a very broad meaning; this, little by little, has become more limited. This is a normal evolution. The vocabulary of the dance is far from being rational and fixed. It evolves constantly and changes sometimes within one period from one school to the next. However, the law of the specialization of terms is a general law. And so, although the term *cabriole* was, in the beginning, a synonym for *batterie de choc,* it has come to signify in the modern sense: *batterie de choc à jambes tendues* (beats with striking, with the legs outstretched). Lachâtre's dictionary shows us that in 1880 the word still had the meaning of *batterie* (beats) in general, since it included the *entrechats*. It may be that the future will witness the appearance of a still narrower interpretation.

362

The **principle of the cabriole** is the *batterie* of the *soubresaut* in derivative position *à la hauteur* (§ 251). There are three types of *cabrioles* corresponding to the *quatrième devant à la hauteur*, the second *à la hauteur*, and the *quatrième derrière à la hauteur*.

A very complex fourth type came to be added to the three preceding ones. It is mainly a development of the first and last types and has become the most popular.

All *cabrioles* are preceded by a step that provides momentum. As with all the other *sauts,* it is necessary to perform a *plié* before leaping, and the dancer always alights on a leg that is *pliée*. We shall study the technique of each step.

363

Cabriole en quatrième devant: the dancer, on his left leg with the right leg *en quatrième devant à la hauteur*, jumps and strikes the calf of the right leg with the top of the shinbone of the left leg; he alights on the left leg, with the right leg *en quatrième devant à la hauteur*.

In principle, the right leg should not move from its position during the whole execution of the step. In practice, it is always lowered a little, but it must be raised immediately after the contact. The body is bent backward. The arms are in third position (§ 41), the position normally accompanying the *quatrième ouverte* (Fig. 50).

364

In classical dance, the *cabriole* is done *en quatrième ouverte*; it is normally preceded by a *passé* (§ 313) (Fig. 50), or less frequently by a *glissade* (§ 158). The *saut* must be as high as possible and result in a forward progression. This step is executed by female dancers as well as by male, but, as in the case of all *sauts,* men make more frequent use of it. Occasionally they do a double beating—that is, they strike their legs together twice in midair. This movement demands great elevation and, at the same time, a certain speed with the lower leg.

As in all steps *à batterie choc*, this one possesses a characteristic moment: the one in which the two legs strike together.

365

Cabriole in second position: the dancer begins on the left leg with the right leg in second position *à la hauteur*, leaps, strikes the right calf with the left calf, and alights on the left leg with the right leg in second position *à la hauteur*.

Just as for the *cabriole en quatrième devant*, the right leg should not be voluntarily lowered for the *choc*, but it always does so slightly and then rises again immediately afterward. The body remains straight. The arms open into second position, the arm that is on the side of the leg that is in the air at the beginning of the step is lifted higher than the other.

366

This *cabriole* is not only much more difficult than the preceding one, it is the most difficult of all the *cabrioles*. It is never performed twice in succession. Only excellent male dancers achieve it *à la hauteur*. Female dancers do it only very rarely on the stage.

The *cabriole à la hauteur* is preceded by a *glissade en descendant* (§ 158) that supplies the momentum.

The characteristic moment is the *choc* of the two calves against each other.

367

Cabriole en quatrième derrière: the dancer begins on the left leg with the right leg *en quatrième derrière à la hauteur*; he leaps, strikes the shinbone of the right leg with the calf of the left leg, and alights on the left leg with the right leg *en quatrième derrière à la hauteur*.

The right leg, in spite of the principle of immobility, is always definitely lowered. The body is inclined slightly forward.

368

This *cabriole* may occur in pure form in certain masculine steps. For example, a series of *cabrioles en quatrième derrière* without intermediate transition steps is found in *Études* (Harald Lander).

It may also be done *croisée* or *ouverte*. It may be preceded by a sort of *pas de bourrée* (§ 437) or by a light *pas de course*, which is improperly called *pas de bourrée courus*.

The characteristic moment is at the impact of the two legs behind the line of the body.

Figure 50. *Passé-cabriole battu en quatrième devant*

369

The last type of *cabriole* is executed after a *passé* in profile, which earns it the name: **passé-cabriole**.

The dancer begins in fifth position with the right foot forward and executes the *passé* (§ 313); he then lifts the right leg *en quatrième devant* and leaps, while turning the body toward the left, which causes the leg to move *en quatrième derrière*; simultaneously, he strikes the shinbone of the right leg *en quatrième derrière à la hauteur*.

Less frequently, the right calf is struck against the left shinbone.

During the whole step, the body remains straight and the arms make the movement described in § 256 with the *passé-cabriole non battu*.

370

This is the type of *cabriole* that is used most frequently. It does not offer too great a difficulty. Male and female dancers perform it. It must always be very elevated.

The *passé-cabriole* may be performed **battu double** in two manners: two seemingly successive *chocs*; or one *choc* before the turning-around, with the right calf against the left shinbone, and the other afterwards, with the left calf against the right shinbone. The latter type is much more difficult; it is the exclusive province of the great dancers.

371

To **designate the cabrioles**, the name of the step that provides the momentum is normally employed. Thus we say: *passé-cabriole devant*; *glissade-cabriole*; *pas de bourrée-cabriole*; *passé-cabriole*. Only the first type is seen joined to the word *devant* to distinguish it from the latter.

372

The *sissonnes* may also be performed *avec un choc:* the step begins like an ordinary *sissonne,* but after having begun to separate, the legs meet for the *choc*; the step ends normally.

FOUR

The Turns

373

Having seen the *pas à terre* and the *temps sautés*, we shall take up the last group of steps: the *tours*.

They involve a rotation about the axis of the body. They may be executed on both feet, on one foot, or while leaping. The first two types are characterized by a constant contact with the ground and will be classed in the *tours à terre*.

374

Turns are by nature dynamic. Rarely do they have a characteristic moment. This is especially true of the turns performed *à terre*. In the great majority of cases the position does not vary during the period of the rotation, and it is often identified with an essential moment of a non-turning step.

375

They are a universal element of the dance, but many people know only the forms of *tours* on both feet because those on one foot require a very conscious combination of positions of the arms, the trunk, and the head. Only elaborate systems make wide use of them.

Generally speaking, *tours* involve a *plié* at the beginning and at the end.

TOURS A TERRE SUR DEUX PIEDS*

376

As we indicated above, we shall designate as **tours à terre** all those steps in which one or **both feet** are constantly in contact with the ground (*tours à terre sur deux pieds*). We shall first study those for which both feet play a simultaneous and substantially equal role.

Tours are executed *sur la demi-pointe* or *sur la pointe*. In character dances, *tours* may be done *à plat* or *sur le talon* (on the heel).

377

The simplest turns are the **piétinés**. They are executed by little alternate steps on each foot so as to rotate the body around the fixed point of its own vertical axis. In general, *piétinés* are done in place.

The *piétinés* may be executed *à plat*, *sur la demi-pointe,* or *sur la pointe* in the first, second, and fifth positions. Third position will be considered as if it were fifth.

378

Piétinés in first position do not exist in the classical dance but are found in the popular or folkloric dances. Most often they are executed *à plat* by female dancers.

The feet are in first position at *demi-normale*—that is, heels together, toes open. The knees are not bent. In general, the rotation is not rapid.

379

Piétinés in second position do not exist in the classical dance either. They are practiced primarily in Oriental dances, with legs very *en dehors* and with knees bent. They are done slowly, *à plat*. These are rather ungainly steps generally reserved for male dancers.

They are done *sur la pointe* by the Ballerina in *Petrouchka* (Fokine).

380

Piétinés in fifth position are the only ones used in the classical dance. They are executed primarily *sur les pointes* by female dancers and *sur les demi-pointes* by male dancers.

149   *Turns performed on the ground on both feet.

It is practically impossible to execute them *à plat*, given the special position taken by the feet.

Piétinés may be done at varying speeds. They almost always turn toward the side of the forward foot. The step may be accompanied by movements of the body and arms, as, for example, in the so-called variation of the Cigarette from *Suite en Blanc* (Lifar).

381

A particular type of *piétinés en tournant* is executed with one foot *à plat* and one foot *sur la demi-pointe*—that is, in **demi-cinquième**.

The foot that is *à plat* serves as a sort of pivot, while in the preceding cases the axis of the turn was between the two feet. The dancer thus turns with little steps executed *sur la demi-pointe* around the foot that is *à plat*. The step is almost always done while crossing the foot *sur la demi-pointe en cinquième derrière*. The knee of the foot that is *à plat* is straight; the other is slightly bent. This type of step is very popular in Oriental dances, such as those of India, Mongolia, Turkestan, and even China and Japan.

382

Related to the turning *piétinés* is the **ronde** that is done with little sideways movements of the feet—that is, when the characters remain facing the center of the circle. This is a rotation common to a group of persons. The turning, instead of being done by each dancer around his personal axis, is done by all around the common center.

If the dancers are in profile, their movement is akin to the *marche* and no longer has the same character at all.

383

Having concluded the series of *piétinés*, we shall take up the **détourné**. The principle of this step is the rotation of the body on both feet, with or without their moving, according to the individual case; the body pivots toward the foot that happens to be to the rear.

384

The *détourné à terre* is very simple: the dancer, in fifth position, right foot forward, shifts his left foot *en quatrième derrière très croisée* while bending the supporting leg and inclining the body forward in a position very characteristic of the step. Then, leaving the left leg in its place, he pivots toward the left by little shifts of the right foot, which is *à plat*, while this time the left leg turns around on itself toward the left, so that when the dancer has achieved a *demi-tour,* he finds that he has his left leg *à pointe en quatrième devant*. He finishes his complete turn, always with little shifts of the right foot, while letting the left toe, which remains *en quatrième devant*, brush against the ground.

This step is generally performed very slowly. At the beginning of the step, the arms open to the rear half-horizontally; during the rotation they rise *en couronne* at the sides.

At the beginning of the step, the body leans forward and slightly to the side of the forward leg; it becomes erect during the *détourné*.

385

The **détourné sur les deux pointes** is taken in fifth position: the dancer rises *sur les deux pointes* while leaping very slightly in order to cross them more and to prepare for the *tour* to the side of the rear foot. He then pivots—practically without moving the two *pointes*—in order to reassume his place in fifth with the left foot forward.

As opposed to the preceding step, this one is done very rapidly. In the classical dance, it is executed *sur les pointes* by the female dancers and *sur les demi-pointes* by the male.

The arm movement is the same as for the *détourné à terre*.

This step is also called **temps de pointe détourné**.

386

The **pas de bourrée détourné** is executed in a very compact continuous movement; the successive movements are fleeting and slurred together and are hardly distinct one from the other.

The dancer, in fifth position, right foot forward, bends his right knee and steps directly *à la pointe* of his left foot, very decidedly *croisé en quatrième derrière*; while standing erect again and turning toward the left, he points his right foot clearly in second, continuing the turning movement before facing forward again and closing in fifth, left foot forward.

This step may be executed alternately from each side.

387

The **enveloppés** work on a principle that is practically the opposite of the *détournés*: the body turns on two feet, always toward the rear leg, but only after the leg that originally had been behind has been brought forward; this leg turns in the direction of the leg that was originally in front.

388

The term **enveloppé simple** is applied to the step executed as follows: the dancer, in fifth position, right foot forward, shifts his left leg into second position, barely *à la demi-hauteur*; while bending the right leg, the left leg describes a sort of *petit rond de jambe en dedans,* as in an *enveloppé*, and steps directly *sur la pointe* crossed immediately in front of the other foot, which simultaneously rises *sur la pointe*; by the impulse thus given, the body continues to turn to the right as for a *détourné sur les deux pointes*. The dancer then returns to fifth, right foot forward.

Several *enveloppés* may be strung together in series; in this case, the step does not close in fifth, but the leg shifts directly into second position.

Executed a very great number of times in succession, this step is very brilliant. Female dancers do it *sur la pointe,* male dancers *sur la demi-pointe.*

389

The **pas de bourrée enveloppé** resembles the *pas de bourrée détourné.*

The dancer, in fifth position, right foot forward, shifts his left foot into second *à la demi-hauteur* and steps directly *sur la pointe* as for an *enveloppé simple*; while the trunk pivots toward the right, the right foot steps *sur la pointe* in its turn, and at the end of the step the dancer finds himself facing front, right foot forward.

390

This step involves no change of feet, and the dancer could do it several times successively in the same direction, but this is not done because it requires three movements: at the end of the first, the body is being supported by the left leg, which has just stepped on *pointe;* at the end of the second, it is on the right leg, which has shifted; at the end of the third it is on the left. It would thus be difficult, if the dancer executed the step rapidly several times in succession, to shift this leg without pause while bringing the weight of the body onto the other leg. The balance thus obtained would be unstable.

In general, when the dancer wishes to execute a series, he terminates the *pas de bourrée enveloppé* on the left foot, with the right leg *au raccourci en quatrième derrière* to permit the execution of a *pas de bourrée détourné* taken with the left leg forward, thus turning to the right—that is, in the same direction as the *pas de bourrée enveloppé*. The succession *pas de bourrée enveloppé-pas de bourrée détourné* can thus be repeated a great number of times. It is a very brilliant series because it may be executed very rapidly. It is reserved almost exclusively for female dancers, who do it *sur les pointes.*

391

The **demi-tours relevés** (rising half-turns) are composed of two parts: the dancer, in fifth position, right foot forward, raises the right foot *sur la pointe,* bringing the left leg *au raccourci* in front of the right knee while making a *demi-tour* toward the right; he closes in fifth, left foot forward; he then raises the left foot *sur la pointe* while bringing the right leg *au raccourci* in front of the left knee, making a second *demi-tour* toward the right, and closes in fifth, right foot forward.

The arms are in sixth position (§ 44), with the curved arm on the side of the leg *au raccourci.*

This step is most often done in series and on a diagonal, with the shoulders parallel to that diagonal. Actually, if it is done face forward, at the end of the first *demi-tour* the dancer finds himself with his back to the audience, while on a diagonal the dancer is turned only three-quarters of the way around. At the end of the first *demi-tour,* the head is in profile to the side of the curved arm, which permits the audience to see the face; at the end of the second *demi-tour,* the dancer is facing the audience.

392

Demi-tours relevés sans fermeture intermédiaire (rising half-turns without intervening closings) are performed like the preceding ones, but at the end of the first *demi-tour* there is no closing in fifth, and the foot is placed directly *sur la pointe.*

The positions of the arms and of the head are the same. Like the preceding step, this is done in series and on a diagonal. This step can also be done with a *tour et demi,* or even two *tours,* in the place of each *demi-tour.*

393

The **déboulés** (pirouettes) are the final type of turn executed on both feet. They are sometimes called *tours chaînés* (chained turns). It seems that in the modern classical dance they originated in Italy and spread throughout Europe at the end of the nineteenth century, to be imported into Russia by Pierina Legnani and Virginia Zucchi and into France by Carlotta Zambelli.

For a long time they were executed *sur la demi-pointe,* and it is not much more than thirty years that they have been done *sur la pointe.*

Originally, only the leading dancers ventured to execute them in this manner, but eventually *déboulés* came to be expected of the whole *corps de ballet.* At the present time, even the students in the *Ecole de danse de l'Opéra* must be able to do them.

It is generally believed that the *déboulé* was actually invented at the end of the nineteenth century, and that this is an instance of an original step. However, it is much older than that, because the Greeks were already performing it more than two thousand years ago, as is testified to by figurines on vases and by a text.[1]

394

To do the **déboulés**, the dancer, in fifth position, right foot forward, shifts his right foot forward *sur la pointe,* then steps directly *sur la pointe* with a rapid movement *en quatrième très ouverte*; he turns toward the right, and, at the end of a *demi-tour,* places his left foot *sur la pointe* behind the right, which immediately rises, going into the *tour*; the dancer faces front once again, places the right foot in front of the left, and continues his movement.

The rotation is rapid and continuous. These steps are done in series of at least two. The spectator then has the impression of seeing a top spinning steadily, without any jerking, and gliding over the ground without support. The legs are kept as close as possible to each other during the entire step.

The arms do not move—they are generally in an intermediate position between the *position de départ* (§ 38) and first position (§ 39).

---

[1] G. Prudhommeau: *La Danse grecque antique.* Editions du C.N.R.S., 1965. § 526 to 528, pp. 153-154, and Figs. 444-445.

395

In rapid turns, the **movement of the head** is never synchronized with that of the body. It is necessary for the dancer to see where she is going, otherwise she becomes dizzy, loses her sense of direction, and very rapidly loses her balance. To be able to fix her attention instantly upon the point toward which she is headed, at one point during each turn the dancer must allow her head to be immobile with respect to her destination. This technique is called **spotting**. The dancer continues to face toward her destination momentarily while her trunk turns *épaulé* toward the right; her head then swings quickly around to the front again—catching up to and passing the body in the process.

This particular movement is applicable to all rapid turns and, consequently, to most of the turns on one foot that we shall study in succeeding sections. It demands serious training and great independence of movement, but it is the *sine qua non* of good execution. In spite of what one might think, this absence of symmetry between the head and the body is not unaesthetic; on the contrary, it gives the spectators the impression of always seeing the dancer's face.

In general, dancers select a fixed point by which to guide their turns. That is why it is very difficult to turn in the open air, where there is nothing upon which to fix one's glance.

For the *déboulés* the dancer is drawn inescapably to this point of reference; whether she wishes to or not, she moves toward the point she is watching.

396

Some schools have the **déboulés executed with a somewhat different technique**. The dancer, in fifth position, right foot forward, brings that foot *sur la pointe en quatrième très ouverte* while starting to turn toward the right; she moves her left foot while doing an *enveloppé* and steps in front of the right while continuing to turn; the uncrossing of the legs leads her around face forward.

This manner of doing the step seems better adapted to *demi-pointe,* whereas *sur la pointe* the first technique gives more regularity and allows a much greater speed.

397

Ever since their first appearance, *déboulés* have enjoyed a considerable vogue.

Their rapidity made the dancer seem actually weightless—she appeared not to touch the ground. Soon it became customary to terminate every female dancer's variation with *déboulés*. This practice remains in almost general use at the present time.

Déboulés were subsequently introduced into the very midst of variations; they were not always done in a straight line, but sometimes for the length of the footlights to complete a circular series of other turns or on a diagonal.

Then *déboulés* began to appear in the course of a circular series (*manége*, literally, "merry-go-round"), alternately with other steps. Finally, in recent years, certain stars have dared to do complete circular series of *déboulés*. These are currently practiced in classes but are still rare on the stage.

TOURS A TERRE SUR UN PIED*

398

Having seen the *tours à terre sur deux pieds*, we will now consider the *tours* on one foot alone. As for the preceding ones, we find among them *tours* that are executed *à plat, sur la demi-pointe*, and *sur la pointe*. As a general rule, only the slow *tours* can be performed *à plat*; the rapid ones are, in principle, executed *sur la pointe* by female dancers and *sur la demi-pointe* by the men.

Tours à terre on one foot are divided into two categories: *tours à terre* on one foot without change of position of the foot (*tours de promenade* or *sur la pointe,* stepping directly onto the toe); and *tours à terre relevés* on one foot (§ 421-458).

We shall devote a different section to each of these categories.

399

Tours de promenade are very slow and are executed *à plat* on one foot, knee straight, with the other leg in a derivative position. The foot that is on the ground pivots in little shifts but without jumping. The entire body must remain absolutely immobile while turning.

These *tours* are generally executed *en quatrième devant* and in second *à la hauteur, en quatrième devant raccourci, en arabesque*, and *en attitude*. It is much more rare to find them in second position *raccourci*; the *demi-hauteur* is almost never used.

*Turns performed on the ground on one foot.

400

Tours de promenade with change of position are begun in a derivative position and proceed to another position during the turning. They may be done with the leg straight or bent and even with a straight leg bending during the *tour* and vice versa.

This whole group of steps is used in particular in the *adagios*.

Among these we might cite the *tour* beginning *en attitude* and turning to the side of the leg that is in the air, which moves, *au raccourci,* into *quatrième devant*. Eventually, it may be terminated by a *développé* (§ 129) of the leg *au raccourci*.

If, beginning *en attitude*, the dancer turns to the side opposite the working leg, at the end of the turn the leg is extended *en arabesque croisée*.

There are also other forms with similar techniques.

401

The **dètourès à la hauteur** are a form of *tour de promenade* with change of position.

The dancer, in fifth position, right foot forward, makes a *demi-tour* to the left, places the left foot *à plat* in front of him, and lifts his right leg in *battement en quatrième devant à la hauteur*; he continues turning toward the left by little shifts of the left foot; the right leg, which remains in approximately the same place, moves into second, then into *quatrième derrière* to finish in *arabesque croisée*.

The name of the step is derived from the turning of the body.

The opposite movement may be executed starting from the *arabesque,* but in this case, the movement is not started with a *demi-tour.*

402

We now take up the series of **pirouettes**. This is the name for turns in which the body, resting on one foot alone, does one or more turns about itself without the supporting foot moving. *Tours de promenade* in which the supporting foot furnishes movement by means of little shifts may, therefore, not be classed as *pirouettes*. In *pirouettes,* the impulse is given either by the whole body at one single time to begin the *pirouette* or by the working leg in the course of the movement.

The *pirouettes* are very numerous and complex. In the main, they may be divided into *pirouettes piquées* and *pirouettes relevées*. Among the *pirouettes relevées* we distinguish *pirouettes en dedans* and *pirouettes en dehors*.

403

We shall begin our study with the **pirouettes piquées**, which are governed by a general principle: the dancer, starting from the fifth or from a derivative position, steps directly *sur la pointe* and then turns. Filming makes it possible actually to observe that a fraction of a second separates the moment when the *pointe* is placed on the ground from the one in which the turning begins. This separation—imperceptible to the naked eye—helps to create a well-executed turn.

404

The name *pirouette piquée* or, in its shortened form, **piqué**, is particularly applied to the following step: the dancer, in fifth position, right foot forward, bends her left leg and steps directly *sur la pointe* of her right foot *en quatrième devant à peine* (barely) *ouverte*; she does a complete turn to the right with the left leg *au raccourci* in second and the left foot behind the right calf. When the dancer returns to a forward position, she places the left foot *à plat* behind the right while doing a *plié* and immediately shifts the straightened right leg *en quatrième devant à la demi-hauteur*. She may then step directly onto the right toe (*piqué*), starting from fourth position *à la demi-hauteur*. In general, the dancer does a small leap onto the *piqué*.

405

These turns effect a **déplacement** (progression) toward the front. They are generally executed a great number of times consecutively on a diagonal or in a circle. The series is completed almost always by *déboulés* (§ 394).

This step is performed very frequently, and almost exclusively by female dancers. It is the most often employed of the *manèges* (circle routines—literally, "merry-go-round"); it concludes most of the great classical variations: the two variations of Etoile in the ballet from *Faust* (Aveline), that of the first act of *Giselle* (Coralli and Perrot), that of the Flute from *Suite en Blanc* (Lifar), and so on.

In exceptional cases, a variation will begin with a *manège de piqués*: the variation of the Green Fairy from *Divertissement* (version of 12 May 1948 at the [Paris] Opera, choreography after Ivanoff).

406

When in a *tour* the working leg is *au raccourci,* as has been explained, the turn is said to be **dans le jarret** (literally, "in the knee").

If the working leg is barely raised from the ground, bringing the foot to the height of the ankle of the supporting leg, the *tour* is said to be **sur le cou-de-pied** (on the instep).

When *tours* are done very fast they are usually on the instep.

To traverse a larger space, dancers often leap forward *sur la pointe* in the first movement instead of doing a *piqué* in fourth position.

In a *manège de piqués,* each includes only one *tour.* Certain very gifted dancers do one *tour* three times, two *tours* one time, and the like. On a diagonal, a good dancer does one to two *tours.*

407

Piqués en attitude are a little more difficult than the preceding ones and are executed more slowly. They begin like ordinary *piqués,* but the left leg, instead of coming *au raccourci* into second or on the instep, rises *en attitude.* The arms are also in the position of *attitude*—that is, the left arm vertical and the right arm extended horizontally to the side.

408

This step has an aesthetic value that is different from the preceding one. Its merit lies not in brilliance and speed but in elegance and grace.

The position of the body and that of the arms must be impeccable. Good dancers do two *tours en attitude*; three are exceptional. It is rare that several *piqués* are done consecutively *en attitude.*

The conclusion of the step varies according to the circumstances, a fact that may occasionally increase the difficulty. The left leg may come down to close in fifth position behind the right. It may return to the front in order to do a *pas de bourrée enveloppé* (§ 389). The most difficult thing is to complete the two turns *en attitude* while maintaining the position and coming down again simply with the foot *à plat.* This conclusion is found twice in the variation from the first act of *Giselle* (Coralli and Jules Perrot).

Quite often turns *en attitude,* like those *en arabesque* that we shall see later, are preceded by a *failli* (§ 320).

409

Tours piqués en arabesque are encountered as often as turns *en attitude*. They are executed by male dancers as well as by female.

The *tours en arabesque* are executed with an *arabesque ouverte* (§ 69) that is maintained throughout the turning.

410

Actually, we should speak of *tours en demi-arabesque,* because the leg is never lifted very high; however, we shall keep the customary term of *tours en arabesque*.

Good dancers, male and female, perform two *tours*. When the *tour* is done on the right leg, the right arm is, in principle, extended forward and the left backward, but variations may be found. One example is in the tarantella from the *Chevalier errant* (Lifar), the variation of the fourth Dulcinea, during the *manège*. Double turns are also found *piqués en arabesque* with hands on the shoulders.

411

Piqués in second position are much less common. The leg must be *à la hauteur* and immobile during the whole turning in second position; it is difficult not to let it slide *en quatrième derrière*.

These turns, which are nearly always executed double, are preceded by a *failli* (§ 320). They are found in the variation of the Black Swan taken from the third act of *Lac des Cygnes* (Petipa and Ivanoff).

412

In **tours piqués en quatrième devant** or *en raccourci en quatrième devant*, the working leg takes its position by means of an enveloppé.

413

Simple **piqués enveloppés** are executed as follows: the dancer, in fifth position, right foot forward, brings her left foot forward with a small *rond de jambe à terre* (§ 123) and steps directly *sur la pointe en quatrième devant*; she turns to the right, bringing the right leg *au raccourci* in second with the foot in front of the left knee. When the *tour* has been completed and the dancer has resumed a forward position, she places her right foot flat in front of the left while shifting the left leg into second *à la demi-hauteur* in order to start another *piqué enveloppé.*

414

Like *piqués* themselves, the *piqués enveloppés* are executed on a diagonal or *en manège, dans le jarret* or *sur le cou-de-pied.*

They are usually done by women.

One or two *tours* may be done from a single impulse.

The arms are *en couronne* (§ 43) or in a *position de départ* (§ 38).

415

Piqués enveloppés may be made more elaborate by adding, during each turn, a *petit battement sur le cou-de-pied* with the working leg; that is, the working leg, which is in front of the other leg, passes rapidly backward and returns forward. This movement might very well be compared with that done by one leg in an *entrechat*. In the ballet *Giselle* (Coralli and Jules Perrot), diagonals of *piqués enveloppés* with *petits battements sur le cou-de-pied* are found twice in the first act.

It is also possible to do a *développé*—that is, to straighten the working leg during the turning, or to straighten it only at the end of the step, after the foot has come back down *à plat*. Finally, the working leg may move *à l'attitude* at the end of the step.

416

Tours enveloppés piqués en raccourci en quatrième devant are done like the preceding ones, but the working leg is placed *au raccourci en quatrième devant* instead of *au raccourcï* in second, and the angle of the knee is obtuse instead of acute.

These turns are very pretty to watch, but very difficult to execute. They are not really seen to advantage unless there are two of them. They are executed solely by female dancers and must be done very slowly.

The body leans forward; the arms are *en couronne,* but crossed at the level of the wrists.

417

Finally, there are **tours enveloppés piqués en attitude**, in which the leg rises directly *à l'attitude.*

But the arms, instead of being placed in the normal position of *attitude* (§ 41), rise *en couronne* (§ 43).

Like all steps utilizing *attitude,* these turns make a very pretty effect.

418

Tours posés (sitting turns) have a very complex technique. The dancer, in fifth position with the right foot forward, shifts her left foot *en quatrième derrière à la pointe,* then places it *à plat*; turning her body a quarter-turn toward the left, she steps *sur la pointe* of her right foot behind the left, while putting her leg *au raccourci* in second as for the *piqué* (§ 404); in this position she executes a *demi-tour* and, resuming a forward position, she closes the left foot in fifth behind the right foot. She may then commence another *tour posé*. While she is turning, the arms rise *en couronne* above the head.

419

These turns are very easy because they are well balanced. Furthermore, the dancer, taking advantage of a *demi-tour* at the outset, may more easily do two or three *tours.*

The *tours posés* are used by female dancers in numerous classical variations. They may also be done by men.

These *tours* may be concluded with a *développé en quatrième derrière,* bringing the working leg *en arabesque*. In this case, the arms are placed at the sides in a semi-vertical position (§ 520).

420

Tours posés en attitude are done like the preceding ones, but instead of placing the working leg *au raccourci,* the dancer places it *en attitude.* The arms adopt the position of *attitude* These *tours* are more difficult than the preceding ones, since the leg *en attitude* makes the balance less sure.

TOURS A TERRE RELEVES SUR UN PIED*

421

We have concluded the study of turns of the *piqué* type. We are now going to take up that of the **tours relevés** (rising turns). These turns,

*Rising turns performed on the ground on one foot.

when they are executed *sur la pointe,* are more difficult than the preceding ones, but *sur la demi-pointe* they are relatively easy.

In these turns, starting from a position with the foot *à plat*, the dancer rises *sur la pointe* or *demi-pointe* by the sole force of the muscles of the knee (essentially the femoral biceps), at the same time he is turning. The supporting foot is not at its maximum height—that is, either *sur la pointe* or *demi-pointe,* until the working leg leaves the ground.

422

A distinction is made between *tours en dehors* and *tours en dedans* according to the direction of the rotation.

The turn is **en dehors** when the dancer turns to the side of the working leg.

The turn is **en dedans** when the dancer turns to the side of the supporting leg.

423

In *pirouettes,* the **role of the arms** is not as essential as has sometimes been supposed. With certain *tours*—for example, *tours relevés en attitude*—the arms remain absolutely immobile, and yet a good dancer can do two *tours* under these conditions. Furthermore, if the arms move at the beginning or at the end of a *tour,* they must remain fixed in their position during the turning, otherwise they may cause an imbalance.

The impulse—the momentum for the *tour*—thus comes from elsewhere, principally from the shoulder. A supplementary impulse is supplied by the supporting leg, because all the *tours relevés* are taken after a *plié*, which helps not only the rising *sur la pointe* but the turning as well.

In the *tours en dehors,* a supplementary impulse is given by the working leg, which explains why, for a given technique, more *tours* are done *en dehors* than *en dedans* in a single impulse.

424

We have seen that the *tours relevés* are divided into *tours en dehors* and *tours en dedans.* This is the division recognized by dancing masters. But we shall distinguish two further categories: the *tours relevés* that start on both feet; and those that start out on one foot alone.

425

We shall begin by studying the **tours relevés preparé sur deux pieds**. These are differentiated most especially according to their preparation. They are very numerous and are immensely popular. They are executed as often by female dancers as by men in all the variations.

As in the case of *tours piqués*, a good female dancer is not content to make only one *tour*. Normally, every dancer from the corps de ballet of the Opera must do two *tours*. Certain dancing stars do three *tours sur pointe*—and, in exceptional cases, four—on the stage. In class they may attain five or six *tours,* but rarely without an additional leap.

The male dancers, *sur la demi-pointe,* must do three or four *tours*. Good male dancers do five or six; very talented ones do seven or eight. Very exceptionally, a dancer may achieve a dozen turns.

On 27 February 1952, at the opening performance of *Fourberies* (Lifar), the star dancer, Michel Renault, who executed for the first time onstage a masculine variation *sur pointes,* did five *tours sur la pointe* from a single impulse.

426

For **tours prepared in fourth position, en dehors**, the dancer may arrive at this fourth in different ways:

· Beginning in fifth position, right foot forward, he does a *pas de bourrée* (§ 192), but instead of closing in fifth, left foot forward, he closes in fourth, left foot forward.

· Beginning in fifth, right foot forward, he shifts his foot into second position (§ 103), then places it *en quatrième derrière*.

· Beginning in fifth, right foot forward, he does an *échappé sauté* in fourth (§ 302) and brings his left foot down in front (or, less frequently, his right foot).

· Beginning in fifth, right foot forward, he shifts his left foot into second and places it *en quatrième devant*.

· With one leg in the air, he places it *en quatrième devant* or *derrière*.

Generally speaking, the fourth may be arrived at from any step whatever, but the first two preparations that have been pointed out are the most popular. Female dancers are more likely to use the *pas de bourrée*, and male dancers, the *dégagé.*

The dancer, in fourth position, left foot forward, turns toward the right, rising on the left foot and placing the right leg *au raccourci* in second, the *pointe* being slightly forward and below the left knee.

These *tours* may also be done "on the instep" (§ 406). It is mainly male dancers who execute them in this way when they do many of them from a single impulse. Finally, there are *tours relevés en attitude* or *en arabesque.*

When the *tour* or *tours* are completed, the dancer closes *dègagè en cinquième derrière* or in fourth position. In the latter position, he is ready to start a new *tour* in the same direction.

Another, less common method consists of ending on one foot while coming back down simply from the *pointe* or *demi-pointe,* but this is quite difficult. In this case, the dancer may move the working leg toward the rear *en arabesque* or *en attitude.*

These turns are much used; they are found in almost all the variations.

The female dancer may do them in *pas de deux* with a partner who guides her with his hands placed around her waist and keeps her from losing her balance. In this case a dancer does three or four *tours;* a star does five or six—even more with a good partner.

427

Tours relevés prepared in fourth position, en dedans, begin like the preceding ones, with the dancer arriving at fourth. Let us assume, then, that the dancer is in fourth, left foot forward. He will turn to the left on his left foot, leaving his right leg *au raccourci* in second as for the *tour en dehors,* on the knee or on the instep, with the *pointe* of the working leg in front of the other leg *en attitude* or *en arabesque.*

These *tours* are used less often than the preceding ones. As we explained in paragraph 423, one may make fewer turns *en dedans* than *en dehors.* They are, however, practiced in class.

428

Tours relevés en dehors prepared for by a temps de pointe relevé on both feet.

The dancer, in fifth position, right foot forward, executes a *temps de pointe relevé* on both feet (§ 173), then closes again in fifth and turns on her left foot toward the right, while bringing the right leg *au raccourci* in second with the *pointe* in front of the left knee. When the turn is completed, the right foot closes *en cinquième derrière* (Fig. 51) or in front of the left foot. If the closing was to the rear, another *tour* can be started in the other direction; if it was closed forward, a *tour* can be begun in the same direction. A series may be done in this fashion—for example, sixteen.

Figure 51. *Tour en dehors*

This type of *tour* is used more by female than by male dancers. A good female dancer makes two *tours*; stars may make three.

Male dancers prefer turns in fourth. When they do these turns, they execute them on the instep.

429

Turns involving the same technique may be taken starting from **another preparation terminating in fifth**: *echappé sur les pointes* (§ 299), *dégagé en quatrième devant* (§ 107), and, less frequently, *quatrième derrière* (§ 108), closed in fifth; *temps de pointe piqué* (§ 165), *relevé* on the anterior foot while bringing the working leg *au raccourci* in second, *pointe* behind the supporting leg (§ 17), and so forth.

One can even begin these *tours* with an *agenouillement* (kneeling movement) (§ 231), but it is very difficult.

Certain very gifted dancers execute them with a movement taken from an ice-skating step: beginning with knees bent, then straightening them, then finishing *plié*. These require both excellent balance and the ability to perform many turns from a single impulse.

430

The **tours relevés en dedans prepared for by a temps de pointe relevé on both feet** would be done, after the same preparation, to the left on the left foot.

They are almost never used, since they have little aesthetic value and are very difficult to execute.

431

Tours fouettés enveloppés start from a fourth position. Assume that the right foot is forward. The left leg is lifted into second *à la hauteur*, then does a *fouetté* (whipping motion) (§ 130), with the *pointe* of the foot placed in front of the right knee while the right foot is raised *sur la pointe* and the dancer turns toward the right. The left foot closes in front of the right foot.

These *tours*, which are very spectacular, are not particularly difficult. It is possible to perform two or three *tours* from a single impulse.

They are often used in the ballets. For example, in the variation from the first act of *Giselle*, she does them to the right and to the left.

Male dancers also perform them.

In the *adagio*, the female dancer may execute them while being held at the waist (as in § 426) or by holding with one hand the male dancer's finger, which is held above her head pointing straight down. This serves as a sort of pivot for her. In the first instance, she may complete them *en poisson* (§ 699).

432

A **variation** consists of causing the working leg to move *en attitude* at the end of the turn. In this case, the foot closes immediately *en cinquième derrière*, or remains *en attitude*, with the supporting foot coming back down *à plat*.

Like all turns ending on one foot, this one is very difficult.

The dancer may also finish with the working leg in second position in order to link the *tour* immediately to another step.

433

In general, during these *tours* the **trunk** is inclined to the side of the working leg, and the head is in profile on the same side. At the end, the trunk becomes erect and even arched back, with the turn concluded *en attitude.*

The arms rise *en couronne* (§ 43) toward the front at the same time that the *fouetté* (§ 130) is being performed.

434

Fouettés détournés are sometimes called simply *fouettés,* but this leads to confusion, because this name is more often used as an abbreviation for *ronds de jambes fouettés* (§ 455).

The *fouetté détourné* has nothing in common with the *fouettés* seen in paragraph 130. It is executed as follows: the dancer, in fifth position with the right foot forward, lifts her left leg in *quatrième derrière ouverte à la hauteur* and does a *soubresaut* on the right foot while turning about a quarter of the way to the right; simultaneously, the left leg does a *battement en cloche,* which brings it into *quatrième croisée.* The right foot is raised immediately *sur la pointe,* and, taking advantage of the impulse received, the body concludes the turn toward the right. The left leg remains more or less pointed in the same direction, which causes it to move into second position, then into *quatrième derrière ouverte.* The supporting foot remains *à plat,* and the final pose is an *arabesque.*

The arms rise at the sides in second at the start, then come back down low and rise *en couronne* to the front. They open to the sides to take the *arabesque* position at the end of the step, with the arm on the side of the working leg extended forward.

435

These complex turns are very difficult, but they do create an effect and have found a place in the ballet. They may be used by male dancers as well as by female. It is rare that more than one *tour* is done from a single impulse.

They are almost always done on a diagonal, with the leg that is on the side toward the audience the one that will do the *battement en cloche.*

It is probably this *battement* that has given its name of *fouetté* to the *tour,* because at the moment the leg moves into first position, it lightly touches the ground; because the movement is very rapid, one has the impression that it is a *fouetté*.

Several *fouettés détournés* may be executed in sequence.

436

A rather infrequent variation consists of executing these same *tours* by bending the working leg after the *battement en cloche*—that is, by doing them **en attitude**. In this case, the arms quite naturally take the position of *attitude* at the end of the step (§ 41).

437

The **pas de bourrée relevé détourné** is closely akin to the *fouetté détourné* (§ 434).

The *pas de bourrée*, which begins this step, is quite different from those we studied in paragraphs 191 through 203.

The dancer in fifth position, right foot forward, shifts her left foot into *quatrième derrière*, then places it *à plat*; she brings her right foot closer while causing her body to make a quarter-turn toward the left; she shifts the left foot once again into second position, places it *à plat*, then—while having her body do a quarter-turn toward the left—she raises her right foot vigorously into *quatrième devant* and simultaneously lifts her left foot *sur la pointe*; she uses this impulse to continue turning her body, making a *demi-tour* toward the left. The right leg stays pointed in the same direction, which causes it to pass into second position, then into *quatrième derrière*. The tour completed, the left foot remains *à plat*, the final pose is an *arabesque*.

The movement of the arms is the same as for the *fouettés détournés* (§ 434).

438

This step begins and ends with the dancer facing the audience, and results in the dancer's moving back away from the audience. It is executed almost solely by female dancers; male dancers substitute the *pas de bourrée cabriole* (§ 478), which produces a similar "retreat."

We note the quite general tendency at the present time to have the male dancers replace the *temps relevés sur les pointes* with *temps sautés* whenever possible.

439

Tours en changeant de pied (with change of feet). The female dancer, having executed one or two *tours en dehors* from a single impulse, finds herself at the end *sur la pointe* of the supporting foot with the other leg *au raccourci*. Without closing and without coming back down with her foot *à plat*, she places the working foot *sur la pointe* in front of the other, which she lifts in order to bring the leg *au raccourci,* while executing one or two *tours en dedans* before closing.

These *tours* are done without interrupting the movement when the feet are changed; it is necessary that they keep the same rhythm as if they had been done from a single impulse.

440

These *tours* with change of feet are very difficult to do *sur la pointe,* because if the dancer has not kept her balance well at the end of the *tours en dehors,* she completely misses the *tours en dedans*; but they do have quite an effect, because, if well-executed, they double the possibilities of *tours* the dancer can achieve.

Done *sur la demi-pointe* the turns are less difficult. Russian dancers quite often do them in this manner, which permits them to make ten or twelve turns. In the *Danses Polovtsiennes* from *Prince Igor* (Fokine), Alexandre Kalioujny, a star dancer at the Opera, used to do fourteen or fifteen turns in this fashion.

The dancer may also begin with *tours en dedans* and continue with *tours en dehors.*

441

The **tours relevés in second position en dehors** are done starting from a fifth position. The right foot begins in front, is shifted *à la pointe* in second, and is then placed *à plat*; both knees are bent; the right leg is raised in second *à la hauteur* with the left foot simultaneously lifted *sur la pointe,* while the knees are straightened. The turning is to the right. Throughout the *tour,* the leg must remain in its position in second. When the *tour* is completed, the right leg closes in *cinquième devant or derrière.*

The arms are placed in second position (§ 40) and remain there.

442

These *tours* are very difficult, especially when a dancer wants to do two of them from a single impulse. They are relatively slow and very spectacular; they have, therefore, found a place in the variations of the leading dancers.

They may also be executed by male dancers *sur la demi-pointe.*

What causes the principal difficulty of this *tour* is the necessity to keep the leg always *à la hauteur.* Actually, the leg has a tendency either to descend *à la demi-hauteur* or to glide into *quatrième devant.* Then, too, the very position of the leg restrains the *tour* and the impulse, therefore, must be greater than for a *tour au raccourci.*

443

The **tours in second position en dedans** also begin with a *dégagé,* but they begin with the left foot when the fifth position is with the right foot forward. It is the left foot that rises into second *à la hauteur* and the *tour* is made toward the right.

As in the preceding *tours* the working leg must maintain its position throughout the *tour*—closing is *en cinquième devant* or *derrière.* Arms are in second position.

444

All the *tours* we have just discussed are *relevés* on one foot, but they are prepared on both feet. These preparations generally consist of one step or one position already studied: *temps de pointe, échappé,* fourth position, or second position. The *temps de pointe* and *échappé* end in fifth, and practically all the *tours* we have seen start from a second, a fourth, or a fifth position.

The basic positions are normally taken with the weight of the body evenly distributed between the two legs. The vertical axis extending through the center of gravity must fall in the center of the polygon of support. At the moment of the *relevé* there is a shifting of the axis, bringing the weight of the body onto the supporting leg. When the working leg rises, it automatically projects the body in the opposite direction. If the vertical axis of the center of gravity is too near the future supporting leg, the weight of the body moves beyond that leg at the moment of the *relevé,* which causes an imbalance.

Dancing masters generally watch the quality of the preparations very carefully, because the cleanness and even the success of the *tours* depend upon these preparations.

445

There are, however, some few persons who can execute *tours* starting from an awkward or improper preparation. It happens rarely, but it does happen. This can be explained by the distinction that can be made between two manners of doing *tours*.

The first, which is the most popular, permits anyone to execute *tours* correctly after systematic training: the dancer, having prepared very exactly, establishes the body axis around which he will turn. His efforts will therefore be directed toward placing this axis well, as indicated above, and not letting it move; the dancer will therefore make his muscles as firm as possible, particularly those of his upper and lower back, in order to turn his body into a rigid block revolving rigorously about itself.

The second manner is reserved for those privileged few who have a talent for doing *tours*. It consists of initiating the turn as fast as possible, with the speed of rotation bringing the axis to its position of balance; this is the principle of spinning tops, which, started at an angle, immediately become erect. But this procedure is dangerous, because the margin of security is very slight despite the fact that the speed of rotation is quite moderate; the deviation from balance must be slight, otherwise the straightening-up is impossible. Young students who possess this faculty do not necessarily become the most adept at doing *tours*, because, relying on their facility, they do not try rigorously to establish their balance and are not able to progress. They may perhaps do two *tours* immediately, but thereafter will be unable to do more. Furthermore, these *tours* are not aesthetically attractive because, even when done successfully, they always give the spectator the impression of the dancer being off balance. That is why, since there is always the possibility of an accident, the dancing master must always recommend to his students the use of the first method, without losing sight of the fact that occasionally a student's particular gift will allow him to conceal a slight fault in preparation.

446

We shall conclude the study of *tours* performed on the ground with **tours relevés sur un pied pris directement** (rising turns taken directly on one foot). We shall encounter once again a number of types already considered. We can establish as a general rule that the *tour relevé* taken directly on one foot is always much more difficult than the same *tour* taken on both feet. It requires very lengthy training to execute correctly. Dancing masters begin teaching *tours relevés* to their pupils by breaking them up into quarter-turns, then into half-turns.

The principal difficulty lies in the total absence of an impetus. The body, in a given position, keeps that position in order to start moving, then turning. The turning is set in motion by the tension of the supporting knee, which bends before the *tour,* and the movement of the shoulder contributes to it.

447

We shall study first the **tours relevés sur un pied au raccourci**; the most frequent are those in **second position**, with the *pointe* of the working leg at the knee of the supporting leg, almost always behind it. These *tours* start from a *raccourci* that may have its origin in various steps.

They may be done *en dehors* while turning to the side of the working leg or *en dedans* while turning to the side of the supporting leg. They may be joined in a series of eight or of sixteen successive turns.

448

Tours au raccourci en quatrième devant are executed in the same manner as the preceding ones, *en dedans* or *en dehors.*

449

Tours en attitude are more frequent. They are mainly done *en dehors* but are also seen occasionally *en dedans.* The positions of the working leg and of the arms (that of the working leg vertical, of the arms, horizontal at the sides) permit the impetus to be created with greater facility. In certain variations for the lead dancers we find two *tours d'attitude,* very often taken after two *tours piqués posés en attitude* (§ 420). One *tour* may be done several times in succession.

Like all *tours en attitude,* these are very elegant. They are executed very slowly.

450

Tours à l'Italienne are *tours relevés* in second position, taken directly on one foot, by thirds of a turn performed very rapidly *sur la demi-pointe.* Three *relevés* are thus necessary to a complete *tour.* In general, therefore, a great number of *tours* are done in succession. The supporting leg always remains *pliée.*

The arms are in second position.

This step is used more often by male than by female dancers. It is effective and has found a place in codas.

It does not differ greatly from *petits soubresauts tournés* in derivative position; it happens that certain dancers substitute *sou-bresauts* (§ 464) for true *tours à l'Italienne relevés*.

451

Tours relevés in second position sur un pied pris directement (rising turns in second taken directly on one foot) are rare. They are found mainly after *tours à l'Italienne* (§ 450), *en dehors*. The impetus given by the *tours à l'Italienne* makes it possible to do two and occasionally even three *tours*. Male dancers do them *sur la demi-pointe*; female dancers, *sur la pointe*.

As we have said above, the second position *à la hauteur* is the one that lends itself least well to *tours*. Theoretically there could be tours in second *relevés* on one foot *en dedans*. In practice they are not in common use.

We note, furthermore, that steps terminating in a second derivative are rare, while a great number of steps end *au raccourci, en attitude,* or *en arabesque*. That, more than the question of difficulty, explains the greater frequency of the other *tours relevés* on one foot.

452

Tours relevés sur un pied en quatrième devant are not in common use. They would be very difficult and not at all pretty. The *quatrième devant à la hauteur* is the least aesthetic of the derivative positions, hence it is used almost exclusively as a transition. The *tours* we have studied keep the position of the dancer identical throughout their duration. There is no interest in maintaining this position, which is hardly elegant, for such a long time.

453

Tours relevés sur un pied en arabesque occur very frequently. They are executed more *en dedans* than *en dehors,* contrary to what we have seen so far. Being graceful, they have a place in several ballets, in the masculine variations as well as in the feminine. They are also found in quarter-turns and thirds of a turn.

In addition, they are used after *sautillements* (hops or skips) while turning *en arabesque* (§ 464)—for example, in the second act of *Giselle*.

454

Tours relevés sur un pied enveloppés fouettés proceed from the same principle as the *tours fouettés enveloppés* (§ 431), but instead of starting from a fourth, the dancer starts from a derivative position, most often a second *à la hauteur* or *demi-hauteur*, or *en attitude*. These *tours* are used after *sautillements* while doing *tours* in second position (§ 464). The impetus thus given permits the execution of two, three, or even more *tours*. Both male and female dancers perform these.

They may also conclude a series of quarter-turns or thirds of a turn *relevés* on one foot *en arabesque*.

455

We shall conclude this long series of *tours à terre* with the **ronds de jambe fouettés**. The dancer, in fifth position, right foot forward, first executes two *tours en dehors* prepared for in fourth (§ 426) on the left foot. At the end of the *tours* she extends her right leg *en quatrième devant,* causes it to move rapidly into second, then into *quatrième derrière*, and brings it back *au raccourci;* these different movements are produced within the space of one *tour* and are repeated a certain number of times. Each time the dancer comes around to face forward, she rests her left foot *à plat* and rises immediately *sur la pointe*. The movement of the right leg keeps up the turning for as long as it is desired. In executing this step it is necessary to take care actually to do a *rond de jambe* and not a simple *fouetté à la seconde* (§ 130).

Originally it seems that the *fouettés* during a *tour* were done with a simple *fouetté à la seconde*; a few foreign schools have conserved this method.

456

This step, under the name **fouetté**, enjoys a considerable vogue at the present time. It was introduced quite recently into the classical dance. It seems to have appeared toward the end of the nineteenth century, under the influence of the Italian style. The Italian dancer Pierina Legnani executed for the first time, it is said, the thirty-two *fouettés* in *La Tulipe de Harlem* (Ivanoff) presented at the Théâtre Marie in St. Petersburg on 4 October 1887.

Since that period, *fouettés* have spread all over the world. They have found a place in most of the ballets but have remained almost exclusively feminine. However, in *Etudes* (Lander) a male dancing star does thirty-two *fouettés*.

At the present time, the step is quite effective: the dancer seems to execute a remarkable *tour de force* by turning always on one foot for a very long time. A series of thirty-two *fouettés* is bound to generate applause from the audience. This rapid step is generally found in the coda of a classical *pas de deux*. But it is becoming more and more the tendency to integrate it into the variations; it is thus found in the first movement of *The Crystal Palace* (Symphony in C by Georges Bizet, choreography by George Balanchine), in the *grand pas de trois* of *Suite en Blanc* (theme and variations from the second act of *Namouna* by Edouard Lalo, choreography by Serge Lifar), and so forth.

Fouettés are usually executed sixteen consecutive times; stars do thirty-two of them; the case is cited of Mia Slavenska who used to do sixty-four.

457

Originally this step seemed to be of such great difficulty that no one considered making it more elaborate. However, at the end of *Suite en Blanc,*[2] Serge Lifar, in 1942, had Lycette Darsonval execute double *fouettés* in the following manner: three single, one double, three single, one double, and so on, in a series of twenty-four *fouettés* completed by a double or triple *fouetté.* An English dancer, Rowena Jackson, in the *Pas des Patineurs* (F. Ashton), executes three single *fouettés,* one double, three single, one triple, twice in a sequence—that is, in a series of sixteen *fouettés.* In the first movement of *The Crystal Palace* are found *fouettés en attitude*: three single, one *en attitude,* and so on, in a series of sixteen *fouettés.*

In class, the very good female dancers do double *fouettés* in series.

In *Etudes,* Harald Lander introduced, in a series of *fouettés, soubresauts sur pointe* by thirds of a turn.

458

After this study of *tours à terre,* we realize how varied and complex are their respective techniques. It seems that since the end of the nineteenth century the vogue for *tours* has not diminished. They are an essential element in choreography, and new forms and new uses of them continue to be invented.

TOURS SAUTES*

459

In all the *tours* we have seen thus far, constant contact with the ground was maintained. In this section we are going to move on to the *tours* in which the turning is accompanied by a *saut.* Most of the time these

[2] *Fouettés* appear three times in this ballet: in the *Grand Pas de trois,* in the *Mandolins* (balcony scene), and in the *Finale.*
*Leaping turns.

tours will be related to the types studied in Chapter Three. As a general rule, the majority of *tours sautés* can be considered variations of *sauts.* We shall follow substantially the plan of Chapter Three.

460

The first type we shall consider is the *soubresaut,* which will give rise to a very large number of *tours sautés.* We shall first see those in which several *soubresauts* are required to produce a complete *tour.*

In all the basic positions except the fourth, it is possible to execute **petits soubresauts tournés** that are scarcely raised above the ground and are always oriented in the same direction. Four or more of these *soubresauts* form a complete *tour.*

These *soubresauts* are found in second position in certain character ballets: for example, the first tableau of *Petrouchka* (Fokine). Primitive dances make use of *soubresauts en tournant* in first or second position.

461

Much more important is the *tour en l'air.* It is a *soubresaut* in fifth position (§ 249) in which the body does a complete revolution. This *soubresaut* is taken in fifth by classical dancers, but in the folk dances it is done in first position. The *soubresaut* can have the form of a *changement de pied* (§ 336) when the *tour* is done on the side of the rear leg. With more than one *tour* in a single leap, the *changement de pied* is obligatory.

This movement, which some years ago was essentially masculine, is now occasionally performed by female dancers, but with a single *tour,* as in the variation of the Emerald from *The Crystal Place* (Balanchine).

Male dancers execute two *tours* to each *saut.* Especially gifted dancers do three of them. At the present time, in order to be engaged in the corps de ballet of the Opera, male students of the Ecole de danse must be able to do two *tours en l'air.*

The **tours en l'air may terminate on one foot,** *en raccourci, en attitude, en arabesque,* or in a derivative position *à la hauteur* or *demi-hauteur.*

In this case, the technique is no longer that of a *soubresaut,* but that of a *sissonne,* since the dancer starts the *saut* on both feet and completes it on one foot.

But the term *sissonne en tournant* is never employed here.

One may also have *tours en l'air* that end with an *agenouille- ment*—variation of the Prince from the first act of *Lac des Cygnes*

(Bourmeister)—or even a fall for a particular purpose—Prince Albert becoming exhausted in the second act of *Giselle* (Coralli and Perrot).

462

In the ballets of the second half of the twentieth century may be found **entrechats en tournant**: for example, the two dancers of the *Grand Pas de trois* from *Suite en Blanc* (Lifar) do some *entrechats 6* (§ 340) with a *demi-tour.*

These *entrechats* are rarely done with a complete *tour;* usually they are done with a *demi-tour.*

463

Brisés en tournant are done by fractions of turns, often by quarter-turns.

They are *en dehors* if the dancer is turning to the side of the rear leg, *en dedans* if he is turning to the side of the forward leg, according to the principle stated for *tours relevés* (§ 422). The arms are in third position, with the raised arm on the side of the rear leg.

En dedans, the trunk leans gently forward and the head is in profile to the side of the raised arm.

464

Soubresauts tournés in derivative positions may be done in all the positions *à la demi-hauteur, à la hauteur, en raccourci, en attitude*, and *en arabesque*. They are rare in classical dance but may be found in modern and character ballets.

Often dancers have a tendency to substitute *soubresauts tournés* for *tours à l'Italienne* (§ 450). This is a reprehensible practice.

If *sautillements* are apparently easier to execute, they definitely do not permit the dancer to attain the same rapidity or the same regularity.

465

At a relatively recent date, **soubresauts tournés sur la pointe** have appeared.

Thus we find a *tour de soubresauts en raccourci en quatrième devant* in the variation from the ballet of *Guillaume Tell* (Aveline), *en arabesque* in this same variation and in the *pizzicati* of *Sylvia* as it was presented in February 1941 at the Opera, *en attitude* in *Guignol et*

Pandore (Lifar), and so forth. In *Phèdre* (Lifar), we find two *tours de soubresauts en arabesque.*

466

Closely akin to the *soubresauts tournés sur la pointe* are the **tours ressautés**. These *tours* have their origin in an error of dancers who, instead of carrying out their *tours*, become disoriented, lose their balance, and leap *sur la pointe* to retain it.

467

Petits jetés dessus may be executed while turning. The dancer begins in fifth position, right foot forward, then does a *plié* and leaps onto the right foot while doing a *demi-tour* toward the right and while bringing his left leg *au raccourci* in slightly raised *quatrième devant*. He immediately leaps onto the left foot while doing another *demi-tour* toward the right, which brings him around face front, with the right leg *au raccourci* in slightly raised *quatrième devant*. The dancer does several of these *petits jetés en tournant* in series.

The arms move from one sixth position (§ 44) to the other, with the curved arm on the side of the working leg.

These *petits jetés en tournant* are quite effective and are not too difficult. They are executed as well by male dancers as by female, on a diagonal or in a circle. The present tendency is to reserve them mainly for female dancers.

A dancer may do series of three *petits jetés en tournant*, then a *grand jeté*. A diagonal of this type is found at the end of the variation of the Star from the divertissement in *Roméo et Juliette* (music by Charles Gounod, choreography by A. Aveline).

For the step to have all its brilliance it must be done rapidly.

468

The technique of the **grand jeté en tournant** is the same as that of the *grand jeté*. The dancer does not start out from the fifth position, but from a *quatrième devant à la demi-hauteur* or from a *raccourci en quatrième devant*. Taking the right leg as the working leg, the dancer will leap onto this leg toward the right and will alight upon it after having done a complete *tour*, with the left leg *en arabesque*, or more often *en attitude*.

469

This type of *grand jeté* is relatively rarely done alone. It is performed mainly by men, and its difficulty is considerable. It is used most frequently in the form of a *demi-tour* after a *coupé tourné* (§ 479) or from three-quarters of a turn after the first movement of a *petit jeté en tournant*. In these two cases, the *jeté* is done *en attitude*. Female dancers perform it mainly in the latter manner. Male dancers, conversely, do diagonals of **coupés jetés** (*Suite en Blanc*) or circles of **pas tombés tournés, coupés tournés, jetés** (*Soir de Fête*) (Fig. 53). Female dancers also do these circles occasionally.

In sequences, the *pas tombé, coupé,* and *petit jeté* must be barely *sautés* (the leaps must be very low), whereas the *grand jeté* is very high.

For the *pas tombé* the arms open gently; then rise *en attitude* for the *grand jeté*.

470

The **failli grand jeté** uses another type of *grand jeté*: the *grand jeté enveloppé*. The step is normally preceded by a *failli* (§ 320). The *failli* having been executed with right foot forward, the dancer places this foot *à plat en quatrième ouverte* and, having raised the left leg in second position *à la hauteur*, he bends the right leg and leaps while doing an *enveloppé* with his left leg—that is, he turns toward the right while bringing the left leg *en quatrième devant croisée à la hauteur*. He descends on the left leg, having made a complete *tour*, with the right leg *au raccourci en quatrième devant*. He may repeat the step in the same direction.

In the *failli* the arms are in sixth position (§ 44), with the curved arm on the side of the working leg; they open immediately, half-horizontal to the sides (§ 518), descend low, then rise *en couronne* (§ 43) passing through first position (§ 39). They open in second position (§ 40) at the end of the step.

471

This is as much a masculine as a feminine step; it is very pretty and lends itself to a certain number of combinations. It may be employed alone on a diagonal, as in the variation of the Queen of the Wilis in the second act of *Giselle* (Coralli and Perrot). Circles of *fallis grands jetés* are rarely done, but circles may be made in which this step is combined with other steps.

In contrast to the *grand jeté en tournant*, in which the dancer should travel as far horizontally as vertically, the *falli grand jeté* must above all be executed vertically.

472

The **saut de chat** may be executed while turning. It is now taken with the forward foot, and the dancer does a *demi-tour* to the side of the forward leg while in midair and ends with an *enveloppé* (§ 388) that brings him back with the same foot forward as when he began. This step is employed by male as well as by female dancers, but it is not in wide use. An example of its use by men is found in the third movement of *The Crystal Palace* (Balanchine).

The arms rise *en couronne,* passing through first position (§ 39), and open to the sides.

473

The only **sissonne en tournant** possible is the *sissonne en descendant* (§ 279). The dancer does a complete *tour* in midair and turns to the side of the forward leg.

The arms take the position for *arabesque.*

This is a uniquely masculine step, very difficult to execute. There is an example of it in the Mazurka from *Suite en Blanc* (Lifar).

474

The **assemblées soutenues** only vaguely resemble the *assemblées* (§ 288). The dancer begins in fifth position with the right foot forward, moves her right leg swiftly into fourth, and jumps to descend *sur la pointe* while bringing the left foot *sur la pointe* in front of the right; she turns *sur les deux pointes* without moving her feet and regains her face-forward position with right foot in front. She now comes back down from her *pointes* in fifth, *à plat,* and can start over again (Fig. 52).

The *saut* is very light, scarcely noticeable. The arms follow the movement of the legs. They open when the right foot steps directly *sur la pointe* and close during the *tour.*

475

The **pas de bourrée grand jeté en tournant** is executed as follows: in fifth position, right foot forward. the dancer executes the *pas de bourrée* described in paragraph 437, which causes him to do a

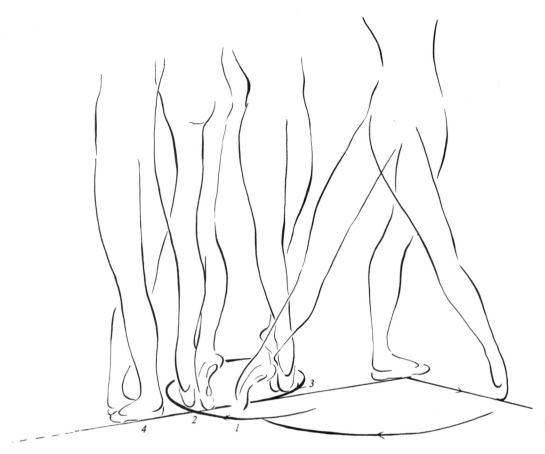

Figure 52. *Assemblée soutenue*

demi-tour. He then raises the right leg in *en quatrième devant,* bends, and leaps and descends on the right leg; the left leg is *en quatrième derrière à la hauteur* after having executed, while in midair, a *demi-tour* to the left, which concludes the complete *tour.*

The dancer can link it directly to another *pas de bourrée jeté* by placing his left leg *en quatrième derrière* without going through fifth position.

The arms rise *en couronne* (§ 43), passing through first position (§ 39), and come back down through second position (§ 40).

The ensemble of the movement is distributed over the complete step in such a way that the arms are *en couronne* at the moment when the dancer reaches the height of his trajectory.

476

To be seen at best advantage, this step must have a very high *saut,* with very clean-cut positions. It is not very difficult and is impressive, so it is often used by male as well as by female dancers. It is employed by itself, on a diagonal, or in a circle. We might point out that it results in a withdrawal upstage; it is therefore executed on a diagonal, in the opposite direction from *déboulés,* for example.

In times past the second leg remained *en attitude*—now it is required that it be *en arabesque.*

This step had already been discovered by the ancient Greeks, who seem to have held it in high esteem.[3]

477

The **pas de bourrée assemblée** differs very little from the *pas de bourrée jeté.* Instead of ending *en arabesque* or *en attitude,* it ends in fifth position. After having performed the step as indicated in paragraph 475, the dancer lands on both feet at the same time, with the same foot forward as at the start.

The arms do the same movements as for the *pas de bourrée jeté.*

It is used in place of the *pas de bourrée jeté* when the latter must be followed by a step beginning in fifth position. It normally ends on a diagonal or in a circle of *pas de bourrée jetés.*

It may also be performed by itself.

478

The **pas de bourrée cabriole** always begins with the same type of *pas de bourrée* (§ 437); the dancer raises his right leg in fourth position, bends, leaps, and does a *demi-tour* toward the left, while leaving his leg pointing in the same direction, which causes it to move into second *à la hauteur,* then into *quatrième derrière.* He descends on the left foot. He may start out anew in the opposite direction.

The movement of the arms is the same as for the *pas de bourrée jeté* (§ 475).

This step is used as often by women as by men.

479

The **coupé en tournant** is executed like the *coupé sauté* (§ 314), but the dancer turns once around toward the side of the forward leg while in midair. He descends with that leg *au raccourci en quatrième devant* or, most often, with the working foot in front of the shinbone of the supporting leg.

[3] G. Prudhommeau: *La Danse grecque antique.* Editions du C.N.R.S., 1965. Vol. I, p. 182, § 651.

Like the *coupé sauté*, the *coupé en tournant* is a transition step that is never used for its own sake; it is used a great deal by male dancers in sequences of *coupés jetés en tournant* (§ 469). In this case, the *coupé* makes only a fraction of a *tour*, which the *jeté* concludes. The *coupé* is a very slight *saut*, and the *jeté* is quite high.

480

The **pas tombés en tournant** are executed like ordinary *pas tombés* (§ 315), but the dancer does a complete turn while in midair. He turns to the side of the forward foot. He extends forward the arm that is on the side of the forward foot at the end of the step, and bends the knee forward while inclining the trunk slightly to the front.

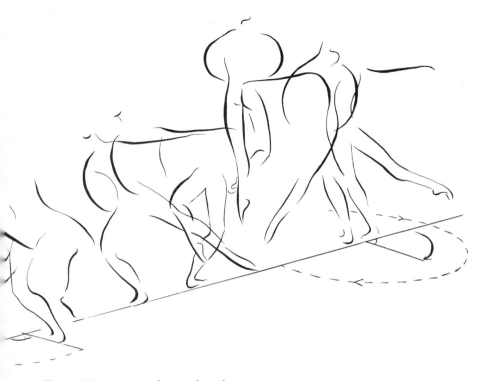

Figure 53. *Pas tombé, coupé, jeté*

Here again we have a transition step. It is, however, used occasionally by itself in the form of a circle or on a diagonal. Most often it is combined with the preceding sequence to form a *pas tombé coupé jeté* (§ 469). The *pas tombé* is always only slightly *sauté* and very close to the ground (Fig. 53).

481

A uniquely masculine *saut* that has been introduced in the ballet comparatively recently is performed in the following manner: the dancer, in fifth position with the right foot forward, raises his right foot extended *en quatrième devant à la hauteur*, then bends his left leg and leaps while causing it to pass over the right leg while doing a *demi-tour* to the right. The right leg remains pointing in the same direction, and the dancer descends on his left leg, with the right leg *en quatrième derrière à la hauteur*.

This leap is difficult and demands a great deal of elevation and precision.

It is found in the second tableau of *Daphnis and Chloé* (Skibine) executed by some pirates and in several instances in *Roméo et Juliette* (Labis), in particular in the dances of Mercutio.

This leap is sometimes called a **revolta**.

<hr/>

482

A few *sauts battus* (beating leaps) can be done while turning. We have seen, in paragraphs 462 and 463, the *entrechats en tournant* and the *brisés en tournant*.

Échappés battus may also be done en tournant. The *échappé* is "beaten," as indicated in paragraph 353, but while in midair the dancer does a quarter-turn, less frequently a half-turn. In general, the dancer turns in the direction of the foot that was in front when he began. With the closing, he does another quarter-turn or half-turn in the same direction.

Because this type of *échappé battu* generally has a change of feet, in this case, the second *échappé* turns to the side of the foot that is to the rear in the beginning.

This is a male dancer's step.

483

The **brisés de volée en tournant** are very difficult and complex steps.

Four of them are necessary for a complete *tour,* but the third, or the third and fourth *brisés* may be replaced by *jetés battus*.

The dancer, in fifth position with the right foot forward, does a *plié*, leaps while lifting the left leg forward, and strikes his left calf against his right shinbone. He alights on the left leg, which is bent, with the right leg *en quatrième devant à la demi-hauteur*, after having done a quarter-turn toward the right while in midair. He then leaps and strikes his left calf against his right shinbone and alights on the right leg, which is bent, with the left leg *en quatrième derrière à la demi-hauteur*, having done another quarter-turn in midair. He leaps and strikes his left calf against his right shinbone; then he alights on the left leg, which is bent, with the right leg *en quatrième devant à la demi-hauteur*, having made still another quarter-turn. He leaps, strikes the left calf against his right shinbone, and alights on the right leg, which is bent, with the left leg *en quatrième derrière à la demi-hauteur*, having achieved his complete *tour*.

This is a man's step, very brilliant and difficult. It is found in *Etudes* (Lander).

484

The **pas de bourrée cabriole battu** is executed according to the description given in paragraph 478, but immediately after the right leg is placed *en quatrième derrière*, the left leg comes to strike it. In this case the *pas de bourrée* causes more turning than a *pas de bourrée cabriole non battu*.

Exceptionally, this *cabriole* is *battu double*. In this case, it will be *battu* once before the turning around and once after.

485

The **pas de bourrée assemblée battu** is done according to the technique described in paragraph 477, but before descending in fifth, the foot that was in front in the beginning crosses in front, moves behind, and returns to close in front. This step is therefore *battu* with an *entrechat* of type 5.

486

Other steps may also be done while turning, such as the *ballonné* (§ 309), the *pas de basque* (§ 189), and the *saut de basque* (§ 311).

We have seen that the techniques of the *tours sautés* are quite varied. Generally, one is dealing with steps that are difficult but that make a dramatic effect. The most difficult of them are executed only by male dancers. They are used often in the ballets. There are constant innovations in this field, and it is probable that this category of step will continue to be enriched.

FIVE

Acrobatics

487

Many authors and lovers of the ballet refuse to recognize acrobatics among the movements of the dance. For this reason we are discussing it separately. Nevertheless, the boundaries are difficult to establish in certain cases.

At the present time, acrobatics are becoming increasingly prominent in the classical ballets. Many of the ballets, even on the stage of the Opera, include acrobatic movements in their choreographies.

488

We shall not study acrobatics in detail, because this would lead us too far from our subject. We shall confine ourselves to describing a certain number of movements that have found a place in the classical ballet. This selection is thus incomplete, and it is possible that other acrobatics than those we shall describe figure in certain ballets; new ones are constantly being added. Farther along (in Chapter Seven, the first section), we shall speak of acrobatics in the *adagio*.

489

One of the acrobatic movements that has been included longest in the ballet is the **grand écart**. Basically, this position consists of having the forward leg in fourth position *à la hauteur* and the rear leg the same, with both legs touching the ground over their entire length (the "split"). In classical dance, the legs must remain *en dehors*.

This was originally an essentially feminine acrobatic movement. Used at first in character ballets such as *La Grande Jatte* (Aveline), it is moving more and more into the classical ballet and is found, for example, in *Etudes* (Lander).

It even happens, albeit rarely, that male dancers do the *grand écart*: in comic ballets such as *La Belle Hélène*, variation of the two Ajaxes (Lifar); or even in serious ones: *Le Chemin de Lumière*, entrance of Death (Lifar).

The *grand écart* is practiced daily in class.

490

Less frequent and more difficult is the *grand écart facial*. It is done with both legs in second position *à la hauteur*. It is practiced in class but seldom found on the stage. However, several examples may be found: in *Petrouchka* (Fokine), the ballerina does the *grand écart facial*.

491

Another acrobatic movement that has now become part of the classical exercises is **le pied dans la main** (the foot in the hand).

The dancer, in fifth position with the right foot forward, raises her right leg *au raccourci en quatrième devant*—then, with her right hand, grasps, from the inner side, the sole of her foot or her heel. She then straightens her leg while raising it in front of her and brings it, taut, immediately into second, still holding the foot with her hand—hence the name of the step. She thus obtains a very high second position *à la hauteur*, which can go as high as a vertical position.

In classical dance this is solely a class exercise, used daily to limber up the legs.

In the music hall, on the other hand, it has found great popularity, especially in the French *cancan*. It is so used in executing *petits soubresauts en tournant* (§ 464).

The French *cancan* has occasionally been introduced into certain ballets, such as *La Grande Jatte* (Aveline).

492

In acrobatics as such, **le pied dans la main** designates another, much more difficult movement. The acrobat raises his leg *au raccourci en quatrième derrière* while arching his body backward. He raises one arm above the head and bends it back behind him until he can take the foot in his hand. He then stretches the arm in such a way as to lift the leg as high as possible behind him (Fig. 79). He may take the foot in either hand. When the hand is opposite the foot, the leg is pulled out *croisée*.

An adaptation of this foot-in-hand acrobatic movement is found in certain recent ballets—for example, in *La Symphonie Concertante* (Descombey).

493

To conclude the acrobatic poses introduced into the ballets, we shall cite the **pont** (bridge). The acrobat leans backward until his hands touch the ground, the body forming a semicircle.

This position, which demands great suppleness in the spinal column, is very easily taken by children, who call it *les reins cassés* (the broken back).

It is the key to numerous acrobatic movements, but it is seldom used for its own sake and then almost always as a transition to other movements: *Notre-Dame de Paris* (Petit), *La Symphonie fantastique* (Massine).

494

Acrobatics often require feats of **balance** achieved with the head down, on the hands, the forearms, and the like. These are difficult and necessitate specialized training. But the balancing on the head and hands, commonly called *le poirier* (the pear tree), is relatively easy. A few examples of it are found in ballet, but in general other dancers hold the feet of those who are performing it in order to assure the immobility of the pose: for example, the red devils in the dream of a witches' sabbath from *La Symphonie fantastique* (Massine).

495

Among the acrobatic movements, the most simple is the **culbute en avant** (forward somersault). It is a children's game. It consists of placing the hands and the head on the ground, making the body rock forward, and rolling onto the back. For the somersault to be performed well, the head must be placed not on its top, but as near as possible to the nape of the neck.

Somersaults are found in certain ballets: for example, the panthers in the act of the Savages from the *Indes galantes* (Lifar); the little clowns in the third act of *Lac des Cygnes* (Bourmeister), and so forth.

496

The **culbute en arrière** (backward somersault) is done as follows: the acrobat, lying on his back, raises his legs and passes them over his head while raising his lower back, then his upper back, until he has turned over completely.

This movement is more acrobatic than the preceding one.

In the ballet it is executed mainly by male dancers: *Roméo et Juliette* (Béjart); Briaxis, chief of the pirates, in the second tableau of *Daphnis et Chloé* (Skibine); and so on.

497

The **culbute acrobatique** is decidedly different from the preceding one in that neither the head nor the body touches the ground. The acrobat places both hands on the ground and revolves his body forward around a horizontal axis; his hands remain on the ground and his legs pass over his head to finish *en pont* (§ 493).

498

If, starting from the *pont,* the acrobat executes a movement that is the reverse of the preceding one, he does a **reculbute**, which is clearly more difficult; this acrobatic feat is found only in ballets that include true acrobatic roles: *Les Forains* (Petit); *Le Bal des Blanchisseuses* (Petit).

499

The **flip-flap acrobatique** is also very difficult; it is an acrobatic somersault in which, while turning, the acrobat leaps from his hands to alight on his feet again while righting himself. Although necessitating elaborate training, this movement was included in a classical ballet such as *Roméo et Juliette* (Labis), in which one of the mountebanks executes it in the first tableau of the second act.

500

A little easier, and belonging to the same family, the **saut en avant sur les mains** (forward leap on the hands) consists of jumping forward to alight on the hands, with the arms bending gently and bringing the body into contact with the ground by way of the chest, then the abdomen and the legs.

This leap occurs in ballets that are already of such long standing as *Petrouchka* (Fokine), in which the Moor executes it in the third tableau when he dances with the coconut.

501

The **roue** (cartwheel) is a well-known and relatively easy acrobatic feat; children perform it.

It is a turning of 360 degrees around a horizontal axis that traverses the body approximately at the pit of the stomach—each hand, then each foot touches the ground out to the side in turn.

In spite of its easiness, this movement is not employed frequently in the ballet. A few examples of it are, however, found, as when it is done by the mountebanks in the first tableau of the second act of *Roméo et Juliette* (Labis).

502

We shall conclude this brief review of some acrobatic movements used by the ballet with the **marche sur les mains** (walking on the hands).

This is an acrobatic feat that is difficult to do well. It has rarely been introduced into the ballet.

An example of it was noted in *Zadig* (Lifar), in which a drunken minister, danced by the late Xavier Andreani, walked on his hands.

503

There is no reason why other acrobatic movements should not appear in the ballets, whether for performers who have to use them normally or for the sake of enriching the choreographic vocabulary.

It sometimes happens that the services of professional acrobats are sought—for example, in *Les Noces fantastiques* (Lifar) for the acrobatic stunts on the trapeze and in the rings. But dancers are working more and more in this field and are capable of executing every acrobatic feat their choreography may demand.

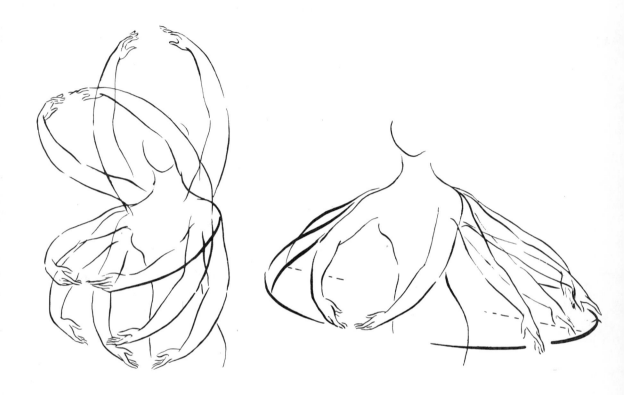

SIX

The Arms

504

Our study has been based up to now on the movements of the legs—*les pas*. These have an essential role in classical dance, although in certain other dance systems this role is minimal, in fact, practically nonexistent: the Hindus accord a very important place to the movements of the hands, the arms, and the various parts of the body or of the head; in the South Sea Islands there are even dances in which the performer is seated.

505

The present tendency is to accord the movements of the arms and hands a much greater importance than they had some fifty years ago. In certain ballets such as the *Symphonie Concertante* (Descombey), there is a veritable choreography of the arms and the hands, with a very rich range of movements and positions.

506

Because the possible movements of the legs are numerous and complex, we had to devote a long study to them, without making any claim to completeness. But the articulation of the shoulder is much more mobile than that of the hip, and the hand movements are infinitely more numerous than those of the feet. It is practically impossible, then, to try to treat exhaustively, within the limits of a work such as this one, the question of the positions and movements of the arms. We shall thus limit ourselves to treating the main points, to pointing out a certain number of facts and rules, and to studying that which is the most important and in widest use.

507

We shall not recapitulate the definition of the seven classical arm positions studied in paragraphs 37 through 44 nor the arm movements that normally accompany the majority of the steps and that were studied along with each of them.

We shall see first the positions of the arms other than the seven classical positions, then the classical *ports de bras*, the other, lesser *mouvements des bras*, and shall conclude with the hands.

508

As we stated in paragraph 37, the classical arm positions were chosen quite arbitrarily. To be able to proceed to a more systematic study, we shall utilize a more precise terminology that does not, however, belong to the choreographic vocabulary.

An arm is "low" (*bas*) (Fig. 54a) when it is vertical, with the hand

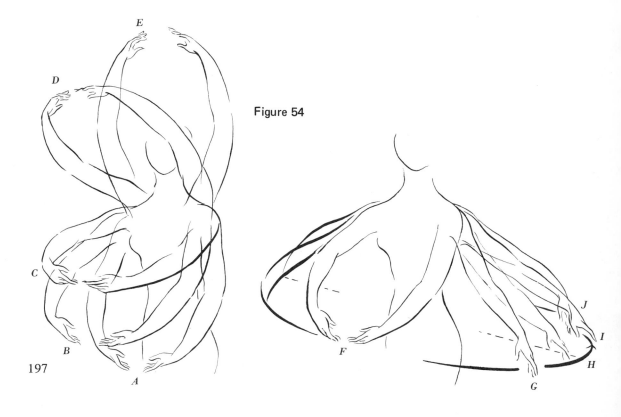

Figure 54

directed downward; "semi-horizontal" (Fig. 54b) when it makes an angle of 45 degrees with the preceding position; "horizontal" (Fig. 54c) with an angle of 90 degrees; "semi-vertical" (Fig. 54d) with an angle of 135 degrees, and, finally, "vertical" (Fig. 54e) when the hand is directed upward (*en haut*).

These positions may be taken with the arms "forward" (Fig. 54f), "lateral" (at the side) (Fig. 54h), or "to the rear" (Fig. 54j) (where it is difficult to go beyond the horizontal level); in a position intermediate between forward and lateral that we shall call "open" (Fig. 54g); and in a position intermediate between lateral and to the rear (Fig. 54i).

509

The arms may be *tendus* (extended) or *pliés* (bent). In the latter case, the upper arm and the forearm will lead in different directions and may be at different levels, but we shall still be able to use the same terms to define them.

If both arms are held in corresponding relationships to the body and at the same level, they are "symmetrical" with relation to the body; curved arms are symmetrical if both upper arm and forearm meet this condition.

There is also symmetry, but on a plane at right angles to the preceding one, when the forward arm and the one to the rear are on the same level.

Last, one final symmetry is produced when the arms are lateral, with one of them semi-vertical and the other semi-horizontal, or when one is leading downward and the other upward, or when one arm is forward and the other to the rear at the same levels. These are symmetries with relation to oblique planes.

Several positions of the classical dance take into account these symmetries.

The arms are "asymmetrical" if, when both are *tendus* or *pliés* they are held at different levels.

Finally, we shall designate as "complex" the positions in which one arm is *tendu*, the other *plié*.

510

When we speak of an **arm tendu**, it does not have quite the same meaning in classical dance as in the layman's language. The rules of linear aesthetics (which are those of the classical dance) prohibit angles, whatever they may be, including the 180-degree angle (which is a straight line). Thus the joints must neither form angles nor be

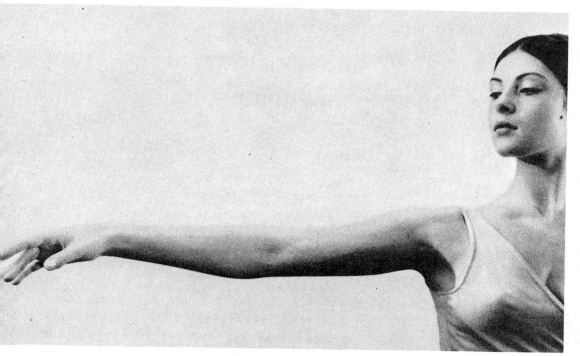

Figure 55 *(Photo: Serge Lido)*

completely straight, but rather "sustained," with the arm forming a gently curved line. When we speak of an arm *tendu* in classical terms, that means with the elbow and the wrist slightly bent (Fig. 55).

Because the vocabulary of the modern dance combines the angular with the linear aesthetic in certain contemporary ballets, it is possible there to have the arms fully outstretched.

511

We shall review the principal arm positions utilized in the ballet, beginning with the arms *tendus,* then the arms *pliés,* and, finally, the arms in complex positions.

In each case we shall first consider the symmetrical positions.

512

The arms tendus low and forward (Fig. 56) corresponds to the rest position or *position de départ* (starting position) that we saw in paragraph 38.

Figure 56

Figure 57

It is obviously very much in use, both as a pose when the dancer is immobile and as a *position de départ* for practically all the arm movements.

This position may also be taken with the hands crossed at the level of the wrists; in this case, it is only a pose. Finally, it may be done with the forearms turned outward and the palms downward. This is a romantic position (Fig. 57).

513

The **arms tendus forward and semi-horizontal position** serves as a substitute for the low position when the dancer is wearing a *tutu*. It would be impossible for her while wearing it to place her arms close to her body without crushing the skirt (Fig. 58).

This position is also intermediate between the *position de départ* and first position, hence it is frequently used.

Like the preceding position, this can be taken with the hands crossed at wrist level (Fig. 59). It is often the rest position of swans—for example, in the second act of *Lac des Cygnes* (Petipa and Ivanoff).

514

The **arms tendus forward and horizontal** constitutes the first classical position (§ 39). We have seen that it is found in the movements that

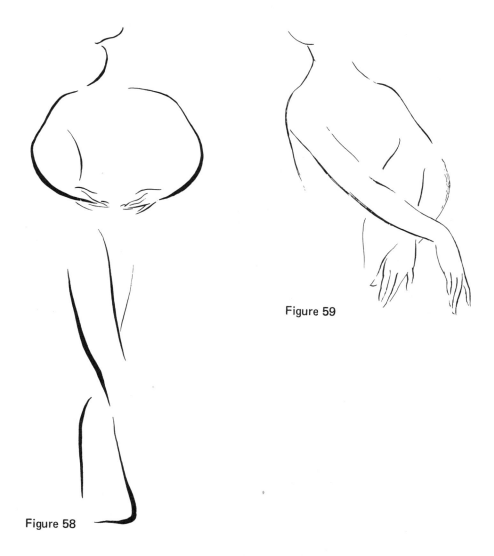

Figure 59

Figure 58

accompany numerous steps; it figures in most of the *ports de bras,* because it is almost always the transition between two classical positions.

In its nonclassical form, this position carries the meaning of arms being extended toward someone. It will thus be found in several ballets—for example, in *Les Noces fantastiques (Lifar) when the* villagers are trying to detain the bride.

515

The **arms tendus forward and semi-vertical position** is not employed in the classical dance; it serves merely as a transition between the first and the fifth positions.

201

With the arms fully outstretched, the position denotes an ascending movement, supplication before a superior, or arms extended toward a divinity.

516

The **arms tendus forward and vertical position** corresponds to the fifth position. The arms are not strictly vertical, as we explained in paragraph 43, but are slightly in front of the plane of the dancer's face.

This is a position that is often used in its own right and one through which a dancer passes when arm movements accompany certain steps, such as the *pas de bourrée jeté* (§ 475), for example.

This position, too, may be taken with the wrists crossed, but it is less frequent than with the arms low or semi-horizontal. It is a romantic position.

The nonclassical arms *tendus* vertical position is found solely in character ballets and modern ballets.

517

The **arms lateral and low** (Fig. 60) is the normal rest position. It is not used in pure classical ballet but is found in character ballets and modern ballets.

518

The **arms lateral and semi-horizontal position** is used often in the classical dance as a rest position. The lifting of the arms away from the body is required by the presence of the *tutu*.

This position is also the transition between the *position de départ* and second position (§ 40), which means that it is frequently used.

It may also be found with several steps: *petites glissades,* for example.

This is the position of the arms in the *Défilé du corps de ballet* (procession) of the Opera.

519

The **arms lateral and horizontal position** (Fig. 61) forms the second classical arm position (§ 40). For this reason it is frequently used, and with numerous steps. It also provides a transition in arm movements that accompany steps and in *ports de bras*.

In the nonclassical form, this position evokes the cross and is found in this capacity in various ballets, from *Giselle* (Coralli and

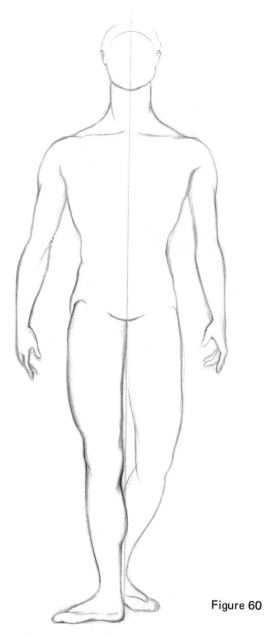

Figure 60

Perrot) to *Notre-Dame de Paris* (Petit). It is also found with no particular significance in character ballets and modern ballets.

520

The **arms lateral and semi-vertical position** is not in very frequent use but is found at the end of certain *tours* (§ 419).

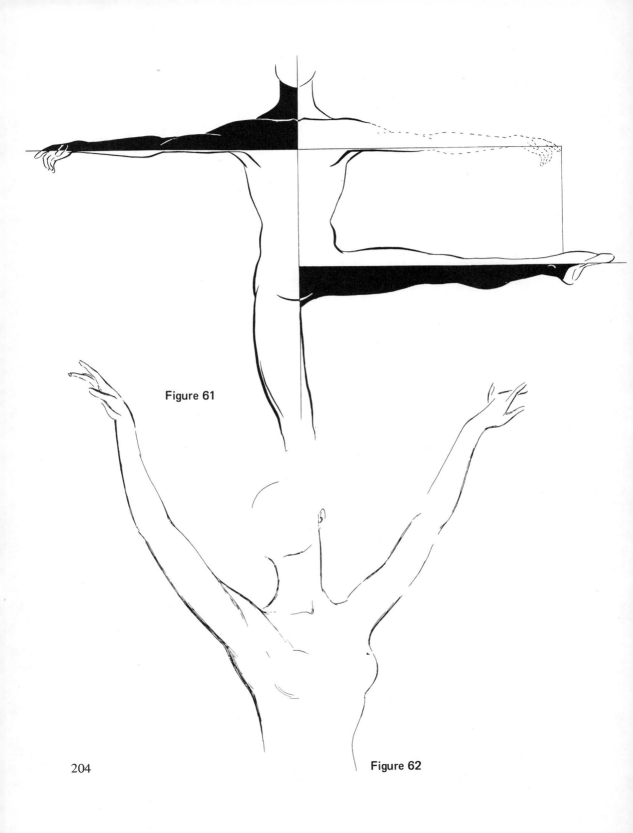

Figure 61

Figure 62

With the palms turned downward (Fig. 62), the arms impart a certain lift: Swanilda, who has taken the place of the doll Coppélia, pretending to come to life in the second act of *Coppélia* (Saint-*Léon*); the flight of *Icare* (Lifar), and so on.

With the palms turned upward, this position is a transition between second and fifth positions—it is used frequently.

It is found in its nonclassical form in a few ballets: adoration of the sun in the last tableau of *Daphnis et Chloé* (Skibine), for example.

521

The **arms lateral and vertical position** is not employed in classical dance. It is rare even in character ballets and modern ballets. It is, however, found occasionally: Petrouchka, in the second tableau of the ballet of the same name (Fokine).

522

The **arms low and to the rear** forms the position popularly called *mains au dos* (hands on back). It is not classical, but may be found even in ballets such as *Giselle* (Coralli and Perrot), where it is supposed to denote the timidity of a young girl; or it may characterize a prisoner: *Guignol et Pandore* (Lifar); the hands may be clasped.

523

The **arms semi-horizontal and to the rear** is the only position of arms to the rear that may have a classical use. It is not, however, very frequent: examples of it are found in *Lac des Cygnes* (Petipa and Ivanoff).

524

The **arms horizontal and to the rear** is a position difficult to execute and very rare. Certain star dancers, such as *Maïa Plissetskaïa*, use it in the positions of the Swan in the second act of *Lac des Cygnes.*

525

We shall not speak of **arms low** for the two **intermediate positions**: the open, and that between lateral and to the rear; actually these are too hard to distinguish from the positions just defined.

526

The **arms open and semi-horizontal position** is sometimes used like the position in which the arms are lateral and immobile.

With the arms *tendus*, this is a frequent position for characters such as dolls or marionnettes: Swanilda in the second act of *Coppélia* (Saint-Léon), the Ballerina in *Petrouchka* (Fokine).

527

The **arms open and horizontal position** does not exist in classical ballet except as a transition between first and second positions.

In its nonclassical form, it may be found in the same situations as in the preceding paragraph, or when one character extends his arm to another to receive him: the Prince and Odette in the finale of the last act of *Lac des Cygnes*.

528

The **arms open and semi-vertical position** is not used in pure classical ballet, but with arms fully extended it constitutes a position similar to that of arms lateral and semi-vertical (§ 520) and has related uses: the gesture of adoration, in particular, in *Le Sacre du Printemps* (Béjart).

529

The **arms in intermediate position between lateral and rearward, semi-horizontal or horizontal,** is rare. In general, this position denotes an idea of thrust or of flight, and it is found with this purpose in, for example, the variations for a bird: *L'Oiseau de Feu* (Fokine); *Lac des Cygnes* (Petipa and Ivanoff).

530

We shall not discuss all the possible combinations of arms *tendus,* but will merely point out a few of those most often used in the ballet.

The **arms tendus forward, one semi-horizontal, the other horizontal or semi-vertical position** is used for a doll, marionnette, or automaton. It will be found among such characters as those in *Guignol et Pandore* (Lifar), the Ballerina of *Petrouchka* (Fokine), *Coppélia* (Saint-Léon), the Pantin of *Elvire* (Aveline), and so forth.

531

The **arms tendus forward, one horizontal, the other semi-vertical position** gives a feeling of lightness and is used quite often with one leg *en quatrième derrière à la hauteur* or *semi-hauteur:* Giselle (Coralli and Perrot), *Les Sylphides* (Fokine), and so forth.

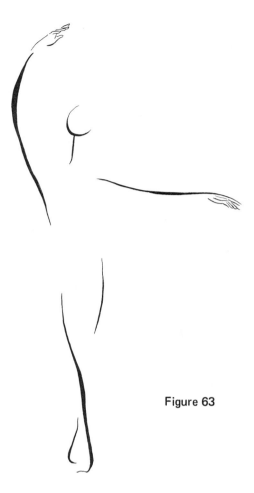

Figure 63

Other combinations of arms *tendus* forward may be found as transitions in the *ports de bras.*

532

The **arms tendus lateral, one semi-horizontal, the other semi-vertical position** is found at the beginning of the classical *révérence*, in the *brisés volés de volée* (§ 352), and the like.

It may also constitute a final pose in a variation, particularly one for male dancers.

533

The **tendus lateral, one horizontal, the other vertical position** (Fig. 63), forms the third classical position (§ 41) or *bras d'attitude*; it is therefore used often with the steps based on the *attitude,* such as *tours*

(§ 407, 420, 426, 449), and also with certain other steps such as *dégagés* (§ 102).

534

The **arms tendus semi-horizontal, one forward, the other lateral position** is employed as an immobile pose—for instance, with simple march-type *déplacements*.

535

The **arms tendus horizontal, one forward, the other lateral** is a position that certain schools adopt with the *arabesque*. This position may be enhanced by raising the rear leg very high.

536

One arm forward and semi-horizontal, the other lateral and semi-vertical (Fig. 64) is used occasionally as a pose.

537

One arm forward and horizontal, slightly crossed in front of the body, **the other semi-vertical and lateral** (Fig. 65) is a position used frequently by female dancers in the adagios, when they are being carried by men, particularly with the *portés cambrés*.

538

One arm forward and semi-vertical, the other lateral, and horizontal may serve as a *position de départ*, particularly for masculine variations; it is also found with a *fondu* (§ 227), with the raised arm on the side of the rear leg.

539

One arm forward and vertical, the other lateral and semi-horizontal, a very infrequent position, was used by Nijinsky in the variation of Prince Albert in the second act of *Giselle* (Coralli and Perrot).

540

One arm forward and vertical, the other lateral and horizontal, with the head turned to the side of the vertical arm and looking behind it, is a position used by male dancers for starting certain steps done on a diagonal.

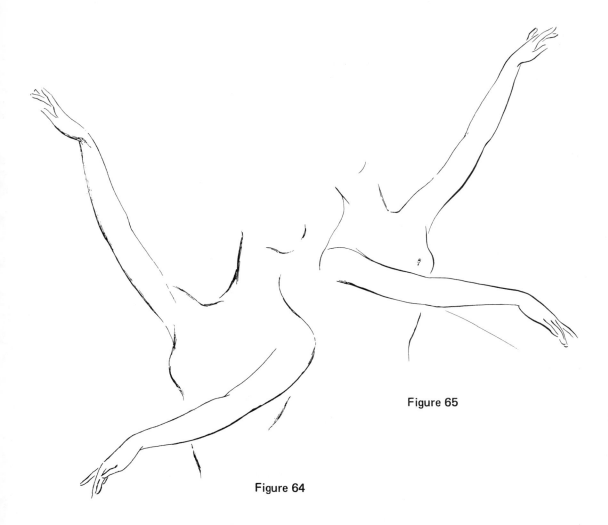

Figure 65

Figure 64

This position is akin to the one we shall describe in paragraph 545, and it may derive from it.

It figures in certain *ports de bras* (§ 586).

541

The **arms semi-vertical, one forward, the other lateral** marks a thrust or a flight.

542

After this whole series of positions in which one arm was forward and the other lateral, we shall see a few positions with one arm forward and one arm to the rear.

One arm forward, the other to the rear, both semi-horizontal is one of the essential moments of the *marche*.

This position is not used in classical dance, but it is found in modern ballets and character ballets. It is the symbolic position of Egyptian ballets: *Khamma* (Jean-Jacques Etchevery).

543

One arm tendu forward and horizontal, the other to the rear and semi-horizontal—a rare position—is found in a few modern ballets and character ballets.

544

One arm tendu forward and semi-vertical, the other to the rear and semi-horitzontal is—as opposed to the preceding ones—a classical position; it accompanies *semi-arabesques* (§ 74), the *dégagés en quatrième derrière* (§ 108), and a certain number of other steps.

545

The same position may be taken croisées—that is, with the head in profile to the side of the raised arm and looking backward behind it.

It is a position as often used by male as by female dancers.

546

One arm tendu forward and horizontal, the other to the rear and semi-horizontal is the arm position for the *arabesque.* But according to the classical rule, the forward arm is slightly above the horizontal, with the hand at eye-level, and the arm to the rear is slightly below it, forming a straight line with the forward arm.

For this reason it is a classical position that is widely used, as much by men as by women. It accompanies not only the *arabesques* (§ 69 through 72) as such, but all steps based on the *arabesque,* such as *tours piqués* (§ 409) and *relevés* (§ 426), and also the *passé-cabriole* (§ 256 through 369), the *fouetté détourné* (§ 434), and the like.

In its nonclassical form, strictly horizontal, it is found in character ballets or with a specific intention: *Istar* (Lifar) shows the door toward which she wishes to proceed (Fig. 66).

547

One arm forward and semi-vertical, the other to the rear and horizontal, a position akin to the preceding one, is sometimes taken by certain

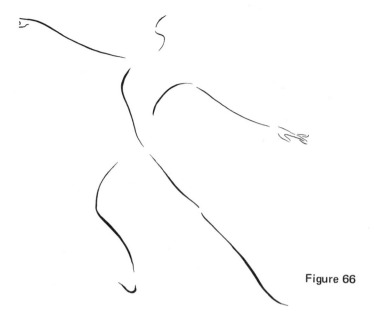

Figure 66

female dancers for the *arabesques,* but in this case it is incorrect because it breaks the line.

It may, on the other hand, suggest an idea of thrust or of soaring.

548

One arm forward and vertical, the other to the rear and semi-horizontal is, on the whole, more used in character dances (Fig. 67).

549

After the arms *tendus,* we shall consider the **arms pliés**. The number of possible combinations is much more significant than for the arms *tendus*[1]

It would thus be out of the question to review all of them within the limits of this work. We shall confine ourselves to analyzing the positions actually used in a normal fashion in the ballet.

[1] In fact, the forearm may be leading downward; semi-horizontal in four different ways in relation to the arm (to the front, to the rear, to the right side, to the left side); horizontal in three different ways (to the front, to the right side, to the left side—the joint of the elbow does not permit the forearm to be horizontal toward the rear); semi-vertical in four ways (as for the semi-horizontal); and, finally, vertical. One of these combinations is to be eliminated in each case because it corresponds to the arm *tendu*: arm horizontal to the front, forearm horizontal to the front. But the number of possible combinations is still considerable.

Figure 67

550

The **arms low and forward, with the forearms horizontal** and *pliés* in front of the body, one against the other (Fig. 68) is the *bras croisés* (crossed arms), a position assigned to pages, domestics, and the like, and particularly to black servants, in numerous ballets. It is also used with character steps: Polonais in the third act of *Lac des Cygnes* (Bourmeister).

551

The **arms low and forward, with the forearms semi-vertical** and *pliés* in front of the body, *croisés* at wrist height, is used as a transition in the *ports de bras,* in *tours* with a partner, or with a specific intention—for example, it is the position of the doubles when they appear in *Les Noces fantastiques* (Lifar). It signifies that they are beings without any real existence. It may be taken with palms turned outward (Fig. 69).

    The same position, but with palms together, is a gesture of prayer (Fig. 70): *Notre-Dame de Paris* (Petit); or a simple position of entreaty: *Giselle* (Coralli and Perrot).

Figure 68 *(Photos: Serge Lido)*

Figure 69

Figure 70

213

Figure 71 *(Photos: Serge Lido)*

552

The **arms low and forward with the forearms vertical** and the hands to the front, palms facing up under the chin, is a symbolic position used, for example, by the Maiden in the *Danses polovtsiennes* from *Prince Igor* (Fokine).

553

The **arms semi-horizontal and forward with the forearms horizontal** in front of the body, one against the other (Fig. 71), is another form of *bras croisés* used with character steps: Mazurka and Hungarian Dance from *Coppélia* (Saint-Léon), for example.

554

The **arms lateral and semi-horizontal with the forearms semi-horizontal** toward the body and the hands on the hips is often used either to characterize women from the lower classes—the fishwives of *Les Noces fantastiques* (Lifar) or peasants, with hands turned inside out, the back of the hand on the hip, for folk dances, especially the Russian: *Petrouchka* (Fokine); or even in a more general way in the ballet: the Chimaera of *Mirages* (Lifar).

This is also the arm position for multiple *tours*.

555

The **arms lateral and semi-horizontal with the forearms horizontal** and folded back in front of the body, hands in front of the chest, is much used in the modern ballet. In this case, the position is often taken with wrists closed: the Symphonie Concertante (Descombey).

556

The **arms lateral and semi-horizontal with the forearms semi-vertical** and bent back on the arms, and the hands on the shoulders is found, for example, in the variation of the fourth Dulcinea of the *Chevalier Errant* (Lifar).

557

The **arms lateral and horizontal with the forearms semi-vertical** and the hands behind the head is used in peasant dances and in certain character dances: *Deuil en 24 Heures* (Petit).

558

The **arms lateral and horizontal, with the forearms vertical** a little to the front, palms upward is the gesture of the supplicant of Greek antiquity. It is found in ballets of Greek character, especially among the bearers of offerings: *Daphnis et Chloé* (Skibine).

559

The **arms lateral and semi-horizontal with the forearms horizontal** and the hands in front of the eyes is rare. There is an example of it in the four Maidens of *Icare* (Lifar).

It may also be used with the hands behind the head, as in the preceding position.

560

The **arms low and to the rear with the forearms horizontal,** one against the other, is the students' position known as *bras au dos* (arms on the back). It is found in a few character ballets.

561

The **arms semi-horizontal to the rear with the forearms semi-horizontal** to the front and the back of the hands against the lower back suggests short wings and for this reason is taken by the Hens in *Les Animaux Modèles* (Lifar).

~~~~~~

562

The **arms pliés and asymmetrical** may take an infinite number of positions, but it should be pointed out that the pure classical dance uses it relatively little. We may find an explanation for that in the fact that, being of a linear aesthetic, the classical dance advocates long, supple lines and eliminates angles. It therefore tends to favor the arms, or at least one arm, *tendus*. Among the classical positions, four are with arms *tendus*, and the only one that has an arm *plié*—the fourth (§ 42)—is used the least.

On the other hand, the harmony of the classical dance is favorable to symmetry. The symmetrical positions will therefore be much employed: three of the five classical arm positions are symmetrical.

The arms *pliés* and asymmetrical therefore corresponds least well to the rules of classical ballet, and that is undoubtedly why it is seldom used. In other types of dance—Spanish and Hindu, for example—these positions are, to the contrary, widely popular.

In the ballet we therefore can find these positions in Spanish dances—*Boléro* (Lifar), the third Dulcinea of the *Chevalier errant* (Lifar), the Spaniards in the third act of *Lac des Cygnes* (Bourmeister)—and in the modern ballets.

563

A few positions, however, belong to the classical repertoire, in particular the one with **both arms forward and low or semi-horizontal with one forearm horizontal in front of the body**, palm down, the other semi-vertical in front of the body, the hand near the chin. This is the romantic position of the Sylphides: *La Sylphide* (Taglioni); *Les Sylphides* (Fokine).

With the forearm semi-vertical and more to the front, palm turned upward, it is a gesture from the Middle Ages—a little precious—which is used, for example, by the Noblewoman of the *Chevalier et la Demoiselle* (Lifar).

564

The ballet also has two positions with the arms *pliés* asymmetrically in which one arm is in front, the other lateral.

Classical *pas de deux* from *Giselle*. Yvette Chauviré and Serge Lifar. (*Photo: Opera Library: Erlanger Archives*)

A classical ballet: *Les Sylphides.* Choreography by Michel Fokine. Yvette Chauviré, Claude Bessy, Peter Van Dyke. (*Photo: Pic*)

Giselle, the mad scene, beautifully expressed by Yvette Chauviré. (*Photo: Pic*)

Kneeling position. Claude Bessy and Georges Skibine in *Daphnis et Chloé*. *(Photo: Pic)*

Icarus. Choreography by Serge Lifar (décor by Picasso).
Saut de l'ange by Attilio Labis. *(Photo: Pic)*

A classical position of Cyril
Atanassoff. (*Photo: Pic*)

A modern position of Cyril
Atanassoff: *Le Sacre
du Printemps.*
Choreography by Maurice Béjart.
(*Photo: Pic*)

Noella Pontois. *(Photo: Lido)*

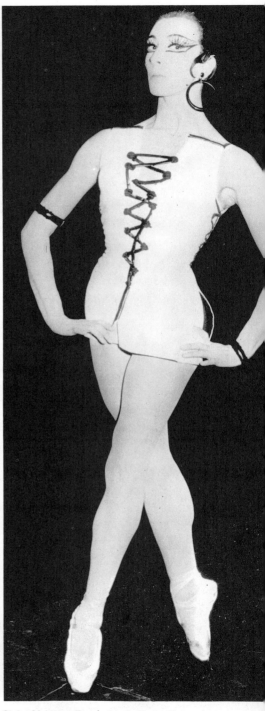

Yvette Chauviré in *Lac des Cygnes.*
(Photo: Mike Davis)

Claire Motte as Esméralda in *Notre Dame de Paris.* Choreography by Roland Petit.
(Photo: Pic)

One arm low and to the front with the forearm horizontal and the hand toward the opposite hip, the other arm lateral and semi-horizontal with the forearm semi-horizontal and the hand on the hip in contact with the other hand is a predominantly masculine position, probably derived from the gesture of having the hands on a sword, ready to draw. It is sometimes found with its original meaning in ballets involving duels, such as *Roméo et Juliette* in its various choreographies. But it may also be found as a pose in very classical ballets.

Used by female dancers, it has a peasant or folk meaning.

565

One arm low and to the front with the forearm semi-vertical and the hand on the opposite shoulder, the other arm lateral and semi-horizontal with the forearm semi-vertical and bent back to the arm, folded back on the arm, hand on the shoulder is a principally masculine position.

It may indicate taking one's coat off the shoulder: Prince Albert in the second act of *Giselle* (Coralli and Perrot).

Female dancers do it, on the whole, with the arm lateral and horizontal (Fig. 72).

Figure 72

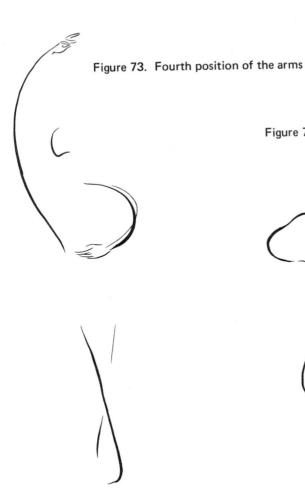

Figure 73. Fourth position of the arms

Figure 74. Sixth position of the arms

566

"Complex" arm positions—that is, with one arm *tendu* and the other *plié*—are more frequent than arms *pliés*. For the reasons we have explained in paragraph 562, they have strictly classical uses, because the fourth position (§ 42) is formed with one arm *tendu* and one arm *plié* (Fig. 73), as is also the sixth position (§ 44), which we have already defined (Fig. 74).

Once again, the number of possible combinations is very great, and we shall cite only a few examples among the most frequently used positions.

567

One arm forward and semi-horizontal, slightly crossed in front of the body, the other semi-horizontal and forward with the forearm

semi-vertical, the hand toward the opposite shoulder, is a position quite often taken by female dancers in the role of a swan.

568

A very ordinary complex position consists of having **one arm lateral and semi-horizontal (usually the left), the other lateral and semi-horizontal with the forearm semi-horizontal and the hand on the hip.** This is principally a masculine position. It is performed by dancers and dancing students of the Ecole de Dance during the procession of the *corps de ballet* at the Opera (directed by Albert Aveline).

569

One arm tendu lateral and semi-horizontal, the other arm low and lateral with the forearm vertical and the hand on the shoulder, is a position used especially used by male dancers but which is not, however, very frequent.

It may be found as an immobile pose, in the *adagios,* and at the beginning or the end of variations.

570

One arm tendu lateral and semi-vertical or vertical, the other lateral and semi-horizontal with the forearm semi-horizontal and the hand on the hip, is a character position used in dances of the Russian type: Mazurka from *Coppélia* (Saint-Léon); or occasionally even in classical variations patterned on folk music—for example, a mazurka.

571

One arm lateral and horizontal, the other lateral and horizontal with the forearm semi-vertical, the hand toward the ear, often signifies listening. It is found in *La Fille mal gardée* (choreography by F. Ashton after Dauberval) (Fig. 75) and in the first act of *Giselle* (Coralli and Perrot).

572

One arm lateral and semi-horizontal, the other low and forward with the forearm semi-vertical in front of the body may be used in two different fashions, according to the position of the hand.

With the hand flat, directed toward the opposite shoulder, it is a masculine position used as an immobile posture: *Suite en Blanc* (Lifar), or as the end of a variation.

Figure 75. Listening gesture

Figure 76. Swan position

When the hand is raised, it is a graceful and feminine gesture—for example, that of the young girl who offers her hand to be kissed while turning away her head. It may also be executed in this way with a burlesque character: Polichinelle disguised as Rosetta, in *Salade* (Lifar).

573

One arm tendu lateral and semi-vertical, the other forward and low with the forearm semi-vertical and bent back in front of the body, is a pose used especially by male dancers at the end of a variation.

220

574

One arm tendu lateral and vertical, the other low and forward with the forearm semi-horizontal, is a swan's position that is found in the second act of *Lac des Cygnes* (Petipa and Ivanoff) (Fig. 76).

575

Finally, **one arm tendu semi-horizontal to the rear, the other forward and semi-horizontal with the forearm horizontal** in front of the body may accompany the *marche* of the male dancers.

576

Here we shall conclude our examination of arm positions. Those we have cited are only a few examples among those that occur most often in the classical ballets.

In the contemporary ballets, the number of arm positions is extremely important and their role is considerable. An exhaustive study of the latter would exceed the scope of this work.

PORTS DE BRAS

577

Port de bras is the name for a movement of both arms executed by a dancer either without any accompanying shifting in position or with minimal shifting that is done by means of very simple steps) *dégagés*, for example (§ 102).

Whatever movement is executed by the legs, it must not become the center of attention, which should be focused above all on the arms.

The *port de bras* may involve a movement of the head or of the body which accompanies or accentuates it.

There are a great number of possible arm movements, but the classical dance has selected a few to form the classical *ports de bras*. These do not have particular meanings in and of themselves [as of welcome, fear, sorrow, for example] their importance results from the beauty of the lines in movement. *Ports de bras* are used particularly in the *adagios*. Unless there is an indication to the contrary, the dancer is in fifth position (§ 29).

578

Port de bras in second position: from the *position de départ* (§ 38), the arms rise forward in first (§ 39), then open into second (§ 40) and come back down laterally to return to the *position de départ*.

The body is facing front; when the arms are in first position, it is inclined slightly forward and is *épaule* toward the rear leg; the body rights itself and returns to face front when the arms are in second position.

The head is facing front; it is bent slightly forward and to the side of the rear foot, accompanying the movement of the body when the arms are in first; the eyes are directed toward the hands. The head then follows the movement of the hand that is on the side of the forward foot and faces front again during the descent of the arms.

This is the simplest of the *ports de bras,* the first that is taught to students at the *Ecole de danse.*

579

Port de bras in third position: from the *position de départ* (§ 38), the arms rise forward in first (§ 39), then find their place in third (§ 41); the vertical arm comes back down in second (§ 40), and the two arms descend laterally to the *position de départ*.

The trunk and the head have positions similar to those of the preceding *port de bras*, with the head following the movement of the hand that is on the side of the forward foot.

580

Port de bras in fifth position: from the *position de départ* (§ 38), the arms rise forward, move into first (§ 39), and continue into fifth (§ 43). They then open up and descend laterally, passing through second (§ 40) to the *position de départ*.

The positions of the trunk and the head are approximately the same as for the preceding *port de bras*.

581

Port de bras in fifth passing through second position: from the *position de départ*, the arms rise laterally, pass into second (§ 40), and arrive in fifth (§ 43); they then descend in front, pass through first (§ 39), and arrive at the *position de départ* (§ 38).

This *port de bras* has a variation in which the arms bend to come back down in front of the body and pass through the position described in paragraph 551.

This arm movement may also be performed with *détournés sur les deux pieds* (§ 385).

582

Compound port de bras in third position: from the *position de départ* (§ 38), the arms rise forward in first (§ 39) and find their place in third (§ 41), with the vertical arm on the side of the rear foot. This arm is lowered laterally while the other rises, in order to achieve the third position that is the reverse of the preceding one. The arm that is horizontal then descends laterally while the vertical arm descends to the front to return to the *position de départ*.

The head, as in the preceding instance, follows the movement of the hand that is on the side of the rear foot as far as the first of the third positions, then the head turns to the other side and follows the movement of the other hand, facing forward again at the end.

583

Another compound port de bras in third position: from the *position de départ* (§ 38), the arms rise in first (§ 39), then find their place in third (§ 41), with the vertical arm on the side of the rear foot; they take a new position in first (§ 39), then one in third (§ 41) that is the reverse of the preceding one; the vertical arm descends in second (§ 40), and both arms come back down to the *position de départ* (§ 38).

The positions of the trunk and the head correspond to those of the preceding *ports de bras*.

This *port de bras* may be executed with the dancer remaining in fifth position, but it often accompanies a movement of the legs: the dancer starts in fifth with right foot forward, shifts that foot into *quatrième devant croisée* (§ 107) at the same time that the arms arrive in third; the anterior foot is placed *à plat* and the knees bend when the arms are in first position. The knees are straightened once again and the rear foot rises *sur la pointe* with the second of the third positions, and closes *en cinquième derrière* while the arms are descending.

584

Port de bras tournant: beginning in the *position de départ*, the two arms describe a circle in a vertical plane parallel to the line of the shoulders; one of the arms is raised to cross in front of the body, the other is lifted laterally to pass through second position (§ 40).

The two movements are done at the same time in such a way that the arms pass successively through the two positions of third (§ 41) and finish in a *position de départ*. Thus, at the beginning the arm that crosses in front of the body moves more quickly than the other; this is reversed by the end of the movement.

The body is *épaule* a little to one side, then to the other, following the movement of the arm that is rising laterally. The head follows the movement of the body.

This *port de bras* is often executed *en fondu* (§ 227). In this case it may be completed by a first (§ 39), followed by *bras d'arabesque* (§ 546), with the forward arm on the side of the rear leg. The dancer may then return through first and invert the *arabesque.*

585

The same port de bras may be executed with a forward progression. The dancer begins in fourth, with the forward foot *à la pointe* (§ 57), achieves the *port de bras*, and at the end of it places his arm in first (§ 39) while placing his forward foot *à plat* and raising the rear foot *à la pointe*; he then opens his arms into second and moves the rear leg forward by means of a *rond de jambe à terre en dedans* (§ 123), while the arms are finding their place in third, with the raised arm on the side of the rear leg. He is then ready to start the whole movement again in the opposite direction.

Instead of the *rond de jambe,* one may do a *détourné à terre* (§ 384) or close in fifth and do a *dégagé* in second (§ 103).

This *port de bras* may also accompany the *petits pas de bourrée courus* (§ 150).

586

Port de bras en troisième croisée: from the *position de départ* (§ 38), the arms rise in first position (§ 39), shift into third (§ 41), return to first, and then find their place *en troisième croisée* (§ 540), the reverse of the preceding third.

The position of *troisième croisée* may also be used at the end of the *port de bras* described in paragraph 580. It is then a complex movement accompanied by a *battement arrondi* (§ 119) *en dehors,* finished *en quatrième derrière*, during the *port de bras* proper; the forward foot is raised *à la pointe* while the arms are placed in *troisième croisée* (§ 540).

This movement may precede a preparation for *tours en dedans* (§ 427). This preparation is taken with the legs *en quatrième croisée* (§ 28) and the arms in sixth position (§ 44).

This sequence is found in the grand ballet of *Castor et Pollux* (choreography by Nicola Guerra).

587

The eight *ports de bras* we have described are the ones that are considered to be classical and are practiced daily in classes for this reason.

They may be combined with each other to form various sequences. They may similarly be accompanied by varied leg movements, but always while fulfilling the condition stated in paragraph 577.

On the stage these classical *ports de bras* are found in the *adagios* of ballets having no theme: *Suite de Danses* (Clustine), *Suite en Blanc* (Lifar), *The Crystal Palace* (Balanchine); and even in the ballets with a theme: *Giselle, adagio* from the second act (Coralli and Perrot), *Lac des Cygnes* (Petipa and Ivanoff), and the like.

They are often the basis for the arm movements that we shall see in the following section.

MOUVEMENTS DE BRAS

588

The **mouvements de bras** are composed of: simple movements that have no significance in and of themselves but that do not belong to classical *ports de bras;* movements that accompany steps; and gestures that have a particular meaning or that are done with a specific intention.

589

The classical practice of *ports de bras,* seen in the preceding section, and taught from the beginning of instruction in the dance, permits the dancer to acquire good muscular control and to hold his arms in any position for a sustained period. The dancer should be able to execute the movements with the greatest delicacy and precision and at the same time give an impression of ease.

All the joints of the arm are mobilized and at no time should any one of them remain "locked" into position. The movement should be like a wave that flows from the body and goes all the way to the fingertips.

When the dancer has completely mastered the classical *ports de bras,* his gestures will have acquired the desired elegance and his arms will be ready for the most diverse movements.

A *port de bras* may, furthermore, become a *mouvement de bras* by taking on a particular significance. For example, the *port de bras* in second position (§ 578) may mean offering, welcome, greeting, and the like. In this case, the hand opens, palm upward, with the fingers more extended and the trunk more inclined to the front.

590

If the positions of the arms seen in the first section were very numerous, the movements are even more so, because they involve the passage from one position to another. It will, therefore, be just as difficult to imagine the total number of possible movements. To a great extent they are left to the free imagination of the choreographer, who may always invent new ones for the requirements of his ballet. The contemporary dance makes increasing use of varied and complex *mouvements de bras.* In ballets such as *Symphonie Concertante* (Descombey), *Notre-Dame de Paris* (Petit), and *Le Sacre du Printemps* (Béjart), a considerable number of them may be found.

We shall content ourselves with pointing out a certain number of movements that are among the most popular and most meaningful.

591

One movement found in several ballets consists of raising arms that are extended forward from the semi-horizontal position to the semi-vertical position. The movement is done in such a way that one arm is at the peak of the trajectory when the other is at the bottom. *Battements* of this type are done several times in succession. They are found, for example, in the variation of the Shadow from *Mirages* (Lifar) and in *Istar* (Lifar), but in the latter instance the movement has a meaning: Istar shakes her arms up and down while a genie from the Gates of the Dead tries to catch her bracelets.

592

Another movement is done with the arms forward: the arm is extended horizontally, then bends, bringing the hand toward the body, then extends once again. The hand describes a sort of ellipse whose curve above the horizontal is described when the hand comes back toward the body. Both arms make the same movement, so that one arm may be extended when the other is completely curved in toward the body. The positions of the wrists follow those of the arms.

This movement is found in, for example, the passage of the Sylphides from *Etudes* (Lander). It may also suggest pushing away when the palms remain turned to the front. On the other hand, with the palms turned toward the body, it is the gesture of drawing toward oneself: the Shadow draws in the Young Man in *Mirages* (Lifar) as if she held him at the end of her line.

The rhythm of the movement may be varied.

593

Another movement of both arms: the arms, held in front of the body, move from right to left and from left to right very rapidly. This movement is found in the ballet of *Thaïs*.

594

Related movement: as before, the arms go from right to left and from left to right in front of the body, but here they scarcely pass beyond the middle of the body, and the movement of one sets off the other. This movement is found in the waltz of the little dog from *Suite de Danses* (Clustine).

595

The **rouleau** (roll) is done with the arms semi-horizontal to the front; the forearms turn horizontally one about the other in front of the body.

This movement is found in, for example, *Les Patineurs* (Ashton).

596

Another turning movement of both arms is performed as follows: both arms rise slowly in front from the *position de départ* (§ 38) until they are *en couronne* (§ 43), with each hand describing a series of circles from the wrist. It is found in the variation of Aurora from *La Belle au Bois dormant* (Petipa).

597

The two arms rise alternately *en couronne* in front of the body and open laterally.

This movement is found in *Les Sylphides* (Fokine).

598

Certain movements of the arms that have no specific meaning are used by preference in character ballets—for example, the gesture of opening the arms half-horizontally (§ 526) and then folding them while bringing the closed hands almost touching each other in front of the body at the level of the pit of the stomach: Trépak from *Casse-Noisette* (Etchevery).

599

Another character movement is done by the Mountebanks of *Divertissement* (Lifar): the arms go from front vertical to rear semi-horizontal; when they are vertical, the body leans backward, and when the arms are to the rear, the body leans forward.

600

For the various movements of both arms that we have just examined briefly we have cited only one example of each. But these movements are among those found most frequently, and the example is intended, above all, as an illustration of the indicated movement.

601

After these few movements of both arms, we shall see others that, on the whole, involve only one arm.

In several ballets we find a movement that consists of causing one extended arm to turn very rapidly around the shoulder; it may be done as well by men as by women: the Young Man and the Shadow of *Mirages* (Lifar), the Pirates from *Daphnis et Chloé* (Skibine).

602

One arm, curved in front of the body, is raised and extended until it is vertical in front: variation of the Shadow in *Mirages* (Lifar).

603

One arm is vertical and lateral, with the hand turning around the wrist: beginning of the variation of the Cigarette in *Suite en Blanc* (Lifar).

604

One arm in front goes from semi-vertical to horizontal: the children's Mazurka in *Suite de Danses* (Clustine).

The same gesture, when the index finger is pointed, assumes the meaning of "pointing out": the two courtesans of *Mirages* (Lifar).

605

One arm curved in front of the body with the hand at the level of the pit of the stomach, is extended in a lateral, semi-horizontal position. This movement may be used in both classical variations and character dances: variation of Djali from the *Deux Pigeons* (Mérante).

606

Similar movement: the arm, curved in the same fashion, is extended open, horizontal. This movement is done more slowly than the preceding one and accompanies, for example, an upstage step: the Nubian women from *Faust* (Aveline); often the other arm has the hand on the hip.

607

The last movements for which we shall give examples belong, on the whole, to character dances: the extended arm describes an oblique line going from low in front of the body and crossing to a half-vertical, lateral position. In *Petrouchka* (Fokine), this gesture is done with a handkerchief in the hand.

608

In the *Danses polovtsiennes* from *Prince Igor* (Fokine), this same type of movement is found, but the arm does not cross in front and goes backward instead of laterally.

609

The **mouvements de bras** we have just seen, although they have no specific meanings, have a validity of their own and are used with a variety of steps. However, the majority of the dance steps we have studied are accompanied by an arm movement that is particular to them—for example, the *pas de basque en descendant* as we described it in paragraph 189.

610

It can happen that a classical *port de bras* serves as a *mouvement de bras* for certain steps: the *pas de bourrée jeté* (§ 475) is accompanied by the *port de bras* in fifth described in paragraph 580.

611

Less frequently, we find steps that can be accompanied by two *mouvements de bras*. In general, one of these is the basic movement —the one taught to students along with the step—but it may eventually be replaced by another, which is well defined, without its constituting a deliberate effect on the part of the choreographer.

For example, the *passé-cabriole en quatrième devant battu* (§ 363) or *non battu* (§ 255) is normally performed as we have indicated in paragraph 363, with the arms rising in third position (§ 41).

But it may also be executed with the arms rising *en couronne* (§ 43), by doing the *port de bras* in fifth (§ 580).

612

Finally, there are a few steps for which there is almost no arm movement: the arms remain in the *position de départ* (§ 38)—for example, during an *entrechat*.

613

Obviously, the arm movement accompanying a step can always be modified, suppressed, or replaced by another when the choreographer wishes to express a particular idea.

But, except when there is such an intention, the failure to execute the desired arm movement constitutes a fault just as surely as any change in the position of the legs.

614

The *mouvements de bras* accompanying the steps may be classified principally as in two categories: those that form a harmonious combination with the positions of the legs and those that facilitate the execution of the step.

The first category accompanies mainly steps performed *à terre*; steps in the *adagios;* and, in general, steps that are either very simple or very slow.

The second category, by contrast, is the normal accompaniment to most leaps and turns. Not only does the movement of the arms make certain steps easier—permitting, for example, a higher *saut*—but, especially with the *tours,* failure to observe the required arm movement can make the execution of the step very difficult, if not impossible.

From this fact it follows that the arm movements belonging to this category will be found to be almost identical for a given *saut* or *tour* whatever the time or place of its execution and whatever dance system it belongs to: for example, in Greek antiquity, the *failli grand jeté* (§ 470) could be identified on a vase that gives a very beautiful analysis of it, but the arm movement that accompanies it is very akin to our own.

615

A final group of arm movements is made up of those that have a particular **meaning**. Depending upon the situation, they may be employed individually—that is, without movement of the legs—or they may replace the arm movement that normally accompanies a step.

We can group these in several categories: certain ones are more or less similar to gestures from everyday life; others are symbols or evocations of ideas or of animals.

616

Before beginning this short study, we might observe that in exceptional cases characters in a ballet may not have arms at all (or may not use them): the fruitworms from the *Festin de l'Araignée* (Aveline) have their arms stuck to their bodies, which are wound around in a spiral; the sea-horses of the *Noces fantastiques* (Lifar) have their arms folded back inside their costumes in such a way that they are not visible at all. The absence of arms precludes the execution of difficult steps and causes a certain clumsiness in the dancers who perform these roles.

617

We shall speak of gestures only in those instances in which the dancer makes the movement without having an object in his hands or at least without that object's normally intervening.

The action of taking a chair, for example, and of setting it down—third act of *Coppélia* (Descombey)—does not constitute a "gesture" in the sense in which we understand this word. On the other hand, in *Mirages* (Lifar), when the Young Man turns the key of dreams—in empty space—to liberate the Chimaera, it is indeed a "gesture," because there is no door nor is there a lock in which to insert the key; the key is only the materialization—equivalent to a veritable play on words—of an abstract idea.

618

We shall simply point out here a few of the gestures that are found most often in the ballets, because their variety is almost infinite, and choreographers are free to make innovations in this field.

619

Gesture of throwing a stone: the dancer reproduces very exactly the movement of picking up and then throwing but, of course, without the object itself. This is a popular gesture and is found in *L'Appel de la Montagne* (Peretti) as well as in *Roméo et Juliette* (Labis).

620

Gesture of fear: one or both hands are brought up in front of the face, palms turned outward, elbows raised: *Daphnis et Chloé* (Skibine).

621

Gesture of drinking: the movement made in taking a glass and lifting it to the lips: the Buffoon in the first act of *Lac des Cygnes* (Bourmeister).

We might note that this gesture is different from the symbolic gesture of drinking in which both hands, clasped together by the little fingers with the palms upward to form cups, rise in front of the body and come up to the mouth. It is different also from the gesture that mimics drinking: with the fingers curved and the thumb spread wide, the hand moves close to the mouth and stops short.

622

One group of gestures has to do with sailors' movements.

To hoist up sail: beginning with both arms folded in front of the body, each hand in turn opens, rises about the other, and closes while descending vertically as the other rises in its turn. The movement is that of pulling on a rope. It is found in all sailors' dances: *Danse du Marin* (Jean Guélis), *Fancy Free* (Jerome Robbins), *'Adame Miroir* (Janine Charrat), *Les Noces fantastiques* (Lifar), and the like.

623

The **gesture of the watch**: the hand is brought up above the eyes, with thumb drawn back, fingers taut, and palm down. This is the movement of someone who is shading his eyes to see better.

It is found in the same dances as the preceding one.

624

The **gesture of rowing**: somewhat stylized; this is a little less frequent than the other two. It is found with the sailors in *Les Noces* *fantastiques* (Lifar), the oarsmen in *Le Chevalier errant* (Lifar), and the rowers of *La Grande-Jatte* (Aveline).

625

We come to another group of gestures, those involving weapons. We are all familiar with the gestures of children pretending to draw revolvers during their games.

The **gesture of the revolver** has only rarely been utilized in ballets—however, an example of it is found in *L'Inconnue* (Lifar).

626

On the other hand, gestures relating to more ancient types of arms have often had a place in the ballet.

Gesture of the slingshot: This is quite rare because the weapon itself is seldom used. Being the characteristic weapon of David, the slingshot may be suggested or depicted in dances pertaining to the king: for example, *David triomphant* (Lifar).

627

The **gesture of drawing a bow** is the most frequently represented of the movements with weapons. The archer's bow is an elegant weapon that, by characterizing a divinity such as Cupid, is pleasing—whence a whole series of extended uses. It is also utilized by other gods from mythology—Diana, Apollo, and the like. Finally, the hunter often has a bow in his hand. This is so clearly understood that in *Giselle,* when in the first act Prince Albert intends to say "I am going hunting," he makes the gesture of drawing a bow.

This same gesture is found, for example, when the Prince, at the beginning of the second act of *Lac des Cygnes,* wishes to assure Odette of his good intentions regarding her and therefore follows the gesture of drawing the bow with the gesture, "No."

In its mythological aspect, we have the gesture in the *pizzicati* of the third act of *Sylvia* (Mérante).

628

In the latter instance, it is very important to distinguish between the gesture made without using any accessory and the movement made with the actual weapon. For example, the entrance of the Huntresses in the first act of *Sylvia* is made with bows; *L'Amour* from *Caprices de*

233

Cupidon (Lander) does not relinquish his; the Mongols in *Danses polovtsiennes* from *Prince Igor* also have their bows in hand.

In the same connection, there is no need to speak of gestures with the lance or the sword, because they do in fact figure in the ballets in which they are found.

629

Other gestures inspired by those from real life are, however, becoming stylized. For example, the **gesture of pointing the finger**, which is found in *Istar* when she shows the door through which she wishes to pass (Fig. 66), becomes symbolic in the variation of the Shadow from *Mirages* (Lifar).

630

Similarly, the **gesture of gathering up** or of picking a flower, found, for example, in the first act of *Giselle*, becomes symbolic when the body bends forward, the hand remaining at a distance from the ground, and ends by being only a movement of the arm devoid of meaning.

631

Certain of these gestures may be intended to underscore the character of the personage—for example, the **gesture of rocking** that is given to the nurses in *Petrouchka* (Fokine); the **gesture of hooking the thumbs under the suspenders** or in the vest, with the arms lateral and horizontal and the forearms bent back toward the arm—given to the peasants in *Le Baiser de la Fée* (Balanchine), and so on.

632

The symbol of a gesture may be very simple—for example, the one for "no": the hand, with the palm to the front (occasionally closed, with the index finger pointing), is shaken from right to left in front of the body; this gesture is often accompanied by one with the head.

633

At other times the symbol is more subtle, being composed of a mixture of real and adapted gestures. This is especially discernible when the dancer represents a **character on horseback**. In the position of a horseman holding the reins, he combines movements that are evocative of the rider with others evocative of the horse: Phoebus, in *Notre-Dam de Paris* (Petit).

634

And so we come to the last category—a very rich and abundan₁ one—the **gestures of animals**. These have always been an inspiration tc choreographers. Without going as far back as Greek antiquity, where the comedies had choruses of animals—birds, dolphins, frogs, and so on[1]—we find some of them in the classical ballet from its very beginnings. By 1830, Pushkin alludes, in *Eugene Onegin,* to the "swans" who hopped about on the stage of the Bolshoi Theatre of St. Petersburg, of which Avdotia Istomina was at that time the great star.

635

Historically it appears that it was the winged animals who were the first to have a place in the ballet. This is easily understood: their grace, their lightness accord perfectly with the striving for lightness that is characteristic of the classical aesthetic: the only choreography arranged by Marie Taglioni for Emma Livry in 1860 was *Le Papillon (The Butterfly).*

No part of it has survived, and we do not know which characteristic gestures may have been employed in this ballet.

636

The birds: swans (*Lac des Cygnes,* 1877) and other birds (the Bluebird from *La Belle au Bois dormant,* 1890) became very numerous toward the end of the nineteenth century and remain so (*La Mort du Cygne [The Death of the Swan],* 1905; *L'Osieau de Feu [The Firebird],* 1910; *Le Cigogneau [The Young Stork],* 1937) up to the middle of the twentieth. It seems that at the present time fewer choreographies are being written in which they appear.

We shall relate to the birds all characters with wings: Sylphides (*La Sylphide,* 1832), Wilis (*Giselle,* 1841), Elves (*Les Elfes,* 1856), Chimaeras (*Les Mirages,* 1944-1947), and even Icarus (*Icare,* 1935).

This profusion of wings will give rise to several characteristic arm movements.

[1] See G. PRUDHOMMEAU: *La Danse grecque.* Editions du C.N.R.S., 1965, p. 537, § 1501 ff.

637

The most frequent are: the **battements d'ailes** (beating of wings) represented by the arms in lateral position, whether they move alternately from semi-horizontal to semi-vertical and vice versa with wrist movement (hand raised when the arm descends, lowered when it rises), or whether the elbow bends, bringing the hand toward the shoulder, then opens out once again in second (§ 40) with wrist movement (hand lowered when the arm bends, raised when it is extended).

These movements may also be done with a single arm.

638

The **bird tucking its head under its wing** is represented with the arms forward and semi-vertical, crossed at the wrist, with the head near the right arm and slightly below it. This movement is often used by swans.

639

Another swan movement consists of **rubbing the head against the feathers**: the right arm, extended in front of the head, rubs against the shoulder.

640

Occasionally the arm represents the **neck and the head of the swan**: it is lateral and vertical, with the elbow slightly bent and the wrist flexed at a right angle, fingers closed tight, thumbs down. This position may be found in *Lac des Cygnes* (Fig. 76) as well as in *Endymion* (Lifar).

641

The **flutterings of the wings of** smaller birds are evoked by a very rapid and constant movement of the outstretched hand: Colibri, the Bluebird in *La Belle au Bois dormant* (Petipa). The same gesture is performed by the Chimaeras of *Mirages* (Lifar).

642

Hens, having only short wings that hardly permit them to fly, have a special movement: the arms are to the rear, bent back, with hands closed on the lower part of the back (§ 561), and they sway from right to the left without the hands moving: *Les Animaux modeles* (Lifar).

The rooster has a different gesture: with his upper arms horizontal to the rear, he bend his forearms horizontally forward along the upper arms; thumbs in armpits, he shakes his elbows. The idea is the same, however: short wings (*Renard,* Béjart).

643

Flying insects: butterfly and mayfly in *Le Festin de l'Araignée* (Aveline); Iphias and Morphide in *Piège de Lumière [Lure of Light]* (Taras); dragonflies in *Blanche-Neige* (Lifar), and the like. These most often have as a characteristic the beating of their wings represented by the first movement described in paragraph 637.

644

From the nineteenth century on, animals other than those with wings have made their entry into the ballet: *Le Petit Cheval bossu [The Little Crippled Horse]* ,1864, is the ancestor of a long line of horses leading up to *Idylle*, 1954 (Skibine) and *Le Massacre des Amazones*, 1956 (Janine Charrat), including even mythical horses such as unicorns: *La Dame à la Licorne [The Lady with the Unicorn]*, 1953 (H. Rosen).

Horses are usually characterized by a movement of the legs (§ 133). Generally, dancers representing horses hold their arms bent in front of them, hands at the height of the chest, palms down, fingers flexed. This movement may evoke the rider who holds the reins, the dancer then being both horse and rider at the same time: Phoebus in *Notre-Dame de Paris* (Petit); or it may indicate the front hooves of the horse when he has reared up on his hind legs: *Idylle* (Skibine).

645

The same leg movement is accompanied by a different movement of the arms to characterize **deer**: the arms are lateral and horizontal, with the forearm semi-vertical and the hands vertical near the forehead, turned back toward the outside, wrists bent, fingers spread apart and slightly bent, the second finger lowered, thumb turned inward representing the horns. The hands shake gently without changing position: *Le Chevalier et la Damoiselle* (Lifar).

The same type of gesture characterizes all the deer family: *Actéon* in *La Symphonie fantastique* (Massine), *Endymion* (Lifar), and so on.

Very closely akin is the symbol of the **reindeer**: the fingers are taut, the index finger lowered, the hands held away from the head, and the arms able to assume various poses, the most characteristic position being arms vertical: *Maanerenen* (Birgit Cullberg).

646

Another animal that has very often attracted choreographers is the **cat.** He is characterized by several gestures, of which the principal ones are passing the paw behind the ear and scratching.

Although we find tabby-cats for the most part—*The Tabby-Cat* (Balanchine), *Le Demoiselles de la Nuit* (Petit), and the like—we also find a few tomcats: the third act of *La Belle au Bois dormant* (Petipa), *Renard* (Béjart). But this last cat is characterized only by his whiskers and not by his gestures.

647

The **dog** appears much less frequently in ballets. Generally he takes an arm position similar to that of the horse (§ 644), representing the dog sitting on his haunches: *Les Malheurs de Sophie* (Quinault).

648

The **bear,** on the other hand, figures quite often in ballets: he is a clumsy, grotesque personage inviting caricature. Usually he holds his arms to the side and semi-horizontal with the forearm vertical, as if he were supporting his hands on a stick placed on his shoulders. He may have movements that are simply imitative: *Petrouchka* (Fokine); or that have an actually caricatured variation: *Les Animaux modèles* (Lifar).

649

Other quadrupeds figure here and there in the ballets with more or less characteristic gestures. The wolf: *Le Loup* (Petit); panthers: entrance of the Savages from the *Indes galantes* (Lifar); fox, billy-goat: *Renard* (Béjart); lion: *Les Animaux modéles* (Lifar), and so on.

650

We have already mentioned (§ 643) **winged insects**; wingless insects are less frequent. They are encountered in a few ballets such as The Cage (Robbins) and Le Festin de l'Araignée, the spider being characterized by her elbows rising higher than her head to represent her legs; the dung-beetle, usually noticeable for its clumsy gait; the ant with rapid and precise gestures; the praying mantis, and the like.

651

Finally, we shall conclude with the **animals that live in water.** Occasionally they may be represented directly: in *Les Noces fantastiques* (Lifar) one can identify shellfish with snapping movements, fish who glide, and sea-horses with no arms; but most often a female dancer will have very supple movements flowing throughout her body, and usually her arms wave, evoking fish, to represent water personages: the Ocean Nymph of *Les Noces fantastiques* and the Nereid of *Nautéos* (both by Lifar).

652

Whereas an animal may play an isolated part in certain ballets—the Dog of *Les Malheurs de Sophie,* the Bear of *Petrouchka,* and so on—there are also a few **ballets grouping numerous animals.**

The scene that opens at the bottom of the sea in *Les Noces fantastiques,* as we said in the preceding paragraph, makes use of everything that lives in water.

Certain of these ballets are realistic and imitative, such as *Le Festin de l'Araignée* (Aveline); others are much more stylized, as, for example, *Les Animaux modèles* (Lifar), where the Ant and the Grasshopper are not like animals at all; or else they become symbolic, as in *The Cage* (Robbins).

653

Related to the animals are the **monsters,** fantastic figures with contorted gestures whose hands, by their pose and their gestures, often suggest claws. These are creatures with evil spirits: the sorceresses of *L'Oiseau de Feu* (Fokine); or creatures out of Hell: *La Symphonie fantastique* (Massine), *Lucifer* (Lifar), and the like.

654

As we stated in paragraph 590, the *mouvements de bras* may be infinitely varied. We have tried to give an idea of their principal categories and of what they may be. It is wrong—and will become more so—to think that the classical ballet is concerned only with legs or to think that the dancer is an automaton devoid of meaning. All the elements in the bodily schema participate in the execution and expression of the steps.

The arms make it possible to underscore and intensify this latter fact. Nothing in the ballet is left to chance: the smallest movement, the most insignificant glance is perceived as a function of a precise idea and contributes to the perfection of an art whose high elaboration must, in the end, give the impression of being perfectly natural.

THE HANDS

655

To complete our study of arm movements we shall devote a few paragraphs to the **hands** (*les mains*).

It appears that the classical dance of the nineteenth century had accorded them little importance, being satisfied with arranging them in a graceful pose, while other forms of the dance, especially in Asia, made them an important element of the choreographic art. However, the present tendency is to give an increasingly larger place to the movements of the hands and to make of them a positive element of the choreography.

656

We shall first define the classical hand positions. There is one for female dancers and a somewhat different one for male dancers.

La main classique féminine has all the fingers supple, neither bent nor taut. The thumb is slightly in toward the palm, the second finger close to the thumb but not touching it, the index finger a little higher than the ring finger, and the little finger still higher yet (Fig. 55).

This position is taken automatically when no other is mentioned. It accompanies exercises. It must become perfectly natural.

657

La main classique masculine has the fingers more extended, with the difference of levels only very slightly marked and the thumb in toward the palm (Fig. 17).

The idea of this position is that of a greater restraint, since the masculine dance is supposed to give an impression of vigor and clarity.

658

When the **arms are in second position**, the female dancers turn their palms toward the front, whereas male dancers turn them downward.

240

Figure 77 *(Photo: Serge Lido)*

659

For the **arabesque,** the female dancer's hand position resembles that of the male, and the palm is turned downward (Fig. 77).

660

In modern ballet and in certain character ballets, the **hand is stiff** *(raide)* with the fingers extended taut and closely together: *The Street* (Mary Wigman). This involves a systematic position such as the one we defined for the classical and not one resulting from a deliberate intention, as for example the stiff hands of the puppets; *Petrouchka* (Fokine); *Guignol et Pandore* (Lifar).

661

In the course of our study of the positions and movements of the arms, we had occasion several times to mention positions and movements of the hands (§ 596 and 603, for example). We shall not repeat what has already been said, but we shall make a few supplementary remarks, starting with those hand positions or movements that have no special meaning.

662

Les doigts tendus et écartés (fingers extended and spread apart): this is a frequent position—adoration of the sun, in *Daphnis et Chloé* (Skibine); and again in the modern or contemporary dance—*La Symphonie Concertante* (Descombey). Generally, this position alternates with *les doigts tendus serrés* (fingers extended and close together) (§ 660) or with the fist (*le poing*) (§ 664). But it may also be found as a pose: *Symphonie pour un Homme seul* (Béjart).

663

Le pouce seul écarté (the thumb alone held apart), the other fingers extended and close together, is a position also found frequently in modern ballets: The Cage (Robbins) (Fig. 78).

This position has quite systematically been given to fawns since the *Prélude à l'Après-Midi d'un Faune* (Lifar).

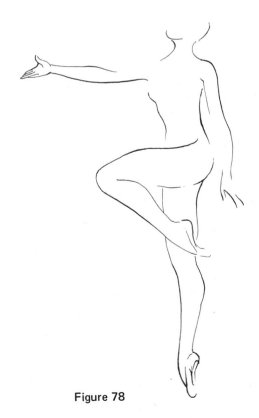

Figure 78

The present Russian school seems also to use it in *sauts portés* (projected leaps) and in all movements representing a flight: *Maïa* Plissetskaia as the Black Swan in the third act of *Lac des Cygnes* (Petipa and Ivanoff); Ludmila Bogomolova in *Eaux printanières* (Assaf Messerer), and the like.

664

Le poing fermé (clenched fist) occurs very frequently in contemporary choreographies: the *Symphonie Concertante* (Descombey), *Le Sacre du Printemps* (Béjart).

Here again it is a case of a fist without any particular significance because, of course, the clenched fist has long figured in choreographies with the meaning of "showing a fist": Swanilda holding out her fists in the direction of the doll in the first act of *Coppélia* (Saint-Léon).

665

A finger movement was recently introduced into the dance and has taken an important place in modern ballets: **les claquements des doigts** (finger-snapping). This had existed for a long time in certain Spanish dances but with a very different use and position: it had been a substitute for castanets, intended to underscore the rhythm, and the palm of the hand was turned downward; now it is rather a means of excitement, and the palm is turned upward or toward the side.

One of the most striking and famous examples of this finger-snapping is found in the film *West Side Story* (Robbins).

But it may be found in ballets even on the stage of the Opera: *Pas de Dieux* (Kelly).

666

Of longer standing than finger-snapping, **claquements des mains** (clapping the hands) is often an aid to the rhythm, but it may be found merely as a movement in character ballets: Mazurka from *Coppélia* (Saint-Léon), dance of the Hungarians in the third act of *Lac des Cygnes* (Bourmeister), and the like.

It is necessary to distinguish this movement from the little Spanish hand-claps in which, both hands being vertical, the fingers of the right hand strike the palm of the left. This is a movement that belongs to the Spanish dance, is characteristic of that dance, and which will find a place for that purpose in the ballets: variation of the third Dulcinea from the *Chevalier errant* (Lifar).

~

667

After the **movements** with no particular significance, we shall find those **that do have a meaning**. Sometimes this meaning is unique for a given pose; at other times there may be several meanings for the same pose.

The best example of this is the pointed index finger that is outstretched while the others are bent. Its most widely used meaning is that of pointing out: Albert chasing Hilarion in the first act of *Giselle* (Coralli and Perrot).

But in another very different meaning it is the characteristic position of the Chinese. In this case, the two index fingers are pointed vertically: variation of the Chinese from *Casse-Noisette* (Ivanoff), *Siang-Sin* (Staats).

Finally, in exceptional cases the position may have no meaning at all: variation of the fingers from *La Belle au Bois dormant* (Petipa).

668

Les doigts interlacés (fingers clasped) are often a symbol of prayer: *Fall River Legend* (Agnes de Mille); but they may also be found in a few other cases: supplication, for example, by Hilarion before the Queen of the Wilis in the second act of *Giselle* (Coralli and Perrot) or by Chloé before Bryaxis, chief of the priates, in the second tableau of *Daphnis et Chloé*; despair: Sylvia in the grotto of Orion in the second act of *Sylvia* (Mérante), and the like.

669

Prayer may also be symbolized by **les mains aux doigts tendus accolés** (hands with fingers extended and joined together). It is a much more symbolic gesture than the preceding one and particularly dear to the romantic ballet: *La Sylphide* (Taglioni) and *Giselle* (Coralli and Perrot); but it is also found in contemporary ballets: *Notre-Dame de Paris* (Petit).

670

We have already mentioned, in connection with monsters (§ 653), **la main en griffe** (the hand representing a claw): it is upright at the wrist and the joints of all the fingers are bent, with the nails turned toward the front. This hand position is also given to maleficent characters: the Fairy Carabosse in *La Belle au Bois dormant* (Petipa), the Gypsies in *Noces fantastiques* (Lifar).

It may also symbolize the ardent desire of characters trying to catch something: the pirates in the second tableau of *Daphnis et Chloé* (Skibine).

671

Finally, the hands, when shaking, may become a symbol of **flames**. One of the better examples is found in the Ritual Fire Dance of *El Amor Brujo,* but the same idea is found in *La Symphonie fantastique* (Massine) at the time of the evocation of the different tortures in prison, over the music of the March to the torture.

Occasionally the same movement may symbolize panic.

672

We could find numerous other movements of the hands and fingers—the more so because the present tendency, as we have already said, is to give a greater importance to these elements in the dance.

In a ballet such as in the *Symphonie Concertante* (Descombey), we have a veritable choreography of hands and fingers. The positions and movements are well determined and chosen with precision with respect to the ensemble of the movement and to the express intention.

MIMICRY

673

Mimicry is a very special phenomenon in the classical dance. Its purpose is to translate for the spectator, in an intelligible fashion, ideas or feelings that would normally be expressed in words.

When the ballet became separated from the opera-ballet, in which an important vocal element intervened, it was confronted with the necessity of expressing itself by itself.

The ballet of action should theoretically be sufficient unto itself, the action being represented on the stage. But very often the action is not sufficiently evident, and the story runs the risk of becoming unintelligible.

In the nineteenth century, this fact brought about the introduction into the dance of a certain number of purely conventional gestures that were intended to play the same role as speech.

674

A clear distinction should be made between **mime** and mimicry.

Mime consists of reproducing actual gestures without the presence of the object to which they apply: for example, to sew, to open a window, and so on; or representing a movement in the most exact manner possible: for example, to run, to march, to climb.

In the latter case, the transformation simply consists of making possible the movement without a shift in space: instead of placing the foot in normal *quatrième devant* for the *marche,* it is brought into normal first while gliding on the ground.

The ballet utilizes gestures from mime, and we have seen a few of them in passing (§ 619 to 627), sometimes with a great deal of realism: the Young Man grasping his purse in his belt in *Mirages* (Lifar).

675

Mimicry, to the contrary, does not utilize real gestures: it searches for a symbol, sometimes clear, at other times more subtle.

Among the **gestures that are easy to understand** we might cite:

· To point to someone with the index finger . . . . you
· To point to the ground with the index finger . . . . here
· To point to one's eyes with the index finger . . . . to see
· To point to one or both ears with the index finger . . . . to hear or listen
· To place the hand flat on the chest . . . . me
· To tap the lower lip with extended fingers, the mouth being open . . . . to speak
· To point to one's mouth with the index finger . . . . to eat
· To point to one's mouth with the thumb, the other fingers cupped . . . . to drink
· To move both hands horizontally, palms down, in front of the neck, starting with the two hands, one on top of the other . . . . to die or kill
· To place both hands, palms together, in front of the right shoulder and bend the head in that direction, gently rocking the shoulders from right to left . . . . to sleep
· To shake both hands, which are vertical, palms forward, from right to left in front of the chest. . . . . No
· To motion with the hand toward the back of the stage, making the gesture start close to the body and extending the arm . . . . far away

· If, in the preceding case, the hand turns twice
around the wrist .... very far
   · To point to one's heart or someone else's heart .... to love
   · To place the right hand on the left hand at the
location of the heart while bending the body from
right to left several times .... great love
   · To extend the right arm, which is horizontal,
in front of oneself, the hand upraised, palm
forward, the index finger and second finger together,
extended, the ring finger and little finger bent,
the thumb on top of them (occasionally one finds
all the fingers extended with the same meaning) .... to swear
   · To rub the thumb of the right hand against the
index finger and second finger .... money
   · To point with the right index finger to the
right temple. .... idea
   · To strike the right temple with little strokes of
the right index finger .... crazy
   · To bring both hands outstretched, the little
fingers and the side of the hands touching, up to
the face, while bending the head forward .... to weep

676

Among the **gestures whose symbolism in more subtle** we can cite:

   · To point with the right index finger to the base
of the left ring finger (The gesture shows the
location of the alliance) .... marriage
   · To trace with the right hand a line going from
the left shoulder to the right hip (This gesture
follows the shoulder-belt, but actually the latter
goes in the opposite direction; i.e., right shoulder
to left hip) .... lord
   · To pass both hands laterally over the whole
length of the body, starting at the armpits and
going as far as the arms can reach (This gesture
shows a very simple dress, by contrast with the
crinolines worn by matrons at the time mimicry
was instituted [in the ballet]) .... young girl

· To move the right hand around the face,
starting from the chin and turning
counterclockwise . . . . pretty
· The same gesture, terminated by a kiss made
by having the thumb, the index finger, and the
second finger together, then spreading them to
throw the kiss . . . . very pretty
· To raise the arms vertically and make the
hands turn around the wrists . . . . to dance
· The two hands go from left to right along a
descending diagonal, starting from approximately
the height of the chest and finishing extended
downward, a gesture accentuated by the body,
which is leaning . . . . to abandon
· With right arm horizontal or semi-horizontal,
lateral or open, and the forearm low, the hand
turns clockwise around the wrist . . . . to steal
· With arms lateral, and semi-horizontal, the
forearm half-vertical, to shake the hands up and
down . . . . to fly
· The right hand, with fingers extended, strikes
with small strokes against the back of the left hand,
which has been placed flat against the left side of
the chest . . . . beating heart

677

It was mainly in the course of the nineteenth century that **mimicry was
developed.**

Born of a need, it grew rapidly.

At the time of *Giselle* (1841), it was widely employed, but in a
manner that was justified: argument between Giselle, Hilarion, and
Albert; dialogue between Giselle and Bathilde; the Queen of the Wilis
indicating to Hilarion the reason for his condemnation, and so on.

But soon this means of compensating for the absence of speech
became an end in itself, and as a result we have very long scenes of
mimicry. In *Coppélia* (1870), for example, certain scenes of mimicry
are related to the action: the scene made by Swanilda before Frantz in
the first act, explanations given by Frantz's mother regarding the
activities of Coppélius, the dialogue of Swanilda and her little friends in

the second act, the dialogue of Frantz and Coppélius, and so on. Others, on the contrary, are far removed from the action: the legend of the ear of corn in the first act.

Mimicry is used and abused, and certain scenes take on the appearance of a conversation between deaf mutes.

A considerable number of symbols are being sought, and an effort made to say things that are increasingly subtle.

In certain cases one actually has the impression that the choreographer is seeking out difficulty to have the pleasure of showing his skill in resolving it.

Toward the end of the nineteenth century and at the beginning of the twentieth, one would no longer conceive of a ballet without mimicry.

Finally it has become so inseparable from the idea one has of the dance that it is found even in ballets having no theme, where there is nothing at all to express: *Soir de Fête*, 1925 (Staats).

678

There was a **reaction** against this state of affairs at the beginning of the twentieth century, dating from the arrival of the *Ballets Russes* of Diaghilev (1909).

We return to the idea that the dance must express itself by itself, not only without words but also without mimicry—which is, after all, an element foreign to the dance.

The action must be combined in such a way that it is self-sufficient, however great its complexity: *Le Chevalier et la Demoiselle,* 1941 (Lifar).

Only gestures of mime are tolerated.

Even the recent ballets, in which the exposition of ideas is often very delicate, do not resort to mimicry: *Mirages* (Lifar), *Symphonie Concertante* (Descombey), *Le Sacre du Printemps* (Béjart), and the like.

679

Mimicry thus presents for the classical dance a quite special case: it is an element that we can follow from its inception through its development to its disappearance.

At the present time, mimicry is no longer included in the ballet, and its presence in a new ballet would be considered ridiculous. The gestures of mime are barely tolerated, and they must still be limited to the absolutely indispensable minimum.

SEVEN

Execution

680

In the last part of this work we shall bring together everything having to do with the application of all the elements of technique we have seen thus far. This application may be made in class or on the stage.

THE ADAGIO

681

The word **adagio** is taken from the musical term. But the present rhythm of the dance adagio is sometimes slower than that of the tempo adagio and thus corresponds to largo or lento.

It is a suite of movements or poses executed to a slow rhythm and necessitating good balance and control of the legs.

682

There are several **forms of adagios**. Those practiced in class for the purpose of exercise are different from those executed on the stage in a quest for formal beauty or for an expression: for example, the love song. There are single adagios and adagios for two. Less frequently, the adagio may be done with three or more.

The meaning and use of the adagio have varied a great deal in the course of the development of the classical dance.

683

The **single adagio** was in existence very early in classical dance. In the class it is an excellent exercise for developing balance and building up control of the legs *à la hauteur*. It also includes much exercise of the arms, the head, and the trunk. Everything in it must be done with suppleness and grace. Every day dancers do an exercise in adagio.

684

The single adagio is relatively rare onstage. It is found in old ballets: *Giselle* in the second act, 1841 (Coralli and Perrot); *Coppélia* in the Slavic Theme, 1870 (Saint-Léon); *La Korrigane*, 1880 (Mérante); or in very recent ballets: *Études*, 1948 (Lander); *La Symphonie Concertante*, 1962 (Descombey).

Generally speaking, the single *adagio* has little specific meaning. Its merit lies chiefly in the beauty of its lines and in the impression, created by its demand for balance, of difficulty overcome.

Nevertheless, for *Giselle* it fits into the whole meaning of the second act: flight.

685

The **adagio for two** is more frequent on the stage than in the class.

It was only in recent times that regular courses in adagio—that is, *pas de deux*—were instituted in a few large theatres such as the *Opéra* and in large companies such as that of the Marquis de Cuevas. These courses usually meet once a week, whereas other classes meet daily.

These courses are intended to develop the movements and poses that will later be used on the stage.

686

As to the **origin** of the adagio *pas de deux*, it seems that it was born of the desire to permit the dancer to execute movements that are impossible to do alone. For example, the dancer could remain a very long time on one *pointe* to do *développés* (§ 129) if someone held her at the waist. This "someone" could be either a man or a woman: Thérèse Elssler (1808-1876), a dancer of moderate ability, acquired her fame by serving as a partner for her sister Fanny (1810-1884). Traces of this conception may be found in the ballet of *Faust* (Aveline) in the passage of the Nubian women, where certain female dancers enable their associates to do turns.

The idea of the couple as male and female partners therefore had no part in the original conception of the *pas de deux*.

687

253 It was probably in Russia, with Marius Petipa (1818-1920), that this idea of the couple was instituted. He includes in his ballets numerous

classical **pas de deux** composed of an adagio, a masculine and then a feminine variation, and concluding with a coda.

In the adagio, the role of the male dancer is always limited to that of setting off his partner to advantage. He holds the female dancer to give her balance and he adds a new element: the *portés* (lifts). The female partner could assist the dancer in her leaps, but the male partner actually lifts her up—indeed, he holds her in the air. From this, we have derived a whole gamut of completely new poses and movements.

688

Beginning with the period of the *Ballets Russes* of Serge de Diaghilev, the adagio has taken on a **new aspect**. Up to that time, the female dancer had been the principal personage of the adagio: her movements alone were important, and her partner was supposed to conduct himself as discreetly as possible. Ideally, he was supposed to be forgotten. One was supposed to have the impression that the female dancer accomplished her feats of balance and elevation by herself.

Then, at that time, one became aware of the existence of the male dancer. This coincided, furthermore, with the revitalizing of choreography, including in particular the resurrection of the importance of the male dancer: ballets such as the *Danses polovtsiennes* from *Prince Igor* require an important masculine contingent, whereas in the ballets at the turn of the century there were almost no male dancers, these being replaced by women disguised as men.

The adagio was thus transformed and became a harmonious combination of lines. Now the male dancer always makes it possible for the female dancer to take poses or to execute movements that she could not do alone, but he must not be careless in his own performance: his movements must harmonize with those of his partner and must prolong or complete them.

The *adagios* that were composed from that time on always took this fact into account: adagio from *Suite en Blanc* (Lifar).

689

The adagio that has become a *pas de deux* has taken on the **meaning of a love song**. From the time of Marius Petipa we find this idea: the second act of *Lac des Cygnes*, for example.

Eventually, except in the *adagios* with no theme whose merit is based on their beauty of form, the idea of love became permanently attached to the *adagio*.

Starting in about 1943, Serge Lifar developed in the adagio a certain sensual side, whose very beautiful expression is found in the adagio of the Young Man and the Woman in *Mirages*.

Finally, certain contemporary ballets have carried it to the point of sexuality: *Le Sacre du Printemps* (*Béjart*).

690

At the outset, the *adagio* utilized only steps known elsewhere. Little by little, particularly starting from the *pas de deux* (§ 687), the *adagio* has developed its own **technique**. It has created for itself poses and movements belonging only to the *pas de deux* that absolutely cannot be performed alone.

The present tendency aims more and more at developing the acrobatic side of the *adagio*; some of these movements reach the limits of performance: *La Valse* (music by Machkowski, choreography by Vassili Vainonen).

691

We have said above that the *adagio* must now achieve a **harmonious relation between the male and the female dancer**. This may be done in three ways:

· The male and the female dancer perform the same movement.

· The male and the female dancer perform symmetrical movements.

· The lines of the female dancer's body form a whole with those of the male dancer.

The last system is the one most often used because it allows greater freedom of action for each of them.

But of course different methods may be found within the same *adagio.*

692

Among the poses and movements proper to the *adagio* that we shall consider in succession are poses, movements on the ground, *les pas à terre sauts,* and *portés*.

Departing from the plan followed in the rest of the book, here we shall discuss *sauts* after *tours*. Actually, certain *sauts* are only the prelude to or the preparation for a *porté*.

693

In the **single adagio** the poses employed are those we have already considered: *arabesque* (§ 67 to 76), *attitude* (§ 81 to 84), *effacé* (§ 89), and *écarté* (§ 91); and the derivative positions *à la hauteur*: *quatrième devant*, second, and *quatrième derrière*.

These poses may be taken with the supporting leg *tendu* or *plié*.

The *fondu* (§ 227) is also much used, but most often with *ports de bras* (§ 580 and 584).

Training for poses, with the leg held in the air, commences at the barre. In the *adagios* executed out on the floor in the dance class, the exercise involves balance and holding the leg extended at the same time. Concurrently, work is directed toward a rigorous correction of the positions of the body, the arms, the head, and their independence. The intensity of the muscular workout caused by the strain of holding out the leg *à la hauteur* must not cause a general contraction of the other muscles. For this reason the dancer will be directed to perform, for example, certain movements or *ports de bras* while the leg is extended.

The poses are taken with the foot *à plat*, but exercises in balancing may also be done on one *pointe*. These will then include the *raccourcis* (§ 64).

All this training has as its aim not only the single adagio onstage, but the *pas de deux* as well. As a matter of fact, for it to be perfect the dancer must achieve her own balance; her partner is there only to help her maintain it.

694

The **pas de deux** adds to the preceding **poses** all the "pushed" or "drawn" positions—that is, positions taken with a supporting leg oblique. These poses cannot be executed alone. They must have to be taken in different manners:

· The dancer holds her partner's hand or hands.

· The dancer supports herself upon her partner by holding his arm, or less frequently, his shoulders or his waist.

· The dancer is held at the waist by her partner.

· The dancer is held by her partner, with one or both hands, by some other part of her body: arm, shoulder, leg, nape of the neck, and so on.

These may be executed with the supporting leg *pliée* or *tendue*.

To the classical poses contemporary choreography adds some that are more original—for example: the dancer, on her right *pointe,* raises

Figure 79

the left leg *au raccourci en quatrième derrière* as high as possible and takes her left *pointe* in her left hand, with the arm horizontal to the rear, a position akin to the acrobatic foot in hand (§ 492). She then leans forward and is supported by the partner, who holds her left wrist: *Symphonie Concertante* (Descombey) (Fig. 79).

695

We may also find **shifting of the axes** in other positions, particularly with the basic positions, and usually the fifth *sur les pointes* (Fig. 80). In this position the dancer, being held by the partner, may descend laterally very low, forming an angle of at least 45 degrees with the ground.

Certain shifts of the center of balance take a particular form—for example, the dancer begins *en quatrième devant à la hauteur* with her hands held by her partner, who is opposite her; she places her foot on the partner's arm or shoulder, and he, by drawing back, causes her to

257

Figure 80

do a *grand écart* in midair: *Symphonie Concertante* (Descombey) (Fig. 81).

696

If the dancer alone were able to take positions with the supporting leg *pliée*, she could not descend very low. In a **plié** on both feet, she could take some low positions with feet *à plat*. But on *pointes*, the *plié*, generally speaking, is still limited. With a partner one can bend down very low while holding up one leg or while on both *pointes*: The Four Temperaments (Balanchine) (Fig. 82).

697

The partner also makes it possible to take **positions of the body** that would be balanced for a dancer alone.

For example: the dancer is on one *pointe* with the other leg *pliée* slightly *en raccourci en quatrième derrière*, arms are lateral and semi-horizontal, and the back is deeply arched. The partner holds her at the waist: *Symphonie Concertante* (Descombey) (Fig. 83).

Figure 81. *Grand écart* with partner

Figure 82. Deep *plié sur pointes*

Figure 83. *Cambré*

The dancer is in second position on the two *pointes,* with arms open semi-vertical and back deeply arched: *Symphonie Concertante* (Fig. 84).

The dancer, *sur une pointe en raccourci* in second position, leans as far as possible to the side opposite the leg *en raccourci,* with the arm of the leg *au raccourci* vertical-lateral and the other arm low in front of the body. The partner holds her with one arm around her waist: finale from *The Crystal Palace* (Balanchine).

698

Finally, there is a whole gamut of poses taken solely in the *pas de deux*: those in which the **female dancer does not touch the ground**. A little farther on (§ 725 to 742) we shall study the *porté,* in which the dancer

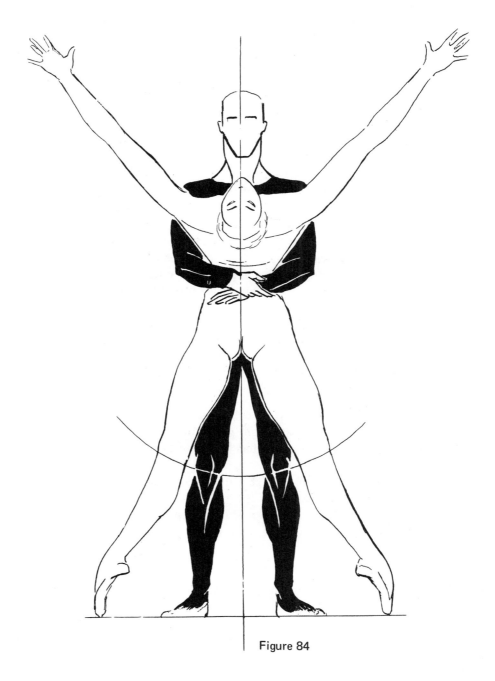

Figure 84

is sustained in the air by the arm or arms of her partner, and the poses in which she rests on his shoulder, which are comparable to the *portés*.

We shall thus see here only the instance in which the dancer supports herself on her partner in a manner other than on his shoulder and where she hangs onto him.

699

One of these special poses has come to be part of the repertory of positions of the classical dance: the **poisson** (fish). The dancer has her arms extended to the front, with wrists crossed, trunk arched, and legs together and extended, crossed at the ankles. She is slanted downward at about a 45-degree angle, with her abdomen supported against the hip of her partner, whose opposite arm is around her waist from below; her partner's arm on the side of the hip on which she is supported reaches to the rear to grasp her legs and helps hold her up.

The male dancer is *en fondu* (§ 227), with the rear leg corresponding to the hip on which the female dancer is supported.

A variation on this pose consists of the female dancer's bending one leg behind the back of her partner and pinning herself to him. He may then release her. This pose creates a great deal of effect because the leg bent behind the back of the male dancer is not seen and the female dancer appears thus to be held up miraculously in midair.

These poses may be taken with the other arm positions.

They are in very wide use in the classical ballet after *tours* and as the final pose of an adagio.

700

A different pose from the same family is taken in the following manner: the female dancer has the same position of the body as in the preceding one, but she spreads her legs apart and places them on either side of her partner's waist; her arms may take various positions. The male dancer brings one arm to the front, under his partner's armpit, and moves the other arm to the rear to grasp her leg while holding her up: *Clairière* (Descombey) (Fig. 85).

701

In another group of poses the female dancer is **supported totally** on some part of the male dancer's body; her balance is such that the male dancer does not hold her.

In *Pour Piccolo et Mandoline* (Descombey), the male dancers, in first position barely open (§ 23), body leaning to the front, horizontal, arms open, carry on their backs the female dancers—who themselves are lying on their backs—hips, knees, ankles bent at a right angle, arms passed over the shoulders of their partners and bent back the length of their bodies. In this manner, the female dancer rests on her partner's back (Fig. 86).

Figure 85. Variation of the "fish"

At other times she rests on her partner's abdomen. For example, in *Carmen* (Petit): Carmen, legs outstretched, lies flat on her stomach on Don José, who is in a "bridge" position—that is, he rests on his feet and hands, knees bent at a right angle, thighs and trunk horizontal, arms behind him making a right angle with the trunk (Fig. 87).

One could find many other comparable poses.

702

In a new series of poses, the female dancer is, as it were, seated on her partner.

The female and male dancers may be face to face as in, for example, *Marines* (Skibine): the male dancer is *en fondu* (§ 227), left leg to the rear; the female dancer is seated on her partner's right thigh, with her right leg running under the whole length of the male dancer's left

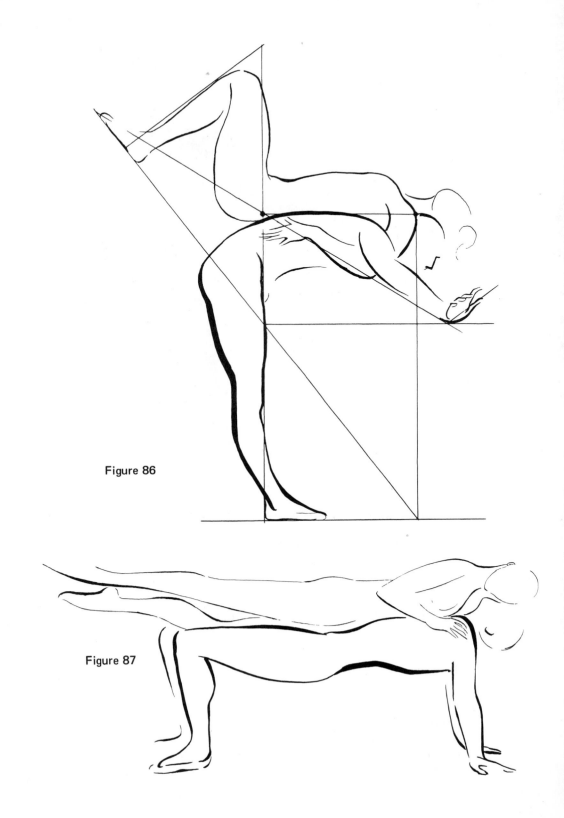

Figure 86

Figure 87

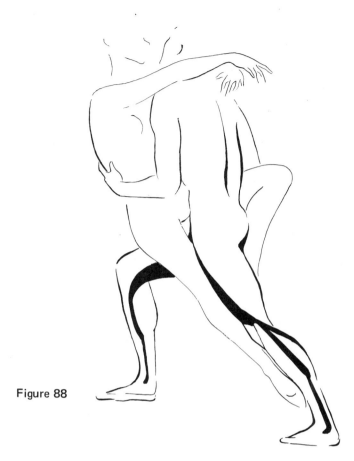

Figure 88

leg and her left thigh rising along the line of the male dancer's right hip
in such a way as to extend the line of his thigh; the lower part of her
left leg is vertical; her hands are around her partner's neck, with wrists
crossed; the male dancer holds the female dancer above the waist, to
the side (Fig. 88).

Female and male dancer may also be one behind the other, with
poses akin to those employed in acrobatics. In *The Cage* (Robbin), the
male dancer is in normal position first, knees and hips flexed at a right
angle; the female dancer is seated on her partner's knees, legs stretched
forward horizontally, trunk quite vertical, arms and hands stretched forward horizontally. The male dancer also has his arms extended forward
horizontally, with his hands under the armpits of his partner (Fig. 89).

703

In another group of poses, the **female dancer is supported by the arm or
arms of the male dancer**, there being no question of *portés* as such.

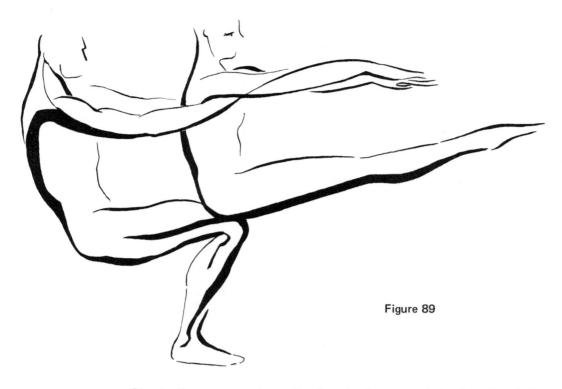

Figure 89

Classically, we may have the female dancer sustained in the air by her partner, who holds her against him. For example, in *Theme and Variations* (Balanchine), the male dancer *en demi-arabesque* has passed his arm around the waist of the female dancer, herself in *demi-arabesque*, and holds her up slightly above the ground (Fig. 90).

In modern character ballets, there may be a great variety of poses.

In *La Rencontre* (David Lichine), the male dancer, in fourth position, has his arm around the waist of the female dancer and holds her against him; she has her left thigh to the front, with her knee bent at a right angle and the foot reaching to the inside surface of her partner's right knee; her right thigh is bent back, making an angle of approximately 90 degrees with the left, the knee bent at a right angle. The right arm is semi-horizontal, toward the rear, with the hand holding the right *pointe*; the left arm, lateral-horizontal, is around her partner's neck, and the hand moves slightly in front of the partner's left arm, which is also lateral-horizontal (Fig. 91).

More familiar is the position in *Pas de Dieux* (Kelly) in which the male dancer holds the female dancer in front of him, his right arm

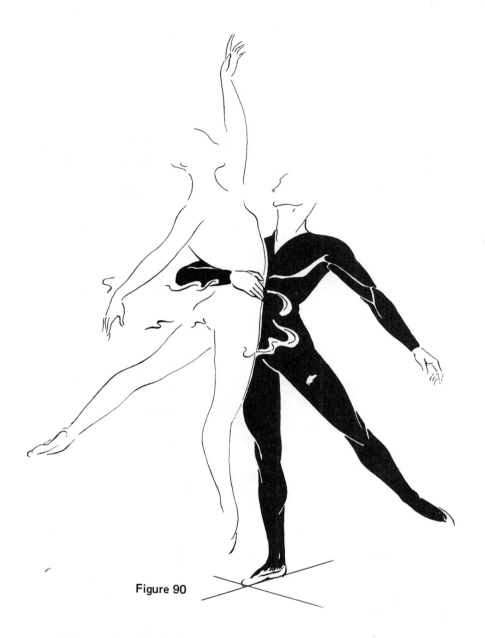

Figure 90

around her waist, his left arm under her knees. The female dancer faces forward, with her legs sharply bent at the hips and at the knees and her arms around the neck of her partner (Fig. 92).

We could give multiple examples of this sort, but this is not the place to draw up a repertoire; this should at least give an idea of the range of poses.

267

Figure 91

704

We shall group in a final category the poses in which the female dancer is in some way clinging to her partner. They are found only in the modern ballets.

At the end of *Le Sacre du Printemps* (Béjart), the female dancer, who faces her partner, has her legs placed on either side of his waist, with her ankles crossed behind him. She is leaning slightly backward.

In *Jungle* (Rudi Van Dantzig), the male dancer is in almost normal second position, knees slightly bent, body erect, arms to the front and semi-horizontal, with forearms semi-vertical and hands lifted, palms toward the front. The female dancer has her legs on either side of her partner's hips, thighs horizontal, knees bent, feet crossed to the

Figure 92   Figure 93

rear at ankle height, body very arched, arms lateral-horizontal, supported on the arms of the male dancer, forearms semi-vertical, hands raised, palms turned out, fingers taut and spread apart, head leaning backward, mouth open. The hands of the male dancer practically frame the mouth of the female dancer (Fig. 93).

In *The Prodigal Son* (Balanchine), the male dancer has a position akin to the *fondu* (§ 227), but with less of a spread: the forward foot is raised *sur la demi-pointe* with the rear leg *en quatrième ouverte* instead of *quatrième croisée*. The trunk is almost face forward, with the arms lateral and semi-vertical and the head turned to the side of the rear leg and leaning slightly backward. The female dancer is literally rolled around the thighs of the male dancer; her arms, horizontal and to the rear, are holding one of her feet, with the other against it, placed at the angle of the thigh and the forward hip (Fig. 94).

Here again the imagination of a choreographer may be permitted to follow its own free will to make innovations.

705

The **movements on the ground** are partly akin to the poses. We have seen—in paragraphs 228 to 236—the *agenouillements* (kneeling) and walking on all fours. The contemporary ballet has, generally speaking, greatly developed the use of movements on the ground: for example, at

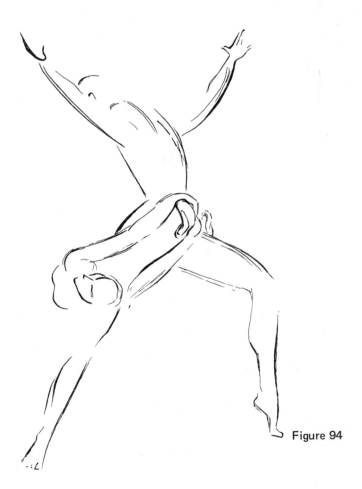

Figure 94

the beginning of the *Symphonie Concertante* (Descombey) a very long passage is executed by the dancers lying on their backs.

In the classical adagio the movements on the ground consist mainly of *agenouillements*. One of the popular forms finds the male dancer kneeling on one knee *au raccourci en quatrième devant* (§ 231) and the female dancer balancing with her foot on the male dancer's horizontal thigh, in a pose of *d'attitude,* or *raccourci en quatrième devant*, or, less frequently, *arabesque*.

The male dancer holds the female dancer's supporting thigh, or she may support herself on one or both of her hands.

706

Here, as before, the contemporary vocabulary has added a considerable number of new elements. We shall cite only a few examples.

In *Le Violon* (Petit), the male dancer is also on one knee, but he has his arms around the body of the female dancer—one at the waist, the other above the thighs—and, leaning forward, he holds her against him, suspended above the ground. The female dancer has her legs stretched in the position of a fifth *sur les pointes*, the trunk and the head inclined backward, arms extended vertically, hands almost touching the ground. This is a position expressing sorrow (Fig. 95).

In *The Crystal Palace* (Balanchine), at the end of the second movement, the male dancer still has the same position but with both arms semi-vertical and lateral and the head and shoulders erect, rather

Figure 95

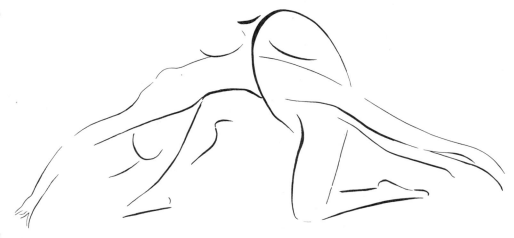

than bent forward. The female dancer is also in almost the same position as in the preceding one, but she rests on the male dancer's thigh, which is placed on a level with her lower back.

707

After some poses in which the male dancer is on one knee, we shall see some where he is on both.

From *Daphnis et Chloé* (Skibine), many examples may be drawn.

For example, the male dancer is seated on his heels (§ 230), trunk *épaulé* toward the left, head leaning to the right; he has his left arm horizontal to the rear, with the forearm semi-horizontal and right arm horizontal to the front, around the waist of the female dancer, who herself is in a position seated on her heels, but on the thighs of her partner; her trunk is *épaulé* to the right, with her head leaning to the left, her right arm *en couronne*, and her left arm horizontal behind her partner (Fig. 96).

In the same ballet, the male dancer, still seated on his heels, has his trunk inclined to the left, head in profile to the left, left arm

Figure 96

Figure 97

outstretched, lateral-horizontal. The female dancer, opposite him, is kneeling on her left knee, with her right leg *en quatrième derrière à la hauteur*, her body arched; her head is in profile to the right, with her cheek against that of her partner. Her arms have positions corresponding to those of her partner, whom she holds by the hands (Fig. 97).

708

After the poses based on kneeling, we shall find some poses in which one of the dancers is **seated**.

In *Jungle* (Van Dantzig), the female dancer is seated on the ground, legs close together and extended, trunk erect, head in profile to the right; the male dancer is seated on his partner's thighs, knees flexed, feet placed in second, *en dehors*, against the female dancer's buttocks. They hold each other in their arms; the head of the male dancer is on the left shoulder of the female dancer (Fig. 98)

This range of positions occurs only in very modern ballets.

Figure 98

709

Finally, one of the dancers may be **lying on the ground**. This is found several times in the Symphonie Concertante (Descombey): at the beginning, the male dancers are stretched out on their backs, knees flexed; the female dancers are seated on their knees and are stretched out behind them (the male dancers), supported at the shoulders by the hands of the male dancers.

In *La Péri* (Skibine), Prince Iskender and la Péri are lying prone on the ground, one on top of the other.

We find poses of the same type in *Le Sacre du Printemps* (Béjart), *Roméo et Juliette* (Béjart), and the like, symbolizing coupling.

710

As we can see, the use of poses on the ground and of movements leading to or proceding from them is becoming more general and more diverse in contemporary ballet. But it should be noted in this connection that it is sometimes hard to distinguish, in such ballets, what is properly "adagio." In the pure classical ballets, as we explained above, the adagio is a well-defined entity, with a tempo and a range of movements and poses of its own. It is not confused with the other parts of the ballet. Furthermore, the latter are clearly separated one from another: the variations and the ensembles are so many pieces with a beginning and an end, and during the interval that separates these elements the audience may applaud. In the contemporary ballet this is not at all the case. Most of the time the pieces are linked together one with another without clear-cut divisions, and there is no applause until the end of an act—or of the ballet, if it has only one act. Because the dance is a total expression, a distinction is no longer made between adagio, variation, and ensemble; the personages step in as a function of internal necessities—where they are supposed to go—without reference to a pre-established plan.

We may, therefore, come to speak of an adagio for parts of a ballet that a purist might not consider as such. We shall simply say that there is an adagio when the movements or poses used are those that correspond to what is customarily called adagio.

711

After having studied matters relating to the poses and movements on the ground, we take up **movements as such,** and first of all, the *pas à terre.* The latter corresponds to steps already studied, but there is a difference between a movement executed in a general way and as it is in an adagio. Actually, in the second case, the passage from position to position is as important as the position itself, because the movement, which is always very slow, acquires a value of its own. For example, in the course of a variation a *battement en quatrième devant* may have for its aim simply to bring the leg into *quatrième devant à la hauteur;* hence, the intermediate movements, though rigorously correct, will somehow be subordinated to the advantage of the essential moments. In the adagio, on the contrary, each secondary moment, each instant of the movement, acquires a value of its own equal to that of the positions of starting and arrival.

Furthermore, in the adagio the movements must be very closely connected. We are no longer dealing with steps which, like colors placed side by side, harmonize while enhancing one another, but rather with a whole, in which each movement is submerged in the succeeding one, like the colors of the rainbow, where one passes imperceptibly from blue to green, for example, without being able to say where one ends and the other begins. This linking of the movements does not, however, mean that the ensemble leads to a dull monotone: the rainbow also possesses striking hues. In the same way the adagio has its high points, but one reaches them by way of a most delicate progression.

If, then, from the outset certain adagio movements may be considered as very easy by comparison with the feats that figure in some variations, they are in the final analysis more difficult because they demand a perfection and a subtle refinement. A good technician can do very difficult variations: only a great artist can truly interpret the adagios.

712

In the **solo adagio** most of the nontraveling steps performed on the ground (*pas à terre sans parcours*) may be utilized. For a certain number of them it is in fact the only situation in which they may be found on the stage.

We shall thus encounter: the *dégagés* (§ 102 to 109), the *battements* (§ 110 to 116), the *ronds de jambe* (§ 122 to 124) utilized separately, the *grands ronds de jambe soutenus* (§ 126), less often than the *petits ronds de jambe soutenus* (§ 127), the *développés* (§ 129), and the *fouettés* (§ 130).

Among these movements, those that will enjoy the greatest favor will be the slow *développés* and the *grands ronds de jambe soutenus,* often terminated by an *arabesque.* To these steps one might add the *relevés sur demi-pointe* or *sur pointe* in the different derivative positions *à la hauteur* and the *raccourcis.*

713

The female dancer of the **pas de deux** will employ the same steps, but taking advantage of her partner's support, she will often execute these movements *sur la pointe.* She may likewise combine them with *cambrés* or shifts of the axis. For example, in the *adagio* in the second movement of the *The Crystal Palace* the dancer does a *battement en quatrième devant* terminated *sur pointe* in fourth, with a forceful *cambré*; in the *adagio* of the second act of *Lac des Cygnes* Odette, *en quatrième devant à la hauteur sur une pointe*, releases her partner's hand, raises her arms *en couronne,* and falls backward by a shift of axis until her partner catches her.

714

Among the **pas à terre avec parcours** performed on the ground, many may appear in the solo adagio, but they will often be executed to a rhythm slower than is customary.

Among the marches will especially be found those with *battement en quatrième devant à la hauteur*: *Les Sylphides* (Fokine); a few marches *sur les demi-pointes,* some *courus sur pointe.* The *glissades* (§ 158 to 161), *temps de pointe piqués* (§ 165 to 171), *temps de pointe relevés* (§ 173), *passé relevé* (§ 186) are thus found as well as the *pas de bourrée* executed very slowly (§ 192 to 197).

715

In the **adagio à deux** the *pas à terre avec parcours* are encountered in two forms: they may occur when the dancers do not touch each other and make movements that are symmetrical or complementary; they may likewise be found when the dancers hold each other while making the same movement or while the partner supports the female dancer during the execution of the step.

In the first case we again encounter its use in the solo adagio.

In the second case we have, on the contrary, the possibilities resulting from the balance assured by the partner—that of slowing down, for example. But *les pas à terre avec parcours* do not lend themselves very well to the *adagio*. We therefore find *glissades,* and the steps cited in the preceding paragraph, especially when they serve as a connection or preparation, for turns, for example.

716

In the **solo adagio, pliés** are used a great deal in class. Quite often the *adagios* begin with a *plié* in fifth position (§ 217), very deep, slow, with sustained balance. *Pliés* are likewise found in all the derivative positions: the *fondu* (§ 227) with *ports de bras* (§ 580 and 584) and occasionally *agenouillements* (§ 231).

On the stage *pliés* are hardly used except for the deep *pliés* in derivative position *à la hauteur*, chiefly *en arabesque*.

717

In the **adagio à deux**, *pliés* many be very deep and may be done for their own sake, especially in derivative positions, or else to introduce a movement: a leap or a turn. They may be executed while the partner is holding the female dancer or while she is using him as a support.

The delicacy of the *pliés* is one of the conditions which are essential to the ease of the *adagios*.

718

In the **solo adagio**, the *tours* appear chiefly in the form of *piétinés* in fifth *sur la pointe* (§ 380), *détournés* (§ 384 to 385) including the *pas de bourrée détourné* (§ 386) done slowly; *enveloppés* (§ 387 and 388) and *pas de bourrée enveloppé* (§ 389).

As regards *tours* on one foot, the *tours de promenade* (§ 399 and 400) are frequent, as are the *détournés à la hauteur* (§ 401), but the other turns seldom appear. Turns in second position (§ 411, 441, 451) are generally preferred, and occasionally those *en arabesque* (§ 409, 453).

Should the need arise, the *pas de bourrée relevé détourné* (§ 437) may also be used.

Thus, in general, it is a question of *tours* that can be performed slowly, with balancing *sur la pointe*.

One may still find *tours en dehors* or *en dedans* terminated by a *fondu*.

719

As regards the **adagio à deux**, on the contrary, **tours** are one of the most important elements. The presence of the partner makes it possible to execute a substantially greater number of turns than can be done alone. The partner's assistance may be rendered in four manners:

• The partner has his hands on each side of the female dancer's waist. He permits her to remain erect without restraining her. He may even by a few judicious movements of the hand maintain her rotation. At the end of the turn, if he sees that his partner will not finish facing forward, he can correct her and with one or both hands cause her to turn.

• The female dancer is sustained by one finger of her partner placed above her head. Here the sole assistance lies in maintaining her balance. In certain cases the point of supplementary support allows the number of *tours* to be increased.

• The female dancer does the *tours* alone, and at the end the male dancer stops her or causes her to take a given position. In this latter case, the male dancer may simply correct a loss of balance at the last moment.

• The partner causes the female dancer to turn in a state of balance while walking around his axis.

720

In the first case will be found the *tours relevés*, in particular those taken starting from a fourth position (§ 426, 427); the *tours enveloppés en dedans* ending *en poisson* (§ 431).

For the second case, these are mainly *tours* of the *enveloppé* or *fouetté* type.

Finally, with the third case, we may have *tours piqués* or *posés*.

The fourth case may occur in two different fashions: the female dancer takes a position—for example, an *attitude;* she gives her hand to her partner, who is in front of her, and he walks while turning on the axis of his partner to cause her to do a complete turn: Adagio of Aurora in *La Belle au Bois dormant* (Petipa).

In the second fashion, the female dancer performs some turns, for example, two turns in second, and at the end of these the male dancer catches her at the waist while she adopts an *arabesque,* and he has her do a complete turn while walking: Adagio of the Bluebird, extracted from *La Belle au Bois dormant.*

721

The **saut**, rare in the solo adagio, is, to the contrary, the second element preferred for the *adagio à deux*.

The leaps might be grouped in three principal categories.

- Those that suggest an idea of soaring.
- Those that are impossible to execute by oneself.
- Those that are intercepted in midair.

722

Soaring may be suggested in principle by all *sauts*. Because the classical dance marks the strong beat at the peak of the trajectory, the emphasis is on "growing lighter" (*allègement*). The idea of soaring will remain present, however, in all aspects of the adagio leap.

However, soaring is much more marked when the partner, suspending or sustaining the female dancer, permits her to leap higher or to remain longer in the air.

This aspect has been found since the period of *Giselle* in the second act.

In this case one may encounter frequently the *grands jetés* (§ 272), the *sissonnes* (§ 278 to 283), and also the *pas de bourrée jeté* (§ 475) or the *pas de bourrée assemblée* (§ 477) in which the male dancer holds the female dancer with one hand, and with the other supports his partner at the waist to prolong and slow down the leap: *Les Sylphides* (Fokine).

723

A certain number of **sauts** utilized in the adagio are impossible to do without a partner. For example, the female dancer might perform some *entrechats* (§ 344) of a very high number—much more than it is normally possible to do.

Because the present tendency is toward the development of acrobatics in the dance, veritable acrobatic leaps will be found in the adagios, the male dancer causing his partner for example to accomplish a sort of complete turn above his head while holding her at the waist.

724

Finally one may very often find **sauts stoppés** in midair by the partner.

At the beginning, there were mainly normal *sauts* in which, by the partner blocking the female dancer at the peak of her trajectory, a much more precise effect of flight was obtained (*Giselle*). But this type of movement subsequently developed in its own right and came to have a greater importance. The leap is taken from farther away, has greater distance, and to the appearance of flight there is added that of difficulty overcome, the male dancer catching the female dancer in what are sometimes delicate conditions. At last danger appears, with the female running certain risk that her partner might not catch her.

Historically, the earliest of these *grands sauts* was executed by Carlotta Grisi, who was hurled through a window into the arms of Lucien Petipa, in *La Péri* (Coralli) in 1843.

In *Suite en Blanc* (Lifar) we find in the adagio a *grand saut*, a sort of *grand jeté* in which the male dancer catches his partner head on.

In the third act of *Lac des Cygnes* Wladimir Bourmeister has prescribed, in the *pas de deux* of the black swan, a *grand saut*, intercepted horizontally, of a clearly acrobatic nature.

One of the most striking examples of an adagio *saut* intercepted in midair with a completely acrobatic character is *La Valse* of Machkowski (Vainonen), danced by the Soviet Russian dancers Raïssa Stroutchkova and Alexandre Lapaouri.

725

From the leap intercepted in the air (*saut bloqué en l'air*) *we must move on to the* **portés**. Many *portés* are in fact taken by means of a leap, and most of the *sauts bloqués en l'air* terminate with a *porté*.

As we stated in paragraph 698, we call *portés* the poses or movements in which the female dancer is held in the air by one or both arms of her partner, or by resting on his shoulder.

726

It appears that *portés* were done at first with **both arms**, which were folded, and with the female dancer supporting herself more or less on her partner.

These *portés* derive directly from the *saut bloqué en l'air*.

The male dancer, usually holding the female dancer at the waist, holds her up and keeps her immobile in the air in front of him, and even shifts his position while holding her thus.

The female dancer has her arms crossed on her chest, or *en couronne;* her feet most often have the position of a fifth *sur pointes.*

We find this *porté* already in the nineteenth century. But it is not very elegant, the effort of the male dancer is great, and it cannot be sustained for very long at a time. It is also found in certain popular dances.

727

Toward the end of the nineteenth century a solution was found which permitted the *porté* to have a lighter, more elegant appearance while making it easier to maintain: the female dancer **sits on her partner's shoulder** (Fig. 99).

The female dancer can then adopt more elegant leg positions, bending them to the side, crossing them, having one leg *pliée* and the other *tendue en demi-arabesque,* etc. The arm positions are quite varied.

Often the male dancer sustains his partner with one hand and has the other arm free: *Les Deux Pigeons* (Mérante).

This pose is still much employed in numerous ballets. It may be found as a starting position for an adagio: for example, in *Suite en Blanc* (Lifar); as a final pose: *pas de deux* from *Don Quichotte* (Petipa), as well as in the course of the adagio.

728

Closely akin to the preceding pose is the one in which the female dancer is **flat on her stomach on the shoulder** of her partner. Her body is arched, her arms stretched forward, often crossed at the wrists, her legs stretched back, crossed at the ankles.

This position is found, for example, in *Suite de Danses* (Clustine).

This pose may be taken at the end of a *pas de bourrée jeté* (§ 475).

Figure 99

729

Finally, the female dancer may **rest her lower back on the shoulder** of the male dancer, her body being very arched. Her legs are in front of the male dancer, extended, crossed at the ankles, or else one leg is extended and the other bent, the arms outstretched and the head held back.

This *porté*, not often found in the classical ballets, occurs mainly in character dances: *Danses polovtsiennes du Prince Igor* (Fokine), or with a precise intention—for example, to suggest abduction: Orion abducting Syliva, in the first act of Syliva (Mérante).

730

Portés tend to develop considerably in the adagio and are becoming more and more varied. In many of them the **female dancer continues to support herself** more or less on her partner to lessen the effort required of her arm.

For example, facing her partner, who holds her at the waist, she supports her knees on the upper part of the male dancer's chest. Usually her knees are bent at a right angle. Her arms and head may have various positions: *Roméo et Juliette* (Lavrovski).

Conversely, the female dancer may turn her back to her partner, who holds her at the waist, and have her knees decidedly bent, and her thighs as well, her body remaining erect; hands in front of the chest: *But* (Descombey).

731

But there are also **portés** in which the female dancer has **no longer any contact with the male dancer,** who keeps her up in the air by holding her in his arms.

These *portés* were first made with arms folded and thus could not be maintained for very long. They were then very similar to adagio leaps (§ 722 to 724).

It appears that until about 1930 the classical adagio consisted essentially of acts of balance, *tours,* and a few *sauts* sustained by the partner, mainly of the *grand jeté* type, with a unique type of leap intercepted in midair (§ 724), to exit from the stage.

André Levinson wrote on this subject in 1929: "The adagio of the opera, an exquisite conquest of the romantic ballet, may be described as a varied succession of unstable balancings on the part of the female dancer, who, positioned on one *pointe,* pirouettes or moves from one position to another. The male dancer [acts as] support, pivot, motor—furnishing impulsion to the star, causes her to turn. In principle, this succession of *attitudes,* through slow *développés* or giddying *tours,* takes place on the ground. It may happen, however, that the male dancer takes up the female dancer by the waist, making her trace, at a height, huge circles of *dégagés.* Occasionally in the finale he intercepts his partner in flight, in order to carry her into the wings—she, having made her thrust, swoops down upon him with a *grand jeté enlevé.*"[1]

732

In the meantime, *portés* had already become well known for some length of time because they figured in **acrobatics.**

Teams composed of a female acrobat and a supporting partner performed exercises in the circus or the music hall in which the man held his partner with arms outstretched in various positions, hurled her into the air, caught her again, etc. It was essentially a question of exercises of strength in which the plastic beauty was not supposed to disguise the necessary effort, because the difficulty that was overcome brought praise from the audience (Fig. 100).

733

For a number of years the classical adagio and double acrobatics (*l'acrobatie en couple*) coexisted without influencing each other.

It would appear that **the action of one genre upon the other** was first made in the first quarter of the twentieth century, by the classical dance upon acrobatics. Indeed, female acrobats were seen performing on their toes: Myrtil, Vronska, Iris Rowe, etc., were inserting dance steps in their acrobatics. Furthermore, certain acrobatic performers had a classical training in the dance.

Between 1925 and 1930, a period in which the decadence of the classical dance was still very pronounced, female dancers with a very classical training were seen (even those coming out of the large state schools) turning toward the most varied genres, in particular, to the music hall.

The acrobatic adagio caused a furor. Dozens of couples performed it more or less successfully.

[1] André Levinson: *La Danse d'aujourd'hui.* Editions Duchartre et van Buggenhoudt, Paris, 1929, p. 377-78.

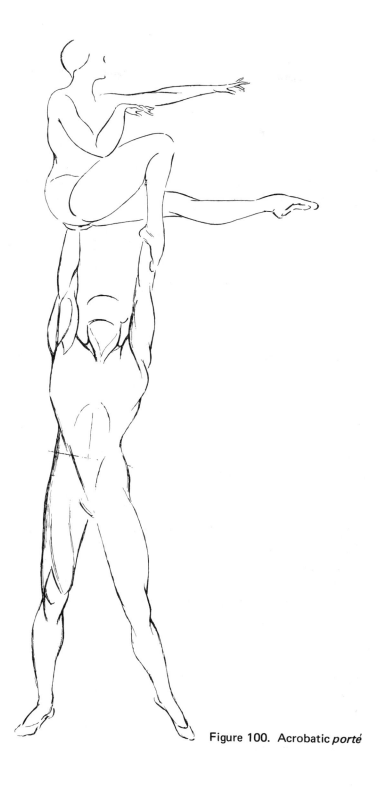

Figure 100. Acrobatic *porté*

285

734

Since that period certain classical dancers, even if they make a few incursions into the music-hall, have applied acrobatic techniques to the adagio.

Robert Quinault, who later become choreographer and professor at the Opera, was one of the first, after Levinson, to undertake the "vertical development of the adagio."[2] He lifted up his partner with arms outstretched and held her by the ankle, the knee, etc.

Levinson insists on the fact that "each group *porté* is conceived in a design of plastic beauty; it is a piece of animated architecture."

This is in fact the capital point differentiating the acrobatic classical adagio from that of the music-hall. It is not a *tour de force*, but is inserted in the aesthetic context of the ballet.

735

The **Russian schools**, particularly that of Moscow, have considerably developed the *portés* with arms extended, sometimes even arriving at a purely acrobatic appearance.

But starting from about 1950, the *porté* with one or both arms extended imposed itself upon the whole classical dance, and is now found by itself everywhere.

We shall not analyze all the possible positions: they are very numerous, and the choreographers are continually adding new ones. We shall cite only a few examples.

736

With **both arms**, the following position is found quite often: the female dancer in **arabesque** bends the vertical leg; the male dancer holds her, with one hand at her waist, the other on her knee. The head and shoulders are usually erect, the arms may take various positions. For example, one arm vertical, the other horizontal to the front; or else one arm horizontal to the front, the other half-horizontal to the front, etc.

737

Also supported by **both arms**, the dancer is in a *demi-arabesque* position, the vertical leg held by the male dancer. The trunk is usually quite vertical, while the arms may have various positions.

[2] Andre LEVINSON: *La Danse d'aujourd'hui*. Editions Duchartre et van Buggenhoudt, Paris, 1929, p. 378.

Figure 101

738

The female dancer, **held at the waist** by her partner, arches herself vigorously while leaning her head backward and having her arms *en couronne*. She may have both legs outstretched, or one outstretched and the other bent. She thus forms the arc of a circle.

739

The female dancer, **held at the thighs**, is literally flat on her stomach in the air, feet crossed, arms lateral-horizontal, head up: *Casse-Noisette* (Petipa, adapted by V. Vainonen) (Fig. 101).

287

740

Related position: the **female dancer flat on her stomach** has one leg vertical, alongside the body of the male dancer, the other leg bent, one arm vertical-lateral, the other horizontal: *Roméo et Juliette* (music by Prokofieff, choreography by Tatiana Gsovsky).

741

Portés with one arm alone, more difficult than those with both arms, are however used in the ballets, where they always make a big effect.

Among them we find a *porté* quite close to the one described in paragraph 738. But the male dancer holds his partner with only one hand placed in the hollow part of her lower back: fourth act of *Lac des Cygnes* (Bourmeister).

742

The **female dancer may also be horizontal,** one leg extended, the other bent, arms lateral in second, carried by the male dancer whose single hand holds her up at the thigh (Fig. 102).

The female dancer may have the position described in paragraph 737, being held by a single hand placed under the buttock corresponding to the vertical leg.

743

The adagio, with its multiple forms, is a choreographic element in full evolution. It is still present in all styles of choreography, including the most modern.

It is the dance passage in which the artistic sense of the performers finds its full expression.

However great its difficulty, the adagio must never prevail over beauty of lines, and the most transcendent technique alone is not sufficient for its perfection.

LES ENCHAINEMENTS*

744

By now we have seen the elements of which the dance is composed— that is, the positions, poses, and steps. These elements combine the variations and ensembles.

*Sequences.

Figure 102

These sequences may be infinitely varied. However, a number of them—grouping together two, three, or four steps—are often found and ultimately form an actual entity which we shall call **classical sequences** (*enchaînements classiques*).

289

745

These classical sequences for the most part date back at least to the nineteenth century, and they had a strong tendency to become stereotyped at the beginning of the twentieth.

Although there is at present great freedom in choreography and even a definite quest for originality, many classical sequences are employed as a complex form of step.

746

We shall first consider the sequences formed of **two elements.** It will be recalled that **a certain number of these sequences have already been discussed** and described as steps: *passé-relevé* (§ 186), *pas de bourrée dessus* and *dessous* (§ 198), *passé-cabriole non battu* (§ 256), *échappé fermé* (§ 299 and 300), *passé-cabriole battu devant* (§ 364), *glissade-cabriole battue* in second (§ 366), *pas de bourrée-cabriole battue derrière* (§ 368), *passé-cabriole battu* (§ 369), *pas de bourrée enveloppé-pas de bourrée détourné* (§ 390), *tours relevés* prepared for in fourth by a *pas de bourrée*, a *dégagé*, an *échappé*, etc. (§ 426 and 427), *tours* prepared for by a *temps de pointe relevé* (§ 428), *tours* prepared in fifth (§ 429 and 430), *fouetté détourné* (§ 434), *pas de bourrée-relevé détourné* (§ 437), *tours* with change of feet (§ 439), *tours relevés* in second prepared for by a *dégagé* (§ 441 and 443), *les petits jetés en tournant* (§ 467), *coupé-jeté en tournant* (469), *failli-grand jeté* (§ 470), *pas de bourrée-grand jeté en tournant* (§ 475), *pas de bourrée-assemblée* (§ 477), *pas de bourrée-cabriole* (§ 478 and 484), *pas de bourrée-entrechat 5* (§ 485).

747

Many sequences formed of **two elements** commence with a **glissade.** The second element is most often a *relevé sur la pointe* or a *saut,* less often a *piqué sur la pointe.*

Thus we have the **glissade-développé**: after a *glissade en descendant* (§ 158), the anterior foot is raised *sur la pointe* while the posterior leg executes a *développé* in second *à la hauteur* (§ 129). The step concludes with a second *à la hauteur*; or else, when the supporting foot comes back down *à plat*, the working leg returns to close in front, and the dancer may start out anew with the other foot.

As an exercise, eight *glissades-développés* may be strung together in sequence, alternating the feet.

They may also be done while ascending. In this case, after a *glissade en remontant* (§ 159), the anterior leg is raised for a *développé* and the closing is done to the back.

748

Very close to the *glissade-développé* is the **glissade-rond de jambe**: it is executed as in the preceding case with a *petit rond de jambe soutenu à la seconde* (§ 127), *en dedans* for a *glissade en descendant, en dehors* for a *glissade en remontant.*

Instead of raising the supporting foot *sur la pointe,* one can do a *soubresaut.*

749

The **glissade-arabesque** may be done in three ways: with a *relevé sur la pointe* (of the posterior foot after a *glissade en descendant,* of the anterior foot after a *glissade en remontant); with a piqué sur la pointe,* or with a *soubresaut.*

The working leg closes to the back after a *glissade en descendant,* and to the front after a *glissade en remontant.* This permits the dancer to start out again on the other foot.

The *glissade-arabesque* is usually done descending.

750

The **glissade-jeté** is very frequent after a *glissade en descendant.* The dancer does a *petit jeté en descendant* (§ 266) and after a *glissade en remontant,* a *petit jeté en remontant* (§ 269).

This combination of steps is found in numerous ballets.

Glissades-jetés may also be done while turning at the rate of a *demi-tour* for each. This step, for example, is found in the variation of Juliet in the *divertissement* from the opera *Roméo et Juliette* by Gounod (Aveline).

751

The *glissade-assemblée,* composed of a *glissade en descendant* and an *assemblée devant* with change of feet (§ 290) or of a *glissade en remontant* and an *assemblée derrière* with change of feet (§ 291), is likewise very frequent. It may be done in its own right or may conclude a series of *glissades-jetés.*

752

The **glissade** may be associated with a **tour piqué** (§ 404), which is most often done *en attitude* (§ 407). It is this sequence which is found in the celebrated variation from the first act of *Giselle* (Coralli and Perrot).

But after the *glissade* one can also have a *piqué en arabesque* (§ 409) or a piqué in second position (§ 411).

753

The **temps de pointe on both feet** (§ 173) often serves as an impulse for *sauts,* in particular for the *entrechats,* especially *entrechat 6* (§ 340); it also provides an impulse for *tours en l'air* (§ 461).

754

The **temps de pointe piqué en remontant** (§ 167) is frequently associated with a **coupé-fouetté** executed in the following manner: after the *temps de pointe* the posterior foot, which has become free, makes a *piqué en cinquième derrière sur la pointe,* and the other leg rises directly into second *à la hauteur* or *demi-hauteur,* then folds while bringing the *pointe* into the hollow of the knee, to the rear. This foot may then do a *piqué en quatrième derrière* to start the step anew with the other leg.

This sequence is very frequent.

755

The *grand rond de jambe-pas de bourrée détourné* actually begins with a *battement arrondi* (§ 119), not closed in fifth but one in which the foot does a *piqué derrière* at the end of the step in order to do the *pas de bourrée détourné* (§ 386).

During the first part of the step the supporting foot may remain *à plat* or rise *sur la pointe.*

756

Jetés give rise to a few combinations.

A *petit jeté en descendant* (§ 266) may, for example, be associated with a **temps de pointe** *piqué en remontant* (§ 167) taken directly starting from the *raccourci* of the working leg. At the end of the *temps de pointe* the working leg closes *en cinquième devant* and the dancer may start over again with the other foot.

757

A **jeté** may also be followed by a **petit rond de jambe sauté**.

With a *jeté en descendant* (§ 266) one can have a *petit rond de jambe en dedans* (§ 127), during which a *soubresaut* may be executed with the supporting foot. The step closes to the front.

With a *jeté en remontant* (§ 269), the *petit rond de jambe* will be *en dehors*. It closes to the rear.

Usually several *jetés-fonds de jambe* are done in succession.

758

With a **grand jeté** there may be associated a **pas de bourrée** enveloppé (§ 389) executed to a very rapid rhythm. This step involves no change of feet. Usually a large number of these are done in sequence: eight or sixteen, on a diagonal or in a circle. This is a brilliant sequence.

The *jeté-pas de bourrée* must not be confused with the *pas de bourrée-jeté* (§ 475), there being no relationship between the techniques of these two sequences.

759

The *ballonné* (§ 309) is often associated with the **pas de basque en descendant** (§ 189). A very large number of these sequences can be executed in series. They were very popular during the nineteenth century.

This step may be done in a symmetrical fashion by two persons holding each other by the hand and alternately facing each other, or back to back.

760

A **temps de bottes** (§ 331) is still very much associated with a **pas de basque en descendant** (§ 189). This is the sequence found at the beginning of the Mazurka of *Coppélia* (Saint-Léon).

761

The **passé-assemblée** is a step related to the *passé-cabriole devant* (§ 255 and 364). It is composed of a *passé* (§ 313), at the end of which the posterior leg moves into *quatrième devant à la hauteur* while the dancer leaps; he alights immediately in fifth, with both feet at the same time.

This step involves no change of feet, and several *passés-assemblées* may be done in sequence.

762

The **passé-entrechat 5** is simply the *batterie* of the preceding step.

In it the *assemblée* is replaced by an *entrechat 5 de volée* (§ 349).

It is a brilliant step which gives a great effect and is executed by male as well as female dancers: second act of *Giselle* (Coralli and Perrot).

763

In the same manner the *glissade-assemblée* (§ 751) may be done as a beating step in the form of **glissade-entrechat 5**.

This step is more difficult than the preceding one. It is brilliant, as are all the steps that include a *batterie*.

It will be recalled that there is also a *pas de bourrée-entrechat 5* which was explained in paragraph 485.

764

The simple *pas de bourrée* (§ 192) is often the second element of a step not involving a change of feet, which makes it possible to do a great number of these sequences in succession: for example, one might do a *saut de chat* (§ 276) and a *pas de bourrée* several times in succession.

Or one might do a **pas tombé** (§ 315) and a **pas de bourrée**, a **sissonne** (§ 279) and a **pas de bourrée**, etc.

765

The **pas tombé** may likewise be followed by a **cabriole en quatrième derrière** (§ 367), *battue*, which terminates by bringing the posterior leg forward to place the foot in fourth. The same sequence can then be repeated with the other foot.

This step is more appropriate for male dancers.

766

As we have seen in the third section of Chapter Four, *tours relevés* are preceded by a preparation.

Certain *tours piqués* may also be preceded by a step serving as an impulse. For example, we have already seen, in paragraph 752, the association of a *glissade* with a *tour piqué en attitude, arabesque,* or second.

These same **tours piqués** may also be preceded by a **failli** (§ 320). The effect is quite close to that obtained with the *tour* preceded by a *glissade.*

767

Finally, a sequence may be formed of a **tour relevé en dehors prepared in fourth position** (§ 426) and a **tour fouetté enveloppé** (§ 431).

The *tour* prepared in fourth closes to the rear, the *tour fouetté enveloppé,* to the front. The dancer may start anew from the other foot.

These two *tours* are done in opposite directions. But if several of these groups are done in sequence, it is customary for the turn in fourth to be done in the same direction as the *tour fouetté enveloppé* that preceded it.

This sequence, like all series of *tours,* is brilliant.

768

We conclude here our examples of sequences composed of two elements. Those which we have cited are among the most popular, but there can be, and in fact, there are many others, and the possible combinations are practically infinite.

769

The **sequences composed of three elements** are definitely not as numerous as those with two elements. The majority of them involve *sauts,* either with two *petits sauts* furnishing the impulse for a *grand saut,* or with a short step between two *sauts,* giving a rebounding effect.

770

The **pas tombé-posé-jeté** joins a *pas tombé* (§ 315), at the end of which the dancer moves the posterior leg forward to place the foot in fourth and raises the foot which at that moment is posterior in order to effect the *grand jeté* (§ 272), open from the point of view of the audience. The *pas tombé* does not involve a high leap, the greatest emphasis being placed on the *grand jeté*, which must be raised very high and cover a great distance. It is mainly a step for a male dancer, as are all those with a *grand saut,* but it may also be performed by women.

771

The **demi-contretemps-posé-jeté** is closely related to it. It commences with a *demi-contretemps* (§ 318). But because the latter step causes a change of feet, the *grand jeté* is *croisé* instead of being *ouvert.*

The effect of this step is very similar to that of the preceding one.

772

The **demi-contretemps-coupé-cabriole** begins with a *demi-contretemps* (§ 318), but whereas in the preceding step the foot was placed *en quatrième devant*, here it is placed *en quatrième ouverte.* The *coupé* (§ 314) brings the anterior leg *au raccourci,* and that leg directly executes the *cabriole* movement (§ 256) while rising *en quatrième devant ouverte à la hauteur*, and the supporting foot executes the *saut* during the reverse movement.

By contrast with the preceding sequences, this one is hardly ever done in series. Rather it is attached to other sequences.

It is rare that the *cabriole* is done as a beating step because the *coupé* gives less of a thrust than the *passé* that normally prepares this *cabriole* (§ 369). Finally, the *saut* may be replaced by a *relevé sur la pointe.*

773

The **double sissonne en descendant** is composed of a *sissonne en descendant* (§ 279) at the end of which the working leg moves forward so that the foot may be placed in fourth position. The posterior leg is then raised in order to do an *assemblée devant* with change of feet (§ 290).

Whereas in the preceding steps only the third element was a *grand saut,* in the *double sissonne* the first and third elements are raised quite high. This is thus a step that produces an effect of rebounding.

774

The **double sissonne en remontant** is composed of a *sissonne en remontant* (§ 281) at the end of which the working leg moves backward to be placed in fourth position. The anterior foot is then lifted to do an *assemblée derrière* with change of feet (§ 291).

This is exactly the reverse of the preceding technique.

~~~

775

We have already spoken, in paragraph 469, of the complex technique of the **pas tombé-coupé-jeté en tournant**, which is composed of a *pas tombé* (§ 480) with one turn, a *coupé* (§ 479) requiring a quarter-turn, and a *grand jeté en attitude* concluding the turn.

At present the tendency is to extend the posterior leg in the *grand jeté*—that is, to do it *en arabesque* rather than *en attitude*. The arms, however, remain *en attitude*.

776

The **failli-posé-tour enveloppé** is executed in the following manner, after a *failli* (§ 320): the anterior foot is placed in fourth for the execution of a *tour fouetté enveloppé* (§ 431), *relevé sur la pointe* of the anterior foot. This turn may also be terminated *en attitude* or *en arabesque*. The *relevé sur la pointe* may be replaced by a *soubresaut* done on the supporting leg during the *tour*.

777

A **tour en l'air** (*simple*) (§ 461) ending *en raccourci devant* may be followed by a *piqué sur la pointe en arabesque croisée*. The working leg closes *en cinquième derrière* with a *plié*.

This sequence involves no change of feet.

Several of these may be executed in series on a diagonal.

This is a woman's step; male dancers may do it with a *double tour en l'air, piqué sur la demi-pointe*.

~~~

778

Here we shall conclude the enumeration of these few examples of sequences with three elements. If there are more sequences with two elements that are considered classic, it is because the greater the number of elements, the greater the variety, and the greater the number of possible combinations. There will therefore be less often a tendency to repeat the same sequences.

779

The **sequences with four elements** may be divided into two groups: one part consisting of those formed of four different elements, hence following the progression of sequences with two and three elements; another part composed of those formed of three identical elements and a fourth, different, one intended either to conclude the series or to effect a change of feet.

This is due to the fact that the classical ballet, especially in the nineteenth and early twentieth century, was based, above all, on the figure *four*. Usually the music is divided into phrases of four measures, to which the steps are adapted. It is said that music and sequences are "square" (*carrés*).

In the great ballets of the nineteenth century one finds multiples of four almost exclusively.

780

There are a few classical sequences with **four different elements.** For the reason already given (§ 778), the greater the number of elements, the greater the variety of possible combinations.

We shall cite only two examples based on *batterie à croisements*.

781

An *entrechat 4 volé* (§ 349)—that is, terminated *en raccourci* behind the leg which would normally have closed *en cinquième derrière*—is followed by an *assemblée derrière* without change of feet (§ 294), an *entrechat 4* (§ 338) and an *entrechat 3* (§ 337).

This is a sequence constituting a good exercise in *petite batterie*. Here we are quite close to the series which we shall study in the third section of this chapter.

782

The following sequence is closely akin to the preceding one: an *entrechat 3 volé*—that is, terminated in the preceding one—is followed by an *assemblée derrière* without change of feet (§ 294) and two *entrechats 4*.

783

Among the sequences formed of **three identical steps** we shall first single out those in which three steps are followed by a fourth, which serves as a conclusion. For example: three *petits jetés en descendant* (§ 266) are followed by an *assemblée devant* with change of feet (§ 290).

This sequence is already found in the step of the wine-harvesters from the first act of *Giselle* (Coralli and Perrot).

784

In other sequences, after **three identical steps** with the same foot, the dancer does a different one that **changes feet**.

For example: three *temps de pointe en remontant* (§ 167) and a *coupé-fouetté* (§ 754). Even with this sequence a veritable series may be done by executing: three *temps de pointe coupé-fouetté* with each leg and four times *temps de pointe coupé-fouetté*.

785

One can also do three **ballonnés** (§ 309) and a **pas de basque en descendant** (§ 189). This sequence is found, for example, in the children's Mazurka of *Suite de Danses* (Clustine).

As in the preceding example, we have already described the simple sequence of two elements (§ 759).

786

This type of sequence can be used also for *pas de batterie:* **three entrechats 4** and an **entrechat 3**. On the basis of *entrechats 4* and an *entrechat 3,* one can compose a series of the same type as that discussed in paragraph 784.

Many examples might be cited.

787

Finally, the last and largest group is formed of the **same step performed three times** without change of feet and a **pas de bourrée** (§ 192).

One may do, for example:

- three *chassés* (§ 152), one *pas de bourrée,*
- three *temps de pointe en remontant* (§ 167), one *pas de bourrée,*
- three *sauts de chat* (§ 276), one *pas de bourrée,*
- three *sissonnes* (§ 279 or 281), one *pas de bourrée,* etc.
- three *brisés* (§ 351), one *pas de bourrée,* etc.

It should be noted, however, that certain steps are rarely combined with the *pas de bourrée*, in particular those using the posterior leg for support: for example, the *ballonnés* (§ 309), which are in fact combined with a *pas de basque*.

Entrechats involving no change of feet are rather combined with an *entrechat* requiring change of feet: the 3 or the 6.

788

To conclude, it should be noted that **four identical steps** may likewise be very often done in sequence:

- four *emboités* (§ 151),
- four *pas de bourrée* (§ 192, 196, 197, 198, 199, 202 or 203),
- four *sissonnés* in second position (§ 283),
- four *assemblées* (§ 290 or 291),
- four *échappés* (§ 299), etc.

The series of identical steps are very systematically used in the class for training purposes and for perfecting the steps, but certain ones are also employed on the stage.

789

Here we shall conclude our study of classical sequences; as we have shown, these sequences allow for an infinite variety. We have tried especially to single out the principle tendencies governing the elaboration of these sequences.

SERIES

790

The **series** are exercises that especially concern the dance class.

These are sequences combining the various aspects of the same technique: for example, the series of *pas de bourrée* or of exercises grouped so as to develop one aptitude or another: for example, the series of balancing acts (*équilibres*).

Series are never executed onstage, but they enable the dancer to acquire a perfect mastery of technique.

Each dancing master may combine some of them according to his own ideas, but certain ones are at present employed in large classical schools. We shall give a few examples of them.

791

We shall begin with a very **elementary series,** that of the **relevés.**

Eight successive times, *en descendant:* starting from a fifth, raise the posterior leg *au raccourci* and close *cinquième devant.* Simultaneously the supporting leg is raised *sur la pointe* and comes back down *à plat* for the closing. Because the step involves a change of feet, each leg is raised alternately.

Eight successive times, *en remontant*: the same step, raising the anterior leg *au raccourci* and closing to the rear. In the first *relevé* the leg that has just closed to the front starts afresh from the back.

Four *relevés en tournant* to the side of the anterior foot, by quarter-turns. The posterior leg rises *au raccourci* and closes to the rear for the first three, to the front for the fourth.

The same thing from the other side.

This very simple series is intended to exercise the instep and to build up force for the *relevés.*

792

The **pas de bourrée** series is much more complex; it reviews the different variants of the *pas de bourrée.* It is executed thus:

- eight *pas de bourrée dessus* (§ 197),
- eight *pas de bourrée dessous* (§ 196),
- one *pas de bourrée dessus et dessous* (§ 198),
- one *pas de bourrée dessus,* but closed to the rear (first part of a *pas de bourrée dessus et dessous*); the anterior leg is raised *en quatrième devant* barely *à la demi-hauteur,* moves rapidly into first (§ 22) while gently striking the floor (second part of a *flic-flac*) (§ 131), to come to rest barely *au raccourci,* foot behind the ankle of the supporting leg. Starting from this position, the dancer immediately does a *saut de chat* (§ 276) without returning to fifth.

Same thing (starting from: a *pas de bourrée dessus et dessous*) on the other side:

- one *pas de bourrée enveloppé* (§ 389),
- one *pas de bourrée détourné* (§ 386),
- one *pas de bourrée enveloppé,* one *gargouillade* (§ 277).

Same thing (starting from: a *pas de bourrée enveloppé*) on the other side:

Six *pas de bourrée bateau* (§ 199). One *pas de bourrée simple* (§ 192). One *temps de pointe relevé* on both feet (§ 173).

One *pas de bourrée dessus* (§ 197). One *pas de bourrée double en descendant* (§ 202), four times in succession.

One *pas de bourrée dessous* (§ 196). One *pas de bourrée double en remontant* (§ 203), four times.

It will be seen that this series calls for steps which are in themselves complicated, such as the *pas de bourrée doubles*. On the one hand, it permits a review of all the *pas de bourrée*; on the other, it allows for a perfect mastery of their use in sequence. It is also a good exercise in muscular control and speed in general.

793

The **series of balancing acts** (*équilibres*) is very simple in principle, but very difficult in its execution. It can only be done correctly by dancers who have already attained quite an advanced level of proficiency.

In fifth position, raise the posterior foot *sur pointe* while the other leg does a *développé* into second (§ 129). The arms move simultaneously from the *position départ* (§ 38) into second (§ 40). The position in second is maintained during two *temps* (movements). Close to the rear.

Same movement on the other side.

Start the whole procedure a second time.

Lift the posterior leg into *attitude* (§ 81), with the corresponding arm position (§ 41), while the anterior foot rises *sur la pointe*, by leaping gently rather than by actually doing a *relevé*. Close by bringing the foot forward.

Same movement on the other side.

Do the same thing on each side, but with an *arabesque ouverte* (§ 69).

In all cases the dancer remains for two beats in each stage of balance.

This series, as its name indicates, is intended to help the dancer acquire balance in the principal positions in which it is practiced on the stage. One can, to be sure, make the tempo progressively slower so that the state of balance is more drawn out.

Exercises of this type must not be done by dancers who are not sufficiently trained, because to keep their balance they risk assuming awkward positions. It is only when one knows how to maintain the correct position through good muscular control that one can undertake the concentrated study of balancing.

794

The **series of échappés**, while reviewing the principal types of *échappés*, requires exercise in balancing on both *pointes* and in dexterity.

An *échappé* in second *sur les deux pointes* (§ 299) closed with change of feet, on which the dancer remains during four beats (calculated as 1 for doing the *échappé* and 2, 3, and 4 for the balancing).

The same thing with the other foot forward.

Twice in succession: an *échappé* on two beats with each foot.

Four *échappés sur la pointe* in second with change of feet, without stopping.

One *échappé* in fourth position (§ 302). One *échappé* in second with change of feet.

The same thing with the other foot forward.

Finally, four *échappés* in second, turning by quarter-turns.

The same thing in the other direction.

795

The series of **petites sissonnes** reviews the different types of *sissonnes*; at the same time it is a jumping exercise, good for breathing, and in its last part exercising precise control over the movements of the leg.

Three *sissonnes en descendant* (§ 279), one change of feet (§ 336).

The same thing on the other side.

Three *sissonnes en remontant* (§ 281), one change of feet (§ 336).

The same thing on the other side.

Four *sissonnes* in second *en descendant* (§ 283).

Four *sissonnes* in second *en remontant* (§ 283).

One *sissonne en remontant* (§ 281), one *sissonne* in second (§ 283), one *sissonne en descendant* (§ 279), one *soubresaut* (§ 249).

The same thing on the other side.

One *sissonne en descendant* (§ 279), one *sissonne* in second (§ 283) taken with the anterior leg which closes to the rear, one *sissonne en remontant* (§ 281), one *soubresaut* (§ 249).

The same thing on the other side.

796

The **series of assemblées** is an exercise in jumping and breathing.

Eight *assemblées* to the front with change of feet (§ 290).

Eight *assemblées* to the rear with change of feet (§ 291).

For each of these sixteen *assemblées* a *temps d'arrêt* (pause) is indicated after the *assemblée*.

Four times in succession: one *assemblée* to the front with change of feet, two changes of feet (§ 336), one *temps d'arrêt*.

Four times in succession: one *assemblée* to the rear with change of feet, two changes of feet, one *temps d'arrêt*.

Eight *assemblées* to the front with change of feet.

Eight *assemblées* to the rear with change of feet.

These last sixteen *assemblées* are connected without *temps d'arrêt*.

The arms open up in second (§ 40) in the *assemblées*, except for the last sixteen, where they remain in the *position de départ* (§ 38).

797

The **series of ronds de jambe** is particularly complex.

Eight times in succession: a *petit jeté en descendant* (§ 266), a *soubresaut* with the supporting leg during which the working leg executes two *petits ronds de jambe* sustained in second, *en dedans* (§ 127); these *ronds de jambe* are terminated in second *à la demi-hauteur* so that it will be possible to connect directly with the *jeté*.

Eight times in succession: a *petit jeté en remontant* (§ 269), a *soubresaut* with two *petits ronds de jambe* sustained in second, *en dehors* (§ 127).

A *petit jeté en descendant* (§ 266), three *soubresauts* turning to the side of the supporting leg, by thirds of a turn, while doing each time a *petit rond de jambe* sustained in second (§ 127) *en dedans,*

The same thing on the other side.

The same sequence on both sides with a *jeté en remontant* (§ 269) and *petits ronds de jambe* sustained in second, *en dehors*, and performed while turning to the side of the working leg.

One *jeté en descendant*, one *soubresaut* with two *petits ronds de jambe* sustained in second, *en dedans. Relevé sur la pointe* of the supporting leg, *développé* (§ 129) and *fouetté* (§ 130) in second with the working leg. Descend with foot *à plat*, keeping the leg *au raccourci,* and start this sequence afresh on the other side.

Begin once again with each leg.

Coupé (§ 314), one *soubresaut* with two *petits ronds de jambe* sustained in second, *en dehors; relevé sur la pointe* of the supporting leg while the working leg is extended *en quatrième devant à la demi-hauteur* and does a *grand rond de jambe soutenu* (§ 126) *à la demi-hauteur*. Descend once more, bending, with foot *à plat*.

The same thing with the other leg.

Begin once again with each leg.

Assemblée derrière (§ 292) without changing feet. The dancer then does a sort of *sissonne en raccourci* in second (§ 284), alighting on the posterior leg, during which action the working leg does a *petit rond de jambe soutenu* in second *en dehors. Glissade en remontant* (§ 159) taken directly starting from the *raccourci* with *rond de jambe.*

Same sequence on the other side.

Begin once again on each side.

The arm movements are as follows:

During the first group of eight sequences the arms are in sixth position (§ 44), alternately on each side, the arm that is bent corresponding to the leg that does the *rond de jambe.*

During the following eight sequences the arms remain in the *position de départ* (§ 38).

During the *ronds de jambe en tournant* the arms are in third (§ 41), the raised arm corresponding to the leg that does the *rond de jambe.*

Next, in the *jeté* followed by the *rond de jambe* the arms are in sixth (§ 44), the arm that is bent corresponding to the leg that does the *rond de jambe.* In the *développé* the arms open in second (§ 40) and move into reverse sixth with the *fouetté;* they are thus in position to do a sequence on the other side.

For the following group, the corresponding arm follows the movement of the leg that does the *grand rond de jambe soutenu* and moves into first (§ 39), into second (§ 40), and finishes *en arabesque* (§ 69), while the other arm rises to the front. During the remainder of the sequence the arms are in the *position de départ* (§ 38).

The arms, in *position de départ* for the *assemblée,* open into second (§ 40), passing through first (§ 39) with the *petit rond de jambe.* For the *glissade* the arm on the side toward which the dancer is going bends, giving a sixth position (§ 44). They remain in this position for the second *rond de jambe.* The arm that is bent opens into second to come back down in the *position de départ* with the following *assemblée.*

The body is leaning slightly forward for the descending steps, the head turned to the side of the working leg.

During the *ronds de jambe en tournant* the body is slightly bent to the side of the supporting leg and the head looks out under the arm that is raised.

In the sequel the trunk remains erect, except during the *fouettés,* in which it leans slightly forward, the head turning a bit toward the arm that is bent.

As is evident, this complicated exercise in its various aspects is simultaneously a test of memory, dexterity, breath control, and of the muscles giving impetus to the leap.

798

We shall now cite two series, much more simple but requiring use of the *batterie*.

The **petit série** is composed as follows:

- eight *entrechat 3s* (§ 337),
- four *entrechat 4s* (§ 338), *entrechat 3,*
- eight *petits jetés en descendant* (§ 266),
- eight *petits jetés en remontant* (§ 269),
- eight *échappés fermés* (§ 299), with high elevation.

This series may be adapted to the strength of the students. Beginners will do it by replacing the *entrechat 3s* with *changements de pied* (changes of feet) (§ 336) and replacing the *entrechat 4s* with *soubresauts* in fifth (§ 249).

Good dancers will use beating steps for the *jetés* (§ 358, 359) and *échappés* (§ 353).

799

Brisés Télémaque are done in the following manner:

Brisé (§ 351), *entrechat 3* (§ 337), *entrechat 4 volé* –that is, terminating with the leg *au raccourci derrière*; *brisé*, but which might be a *glissade en remontant* (§ 159) *battue, entrechat 3, entrechat 4 volé*.

These steps are done along a single diagonal. The dancer then starts out on the same sequence, but does it on the other side and on a diagonal perpendicular to the preceding one.

This is yet another exercise in dexterity, but it is brilliant and may be used on the stage.

800

We shall conclude with the series based on *tours.*

The **série des tours prepared in fourth** *is done in the following* manner:

One *tour relevé en dehors* taken in fourth position (§ 426), prepared for by a *dégagé* in second (§ 103), terminated in second *à la demi-hauteur* (§ 62). A *tour relevé* in second *en dehors* taken directly (§ 451) and closed *en cinquième derrière*.

The same thing with the other foot.

One *tour relevé en dehors* in fourth (§ 246), prepared for by a *dégagé* in second (§ 103) and terminated *en attitude* (§ 83). One *tour relevé en attitude en dehors* taken directly (§ 449), closed *en cinquième derrière*.

The same sequence with an *arabesque* (§ 71) on each side.

A *tour relevé en dehors*, taken in fourth (§ 426), prepared for by a *dégagé* ending in second *à la hauteur* (or *demi-hauteur*), a *tour relevé* in second *en dehors* taken directly (§ 451). A *tour relevé en attitude en dehors* taken directly (§ 449) closed *en cinquième derrière*.

The same thing on the other side.

The same sequence on the other side.

As is evident, this sequence is difficult in itself, because it requires the technique of *tours relevé* taken directly. It is a very concentrated study of *tours* and of balance. In the place of one turn the dancer may do two turns from one impulse.

801

The **série des tours en dedans** is a little less complicated than the preceding one.

Battement arrondi en dehors (§ 119) terminating in fourth (§ 26). At the same time, the arms rise in fifth (§ 43) through the intermediary of the first (§ 39), are opened in second (§ 40), then are placed *en troisième croisée* (§ 540), while the anterior foot is raised *sur la pointe*. The anterior foot rests *à plat*, both knees bend.

A *tour relevé en dedans* (§ 427) but with the leg *en attitude* instead of being *au raccourci;* arms *en attitude* (§ 41). Close *en cinquième derrière*.

The other leg is raised immediately to start afresh on the other side. Do not close in fifth.

The leg that was *en attitude* is extended in *demi-arabesque ouverte* (§ 69); *temps de cuisse* (hip movement) (§ 115). Move the leg forward and place it in fourth (§ 26). Raise the posterior foot *à la pointe*.

At the same time the arms that were *en attitude* move into first (§ 39), then are placed *en arabesque* (§ 69) for the *temps de cuisse*. They descend in the *position de départ* (§ 38) *for the passage of the leg and* are placed once again in third (§ 41) when the posterior foot rises *à la pointe*. The raised arm corresponds to this foot.

The foot remains *à plat*, the knees bend. One *tour en dedans* in second with the arms in second.

From this position move directly into *arabesque* to do a sequence on the other side. This passage into *arabesque* is made by a turning (reversal) of the body.

The dancer then repeats the same sequence on both sides, with a *tour arabesque.*

Like all the series of *tours,* this one is difficult. As in the preceding case, two *tours* may be made from a single impulse.

802

We shall conclude with the **série des tours taken directly**.

One tour *relevé en dehors* (§ 428) taken from a fifth position, without preparation.

This turn is not closed in fifth, but is connected to a second *tour relevé en dehors* taken directly (§ 447), at the end of which there is connected a *tour relevé en attitude en dehors* taken directly (§ 449), then another *tour* of the same type which is terminated *en raccourci,* and the dancer may start the whole sequence anew without closing in fifth.

Because this exercise is always done on the same leg, it will have to be done the next time on the other side.

In these turns, because the working foot never remains on the ground, much balance and precision are required. These turns are therefore very difficult.

803

Here we shall conclude our examples of series. This particular series is classical, but each dancing master can, if he so desires, combines others, more or less difficult, with pauses for rest where needed.

The principle of series has the advantage of requiring the repetition of techniques of the same family.

The series often involve concentrated study of certain types of steps and are almost always excellent training for dexterity and control.

EIGHT

The Dancing Lesson

804

The plan of the dancing lesson is traditional. Let us examine it rapidly and see if it is justified by present-day knowledge of psychology and physiology.

The lesson begins with exercises at the barre. These exercises have a dual purpose: to warm up the muscles and to prepare for the exercises in the middle of the floor and for the actual dance steps.

In their normal condition the muscles are said to be "cold." A cold muscle is not capable of doing good work: it lacks elasticity and runs the risk of becoming cramped if one forces it.

The muscle warms up, in the literal sense, through a workout because the oxygen brought by the blood is burned up in it and releases carbon dioxide, which will be evacuated through the blood up to the lungs. As the temperature of the muscle rises it becomes more elastic, more supple, and the blood in it circulates better.

Therefore the exercises at the barre must begin with a gentle, slow workout, without running any risk of becoming fatigued and thus flooding the muscles with lactic acid.

While this is taking place the second purpose of the barre comes into play: the exercises cause certain muscles in particular to have a workout and prepare for certain particular steps.

After the barre, the muscles must be warm, not overtired, and sufficiently exercised.

805

In general, the *adagio* is introduced at this point, because slow movements do not cause excessive muscular output but are rather based on balance, thus necessitating thorough control, which is impossible in a state of physical or mental fatigue.

After the *adagio* the dancer often does *tours*. These also demand a great deal of balance, and to a certain extent, the *adagio* prepares for some forms of *tours*. It is not tiring, to the muscles, at least.

The sequences based on *tours*, on balancing, and (for girls) on *pointes* are the result of this exercise.

The *sauts,* which require a great physical output and are very tiring, will come next.

The last set of exercises combine all the preceding elements.

The lesson is usually concluded with a few very simple exercises, *battements*, *dégagés*, etc., constituting a return to calm, a renewal of total control over the muscles after the difficult exercises, and a sort of "putting-in-order" until the next lesson.

The traditional plan, which is formed empirically, thus presents a logical succession of exercises and causes a fair amount of fatigue.

806

We shall first consider a type of dance lesson intended for female dancers who have already have a certain amount of training: the lesson taught by Geneviève Guillot at the (Paris) Opera.

Next we shall see a lesson for male dancers, a lesson for girl beginners, and a lesson for boys.

Throughout the lesson the teacher must have his attention focused acutely on each of his pupils. Obviously he must not be content to simply show the exercises, leaving the pupils to their own devices. Not only must every mistake be immediately pointed out and corrected, and every laxity suppressed, but in addition the teacher must stimulate the student (whatever his age or level of attainment) to do his very best in order to make progress. Muscular exercise will be profitable only if it is total, without however striving to exceed the physical possibilities of contraction or stretching, which would have the effect of producing just the opposite of the results desired.

A LESSON FOR FEMALE DANCERS

807

The exercises at the barre which we are going to describe are those of one lesson. If the dancer wishes to work at the barre before going onstage, she will strive only to warm up her muscles without tiring them in order to

levator sca

semispinalis capitis
splenius capitis
splenius cervicis

trapezius – – – –

rhomboideus _ _ _ _ _
extensor carpi radialis longus – – – – – –
extensor carpi radialis brevis – – – – –
extensor policis – – – – – –

ileocostalis dorsi

spinalis dorsi – – – – – – – – –

longissimus dorsi – – – –

erector spinae

sacrospinalis _ _ _ _ _ _ _ _ _

semitendinos
semimembranosus

triceps sural – –

long segment – – – – – –

biceps femoris (crural)

short segment – – – – –

gastrocnemius – – – – –

triceps sural

soleus _ _ _ _ _ _ _ _

Extensor muscles and muscles for the correct
position of the back, shoulders, and head

extensor digitorum brevis – – – – –

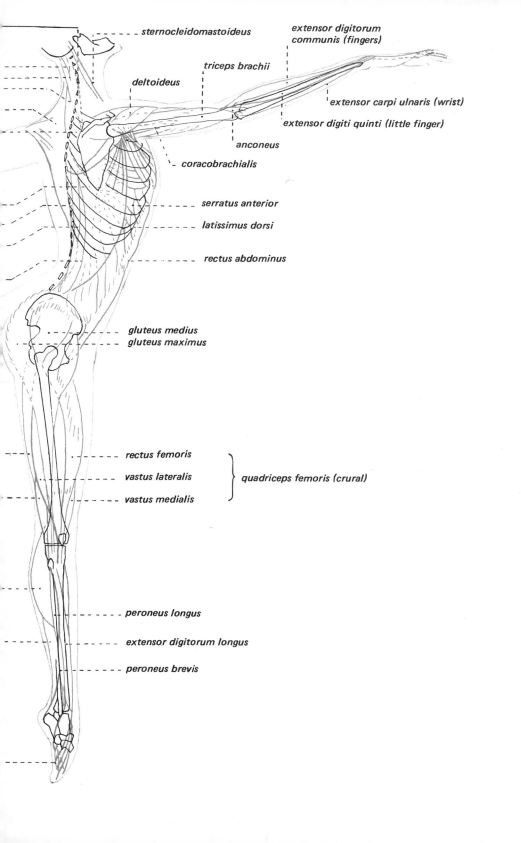

sternocleidomastoideus

extensor digitorum
communis (fingers)

triceps brachii

deltoideus

extensor carpi ulnaris (wrist)

extensor digiti quinti (little finger)

anconeus

coracobrachialis

serratus anterior

latissimus dorsi

rectus abdominus

gluteus medius

gluteus maximus

rectus femoris

vastus lateralis

quadriceps femoris (crural)

vastus medialis

peroneus longus

extensor digitorum longus

peroneus brevis

make them ready to execute the difficult steps of the variation. She will thus work with great suppleness and without forcing.

On the other hand, the work at the barre during the dance class demands a total and continuous effort. Before beginning, the dancer will limber up muscles and take a few deep breaths. Throughout the lesson she must keep in mind what she is in the process of doing: the muscular workout will have far better results if it is accompanied by intense mental effort.

All the exercises for which the dancer is in profile at the barre should be executed a second time, after a *demi-tour* in order to give the symmetrical muscles an identical workout.

At the Barre

808   EXERCISE 1. PLIE, LEAN TO THE SIDE

Back to the barre, in second position, quite wide open. Trunk very erect, pelvis rotated forward. Care should be taken not to pull the shoulders back; the lower back should not be hollowed out (Fig. 103). The toes are *à plat* on the floor, without falling on the big toe (Fig. 104).

The correct position of the pelvis is brought about by the bilateral contraction[3] of the muscles of the antero-lateral wall of the abdomen: the transverse muscle, which maintains the steadiness of the lumbar region, the large and small oblique muscles which, pulling on the pubic bone when they take the thorax as their pivot, and cause the pelvis to rock upward and forward. Simultaneously, the large and the medium buttocks muscles contract with the femur as their pivot, which brings about a downward shifting of the sacrum.

The correct position of the back is obtained by the bilateral contraction of the spinal extensor muscles of the rachis: lumbar vertebrae, spinal transverse muscle, the long dorsal muscle, and the sacro-lumbar or ilio-costal, epispinal, and interspinal muscles.

The shoulders are kept low by the contraction of the sub-clavian taking a pivot on the first side, which lowers the clavicle. The small pectoral muscle, pivoting on the sides, exerts a downward pull on the coracoid apophyse of the scapula, which likewise lowers the shoulder. The angular of the scapula pivoting on the cervical column draws the angle of the scapula and consequently lowers the shoulder. The

---

[3] In scientific parlance, the contraction is the shortening of the muscle, the active organ of the movement that brings about, through the intermediary of the tendons, the shifting of the corresponding bones, the passive organs of the movement. In choreographic parlance, the term *serre* (closed) is often used in this sense, with "contracted" meaning "clenched."

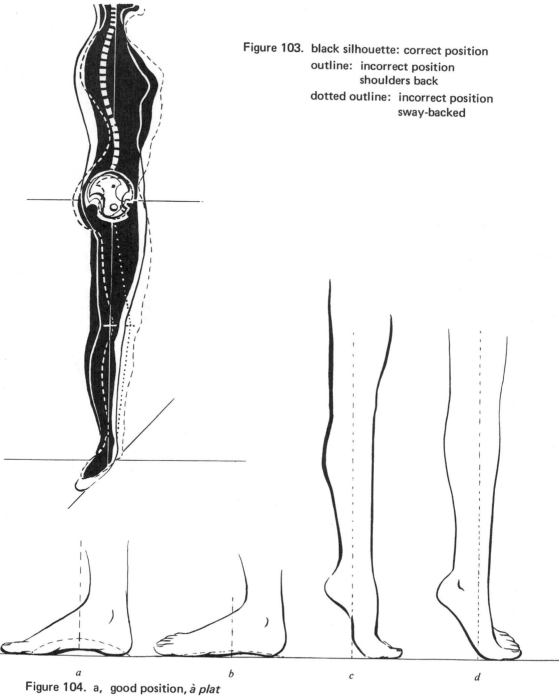

Figure 103. black silhouette: correct position
outline: incorrect position
shoulders back
dotted outline: incorrect position
sway-backed

a   *b*   *c*   *d*

Figure 104.   a,   good position, *à plat*
b,   weight falling on the big toe
c,   good position *sur la demi-pointe*
d,   weight falling on the big toe

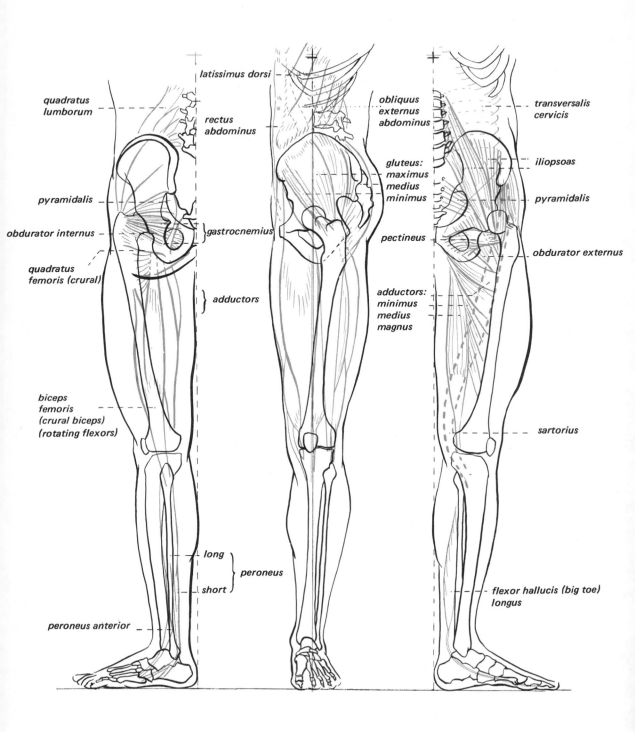

quadratus
lumborum

rectus
abdominus

latissimus dorsi

obliquus
externus
abdominus

transversalis
cervicis

pyramidalis

gluteus:
maximus
medius
minimus

iliopsoas

pyramidalis

obdurator internus

gastrocnemius

pectineus

obdurator externus

quadratus
femoris (crural)

adductors

adductors:
minimus
medius
magnus

biceps
femoris
(crural biceps)
(rotating flexors)

sartorius

long

peroneus

short

flexor hallucis (big toe)
longus

peroneus anterior

Outward rotating muscles and muscles for the tilt of the pelvis

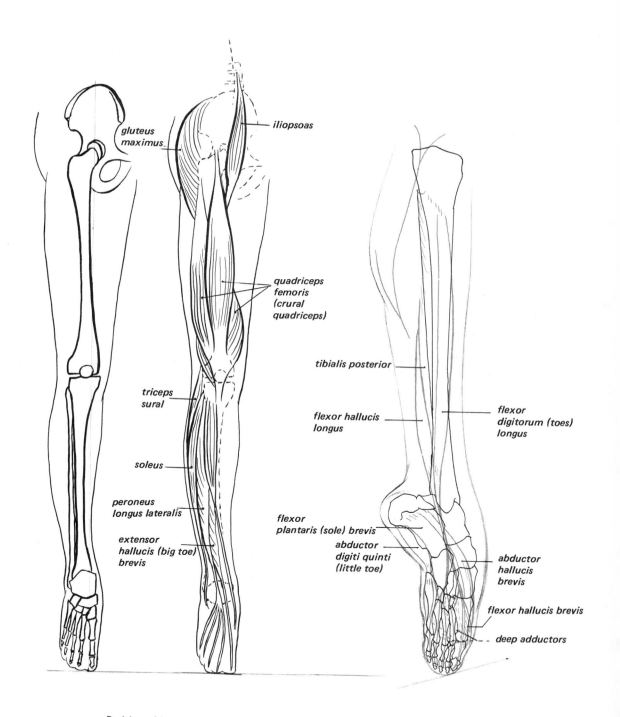

gluteus maximus

iliopsoas

quadriceps femoris (crural quadriceps)

triceps sural

soleus

peroneus longus lateralis

extensor hallucis (big toe) brevis

tibialis posterior

flexor hallucis longus

flexor digitorum (toes) longus

flexor plantaris (sole) brevis

abductor digiti quinti (little toe)

abductor hallucis brevis

flexor hallucis brevis

deep adductors

Position of bones and muscles for the *pointe*

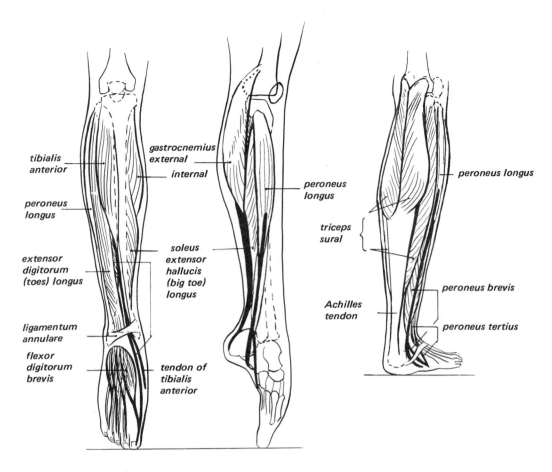

Leg muscles

action of these muscles gives the correct position to be maintained during the various exercises.

The bilateral contraction of the large dorsal and the large pectoral muscles raises up the thorax.

Balance of the head is obtained by controlling the degree of contraction—on the one hand, of the muscles of the nape of the neck, basically the splenial muscle, the large and small complexus;* on the other, by control of the sternocleidomastoid.

The legs are placed *en dehors* by the moderate contraction of the abducent and rotating muscles of the hips outward: posterior fasciculi† of the medium and small buttocks muscles, upper fasciculi of the large buttocks and pyramidal muscles; as well as by a complete contraction of the rotating muscles outward: external obturator, internal obturator, and gemellus muscles. For the legs to be held taut it is necessary to contract the crural quadriceps.

*Complexus—semispinal capitis.
†Fasciculi—bundles of muscles or nerve fibers.

The foot rests with the sole on the ground, the little toes well supported by the contraction of the common extensor of the toes contributing to the abduction and outward rotation of the foot.

Bend slowly: any violent movement at the beginning of a lesson is dangerous. Do not descend too low or stretch a cold muscle too much. The movement may be progressively increased as the muscle warms up. The second position that is more open than is customary in classical dance permits a workout for the muscles with more suppleness.

The *plié* is accomplished by the action of the weight, but if one allowed this to work on its own, one would have a terrible fall. It is therefore necessary to have full control over the buttocks muscles and the external rotators (obturators and gemellus muscles) that work in concentric contraction, as well as control over the quadricep muscle (vastus) and adductors which act as a check. To rise again, the adductors and quadricep (vastus) work in concentric contraction.

To return to the initial position, incline the trunk to one side, then to the other, taking care to make a very clean bend sidewards without making any incline either toward the front or toward the back.

To lean to the side, the trunk must not turn either forward or backward. Its lateral inclination is caused by the unilateral contraction of the spinal muscles of the corresponding side and by the oblique muscles.

Any exercise based on *pliés* may be included at the beginning of a lesson, provided it contains no violent movement or any that demands too great muscular effort:

> · *Pliés* in all the fundamental positions,
> · *Dégagés* followed by a *plié*, etc.

809   EXERCISE 2. ANKLE WORK

Back to the bar, in first position.

Battement in second, at barely *demi-hauteur* with the *pointe* raised. Lower the *pointe*. Place the *pointe* in second. Close in first. The same exercise with the other leg (Fig. 105).

To bring the leg *à la demi-hauteur*, the femoral quadriceps muscle is fully operative, as is the iliopsoas.

The bending of the foot on the leg[4] is due to the contraction of the anterior peroneal muscle and of the common extensor muscle of the toes which likewise cause the outward rotation and abduction of the foot. The anterior tibial and

---

[4] In anatomy, the leg is the part of the lower member included between the ankle and the knee. The part included between the knee and the hip is the thigh.

Figure 105. *(Photo: Jacques Aubin)*

extensor of the big toe are moderately contracted so as not to bring about the inward rotation of the foot. The sural triceps* is in extension.

When the foot is stretched, the sural triceps contracts and the pedal muscle, situated in the dorsal region of the foot, contributes to the extension of the toes. The lateral peroneal muscle contributes to the extension, abduction, and outward rotation of the foot. In addition, it plays an important role in the formation of the instep by pulling backward the first metatarsal.

Throughout the exercise, care should be taken to maintain the correct position of the body described at the beginning of the preceding exercise.

This exercise warms up the knee muscles while giving the ankle and instep a workout.

810   EXERCISE 3. RACCOURCIS

Back to the bar, in first position.

Bring up each leg alternately *au raccourci* in second, the *pointe* quite taut. Close in first.

*calf muscles

320

Figure 106 *(Photo: Jacques Aubin)*

The lateral bending of the hip on the pelvis is essentially caused by the unilateral contraction of the iliopsoas pivoting on the pelvis and by the contraction of the right anterior of the crural quadriceps.

Bring up each leg alternately *au raccourci en quatrième devant très croisée*, then open into second while remaining *au raccourci*. Close in first (Fig. 106).

The *quatrième devant très croisée* is accomplished because of the contraction of the adductor muscles of the thigh located in the internal region of the latter: pectinal and medium adductor muscles in a shallow plane; small adductor in a middle plane; large adductor in a deep plane. With the exception of the latter, these muscles also contribute to the bending of the thigh on the pelvis.

The passage from the *quatrième croisée* into the *seconde* is brought about by the contraction of the abductors and the external rotators.

This exercise forces the articulation of the hip.

The same exercise, leaving the *pointe* of the working leg constantly in contact with the other leg. This exercise causes less work for the hip, but more work for the muscles.

321

These exercises may be accompanied by a *plié* of the supporting leg during the movement with the starting and closing in first position, legs extended.

In the second part of the exercise, one can also lift the thigh higher after having come *au raccourci* in second, before closing in first.

These first three exercises have warmed up the muscles and limbered the joints. Now the preparation for the dance steps is going to be added.

811   EXERCISE 4. DEGAGES

In profile at the bar, in fifth.

Placing in position: the working arm, in rest position, rises in first, then opens into second.

For exercise 1 we indicated the muscles that give a correct position to the shoulder.

The arm rises in first by contraction of the anterior fasciculi of the deltoid muscle. It opens into second position by contracting the posterior fasciculi of the same muscle, which action is completed by the contraction of the supra-spinal, sub-spinal, and *petit rond* muscles.

The extension of the forearm with relation to the arm is due to the contraction of the brachial triceps and the elbow. Because the classical dance prohibits all angles, the straight angle included, this contraction is not total and at the same time the brachial biceps and anterior brachials are slightly contracted.

THE HAND IS IN "indifferent position." The extension of the hand with relation to the forearm is due to the action of the long and the short radial muscles.

The correct position of the thumb is obtained by a moderate contraction of the opponens pollicis.

The extensor muscle of the fingers is slightly contracted. The interossei controlling the middle finger are slightly more contracted than those connected with the other fingers. The natural extensor for the little finger is weakly contracted.

The arm must not be either too high or too low, and the hand must not fall (Fig. 107).

The fifth position imposes a strong bilateral contraction of the adductor and rotator muscles outside the thigh: pectinal, crural quadrate; small, medium, and large adductor of the thigh; as well as of the rotator muscles.

At the same time the arm is being placed in position, the head bent slightly forward and toward the bar moves, face front, then in profile to the side of the working arm. The eyes follow the movement of the hand. The head comes back face front for the exercise.

The head is placed in profile by the unilateral contraction of the large oblique muscle, of the large right anterior, and of the upper external fasciculus of the length

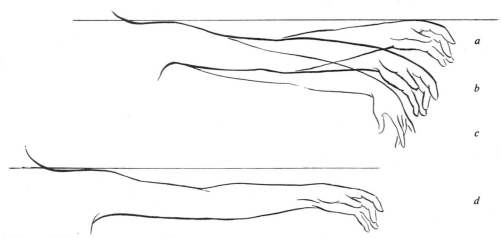

Figure 107. a, b, c, poor positions
d, good position

of the neck, corresponding to the side toward which the head is turned. At the same time the head is bent by the action of the large right anterior muscle and of the three fasciculi of the length of the neck.

The head becomes erect through release of the contraction of these muscles and by the action of the small right anterior muscle, on the side toward which the head is turned.

Finally, the head moves from one profile to the other by the contraction of the large oblique muscle of the opposite side.

This assuming of position repeats itself before all the exercises executed in profile at the barre.

During the exercises, failing any directions to the contrary, the working arm remains in second position.

The anterior foot moves in second *à la pointe*, is placed *à pointe*, is placed *à plat*, rises again *à la pointe*, and closes *en cinquième derrière* while both knees do a *plié*. Tighten again to resume the exercise with the same foot closing forward (Fig. 108).

The dancer may likewise do a *plié* in second and return *tendu* in fifth position.

This exercise may be done *en quatrième devant, en quatrième derrière,* or *en croix* (in a cross) (*quatrième devant*; second; *quatrième derrière*, second).

For the *dégagé* the *pointe* must remain in constant contact with the floor while the dancer is gliding on it. For the foot to remain fully *en dehors* it is necessary to give the impression of pushing the heel forward.

The impression of pushing the heel forward is obtained through the contraction of the short lateral peroneal muscle and of the long lateral peroneal muscle, whose tendons are inserted on the external side of the heel-bone.

Figure 108 *(Photo: Jacques Aubin)*

When the foot is placed *à plat* in second, care should be taken that the movement go progressively from the *pointe* toward the heel.

At this point there may be inserted any other exercise at the barre that is based on *dégagés*.

812   EXERCISE 5a. RONDS DE JAMBE A TERRE

In profile at the barre, in fifth position.

Eight *ronds de jambe à terre en dehors*, eight *en dedans*.

This exercise gives a workout for the hips and the toes and contributes to the opening-up of the leg.

Care must be taken not to do a *quatrième croisée devant* and, on the other hand, not to be satisfied with a *quatrième ouverte derrière*. During the passage into first the leg should be strongly forced *en dehors*. The *pointe* must glide neatly on the floor for the *dégagé* and during the half-circle.

During the exercises the muscular control must be precise so that no confusion will occur. In the *ronds de jambe,* the contractions of the muscles of the lesser member that is in movement have a tendency to cause an external rotation of the arm.

The working leg should rub gently on the floor but not be placed *à plat* the work of the transverse muscles, the large abdominal, and right pyramidal muscles of the abdomen are most important.

813   EXERCISE 5b. RONDS DE JAMBE A TERRE PLIES

The supporting leg does a *plié* during the half-circle and is stretched out once again in the passage into first position. A pause may be made between each one, or at every fourth.

This exercise provides a workout not only to the muscles and joints cited above but also to the muscles of the supporting hip and, in a more intense manner, to the opening-up of the legs.

To the exercising of the muscles of the working leg there is added the static contraction of the vastus muscles of the supporting leg.

Ronds de jambe à terre pliés are usually concluded with *penchés en avant* and *en arrière* with one foot *à la pointe, en quatrième devant* or *derrière.*

These exercises give a workout to the muscles of the trunk and gently soothe the spinal column.

For the *penché en avant*, the muscles of the back—large dorsal, spinal, quadrate of the lumbar region—work with restraint. Care must be taken to maintain the contraction of the spinal muscles in order to avoid a rounded back. The movement must start from the level of the pelvis and not from the shoulder.

For the *penché en arrière* there is the bilateral contraction of the spinal muscles, in particular the long dorsal and sacro-lumbar, at the beginning of the movement. Next the abdominal muscles (large right and oblique) work under restraint. The movement is limited by the meeting of the posterior apophyses of the spinal column. Persons whose dorsal and lumbar posterior apophyses are naturally too oblique will never be able to arch themselves very much.

814   EXERCISE 6a. FOOT ON THE BARRE

In profile at the barre, in fifth position.

Raise the anterior leg *au raccourci en quatrième devant*, then do a *développé en quatrième devant à la hauteur* and place the foot on the barre.

To place the foot on the barre *en quatrième devant,* the flexing of the hip on the pelvis is due to the iliopsoas. It contributes to the external rotation of the hip at the same time as do the posterior fasciculi of the small and medium buttocks muscles.

the upper fasciculi of the large buttocks muscle, the internal and external obturators, the upper and lower gemellus muscles, and the right anterior of the crural quadriceps.

The extension of the leg with relation to the hip is wholly governed by the crural quadriceps. The extension of the foot with relation to the leg is due to the contraction of the sural triceps and of the long lateral peroneal muscle.

The dancer does a *plié*, then extends the supporting foot twice.
The dancer leans the trunk forward, then backward.

When the body is leaning forward, the contraction of the spinal muscles avoids curving the spinal column. The contraction of the sub-clavian and of the small pectoral muscle must be very strong to keep the shoulders low.

After having done this exercise with feet *à plat*, it is executed *sur la demi-pointe*.

Next the dancer does a quarter-turn toward the barre and finds herself opposite it ready to do the same exercise in second position. A *penché de côté* is then done on alternate sides.

The *penché de côté* is accomplished by the unilateral contraction of the spinal muscles, especially the sacro-lumbar, the long dorsal, and the oblique muscles.

Finally, with another quarter-turn the dancer will be in profile at the bar, but on the other side, and will do the exercise *en quatrième derrière*. The *penché* will be done forward and backward.

This exercise provides a workout in extension for the muscle of the lower part of the hip, the opening-up of the legs (especially when it is done in second), and the limbering-up of the thigh. It prepares for the elevation of the leg.

For the whole time a leg is on the bar the hips must remain horizontal: the hip of the working leg has a tendency to be raised (Fig. 109).

During the *plié* the knee of the supporting leg must be pushed *en dehors* to the maximum. The toes are pressed quite flat; care must be taken not to fall on the big toe (Fig. 104).

The working leg rests with the heel on the barre and must remain perfectly *en dehors, tendue,* the *pointe* tight (*serrée*). The knee and the *pointe* have a tendency to relax during the movements of the trunk.

The abdominal muscles must be contracted. To derive the maximum benefit from this exercise it is important to make the muscles work while completely contracted. This strong contraction, followed by a total lengthening, develops the muscles in length rather than in thickness.

We have given directions to do two *pliés*. The dancer may do more. But the number is dependent upon the degree of training of the

Figure 109 *(Photo: Jacques Aubin)*

dancer. Muscular fatigue must not become too great. It is recommended that the dancer do no more than eight *pliés* on the same leg.

Each *plié* may be followed with a *relevé sur la demi-pointe*. In this case, the dancer remains *sur la demi-pointe* for the *penchés*.

When the foot on the bar is *en quatrième devant* or in second, the dancer may attach the toes to the barre as is indicated in paragraph 864.

En quatrième devant the working arm is in second position for the *pliés*. It rises *en couronne* for the *penchés*.

When the dancer is opposite the barre, both hands are on it during the *pliés*. The arm corresponding to the leg on the barre then rises *en couronne* through the intermediary of the second position. It remains in this position during the *penché*, the trunk leaning toward the side opposite that of the working leg. When the body becomes erect again, the working arm comes down through the intermediary of the second, the hand is placed on the barre, and the other arm carries out the same movement for the other *penché*.

327

Figure 110 *(Photo: Jacques Aubin)*

When the leg is on the barre *en quatrième derrière* the arm of the supporting leg is forward horizontal during the *pliés*. It is lowered slightly with relation to the trunk during the *penché en avant* and rises *en couronne* for the *penché en arrière*.

815   EXERCISE 6b. FOOT ON THE BARRE WITH NO SUPPORT

Opposite the barre, *en quatrième devant à la hauteur*, foot on the barre, arms in second.

Bend and extend the supporting leg. For the *pliés*, bear in mind what we have just said above.

The dancer may alternate a *plié* with foot *à plat* and a *plié* followed by a *relevé sur la demi-pointe*.

Penché en avant with the arms *en couronne*. *Penché en arrière* with the arms opening in second.

In profile at the barre, leg in second *à la hauteur*, foot on the barre, arms in second (Fig. 110).

Same exercise. The *penchés* are done to the side. The arm on the side where one is leaning bends behind the back, the other arm rises *en couronne*. The changing of arms is done through the intermediary of the second position.

Back to the barre, leg *en quatrième derrière à la hauteur*, foot on the barre, arms in second (Fig. 111).

Same exercise. During the *penché en avant* the arms descend to the front, rise in first position while the trunk is becoming erect, and rise *en couronne* for the *penché en arrière*. They open in second when the body becomes erect once again.

If the dancer has done *pliés* with *relevés*, in whatever position, the foot descends *à plat* for the *penchés*.

This exercise gives a great deal of work in balancing and requires very great muscular control. It causes much fatigue and it is recommended that the dancer change legs with each position. Particular care must be taken to see that the hips are horizontal on the outside of the leg on the barre (especially in second position) and that they are stretched tight (especially *en quatrième derrière*). In second the trunk must lean toward the barre only to the extent that its movement does not cause the hip to rise.

When the foot on the barre has no support, holding the leg *en dehors* necessitates a more intense contraction of the rotator muscles on the outside of the hip.

All the abdominal muscles play a role in maintaining one's balance.

Figure 111 *(Photo: Jacques Aubin)*

816 EXERCISE 7. BATTEMENTS SUR LE COU-DE-PIED

In profile at the barre, in fifth position.

The anterior foot glides on the floor in second until it is *à la pointe*, then it is lifted barely *à la demi-hauteur*, in continuous movement. The leg bends while striking in order to bring the foot behind the supporting ankle while keeping the *pointe* quite taut. The leg is stretched once again in second *à la demi-hauteur*, then bends while bringing the foot in front of the ankle of the other leg, the *pointe* slightly less taut, but the toes firmly *en dehors* (Fig' 112).

When one stretches the knee, one must contract the crural quadriceps. The extension of the foot with relation to the leg is chiefly due to the contraction of the long lateral peroneal muscle. One brings the foot against the ankle by means of a rapid contraction of the crural biceps. When one bends the ankle, the anterior peroneal muscle contracts.

Figure 112 *(Photo: Jacques Aubin)*

The exercise may be done in series with the supporting leg *tendue*; or with the supporting leg doing a *plié* at the same time as the working leg; or alternating a *battement tendu* and a *battement plié*; or raising the supporting foot *sur la demi-pointe* when the working leg is in second position.

Battements may also be done on the instep *en quatrième devant, quatrième derrière*, or *en croix*.

This exercise is one of those that develop speed in the lower leg. It prepares for the *batterie à croisements*.

The thigh of the working leg, once it has reached its position, must not move during the *battements*.

The degree of contraction of the iliopsoas muscle must be maintained consistently during the whole exercise.

Figure 113 *(Photo: Jacques Aubin)*

The *fouettés* must be done in a precise and rapid manner.

The ankle may also be bent when the dancer brings the working leg in front of or behind the other leg.

The work of the long peroneal muscle is now more intense, and this exercise contributes to the development of the instep.

817 EXERCISE 8a. DEVELOPPES

Back to the barre, in first position.

The leg rises *au raccourci en quatrième devant*. It is extended *en quatrième devant à la hauteur* while the supporting leg does a *plié*. When the position is obtained, the supporting leg is extended again without any lowering—even the slightest—of the working leg. Place the *pointe en quatrième devant*. *Penché* forward; *penché* backward while making the *pointe* glide lightly over the floor toward the front. Close in first position (Fig. 113).

332

Same exercise with the other leg. This ensemble may be repeated twice. If the exercise is done without the *penchés*, it will be repeated four times consecutively.

In profile at the barre, in fifth position.

Same exercise; with *penchés* to the side.

Facing the barre, in first.

Same exercise, but the dancer does a *penché* toward the rear, following which she places the foot to the back, sliding it along the floor so that it recedes from sight, and does a *penché* to the rear in this position.

During the whole exercise the hips must remain quite horizontal.

The balance of the pelvis is maintained by the bilateral contraction of the large right abdominal muscles and of the large buttocks muscles with the femur serving as a pivot, as well as by a controlled contraction of the lesser and medium buttocks muscles, taking the femur (thigh-bone) as a pivot. Care must be taken that this contraction is not more pronounced on one side than on the other, because the hip of the working leg tends to raise itself.

The *pointe* must be extended until it rises off the ground. It rises along the other leg, as if caressing it. The movement of tension is made starting from the *pointe*. The exercise of the *pointe* contributes to the lightening effect toward which the classical dance strives.

In order for the *pointe* of the working leg to be fully extended, the common extensor of the toes and the natural extensor for the big toe must contract. But care must be taken not to exaggerate the contraction of the big toe, because this would cause an inward rotation of the foot, which dancers refer to as "pruning-knife foot" (*pied en serpette*).

When the knee is taut, the knee-cap must be completely hollow.

The act of forcefully extending the leg, brought on by the strong contraction of the crural quadriceps, causes as a reaction a strong extension of the opposing muscles of the latter, situated on the posterior surface of the thigh: the crural biceps, semitendinosus, and semimembranosus.

The purpose of this exercise is to develop strength in the muscles, which allows a leg to be sustained in the air, an indispensable capability in adagios.

The maintenance of the leg *à la hauteur* is due to an intense contraction of the iliopsoas. This muscle, which has already been exercised a great deal since the beginning at the barre, must, at this point in the lesson, be capable of maintaining a degree of raised contraction for quite a long time without any relaxing and while preserving the same degree of abridgement (*raccourcissement*).

This exercise is the one in the series that were described which least contracts the muscles; it permits a more controlled workout.

It is desirable to replace this exercise occasionally with one of the three which we are going to describe. The dancing master will select the gradation of rhythm suitable to the strength of his pupils.

818   EXERCISE 8b. DEVELOPPES WITH PLIES.

In profile at the barre, in fifth position.

Do a *développe a la demi-hauteur* in fourth in front of the anterior leg. Bend the supporting leg, without the working foot touching the floor. Bend the working leg in order to bring the heel in front of the ankle of the other leg, which is always bent; stretch the knee of the supporting leg, but do not place the working foot on the ground.

Continue doing the same exercise in second, *en quatrième derrière,* and again in second.

Next, still without having placed the working foot on the ground, resume the exercise while raising the supporting foot *sur la demi-pointe* before doing *développé* and while resting the heel at the moment when the knee bends. Do not rest the working foot.

Do the same exercise in *développé à la hauteur,* once with the supporting foot *à plat* and once raising it *sur la demi-pointe.*

The *relevé sur la demi-pointe* is accomplished by an extension of the foot with relation to the leg, caused by the contraction of the sural triceps pulling on the heel-bone by way of the Achilles tendon.

Because this exercise is very difficult and is very taxing on the muscles of the supporting leg, it is particularly recommended for male dancers. It builds strength and gives a workout to the ankle and the knee. It is a preparation for the *saut* and it helps the dancer to acquire balance.

Care must be taken not to use up one's strength in pulling on the barre. Pay attention to balance: the vertical of the center of gravity must pass through the supporting foot. This may be checked while releasing the hold on the barre without any change of posture.

Because the *saut* is accomplished by a very strong and very rapid contraction of the sural triceps, this exercise prepares for it by causing those muscles to work.

When the working foot is placed on the ground, the iliopsoas may be totally contracted. But when the foot is not placed, this muscle remains partially contracted. If this exercise is done by a person with insufficient training and whose muscles are not ready for such a workout, there is great risk of muscle shortening.

During this exercise, numerous msucles are called upon to work intensively. This demands a large consumption of oxygen. It is necessary to assure a sufficient irrigation of the muscle, otherwise there would be an accumulation of lactic acid and resulting cramps.

819 EXERCISE 8c. GRANDS RONDS DE JAMBE

In profile at the barre, in fifth position.

En dehors: do a *développé en quatrième devant à la hauteur*, move in second *hauteur* then *en quatrième derrière à la hauteur*. Do a *raccourci* in second in order to move once again *en quatrième devant à la hauteur* or else close *en cinquième derrière*.

The principal muscles concerned are the rotators of the thigh *en dehors*: the iliopsoas muscles during the *développé*, then the posterior fasciculi of the lesser and medium buttocks muscles, the pyramidal muscle, the internal and external obturator muscles, and the quadrate of the lumbar region.

En dedans: do a *développé en quatrième derrière à la hauteur*, move in second *à la hauteur,* then *en quatrième devant à la hauteur*. *Raccourci* in second to move again *en quatrième derrière* or close *en cinquième devant*.

The principal muscles involved are: the crural quadrate and the lower fasciculi of the large buttocks muscle, as well as the adductor muscles of the thigh and of the pectineus.

Throughout the exercise and especially during the passage from *quatrième derrière* into second, one must avoid contraction of the muscles that cause the internal rotation of the thigh: anterior fasciculi of the lesser and middle buttock, and the tensor fascia lata.

The dancer may link together several series of *grands ronds de jambe* of each type or alternate *ronds de jambe en dehors* and *ronds de jambe en dedans*. If she wishes to close during a series of *ronds de jambe* of the same type, she does it in first position.

In the *grand rond de jambe en dedans*, during the passage from *quatrième derrière* to second, the joint of the hip must open up and rotate as soon as possible. Particular care must be taken in this regard.

This exercise requires more strength than the preceding one; it must not be performed, and certainly not in sustained sequence, except by dancers who have already acquired muscular strength and control. Otherwise it could present more drawbacks than advantages.

The *grand rond de jambe* may also be done starting with a *battement* in fourth rather than with a *développé*.

820 EXERCISE 8d. RONDE DE JAMBE SOUTENUS IN SECOND POSITION

In profile at the barre, in fifth position.

Battement or *développé* to obtain a second *à la hauteur*. Sustained *ronds de jambe en dedans* or *en dehors*, according to the various rhythms.

For example: two slow *ronds de jambe en dehors* followed by three fast ones. Same sequence. Two slow *ronds de jambe*, three fast, two slow, two fast, and close in fifth.

Or: two *ronds de jambe en dehors*, close *en cinquième derrière*. Two *ronds de jambe en dedans*, close *en cinquième devant*.

During the *ronds de jambe* the principal muscles in action are the sartorial muscle, the *droit interne* and the popliteal muscle.

The thigh of the working leg must not move once it has reached *hauteur*.

To keep the thigh immobile in second position, it is necessary throughout the exercise to maintain the same degree of contraction of the iliopsoas and of the abductor muscles of the thigh: posterior fasciculi of the small and large buttocks muscles, the upper fasciculi of the large buttocks muscle, the pyramidal muscle.

When the *ronds de jambe* are done slowly, a pause is observed in the most extreme position (the one when the angle formed by the hip and the lower leg is open the widest). In rapid *ronds de jambe*, only the last one in each series (of two, three, or four *ronds de jambe*) has this pause.

The extension of the leg into second position is obtained by a contraction of the femoral quadriceps; a limited contraction because the leg does not attain a total extension with relation to the thigh.

This exercise adds practice in speed to practice in lifting.

821 EXERCISE 9. PETITS BATTEMENTS SUR LE COU-DE-PIED

In profile at the barre, in fifth position.

Slightly raise the anterior leg in order to bring the heel in front of the ankle of the supporting leg. Then move the heel behind the ankle of the supporting leg. *Dégagé pointe à terre* in second. The same exercise but in the backward-forward direction. Continue, alternating the two manners.

After a series of eight or sixteen *petits battements,* do four passages backward-forward, or vice versa, followed by the *dégagé*.

Conclude with a series of *petits battements sans dégagé*, feet *à plat*,then *sur la demi-pointe*. Next, still *sur la demi-pointe,* strike rapidly in front of the ankle.

This exercise may be done while bending the supporting leg at the moment of the *dégagé*; or by rising *sur la demi-pointe* for the *petits battements;* or by doing a *développé à la demi-hauteur* instead of the *dégagé*; or with the *dégagé en croix*.

The ankle is slightly bent during the *petits battements* and is extended at the *dégagé*. The dancer may also keep it always taut. For the *frappés devant* the *pointe* is fully extended.

During the whole exercise, the short lateral peroneal muscle causing the outward abduction and rotation of the foot is contracted.

The flexion of the foot is due to the common extensor of the toes and of the anterior peroneal muscle, which are likewise outward abductors and rotators of the foot. Furthermore, the common extensor muscle of the toes stretches the toes with respect to the corresponding metatarsals. When the foot is extended while remaining *en dehors,* there is a contraction of the lateral peroneal muscle which also augments the concavity of the plantar arch.

The *dégagés* furnish a workout for the extensor and flexors of the thigh: crural quadriceps and biceps.

This exercise develops speed in the lower part of the leg and prepares for the *batterie à croisement*.

822   EXERCISE 10. GRANDS BATTEMENTS

In profile at the barre, in fifth position.

There are a great number of exercises at the base of *grands battements*. We shall give a few examples.

· Eight *grands battements en quatrième devant*, four *grands battements* of which the first is finished *pointe à terre en quatrième devant*; the three that follow fall back in this position. Four *grands battements* separated by a *dégagé en quatrième devant*.

· The same exercise in second, then *en quatrième derrière*.

· One *battement tendu* followed by a *battement* with the supporting leg *pliée* in a series of eight in each position.

· One *battement followed by a battement relevé sur la demi-pointe or sur la pointe*, with a pause for the working leg *à la hauteur*. In series of eight in each position.

· *Battement* with *développé*; supporting leg *tendue* or *pliée*. In series of eight in each position.

Care should be taken that the *pointe* glide along the floor as long as possible before being lifted up and that it glide in the same manner at the closing.

The lifting power must flow from the *pointe* and not from the thigh. This is particularly important for the *battements* ending *pointe à terre*. Attention should be paid to the precision of the positions *à la hauteur* or *à terre*, and to the speed of the intermediary movements.

For the *grands battements en quatrième devant* the contractions are made in the following order: lateral long peroneal muscle and sural triceps; *droit anterieur* of the crural quadriceps, tensor fasciae latae; iliopsoas and more intense contraction of the *droit anterieur* of the crural quadriceps.

For the *battements* in second position there is added the exercise of the abductors of the thigh.

For the *battements en quatrième derrière*, the extension of the thigh is essentially brought on by the contraction of the large buttocks muscle, then of the quadrate of the lumbar region.

The contraction of these different muscles involves the extension of opposing muscles, in particular, the flexor muscles of the leg with relation to the thigh: femoral biceps, semitendinosus, and semimembranosus. In the *grands battements,* because the contraction is intense and rapid, it brings about a sudden and very strong extension of the opposing muscles. If these muscles are insufficiently prepared, injuries may result.

Various combinations of *battements* may be composed by changing position each time.

Example: *battement en quatrième devant croisée*; *battement en quatrième devant ouverte*; *battement* in second; *battement en quatrième derrière ouverte*; *battement en quatrième derrière croisée*; *battement* in second.

For dancers already possessing a sure technique, the *battements* may be embellished with *épaulements* and with varied positions of the trunk, the head, and the working arm.

In no case should the trunk start to bend back during the *battements.*

The first aim of the *battements* is to improve the elevation of the leg. This contributes to the opening up of the hip joint. They make for the lightness which is necessary to the execution of steps involving one leg in the air and for delicacy in the closings in fifth.

There should never be more than sixteen *battements* with the same leg.

The choice of this or that series of battements may be made according to the technical level of the dancers. It is good to continue the same exercise in *battements* for a certain length of time (one week, for example, for dancers exercising every day).

Figure 114. *(Photo: Jacques Aubin)*

823   EXERCISE 11. BATTEMENTS EN CLOCHE*

In profile at the barre, in fifth position.

Battements en cloche may be done with a pause in first, or in succession. They may also be done very rapidly *à la demi-hauteur*.

The body must be kept fully erect, stretched upward. The hips remain fully horizontal. Attention should be paid to the correct passage into first position.

This exercise develops speed in the lower part of the leg.

824   EXERCISE 12. FOOT IN THE HAND

In profile at the barre, in fifth position.

Raccourci en quatrième devant, take the heel in the hand, lengthen *en quatrième devant*, pass into second (Fig. 114), pass again into *quatrième devant*, then into second without releasing the heel; pass *au raccourci* into second and resume the exercise stretching into

*Suggesting the movement of a tolling bell.

quatrième devant, still without releasing the heel. Conclude by releasing the heel in second while keeping the leg as high as possible for a few seconds before closing in fifth.

Keep the leg well *en dehors*. This exercise must be done with a great deal of suppleness, without any use of force, because it can be dangerous and may cause muscular injury.

In this exercise the movement of extending the leg with relation to the thigh and of flexing the thigh on the pelvis is caused by the pulling with the hand on the heel and not by a voluntary contraction of the muscles of the lower limb.

This exercise, then, acts especially to extend the muscles, in particular the flexor muscles of the leg.

The tension of the leg is assured by the crural quadriceps. Its failure to contract would allow the knee to bend.

The leg may be forced backward also by taking the knee in the hand starting from a *raccourci* in second position and pushing the leg into *attitude*.

Care must be taken not to let the shoulder and the hip slide backward.

These various exercises increase the possibility of elevation of the leg.

The foot in the hand is optional. Given the considerable work of extension which it involves, it can only be done with muscles that are warmed up and sufficiently trained.

825   EXERCISE 13. PLIE RELEVE SUR POINTES

Face to the barre.

· In second position. *Demi-plié.* Raise both feet *sur la demi-pointe* or *sur la pointe* while keeping the knees bent. Stretch. Place the heels in position.

Repeat four times.

· In second. Raise both feet *sur la pointe* or *la demi-pointe*. Bend the knees. Place the heels while keeping the knees bent. Stretch (Fig. 115).

Repeat four times.

· In first or in second. *Plier. Relever sur la pointe* while stretching. Remain in balance *sur les pointes* in first or second. Raise the arms *en couronne*.

Echappés may also be done *sur les pointes; relevés* on one foot starting from a first position with release of the working leg in second *à*

Figure 115. *(Photo: Jacques Aubin)*

la demi-hauteur, alternately with each leg: *relevés* on one foot *en raccourci,* to the front or to the back starting from a fifth, etc.

Do not hollow out the back. Care must be taken to remain firmly *sur la pointe* without letting the ankle turn to the left or right. Descend not by falling suddenly on the heel but by successively placing all the parts of the sole of the foot starting from the toe.

This exercise warms up the muscles of the foot and develops the arch of the instep—so necessary to the good execution of *pointes.* It gives strength for *relevés.*

When the foot rises *sur la pointe,* the following muscles contract to stretch the foot on the leg:

· The lateral peroneal muscle, which also promotes the outward rotation of the foot and heightens the arch of the instep while drawing the posterior end of the metatarsus backward and outward.

341

· The sural triceps, whose contraction must be limited in order not to cause adduction and rotation inward.

· The small plantar muscle, whose concomitant action is very weak.

The following muscles assist the rising of the foot *sur la pointe*:

· The short flexor muscle of the big toe, whose action is supported by the abductor muscle of the big toe.

· The lumbricales, which bend the first phalanx of the toes and extend the other two.

· The dorsal and plantar interossei, bending the first phalanges of the toes.

The maintenance of balance *sur la pointe* is favored by the contraction of the foot muscle or the short extensor muscle of the toes, which extends the first phalanges and bends them toward the outside.

The contraction of the long extensor muscle, which flexes the second phalanx against the first, might cause broken toes.

826 EXERCISE 14. SUPPLENESS

Back to the barre, in standard first position.

Relever sur les demi-pointes. Lean the body forward as low as possible. Bring the trunk erect. Place the heels. Bend both knees, keeping one in front of the other. Tighten the knees while arching the back vigorously, the head leaning backward, and while remaining still *sur les demi-pointes.* Return by stages to the erect position. Place the heels.

Do this exercise four times in succession, eight times for dancers in very good form.

Tighten the knees well when the trunk bends forward. Push the trunk as far as possible in the form of an arc for the second part of the movement.

This exercise makes the spinal column supple, warms up and provides a workout for the muscles of the back.

During the *penché en avant* the back remains flat by means of a slight bilateral contraction of the different spinal muscles which are extensors of the spinal column.

The flexing of the trunk toward the front is controlled by the contraction of the posterior muscles of the trunk. Care must be taken not to contract the flexor muscles of the spine: *grand droit*, large and small oblique muscles—this would cause the flexing of the spinal column called "dos rond" (round back).

The second part of the exercise, after the *plié*, extends the thigh with relation to the pelvis: contraction of the buttocks; then the leg, with relation to the thigh:

contraction of the quadriceps; and finally, the foot in relation to the leg: contraction of the sural triceps. It is accompanied by an arching of the spinal column: total bilateral contraction of the spinal muscles: lumbar quadrate, *masse commune,* spinal transverse, long dorsal, sacro-lumbar, epispinal, and interspinal.

The position of the arms involves the bilateral contraction of the long dorsals and of the trapezia.

827 EXERCISE 15. ADAGIO AT THE BARRE

In profile at the barre, in fifth position.

Plier: The arm that was in second descends, then rises *en couronne* while passing in front of the trunk as the dancer is making herself erect. Rise on both *pointes. Développer en quatrième devant,* the arm remaining *en couronne.* Place the leg *en quatrième devant,* lift the other leg extended to the rear; the arm is lowered outstretched toward the front while the leg rises as high as possible to the rear. Stand up straight. Place the leg in fifth *sur la pointe.* Do a quarter-turn in order to arrive facing the barre. *Développer* in second while remaining *sur la pointe. Raccourci in second position.* Pass into *attitude.* Stretch out *en arabesque* while drawing backward until the arms are taut. The supporting leg is still *sur la pointe* and taut. Return to *attitude.* Release the bar with one hand, then with both, while trying to maintain balance.

Care should be taken in the descent from the *arabesque* not to initiate the movement of the shoulders. The line formed by the working arm, the trunk, and the working leg must be considered as rigid and not to be distorted in the course of the movement. The knee of the supporting leg must not bend.

In the *arabesque* the arm is brought forward by the action of the anterior fasciculi of the corresponding deltoid and pectoral muscles. The foot is extended in relation to the leg; the leg in relation to the thigh, and the thigh in relation to the pelvis; the arm is extended in relation to the trunk, in such a way that these different segments form a continuous line. When this position is obtained, the contraction of the muscles absolutely must not vary. In particular, care must be taken not to relax the anterior fasciculi of the deltoid, because this would cause the arms to fall.

In *attitude* the trunk is vertical. The spinal muscles—lumbar quadrate, spinal transverse, long dorsal, sacro-lumbar or ilio-costal, epispinal, and interspinal—are contracted bilaterally in an equal fashion. The thigh and the leg are on the same horizontal plane perpendicular to the trunk. The position of the thigh is obtained by the contraction of the adductors and rotators outward: posterior fasciculi of the small and medium buttocks muscles, superior fasciculi of the large buttocks muscle, and pyramidal to which there is added the action of the external and internal obturators and of the gemini muscles which are solely outward rotators from the thigh.

828

All the exercises we have just described must be done identically with each leg.

After the barre exercises themselves, the dancer may do a few exercises still using it as a support, either to gain suppleness or to prepare for steps.

EXERCISE 16. TO GAIN SUPPLENESS

Back to the barre.

Lift one leg *en attitude*. Place the knee on the barre while keeping the trunk straight but without drawing the shoulders back, which the dancer tends to do, because she holds onto the barre from both sides of the body and from behind it. *Plier* and stretch the supporting leg.

Face to the barre.

Same exercise with the leg *au raccourci en quatrième devant*, very much *en dehors* the lower part of the leg placed on the barre, full-length.

These exercises may also be done while doing a *relevé sur la pointe* or *demi-pointe.*

Face to the barre.

Raise one leg in second *à la hauteur*, place the foot on the barre. Slide the foot along the barre as far as possible. Straighten up again and slide in the other direction, again as far as possible.

When all these exercises have been done with one leg they must be done with the other. It is not necessary to do all these exercises at each lesson. The decision is up to the dancing master.

829   EXERCISE 17. PREPARATION FOR *FOUETTES*

In profile at the barre, in fifth position.

Raise the anterior foot *au raccourci. Développer* while bending the supporting leg. Rise *sur la pointe* while causing the working leg to do a *rond de jambe* which will bring it into *attitude*. Descend while doing a *plié*, foot *à plat*. Do a *tour* on the side of the working leg while doing a *relevé*. This turn, having the technique of *détournés*, brings the free leg *au raccourci en quatrième devant*. Close *en cinquième devant.*

Care should be taken to poise the trunk well, the shoulder remaining on the same plane as the thigh, which must stay strictly in second.

830   EXERCISE 18. PREPARATION FOR *TEMPS DE FLECHE* *

Back to the barre, in fifth position.

Temps de flèche with each leg, alternately.

Care should be taken not to let the trunk draw back toward the rear.

The dancer may likewise exercise at the barre for *entrechats*, *cabrioles*, etc.

In the Center of the Floor**

831

Work in the center of the dance floor usually begins with **little exercises** akin to those done at first at the barre, but often involving a shifting in space. This allows the dancer to acquire good control of balance without the barre and also exercises the ankles.

· *Dégagés* in second position with the posterior foot closing in front, alternately with each leg. Eight *en descendant*, then eight *en remontant* (anterior foot, closing to the rear).

These *dégagés* may also be combined with *pliés*.

· Lift the posterior leg alternately *au raccourci* in second position and close forward. Eight times *en descendant* and eight times *en remontant*.

· The same thing with *battements*.

These different exercises may also be done with various rhythms—for example, two slow and four rapid beats.

There can be an infinite number of variations from more complex exercises.

· Four *battements* in second position *à la demi-hauteur* on the instep, without closing

four *petits battements* on the instep, with the same leg

four *petits ronds de jambe soutenus en dedans in second position*, with the same leg

four *battements* in second position *à la demi-hauteur* on the instep, closing in fifth.

*Arrow movement.
**Milieu.

· Same thing with the other leg, then a repeat of the whole exercise, *en remontant,* with *ronds de jambe en dehors.*

832

Next come the **ports de bras.** They are at the basis of the series of the classical *ports de bras* described in paragraphs 577 to 587, and executed in place or with simple shifts utilizing *dégagés, temps de cuisse, battements, fondu,* etc.

Example of *ports de bras* without shifting:

In fifth position, right foot forward. Raise the arms in first and open into second (§ 578). Lean forward and, in straightening up, do the *port de bras* in fifth (§ 580). *Port de bras* in third (§ 579) successively with each arm. *Port de bras composé* (compound) in third (§ 582).

833

The *ports de bras* constitute a preparation for the adagio. The other element making up the adagios will be practiced more specially with the **exercises in balance.** Here are a few examples.

· *Développé en quatrième devant à la demi-hauteur.* Place the *pointe à terre en quatrième devant* while doing a *plié* with the supporting leg. Pass the working leg into first position while bending it and while leaving the supporting leg *pliée. Relever sur la demi-pointe* while stretching as the working leg rises *en quatrième derrière.* Close *en cinquième derrière.*

The same thing with the other leg.

· *Dégagé en quatrième devant.* Lift the supporting leg *sur la demi-pointe* without causing the angle it makes with the working leg to vary. Close in first position while bending both legs and descending gently from the *demi-pointe.* Stretch.

The same thing to the rear. Repeat the whole exercise on the other side.

· *Développé en quatrième devant à la demi-hauteur. Relever sur la demi-pointe. Grand rond de jambe soutenu à la demi-hauteur en dehors* ending *en arabesque,* the foot of the supporting leg being still *sur la demi-pointe.* Descend gently, foot *à plat,* with a *plié.* Close *en cinquième derrière,* stretching once again.

The same thing from the other side.

· *Plier* in first position. *Relever sur les demi-pointes. Développer en quatrième devant à la hauteur.* Close in first position *sur les demi-pointes.* Descend, feet *à plat*, doing a *plié* and extending once more.

The same thing with the other leg.

Same exercise *in second position* with *plié* in second.

In fifth, *plier*. Rise up again *sur les demi-pointes.* Do a quarter-turn on the side of the anterior foot, taking that foot as a pivot. *Développer en arabesque ouverte.* Gently bring down the supporting foot *à plat.* Half a promenade turn in order to be placed *en arabesque croisée.* Place the *pointe* of the working leg *en quatrième derrière.* Close in fifth.

The same thing on the other side.

Very experienced dancers will do balancing steps *sur les pointes.* Exercises of this type may likewise be placed after the adagio and before the turn.

834

After all these preparations comes the **adagio composé**, of which we shall give a few examples.

In fifth, right foot forward. *Plier* (§ 217). Rising up again, do a *port de bras* in fifth (§ 580) and bring the arms down in the *position de départ* (§ 38).

Disengage the right foot and place it *en quatrième devant croisée.* Raise the left leg *en arabesque.* Bend back *au raccourci* in second position and then extend into *quatrième devant à la hauteur.* The arms, after being passed through the *position de départ,* while coming from the *arabesque,* rise in third, the upraised arm corresponding to the supporting leg.

Place the left foot forward and raise the right leg *en arabesque,* the arms taking the *arabesque* position. *Grand rond de jambe soutenu à la hauteur* with the right leg; the arms open into second. Place the right foot in fourth and raise the left leg *en attitude croisée. Relever sur la pointe. Fondu* with *port de bras tournant* (§ 584).

Rise while keeping the posterior foot *sur la pointe* and lift the left leg *en arabesque* as soon as the right leg is taut. Promenade turn. *Relever sur pointe.* Close in fifth.

835

In fifth, right foot forward. *Dégager* the right foot *en quatriéme croisée*; place it *à plat.* Raise the left foot onto *pointe,* slide it toward the back while flexing the right knee. Do a *détourné à terre* (§ 384).

347

Pass the left leg into *arabesque* going through the first position while raising the right foot *sur la pointe*. Rest it again *à plat*.

Lean forward while simultaneously raising the leg to the rear (the arm, the trunk, and the working leg form a rigid line which pivots as a whole about the hip-joint). Rise up again. *Temps de cuisse* (§ 114). Pass the left leg into *quatrième devant*. Place the foot *à plat*. Two *tours* in a single impulse, *relevés en dehors* taken in fourth (§ 426), terminated *en fondu croisé*. *Ports de bras*. Rise again with the right foot *à la pointe*. Final pose: trunk slightly *épaulé* to the left, head in profile to the left, arms in third, the right arm raised.

836

In fifth, right foot forward. Start a *battement arrondi* (§ 119), which stops in second *à la hauteur*. Reversing the trunk, pass into *arabesque* without changing the direction of the right leg. Close *en cinquième derrière*. Same thing on the other side, but when *en arabesque* lean the trunk forward (taking into account the directions given in the preceding paragraph concerning such a *penché en avant*). Rise up again. *Temps de cuisse* (§ 114). Pass the left foot to the front, place it *à plat* in fourth. Raise the right leg *en arabesque*. *Détourné à la hauteur*. The right leg is then *en arabesque quatrième devant à la hauteur*: it passes into first and rises to the rear *en arabesque*. *Pas de bourrée* (§ 192) terminating in fourth.
Raise the left foot (the one that is posterior) *sur la pointe* while opening the arms in second. Place the left foot *à plat*. Raise the right foot *sur la pointe* while putting the arms in third, the raised arm corresponding to the posterior foot. Raise the right arm forward *en couronne*. Open the arms in second while placing the right foot *à plat*. Bend back the right arm in sixth position (§ 44). The dancer is thus in preparation in fourth for the *tours*. Do a *tour enveloppé relevé* (§ 431). This turn can be finished while placing the left foot *sur la pointe* to the rear, in *demi-quatrième* (§ 57) with the arms lateral, half-vertical (§ 520).

837

Next comes the practice for **tours**.

The dancer may do either sequences of *tours* of the same type: *pas de bourrée, tour relevé en dehors* (§ 426) or *en dedans* (§ 427), etc. alternately with each foot, with one, two, or three *tours* from the same impulse; or more complex sequences in combination with varied techniques or while making use of the series studied in paragraphs 800 through 802.

It will be recalled that in turns the correct position of the trunk must be maintained, with no relaxation during the rotation.

838

The former sequences are practiced more or less in position. Then the dancer will do diagonals of *piqués* (§ 404), *enveloppés* (§ 413), *tours posés* (§ 418), etc. Occasionally several types of *tours* will be combined:

· A *tour fouetté enveloppé* (§ 431). Close *en cinquième devant*. *Pas de bourrée détourné* (§ 386). Repeat.

· *Relevé*, bringing the posterior foot *au raccourci*. Close *en cinquième derrière* while placing the arms in sixth (§ 44). Do two *tours relevés en dehors* (428) in a single thrust. Close *en cinquième derrière*. *Détourné* on both feet (§ 385). *Echappé sur les pointes* in second position with change of feet. Repeat.

839

Next come the **pas composés** (compound steps), with *tours* and *pointes* as their basis. These consist of varied sequences, combinations of classical sequences (§ 744 to 789), or inventions of the dancing master.

· A *tour fouetté détourné* (§ 434) ending *en arabesque* followed by two *relevés en arabesque* without moving the working leg. *Passé-relevé-arabesque* (§ 186) joined directly with the working leg. Two *relevés en arabesque* without moving the working leg.

The same thing on the other side.

At this point in the lesson certain series will be found, such as that of the *pas de bourrée* (§ 792), *ronds de jambe* (§ 797), etc. One may even practice fragments from classical variations, or actual variations for the purpose of exercise.

840

Jumping exercises may begin with simple series: *changements de pied, sissonnes, échappés, assemblées*, etc.

Next come the steps involving the *batterie* and the *grands sauts*.

We shall give only one example of a jumping exercise, but the variety is great and the combinations infinite, each teacher adapting his exercises to the level of his pupils and to the intended purpose of the particular lesson.

Échappé sauté (§ 299), *fermé* (§ 300). *Temps de pointe relevé* on both *pointes* (§ 173). *Changement de pied* (§ 336).

The same thing on the other side.

Passé-cabriole en quatrième devant (§ 255). Place the working foot *à plat en quatrième devant. Pas de bourrée* (§ 192), terminating in fourth. *Relever* on the anterior foot *en arabesque croisée* (§ 71).

Pas de bourrée-jeté (§ 475). *Pas de bourrée détourné* (§ 386). *Pas de bourrée* (§ 192).

The same thing on the other side.

Temps de pointe relevé on both feet (§ 173). *Changement de pied* (§ 336). Repeat.

Three *changements des pieds*. One *temps de pointe relevé* on both feet while raising the arms in first position (§ 39) and opening them in second (§ 40). Descend *à plat* in fifth.

This exercise may be done as we have just described it—that is, with *batterie.* It is made more difficult by doing an *échappé battu 3* (§ 353), replacing the *changements de pieds* with *entrechats 3* (§ 337) and doing the *cabriole* with beating step (§ 364).

Finally, dancers possessing a very good technique may be asked to do *échappés battus 5* (§ 353) and *entrechats 6* (§ 340).

Thus one can, with the same exercise, show a progression in practice, whether the same dancer, after having familiarized herself with the simple form, executes the more difficult forms, or in a class in which the dancers are at different levels and each one is required to exercise according to her ability.

841

The following exercise will combine *sauts* and *tours,* making the synthesis of the preceding exercise.

Échappé on both *pointes* (§ 299), *fermé* (§ 300). *Temps de pointe relevé* on both feet (§ 173). *Changement de pied* (§ 336).

The same thing on the other side.

Passé, développé relevé en quatrième ouverte devant (§ 183). Place the working foot *à plat en quatrième devant. Pas de bourrée* terminating in fourth. *Relever* on the anterior foot *en arabesque croisée* (§ 71). *Pas de bourrée-jeté* (§ 475). Two *tours posés* (§ 418).

The same thing on the other side.

Pas de bourrée détourné ending in fourth (§ 386). *Relever* on both *pointes* while remaining in fourth. Descend *à plat,* bending the knees and placing the arms in sixth (§ 44), the preparatory position for a turn. Two *tours en dehors* (§ 426). *Pas de bourrée détourné* (§ 386).

Final pose while disengaging the anterior foot *en quatrième devant* (§ 107) and opening the arms in second (§ 40) by way of the first position (§ 39).

It will be noted that this exercise contains elements dependent on similar techniques, but some of them belong to the *sauts*, others to the *pas à terre* or to the *tours*. For example, the *échappé* which is *sauté* in paragraph 840 is on both *pointes* in paragraph 841; the *passé-cabriole en quatrième devant* of paragraph 840 is replaced by a *passé relevé* in paragraph 841, etc.

This procedure makes it possible to exercise on a precise point in the midst of a sequence without part of the attention being diverted by the effort of memory which the execution of a new exercise necessitates.

At this point in the lesson may be placed the exercise in variations or fragments of variations from the repertoire.

842

Next comes the exercise in speed, quick and brilliant little steps belonging usually to the categories of *pas à terre, sauts simple,* and the *petite batterie: relevés sur une pointe* with *développés* with the other leg (§ 183) *en quatrième* devant—*ouverte* or *croisée*—or in second, the *développé* done at a low elevation, the rhythm very rapid; clicking steps *sur les pointes: temps de pointe piqués en descendant* (§ 165) or *en remontant* (§ 167); *emboîtes* (§ 151); *échappés sur pointes* (§ 299); *petits pas de bourrée enchaînés* without descending from the *pointe* (§ 193); *petits soubresauts* on both *pointes* (§ 249); *petits jetés* (§ 266 and 269); *petites sissonnes* (§ 279 to 283); *entrechats 3* and *4* (§ 337 and 338); *brisés* (§ 351); *échappés battus* (§ 353); *petites cabrioles battues* very low (§ 363 to 367); etc.

Afterward, these elements are combined in sequences.

One may be surprised to see at this point in the lesson a particularly tiring workout and one that requires a great deal of breath. This particular order of exercise is deliberate. In fact, very brilliant and rapid sequences are used on the stage especially in codas, particularly at the end of the classical *pas de deux.* They therefore are brought in after the variations and the dancer must in due course be trained to do them without tiring.

843

Toward the end of the lesson is the exercise in circular series (*manèges*). *Manèges* may be composed of always the same step: *piqués*

(§ 404), *pas de bourrée-jeté* (§ 475), *pas tombé-coupé-jeté* (§ 469), *petits jetés en tournant* (§ 467), *déboulés* (§ 394), etc.

There are other *manèges* composed of different steps—for example, two *piqués* and two *déboulés*. Certain circular series, such as those of the ballet *Suite en Blanc* (Lifar), are veritable *petites variations*.

As in the preceding paragraph, the placing of the *manège* in the lesson is determined by the use of circular steps on the stage: traditionally they conclude the variations and codas.

844

After the exercise in *manège*, or occasionally in place of it, may be found the exercise in *fouettés* (§ 455).

One might start out by exercising with simple *relevés* accompanied by a *rond de jambe soutenu* with the working leg, but without turning. Then there might follow some series of *fouettés*—8, 16, 24, 32— according to the strength of the dancer. Eventually, one might have some *fouettés* executed with variations (§ 457) by those dancers who already possess an excellent technique.

As in the other exercises, the *fouettés* may be done on both sides, but it is certain—as is true of other *tours*—that the dancer will not be able to achieve the same performance with both legs, because the greater dexterity in one direction or the other will make itself quite evident.

Once again we find a step whose location in the lesson is determined by the moment of its execution on the stage: the *fouettés*—among the most brilliant steps in the present vocabulary of the classical dance—are generally done at the coda of the classical *pas de deux: Le Cygne Noir* (Petipa and Ivanoff); or toward the end of a ballet: *Suite en Blanc (Lifar)*. Thus, the dancer, even though tired, must be capable of executing them in impeccable fashion.

845

Two types of exercises might be considered for terminating the lesson:

· A series of *sauts*. They may be executed by rising as high as possible to a sustained rhythm in order to develop elevation and to push the dancer's endurance to its outer limits.

· A series of simple, short exercises such as *dégagés*; *petits battements* in second position alternately with each foot while lifting the posterior foot and closing forward eight times in succession, then doing the reverse eight times in succession; *raccourcis* executed in the same manner, etc.

The purpose of these exercises is to put the body in the proper condition until the next lesson.

The two types of exercises might be alternated on the basis of the greater or lesser amount of fatigue generated by the exercises that have been done during the lesson, on the basis of a pre-established plan, or according to various circumstances such as the temperature, etc.

846

Traditionally the dance lesson is concluded by a *révérence* (bow) executed according to the classical form.

In fifth position. Right foot forward.

Shift the left foot into second position (§ 103) while "shouldering" and turning the head toward the left. The arms rise in third (§ 41), the left arm raised. Place the left foot *à plat* and raise the right *à la pointe* while reversing the *épaulement,* the position of the head, and that of the arms. Bring the right foot into first (§ 22) while doing a *plié* and place it *à plat en quatrième derrière* (§ 26), stretching it while the left foot rises *sur la pointe.* In passing into first position, the trunk leans forward and the arms descend into the *position de départ* (§ 38). They rise laterally into second (§ 40) when the legs are extended. Close the left foot *en cinquième devant* and begin anew from the other side.

The dancer may embellish the passage into first by a *petit battement* on the instep (§ 212) forward-backward.

There are those who might consider that this practice of *révérence* is out of style. However, it symbolizes the acknowledgement of the pupil to his teacher and demonstrates the respect that is due him. In an exercise as difficult as that of the dance at the professional level (the level of this lesson), it is important that the pupil do his best and constantly surpass himself. It is therefore necessary that he have great confidence in his teacher and show a respectful admiration for him—sentiments of which the *révérence* is testimony.

847

The lesson for the female dancer which we have just explained is a typical lesson, but it does not contain all the answers. Training in the dance must be ordered and constructive. A good dancing master does not improvise: he has a plan for the whole, relating on the one hand to the year's work, on the other to that of the week.

At the beginning of each year, after the vacation, one commences with a simple, elementary exercise, progressively restoring to the muscles the possibility of executing the difficulties up to which the dancer had arrived at the year's end. If one wished to start out immediately at this level, the dancer, compensating by means of incorrect positions and movements for the temporary inadequacy of her muscles, would risk committing serious mistakes which would later be very difficult to correct.

The higher the previous level attained, the more rapid this sort of review may be, but it is indispensable. Later on, the annual progression should take into account the groups of muscles concerned with a specific movement in order to obtain an harmonious and balanced development. It should take into account categories of steps, introducing them judiciously. And it should make allowance for techniques by preparing through simple exercises for the acquisition of a given technique, then by considering the applications of the latter in different types of steps; and finally, by making the point of departure of techniques more complex or difficult, etc.

The training plan must not be too rigid and can be adapted to each particular dancer. Human material cannot be modeled in the same way as inert matter.

The teacher should not lose sight of the fact that technique is not an end in itself, but a means to reaching artistic expression. Only a perfect mastery of the techniques of the dance can liberate the dancer sufficiently for her to devote herself totally to aesthetic and expressive pursuits. But training in technique for its own sake would be sterile. To technical progression must therefore be added artistic advancement. This training will be brought about in the relatively simple exercises by insisting on the harmonious combination of the lines and on facial expression (Fig. 116).

848

While courses at the professional level meet every day, a weekly program must also be established.

· *Monday:* Exercises that are relatively simple (this does not mean "easy") to put all the muscles in the correct place. This work must be done very much in depth, and the teacher must demand perfection.

The *adagio* will have great importance, in particular in the effort to acquire balance.

Series will be executed which permit various techniques to be perfected.

This whole exercise must be done in depth and at the same time with suppleness, in order to avoid contorting muscles.

Figure 116

· *Tuesday:* More closely related and more varied exercises. Practice in steps that will be included later in variations. They will be studied separately at first, then in simple sequences.

· *Wednesday:* Study of new steps; longer and more complex sequences based on the steps and techniques taken up on the preceding days.

· *Thursday:* Traditionally this is the day of rest at the Opera.

· *Friday:* Study of difficult steps. This is the day when the most complicated variants of the classical steps will be studied, or the steps requiring the greatest mastery of technique.

Complex and lengthy sequences.

· *Saturday:* Synthesis of the week's work: the new steps and techniques will be included in variations. Work on style and expression.

The dancing master should then to a certain extent conceive his plan of work well in advance. Knowing that he intends to work on a certain variation on Saturday, he will see that its elements are studied on the preceding days.

849

As an example we shall consider the work for one week on the variation from the first act of *Giselle* in the choreography currently being executed at the Opera.

· *Monday:* Among other exercises, work on balancing *en arabesque sur la pointe* and easy descent of the foot, which rests *à plat*, through the intermediary of the *demi-pointe*; rounded *battements relevés sur la pointe* (§ 180).

· *Tuesday:* Sequences with *failli* (§ 320), *piqué sur la pointe en arabesque, failli, piqué sur la pointe en attitude.*

In the exercise in *tours,* the dancer might do *tours relevés en dedans* (§ 427) eight times successively alternating legs, with a *temps d'arrêt* (pause) after each turn or each group of turns from a single impulse.

Tours piqués en attitude (§ 407), practiced in the same manner.

Changements de pieds sur les deux pointes.

· *Wednesday:* Sequence: *failli, piqué sur la pointe en arabesque,* sitting (*posé*), *saut de chat,* rising up (*pointé*), *temps de pointe piqué en descendant* with *petit battement* on the instep, twice in succession, *battement arrondi relevé sur la pointe.*

Tours en dedans preceded by a *failli* and linked together without a pause.

Petits soubresauts sur une pointe.

Circle (*manège*) of *piqués.*

· *Friday: Tours en attitude* terminating by descending on the toe without moving the leg *en attitude.*

Diagonal of *soubresauts sur une pointe.*

Sequences constituting fragments of the variation.

· *Saturday:* The variation in its entirety, then a study of expression and style.

A LESSON FOR MALE DANCERS

850

The basic exercise is common to male and female dancers. Both must strengthen their muscles and make them more supple; both must acquire balance, elevation, learn to do *tours,* etc. Finally, however, a man and a woman will not actually dance in the same manner. There are steps that the one will do but not the other: even when they are doing the same step they execute it in different ways: for example, the *sissonnes* (§ 279). Men can leap higher than women, do more beating steps, more turns from a single impulse; but they do not dance on *pointes.*

To strengthen the muscles bringing about the easing of the *saut,* the *pliés* will be stressed, with descent and ascent *sur la demi-pointe.* Much work will be done with the foot muscles: for example, when the dancer descends from a *demi-pointe,* he must have the feeling that his heel is crushing a resistant object; or he may make the movement of picking up something with his toes. These two movements are facilitated by the type of slipper worn by male dancers: the sole is much more flexible than that of the slipper worn in toe-dancing, and the toe of the slipper is also flexible.

The means of descending from the *demi-pointe* used by men gives a special workout for the anterior muscles of the leg: the long and short lateral peroneal muscles as well as the extensors of the toes. It contributes to the development of all the levator muscles of the foot. Finally, it likewise involves the plantar arch by the contraction of the flexor of the toes.

In the movement of picking up something with the toes, apart from the sural triceps, the flexor of the toes is developed, contributing to the formation of a plantar arch that is very muscular and particularly suited to the *saut.*

To acquire a good notion of balance, the teacher will frequently give unannounced instructions for the dancer to let go of the barre. He will also have the dancer release it regularly during certain exercises.

851

We shall give as an example a lesson conducted at the Opera by Raymond Franchetti for male dancers seventeen to eighteen years old.

As we have already pointed out for the female dancers (§ 807), each exercise for which the dancer is in profile at the barre should be done a second time from the other side after a *demi-tour.*

At the Barre

852   EXERCISE 1. PLIES.

357

In profile at the barre. In second position. Arms in *position de départ* (§ 38).

Port de bras in second position, at the end of which the hand is placed on the barre.

Plier; rise *sur les demi-pointes*; balance with the arms *en couronne* (§ 43). Descend gently while resting the hand on the barre. A slight *demi-plié*; stretch. Pass into first position.

Plier. Straighten up. Lean forward. Straighten up. *Port de bras:* first, second, with the working arm. Pass into *quatrième devant*.

Plier. Straighten up. Lean forward. Move the anterior leg into *quatrième derrière* by means of a *rond de jambe à terre en dehors*.

Plier. Straighten up. Lean backwards. By means of a *rond de jambe à terre en dedans* bring the posterior leg forward and close in fifth.

Plier. Straighten up. Rise *sur les demi-pointes,* balance with the arms *en couronne.* Turn in the other direction, on the side of the barre, *sur les deux demi-pointes,* in order to do a *demi-tour* and start anew from the other side.

853   EXERCISE 2. DEGAGE PLIES

In profile at the barre, in fifth position.

Dégagé. Place the foot *à plat.* Plier. Close, leaving the foot *à plat* and remaining *plié.* Stretch. *Dégagé.* Close.

This exercise is done *en croix* (§ 811).

The same exercise is started again *en croix*, without the *plié*, hence in the following form: *dégager*; place the foot *à plat*; close, leaving the foot *à plat*.

The teacher may direct that the barre be released in fourth or in second.

When the exercise is done in fourth, the working arm is forward horizontal; it is in second position for the *dégagés* in second position.

854   EXERCISE 3. PRACTICE FOR THE ANKLES

In profile at the barre, in fifth position.

Dégager. Place the foot *à plat.* Raise it *sur la pointe.* Raise the leg *à la demi-hauteur.* Lift the *pointe* while bending the ankle. Stretch the ankle, but while leaving the toes raised up: the foot in the air in the position for the *demi-pointe.* Stretch the toes. Place the *pointe* on the ground. Close.

When the working foot is placed *à plat* there is a shifting of the axis and the weight of the body is distributed equally between the two legs (it can be controlled by having the dancer release the barre). When the working leg is raised *sur la pointe*, the weight of the body is moved back onto the supporting leg.

This exercise is done *en croix*.

855   EXERCISE 4. DÉGAGÉS

In profile at the barre, in fifth position.

Dégager. Place the foot *à plat* while bringing the weight of the trunk between the two legs. *Plier.* Stretch. Lift the working foot *sur la pointe* while causing the weight of the body to be shifted onto the supporting leg. Close. *Dégager.* Close. *Dégager.* Close.

This exercise is done *en croix*.

Next, do four *dégagés en croix* in each direction while raising the working leg *à la demi-hauteur* (a movement analogous to *petits battements à la demi-hauteur*, but with care being taken to have the foot execute the movements proper to the *dégagé* before it leaves the floor and as soon as it has touched it).

856   EXERCISE 5. SUPPLENESS

Back to the barre, in first position.

Lean the trunk forward until the head touches the knees. Straighten up. *Plier* as low as possible. Make the knees taut while throwing out the chest and leaning the head backward. This movement is made while stretching first at the height of the hip, then of the knee, then of the ankle. Return progressively to the upright position.

This exercise is done twice in succession, or four times, or eight for dancers who are very well-trained.

It will be observed that this movement is akin to the one described in paragraph 826 for female dancers, but it is done in classical first and not in standard first position.

857   EXERCISE 6. RONDS DE JAMBE A TERRE

In profile at the barre, in fifth position.

One *rond de jambe a terre en dehors* broken down (*décomposé*) with pause *en quatrième devant*, in second, *en quatrième derrière*, and in first.

Two *ronds de jambe en dehors* with pause *en quatrième devant* and *en quatrième derrière*. At each pause the trunk leans slightly in the direction opposite to that of the leg in order to be in line with the extension of the leg.

Four *ronds de jambe en dehors*.

One *battement arrondi en dehors*.

Start afresh with *ronds de jambe en dedans*.

Plier. Move the foot forward *en quatrième devant* while leaving the supporting knee *plié*.

One *rond de jambe en dehors* leading the working foot into *quatrième derrière*. Place the foot *à plat*. Lean the trunk forward, then backward.

One *rond de jambe en dedans* bringing the foot into *quatrième devant*. Lean the trunk forward, then backward.

Close in fifth. Lean the trunk forward. Straighten up. *Port de bras* in first and second with the working arm.

858 EXERCISE 7. RONDS DE JAMBE SOUTENUS

In profile at the barre, in fifth position.

Raise the working leg in second *à la hauteur*. Do a *petit rond de jambe soutenu* in second position *en dehors*. Stretch the leg in second *à la hauteur*. Close.

Start afresh with two *petits ronds de jambe soutenus* in succession.

The same thing with two *petits ronds de jambe soutenus* in succession.

Raise the working leg *en quatrième devant à la hauteur*. Bend the supporting knee. Move the leg into second *à la hauteur* and stretch the supporting knee. Two *petits ronds de jambe soutenus à la hauteur en dehors*. Close to the rear.

Raise the working leg *en quatrième derrière à la hauteur*. Bend the supporting knee. Move the leg into second *à la hauteur* and stretch the supporting knee. Two *petits ronds de jambe soutenus* in second position *en dedans*. Close to the front.

Foot in the hand.

Knee in the hand to force *attitude*.

Release the knee. Stretch the working leg *en arabesque*. Balance *en arabesque*.

859 EXERCISE 8. RELEVES PLIES

In profile at the barre, in fifth position.

Dégager and raise the leg *à la demi-hauteur*. *Plier*, bringing the heel of the working leg onto the ankle of the supporting leg. *Relever sur la demi-pointe* while keeping the knee of the supporting leg flexed. Stretch the working leg while bringing it *à la demi-hauteur* and simultaneously stretch the supporting leg. Two *battements* on the instep while raising the supporting foot *sur la demi-pointe* and while bending the supporting knee at the time of the closing on the instep. Close in fifth.

This exercise is done *en croix*.

Four times in succession: three *battements* on the instep without *relever,* with a pause in *plié* on the last one.

Relever sur les deux demi-pointes. Raccourci in second. Balance *en raccourci sur la demi-pointe.*

860 EXERCISE 9. PETITS BATTEMENTS

In profile at the barre, in fifth position.

Dégager into second. Do a *petit battement* on the instep front-to-back. *Petit battement* back-to-front at the bend of the knee. Close *en cinquième devant*.

Start afresh a second time.

Four *petits battements* on the instep. *Pointer* in second.

Start over a second time.

Sixteen *petits battements* on the instep.

Relever sur les deux demi-pointes. Raise the working leg *au raccourci in second position,* move it into *attitude,* extend it *en arabesque* while bringing the supporting foot back down *à plat. Relever sur la demi-pointe.* Balance *en arabesque sur la demi-pointe.*

861 EXERCISE 10. BATTEMENTS

In profile at the barre, in fifth position.

Dégager. One *battement* terminating *sur la pointe.* Close in fifth. One *battement* closing in fifth.

The first *battement* is twice as slow as the others.

This exercise is done *en croix*.

For the *battements en quatrième devant*, the working arm is *en couronne.* For those in second, it is in second. For those *en quatrième derrière*, it is extended horizontally to the front.

862 EXERCISE 11. ADAGIO AT THE BARRE

In profile at the barre, in fifth position.

Développer; raise the leg as high as possible. Place the leg extended *à la pointe*. Close in fifth.

Execute this movement *en croix*.

Développer en quatrième devant while bending the supporting leg. Move the working leg into second *à la hauteur* while stretching the supporting leg. Bring the working leg into *quatrième devant à la hauteur*. Bend the supporting leg. Place the working foot *en quatrième devant à la pointe*. Close in fifth. Stretch.

The working arm follows the movement of the leg. In the *développé en quatrième devant* it is in second at the moment of the *raccourci* and rises *en couronne* when the leg is stretched. In the *développé* in second position the arm is in first for the *raccourci* and in second when the leg is stretched. In the *développé en quatrième derrière* it remains in first position.

863   EXERCISE 12. FOOT ON THE BARRE

In profile at the barre, in fifth position.

Raise the leg that is not on the side of the barre *en quatrième devant à la hauteur* and place the foot on the barre. Raise the working arm *en couronne* while passing through the *position de départ* and first.

Lean the trunk forward until it touches the leg. Straighten up. Lean the trunk backward until it is horizontal. Straighten up. Rise *sur la demi-pointe*. Balance.

Pivot a quarter-turn in order to be facing the barre and in second position *à la hauteur* with the foot still on the barre. Descend, foot *à plat*. Lean to the side, first toward the supporting leg, then to the other side. The working arm, corresponding to the leg on the barre, remains *en couronne*. Straighten up and change the supporting hand. Raise the new working arm *en couronne* and lean the trunk to the side of the supporting leg, then to the other side. Straighten up. Rise *sur la demi-pointe*. Balance.

Pivot a quarter-turn in order to be in profile at the barre, the working leg *en quatrième derrière à la hauteur* with the foot still on the barre. Descend, foot *à plat*.

Lean the trunk backward. Straighten up. Lean the trunk forward while lifting the working leg as high as possible above the barre. Straighten up while resting the foot on the barre. Rise *sur la demi-pointe*. Balance.

Pivot a quarter-turn in order to have the back to the barre, in second *à la hauteur*, the foot on the barre. Descend, foot *à plat*. Move the working leg into *quatrième devant à la hauteur*. Release the barre. *Grand écart*.

864   EXERCISE 13. OPENING OF THE FEET

Face to the barre, in second position *à la hauteur*, foot on the barre.

Attach the *pointe* of the foot to the barre by means of a strap tied around the toes and the barre.

Plier slowly four or eight times in succession.
Do the same exercise with the other foot.
Good dancers in regular training no longer need this exercise.

865   EXERCISE 14. BATTEMENTS EN CLOCHE

In profile at the barre, in fifth position.
Two *battements en cloche* with pause at the passage into first.
Four connected *battements en cloche.*

866   EXERCISE 15. OPENING OF THE LEGS

The dancer sits on the floor, facing the barre. He leans the trunk slightly backward and rests on the forearms. He bends the knees, then opens them, placing the soles of his feet one against the other. Another male dancer places a foot on each knee while using both hands on the barre for support. He gradually bears down on the dancer's knees until they touch the floor.

Good dancers who are in fine condition have a wide enough spread to touch the ground with their knees without forcing. They no longer have the need of this exercise.

In the Center of the Floor

867   DEGAGES and TOURS

In fifth, right foot forward.
Dégager the right foot *en quatrième devant* slightly *croisée.* Place the foot *à plat. Plier.* Stretch. Raise the posterior foot *sur la pointe.* Close in fifth. *Dégager* the right foot in second. Place it *à plat en quatrième derrière,* the arms moving into sixth position. Two or more *tours relevés en dehors en cinquième derrière.*
Start afresh from the other side.

868   ADAGIO

In fifth, right foot forward.
Développer the right leg *en quatrième devant* while bending the supporting knee. *Grand rond de jambe soutenu à la hauteur en dehors,* while stretching the supporting leg. When the working leg is *en arabesque,* bend the supporting leg. *Pas de bourrée détourné.* One *tour relevé en arabesque en dedans,* terminating *en arabesque.* One promenade *tour en arabesque,* breaking *en arabesque ouverte. Pas de bourrée.*
Start afresh from the other side.

869 BALANCING

In fifth position, right foot forward.

Plier. Développer en quatrième devant à la hauteur while bringing up the supporting foot *sur la demi-pointe.* Descend *à plat* and flex the supporting leg while bringing the working leg *pliée* on the instep. *Développer* in second and thus continue the movement *en croix.*

The working foot does not rest on the floor during the whole exercise. It is only after the last *développé* in second position that one closes *en cinquième derrière.* Then start the whole exercise anew with the other foot.

870 TOURS

Tours relevés en dehors taken starting from a fourth position obtained by way of a *pas de bourrée.* The dancers do two, three, four, or more *tours* from a single impulse. One should begin with two *tours* in order to be sure that they are well "tuned." Afterward, the dancer may try to increase his number of *tours,* but while taking care to maintain a correct position.

871

In fifth position, right foot forward.

Dégager en quatrième devant. Place the foot *à plat.* Raise the posterior leg in order to do two *tours* in second position *en dedans relevés,* terminating *en arabesque.*

Pas de bourrée ending in fourth. Two *tours en dehors relevés,* closing in fifth.

The same exercise, on the other side.

872 SAUTS

In fifth position, right foot forward.

Échappé sauté, closing with *changement de pied.* Two *changements de pied.* Twice in succession: *brisé, entrechat 4.*

Start afresh on the other side.

Repeat the same exercise after a pause for rest (while the other students are working), doing a beaten *échappé 3* or *5* as well as a beaten close; replacing the *changements de pied* with *entrechats 3* or *6,* and the *entrechats 4* with *entrechats 5.*

873 SEQUENCES

In fifth position, right foot forward.

Two *passés-assemblées*. Four *entrechats 6*. *Pas de basque en descendant*. *Relever en arabesque*. *Pas de bourrée-jeté*. *Pas de bourrée-relevé en arabesque*. *Chassé*. *Pas de bourrée*.

Care should be taken during this exercise that the positions of the arms and shoulders are correct.

874 TOURS EN L'AIR

Dancers who are not highly trained do these in the following manner:

In fifth position, right foot forward.

Plier. A quarter-turn in the air with change of feet. *Plier*. A quarter-turn in the air with change of feet which brings the dancer opposite his initial position.

The same thing with a half-turn, three-quarter turn, whole turn.

Professional dancers in normal practice may exercise thus: one turn, a turn and a half, two turns, in the same manner.

875 FINAL EXERCISE

In first position.

Lean the trunk forward. Straighten up while raising the arms in first, then opening them in second.

Port de bras in first, fifth, second.

Port de bras tournant, while leaning the trunk forward.

Bow.

The male dancers' bow (*salut*) is different from that of the female dancers (*révérence*) (§ 846): the dancer shifts his left foot into second, then he moves it into first and places it *à plat en quatrième derrière* while leaning the head and the trunk slightly forward, while the right foot is raised *à la pointe*. The left arm alongside the body, the right arm rises a little higher than the second position, palm upward. It is gently lowered when the body is leaning forward. Close; the arm descends alongside the body (Fig. 117).

Start anew from the other side.

876

The observations made in paragraph 847 and 848 may be applied to exercises for male, as well as for female dancers.

To the customary exercises might be added certain arm move-

Figure 117. Bow

ments in order to allow the dancer to execute the *portés*, and especially those with arms extended, which present choreographies prescribe.

In specialized courses, the dancers may be trained for their role as partner in the *pas de deux*.

Like the female dancers, male dancers are supposed to work on their expression and style. They should develop breadth of movement and assert their presence with authority and nobility. Their art must be dignified and their movements clean and precise, without flourishes.

LESSON FOR BEGINNING GIRLS

877

For a long time it was thought that dance lessons for beginning girls should consist of teaching the steps, beginning with the easiest. The dancing master would illustrate the steps and the pupil would reproduce them as best she could. If she did not succeed in doing them, the teacher would have her do them over until perfect execution was reached.

In recent times dancing masters began to dissect the steps, marking pauses in their execution, as we have explained—for example, for the *ronds de jambe à terre* (§ 857). But if there are some movements which lend themselves easily to dissection, there are others for which dissection is delicate; they would require pauses in awkward if not impossible positions, in the case of *sauts* or *tours*.

Today the teachers apply to the dance some methods akin to those which have been tested in athletics. Before having a step executed, the teacher prepares for it, the ideal being that the pupil should not ever fail in an attempt. He will thus have those muscles exercised first which will permit the acquisition of rigorously correct positions for all the elements in the body: trunk, legs, arms, head. It is only when he is certain that the pupil will assume these positions automatically that he will teach the pupil steps he (she) is fully prepared to execute and for which he (she) will not adopt any faulty position whatever.

It may appear that the teacher is losing time. At the end of a year the pupils of the great dancing schools, such as those of the Opera of Paris, of Russia, Hungary, Denmark, etc., know far fewer steps than their predecessors of fifty years ago. But all the steps they do are impeccable. If one asks the child to do things that are too difficult or for which he is not prepared, he will acquire defects which he will not be able to lose later. Every year the teachers and directors of the great schools are obliged regretfully to eliminate children who have great qualities, but whose early training was poorly directed and who, in spite of the efforts of competent teachers, can no longer eliminate their bad habits.

The great difficulty of the dancing master is to always make the students work to the maximum without ever going beyond their capabilities.

878

We shall give as an example of a lesson for beginners one of those taught by Jacqueline Moreau to the pupils of the Third Division C at *l'école de danse* of the Opera, in the month of October. The pupils are between eight and ten years old. They have passed the probationary period; that is, during the first three months of the school year they have come every day to take a dance lesson at the Opera. They wear soft slippers, and there is no mention (as yet) of their dancing on *pointes*. Theirs is a group lesson (twenty-five pupils) and lasts an hour and a half.

As we indicated previously (§ 807 and 851), when an exercise done in profile at the barre is terminated, the pupil does a *demi-tour* on the side of the barre and resumes the same exercise from the other side.

Each exercise is preceded by the placing in position indicated in paragraph 811.

At the Barre

879 EXERCISE 1. PLIES

In profile at the barre, in first position.

Two times in succession: two *demi-pliés* without lifting the heels, one *plié* with *port de bras:* the working arm descends in the *position de départ* at the moment of the flexing, rises in first and opens into second as it rises the second time.

Dégager in second and place the foot *à plat.* Same exercise, at the end of which the working foot rises *à la pointe* and closes *en cinquième devant.*

Same exercise.

The working arm descends in the *position de départ,* then rises *en couronne* by way of the first position. The other arm rises simultaneously *en couronne* while passing through first. Balance with feet *à plat.*

880 EXERCISE 2. DEGAGES PLIES

In profile at the barre, in fifth position.

Two times in succession: *dégager,* place the foot *à plat, demi-plié,* stretch, lift the working foot *à la pointe,* close.

This exercise is done *en croix* (§ 811).

881 EXERCISE 3. DEGAGES

In profile at the barre, in fifth position.

Two *dégagés* followed by a closing in fifth, in each position, *en croix.*

882 EXERCISE 4. DEGAGES AVEC DEMI-HAUTEUR

In profile at the barre, in fifth position.

Dégagé, at the end of which the leg rises *à la demi-hauteur.* Place the foot back on *pointe* and close.

Two in each position, *en croix.*

The *dégagés* in fourth are closed in fifth, those in second are closed in first.

This exercise is analogous to the second part of the one described in paragraph 855

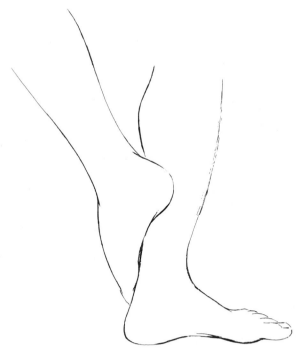

Figure 118. Position of the foot in front of the ankle

883 EXERCISE 5. RONDS DE JAMBE

In profile at the barre, in fifth position, arms in the *position de départ*.

Four *ronds de jambe en dehors,* followed by four *ronds de jambe en dedans,* broken up, with pause at the two fourths, in second, and in first.

The arm rises in first with the first fourth, moves in second with the second, remains there during the second fourth, and descends in the *position de départ* with the first. This movement is as useful for *ronds de jambe en dehors* as for those *en dedans.*

884 EXERCISE 6. BATTEMENTS ON THE INSTEP WITH PLIES

In profile at the barre, in fifth position.

Dégager in second. Lift the leg *à la demi-hauteur.* Bend the working leg while bringing the foot behind the ankle of the supporting leg, toes tightened. Bend the supporting leg. Tighten. Place the *pointe* in second. Raise the leg *à la demi-hauteur.* Bring back the foot in front of the ankle of the supporting leg. This position is unusual: the ankle is slightly flexed, the sole of the foot held close against the other leg, the extremity of the toes reaching to the heel-bone. (Fig. 118).

The exercise is done four times without closing in fifth. The foot is pointed downward in second starting from its position on the ankle.

885   EXERCISE 7. BATTEMENTS FRAPPES

In profile at the barre, in fifth position.

Lift the working leg into second *à la demi-hauteur*. Bend it, bringing the foot behind the supporting ankle. Tighten it.

Repeat eight times in succession, bringing the working foot alternately behind and in front of the supporting ankle. When the working foot strikes in front, it takes the position described in the preceding paragraph.

Conclude with a balancing with the foot *à plat*, with the working foot in front of the supporting ankle and the arms *en couronne*.

A little later in the year, the same exercise may be done with a *relevé sur la demi-pointe* when the working leg rises *à la demi-hauteur*. It may be concluded then by a balancing *sur la demi-pointe*.

886   EXERCISE 8. RACCOURCIS

In profile at the barre, in fifth position.

Raise the working foot in front of the supporting ankle; lift it up to the knee. *Demi-plié*. Tighten. Balance with foot flat *en raccourci* in second. Close in fifth.

Do the exercise four times in succession, closing in fifth alternately before and behind. After a closed *cinquième derrière* the working foot rises behind the supporting ankle.

The student has a tendency to raise the hip at the same time as the leg. Care should be taken that the hips remain fully horizontal.

887   EXERCISE 9. ADAGIO AT THE BARRE.

In profile at the barre, in fifth position.

Dégager. The arm that was in second descends in the *position de départ*, then rises in first and opens in second.

Lift the leg *à la demi-hauteur*.

Balance with foot *à plat* in this position. Place the hand back on the barre. Place the working *pointe*. Close.

Do this exercise twice in succession *en quatrième devant*, then in second.

Demi-tour in order to do the same thing on the other side. Another *demi-tour,* in order to come back to the initial position, and the student does the same exercise twice *en quatrième derrière* and twice in second. *Demi-tour* in order to do the same thing on the other side.

888 EXERCISE 10. DEVELOPPES

In profile at the barre, in fifth position.

Plier, bringing the working foot in front of the supporting ankle. Stretch. *Développer en quatrième devant à la demi-hauteur.* Place the *pointe en quatrième devant.* Close in fifth.

This exercise is done *en croix.*

889 EXERCISE 11. PETITS BATTEMENTS SUR LE COU-DE-PIED

In profile at the barre, in fifth position.

Petits battements forward-backward on the instep; place the *pointe* in second position.

Eight times in succession, alternating forward-backward and backward-forward.

Four times in succession: four *petits battements;* place the *pointe* in second.

Sixteen *petits battements* in succession.

890 EXERCISE 12. BATTEMENTS

In profile at the barre, in fifth position.

Dégager. Battement terminating *à la pointe.* Close.

Four of each, *en croix.*

Next, the *battements* may be done in the following manner:

Four times in succession: *dégager en quatrième devant. Battement en quatrième devant* ending *à la pointe.* Close.

Four times in succession: *dégager en quatrième devant.* Close. Battement.

Demi-tour.

Same thing on the other side.

Demi-tour.

Four times in succession: *dégager* in second. *Battement* in second ending *pointe à terre.* Close in first.

Four times in succession: *dégager.* Close in fifth. *Battement* in second closed in fifth.

Demi-tour.

Same thing on the other side.

Quarter-turn in order to be facing the barre.

Four times in succession: *dégager en quatrième derrière. Battement en quatrième derrière* ending *à la pointe.* Close.

Four times in succession: *dégager en quatrième derrière.* Close. *Battement.*

Dégagé in second with the posterior foot. Close forward.

Do the *battements en quatrième derrière* with the other leg.

891   EXERCISE 13. FOOT ON THE BARRE

Face to the barre.

Place the foot on the barre in second *à la hauteur.*

Four *pliés* with the supporting leg, done slowly.

Lean the trunk toward the working leg while raising the arm *en couronne* on the side of the supporting leg. Lean to the other side. Change hands on the barre. Lean the trunk, "shouldering" toward the working leg while extending the corresponding arm forward, then placing it *en couronne.* Lean the trunk to the other side.

Four *pliés* with the supporting leg.

Lift up the working leg above the barre. Bend the working leg, bringing the foot *au raccourci* in front of the knee of the supporting leg. Close *en cinquième devant.*

Start afresh with the other leg.

Next, the teacher may alternate the foot on the barre in second, the foot on the barre *en quatrième devant,* and the foot on the barre *en quatrième derrière.* For the foot on the barre in fourth, the pupil is in profile at the barre. The working arm is in second; it descends half-horizontally with the *plié* and resumes its position when the supporting knee is tightened. The trunk leans forward, then backward, with the arms *en couronne.*

The exercise may be concluded with a balancing *en raccourci* with foot *à plat.*

The hip of the working leg has a strong inclination to be raised up. Care should be taken that it remains in place.

892   EXERCISE 14. SUPPLENESS

Back to the barre, in standard first position.

Lean the trunk forward while trying to touch the knees, which are quite straight, with the head. Straighten up. Do the movement described in paragraph 856.

Four times in succession.

893   EXERCISE 15. RELEVES

Face to the barre, in first position.

Relever sur les demi-pointes four times, calculating four *temps* for the whole movement. Eight times, calculating two *temps*.

After each *relevé*, place the heels firmly while doing a *demi-plié*, then stretch.

In the Center of the Floor

894   PORTS DE BRAS

In fifth position.

Arms in the *position de départ*. Raise them in first, open them in second. Raise them slightly above the second, returning with the hands palms down. Descend in *position de départ*.

Twice in succession while doing the same third.

The arms in *position de départ* rise in first, then in fifth, open in second, and descend in *position de départ*.

Twice in succession.

The arms in *position de départ* rise in first, are placed in third, reverse the third, pass into first, rise in third, reverse the third, pass into first, and descend in the position de départ.

A *dégagé* in second position permits a change of feet. Start the whole exercise anew from the other side.

895   PORTS DE BRAS MARCHES

In fifth position, arms in *position de départ*.

Dégagé en quatrième derrière with the posterior foot, bending the supporting leg, the arms rise horizontally, stretched out in parallel, the arm on the side of the supporting leg being in second, the other in front of the body. The trunk is leaning slightly forward. The head is turned to the side of the supporting leg.

Rond de jambe en dedans broken *en quatrième devant pointe à terre* while stretching the supporting leg. The arms move through second and descend in the *position de départ*. Without disturbing the position of the legs, lean the trunk forward then straighten it while having the arms move from the *position de départ* into first, then into fifth; open them in second, finally bring them back down in *position de départ* while the foot that was *à la pointe* comes to close *en cinquième devant*.

Do this exercise four times in succession. Because it involves change of feet, the dancer will thus have done it twice on each side.

Care should be taken during the leaning forward that the students keep their backs flat, giving the impression of lengthening it.

The movements must be very precise as to the positions and at the same time very well connected. From the beginning the students must strive for elegance and style in the *ports de bras.*

Next, the exercise may be done twice *en descendant* with *rond de jambe en dedans* and twice *en remontant* with *rond de jambe en dehors.*

896 DEGAGES

There are several exercises that might be done as a basis for *dégagés.* It might be good to vary them often enough that the pupils do not come to execute their movements mechanically. We shall indicate a few of them.

Four *dégagés en quatrième devant.*

Four *dégagés* in second, closing alternately in front and behind.

The same thing with the other leg.

Four *dégagés en quatrième derrière.*

Four *dégagés* in second, closing alternately behind and in front.

The same thing with the other leg.

897

In fifth, arms in second position.

Dégager. Place the foot *à plat. Plier.* Stretch. Raise the working foot *à la pointe.* Close in fifth while bending. Stretch.

During the *dégagés* in fourth, the arm corresponding to the leg that is shifting is extended forward in first; the other remains in second. For the *dégagés* in second, both arms remain in second.

This exercise is done. *en quatrième devant* and in second with each foot, then *en quatrième derrière* and in second, making each leg work in the same order as for the first part of the exercise.

This sytem may be replaced later by that of the cross (§ 811). It keeps the beginners from using the same supporting leg too long and from making the free leg work too much. The exercises are especially slow, because they are so often broken up. The *pliés* take up one *temps,* whereas later they will be done automatically in the sequence of movements. Performed in this manner, the exercises are very tiring because they demand a prolonged effort. Not to change legs risks exceeding the capacity of resistance of young students and causes them to pick up bad habits.

898

In fifth position, arms in the *position de départ*.
>Eight *dégagés en descendant*.
>Eight *dégagés en remontant*.

On each *dégagé* the arms pass through one of the following positions, in this order: first, fifth, second, *position de départ*. Within the whole exercise this *port de bras* is repeated four times. The movement is connected, without pause in each position.

899

In fifth position, arms in *position de départ*.
>Two *dégagés* followed by three *battements à la demi-hauteur* and a *temps d'arrêt*.

In the order indicated in paragraph 897: *quatrième devant*, second, then *quatrième devant* and second with the other foot; *quatrième derrière*, second with the first foot, *quatrième derrière*, second with the other foot.

For the *dégagés* in fourth the arms are in sixth position, the arm that is *plié* corresponding to the working leg. For the *dégagés* in second, both arms are in second.

The first *dégagé* in second position closes to the rear

900 ADAGIO

Several adagios may be combined, but the following rules must be observed: the balancing is done on one foot with the foot *à plat*; on two feet, *sur la demi-pointe*. One leg may be kept lifted above *demi-hauteur;* both legs should exercise alternately in order to avoid tension in certain muscles. Many *ports de bras*. Simple sequences in order that maximum attention may be paid to the execution.

We shall give only one example.

901

In fifth position, arms in *position de départ*.
>*Dégagé en quatrième devant. Ports de bras* in first and second. Raise the leg *à la demi-hauteur*. Balance with *port de bras: position de départ*, first, fifth, second. Place the *pointe* on the ground. Close in fifth while the arms are ascending once again in *position de départ*.

Do the same exercise in second. Close *en cinquième derrière*. The same thing with the other leg.

Next, *en quatrième derrière*, then in second with each leg.

375

902 SAUTS

Sauts are practiced most often in series of identical *sauts*. The *pliés* preceding and following the suspension should be carefully marked out—they will occupy one *temps*. Care should be taken that the heels are set down, that the trunk remains straight and the hips horizontal.

903 SOUBRESAUTS

In fifth position, arms in *position de départ*.

Plier. Soubresaut. Plier. Stretch. One *temps d'arrêt.*
Plier. Changement de pied. Plier. Stretch. One *temps d'arrêt.*

During the *soubresaut* the feet are held close together, one in front of the other during the suspension.

For the *changements des pieds* the feet move in first, *pointes* tightened during the suspension.

904 ECHAPPES

In fifth position, arms in *position de départ*.

One *échappé* in fourth. Two *soubresauts* in fourth. Close in fifth.
The same thing in second, closing to the rear.
Repeat the whole exercise with the other foot.
The legs are not stretched again between the two *sauts*.

905 ASSEMBLEES

In fifth position, arms in *position de départ*.

Eight *assemblées en descendant*.
Eight *assemblées en remontant*.

One *temps d'arrêt* separates two *assemblées*. The arms open in second by way of the first, then descend in the *position de départ*.

906 JETES

In fifth position, arms in *position de départ*.

Eight *petits jetés en descendant*.
Eight *petits jetés en remontant*.

907 GLISSADES

In fifth position, arms in *position de départ*.

Three *glissades en descendant*, without change of feet, one with change of feet.

Repeat from the other side.

Four *glissades* with change of feet.

Each *glissade* is broken up, but without pause in the various positions. The movement remains connected. The *glissades* are done in the following manner.

Plier in fifth. *Dégager* the posterior foot in second, the supporting leg remaining *pliée*. Place the foot *à plat*, bringing onto it the weight of the body. Raise the other foot *à la pointe*. Make it glide on the floor to close in fifth while doing a *demi-plié*. Stretch.

For the *glissades,* the arms are placed in sixth position.

908

Very young pupils will simply do eight *glissades en descendant* and eight *glissades en remontant,* executed as indicated in the preceding paragraph, broken up but connected.

Children must not get into the habit of exercising by fits and starts under the pretext of breaking into constituent parts.

909 GLISSADES COMPOSEES

Four *glissades assemblées en descendant.*

Four *glissades assemblées en remontant.*

One *temps d'arrêt* separates two *glissades assemblées.*

The arms move from the second to the *position de départ* during the *plié.* They rise in first with the *glissade* and open in second for the *assemblée.*

The *glissades-jetés* may be done in the same manner.

Only steps that have already been studied separately and perfectly assimilated may be combined.

910 PREPARATION FOR THE COUPES

The pupil, in fifth position, raises his anterior leg *pliée au raccourci* with a rapid gesture, bringing the foot in front of the other leg *à la demi-hauteur.* Simultaneously the supporting leg is *pliée.* The movement must be quick and clean. Close in fifth while stretching.

Do the same thing while lifting the posterior leg, which is brought behind the calf.

Eight times in succession.

Resume the whole exercise for the other side.

911   PREPARATION FOR COUPES FOUETTES

In fifth position.

Do the movement described in the preceding paragraph, with the posterior foot. Close *en cinquième derrière* while the other leg rises immediately into second *à la demi-hauteur*. Bend this leg while "lashing" (*fouettant*); the supporting leg does a *plié* at the same time. Close *en cinquième derrière* while stretching the knees.

The arm corresponding to the foot that is raised for the *coupé* is in second position. The other arm is in first. When the leg is in second the arm opens into second. The arms descend in the *position de départ* at the closing.

Start afresh with the other leg. Four times altogether.

912

In fifth position.

Do a *coupé non sauté* (a nonleaping *coupé*) (§ 910) with the anterior foot and *sauter* to do an *assemblée*. Fall back *en plié* and stretch only afterwards. The *assemblée* has no change of feet.

Do the same thing by lifting the posterior foot. Repeat the whole thing four times.

After a pause for rest, the same exercise with the other foot forward.

The student has a tendency to do several little *pliés*. It is necessary that the movements be clean and precise.

913   RELEVES

In first position, arms in second position.

Relevé sur les deux demi-pointes, paying attention that the movement is perfectly symmetrical. Descend, foot *à plat*.

Four times in succession to a slow rhythm.

Do the same thing four times, but with *plié* when the feet are placed *à plat*.

Repeat the whole thing in second (obtained through a *dégagé*), then close in fifth while lowering the arms.

Eight *échappés sur les demi-pointes* with change of feet. The arms remain in the *position de départ*.

Relevé sur les deux demi-pointes in fifth; the arms rise *en couronne*. One *échappé* with change of feet; the arms open in second and descend in *position de départ* with the closing of the *échappé*.

The head is turned to the side of the anterior foot, the eyes are directed toward the corresponding hand.

914

In fifth position.

Eight *relevés* while bringing the anterior leg *au raccourci* in second position and closing to the rear.

Eight while lifting the posterior leg and closing forward.

The arms remain low, the head is turned to the side of the working leg.

Care should be taken that the trunk remains straight, the hips horizontal, and that the hip of the working leg does not rise. The pupil has a tendency to balance himself.

Before and after each *relevé* the knees flex. Care should be paid to the correctness of this *plié*. The heels must not "prepare for" the *relevé* by rising up. The supporting foot rises *sur la demi-pointe* when the working foot leaves the floor, and not beforehand. It is necessary, from the beginning, that children acquire the habit of correct movement, otherwise they will "cheat" to rise *à la pointe*. This is a very serious fault and, once acquired, is almost impossible to correct.

One can also do: four times one *raccourci* with the anterior foot closing forward followed by one *raccourci* with the posterior foot closing behind. After a pause for rest, the pupil may do the same thing on the other side.

915   PIQUES

In fifth, arms in third position, the raised arm corresponding to the future working leg.

Plier in fifth position. Raise the anterior foot *à la demi-hauteur* in second, while remaining *plié*. *Piquer* (point) it *sur la demi-pointe* in second. The trunk remains face front. Cause the weight of the body to pass onto the leg *sur la demi-pointe* and bring the other leg *à la demi-pointe en cinquième derrière*. Descend, foot *à plat*, in fifth while bending. Stretch, lowering the vertical arm in first position and bending it to obtain a sixth. The other arm does not move.

Plier, raise the anterior foot again *à la demi-hauteur* in second, the supporting leg remaining *pliée*. *Piquer sur la demi-pointe* in second while bringing the other leg *au raccourci*, the *pointe* quite taut behind the calf of the supporting leg. Close *en cinquième derrière* while bending. Stretch while raising the folded arm *en couronne*.

Do this combination four times in succession.

After a pause for rest (during which the other students do the exercise), the whole thing should be repeated on the other side.

Next, the teacher will have the same exercise done on a diagonal in *position effacé*.

916   PREPARATION FOR TOURS

In fifth position.

Dégager the anterior foot in second. The arms move through first and open in second. Close the foot forward while bending, and place the arms in sixth, the bent arm corresponding to the working leg.

Relever à la demi-pointe while bringing the anterior leg *au raccourci*. The arms are placed in first position.

Close *en cinquième derrière* while bending. Stretch.

Repeat on the other side.

Do this combination four times in succession.

917   TOURS

Whenever the teacher may decide that the time is appropriate he may have the preceding exercise done with quarter-turns.

Next, he will proceed to half-turns.

Care must be taken to avoid undue haste in the teaching of *tours*. Talented students run the risk of doing *tours* carelessly, with flaws that they will never be able to lose and that will make their *tours* uncertain. The others will compensate for their failures or the uncertainty of their balance by the use of defective positions which will be very troublesome to correct.

Tours are mastered very slowly and very gradually. But a student who has practiced correctly will never fail in her *tours* thereafter.

918   REVERENCE

In fifth position, right foot forward, arms in the *position de départ*.

Plier. Dégager the left foot in second while tightening the knees and raising the arms in second position. Place the foot *à plat. Plier* in second, *à plat*. Stretch while raising the right foot *à la pointe*. The left arm comes into first and the right does not move. Move the right foot into first while bending and place it *en quatrième derrière à plat*. The arms are in first position. Raise the left foot *à la pointe* while tightening the knees and open the arms in second. Close in fifth, left foot forward, arms in the *position de départ*.

Start afresh from the other side.

919

The lessons given to girl beginners are extremely important. Upon them the dancer's whole future depends. One of the first concerns of the teacher is to make sure that the pupil becomes aware of the balance of her body in the unaccustomed form of the *dehors*. He will pay close attention to the positioning described in paragraph 808 and will see to it that the child alway keeps her hips and shoulders horizontal. In a later section we shall see how the positioning is done from the first dance lesson.

Pliés are exceedingly important. During the course of the exercises the *plié* occupies a certain amount of time in order that the pupil may acquire the correct habits and that thereafter it may be the natural accompaniment of movements. At the same time this will discourage parasitic movements: *petits pliés* or *sursauts* that are often grafted onto the preparations or alighting from *sauts*.

The teacher should not let the pupil exercise the legs alone under the pretext of avoiding getting "tangled up." From the beginning it is necessary that she learn that the dance is an *ensemble* which involves the arms, the trunk, and the head as well as the legs.

While learning the technique, the pupil must learn style and interpretation. In the course of the first year she should learn to give meaning to certain movements which are perfectly assimilated.

On the examination at the end of the year of the Third Division C of *l'école de danse* of the Opera, the students have, among other exercises, a short expressive variation. For example, in 1967: the child holds in her hands a little bird, embraces it, cajoles it, then permits it to fly, follows it with her eyes, and becomes sad for having lost it.

LESSON FOR BEGINNING BOYS

920

Just as we noted in paragraph 850, the training for male dancers and for female dancers is not identical. This difference is observable from the beginning, and the little boy's lesson is preparation for the exercise of male dancers, just as that of the little girls prepares for the female dancers' exercise.

Already we shall find the training intended to cause them to acquire the *ballon* (elevation); in the *pliés*, the boy should conserve his movement, yielding only gradually to the weight, and when he rises he must have the impression of struggling against a force that presses him toward the ground. Thus, he will cause groups of opposing muscles to exercise. The teacher will frequently instruct him to release the barre to prepare for balances, etc.

We shall give as an example a lesson taught by Christiane Vaussard to the students of the Third Division B of *l'école de danse* of the Opera in the month of October. The students are from eight to ten years old.

They have passed the probationary period, as indicated in paragraph 878 for the girls. This is a group lesson (fifteen students) and it lasts an hour and a half.

As we indicated in paragraphs 807, 851, and 878, when an exercise done in profile at the barre is terminated, the pupil does a *demi-tour* and resumes the same exercise from the other side. Each exercise is preceded by the positioning indicated in paragraph 811.

At the Barre

921   EXERCISE 1 PLIES

In profile at the barre, in first position.

Demi-plié. Free *port du bras: position de départ*, first, second. *Plié.* Free *port du bras: position de départ*, first, second. Each *plié* with its *port du bras* takes four *temps*.

Raise the arms *en couronne*. Balance, feet *à plat*. Rise *sur les demi-pointes*. Balance.

One *dégagé* in second position and start the whole exercise again in second.

Close *en cinquième devant* and resume the whole exercise in fifth.

Do a *dégagé* in second position with the anterior foot and close to the rear. Start the exercise afresh in fifth.

Small boys should make a special effort in these *pliés* to put into practice the rules set forth in paragraph 920.

922   EXERCISE 2. DEGAGES

In profile at the barre, in fifth position.

Four *dégagés* in each position, *en croix*.

Each *dégagé* takes four *temps*.

The working arm is in second position except for the *dégagés en quatrième derrière*, where it is extended forward horizontally.

923   EXERCISE 3. DEGAGES PLIES

The same exercise as the preceding one, with *plié* at each closing and tightening for the *dégagé*.

924   DEGAGES AVEC DEMI-HAUTER

In profile at the barre, in fifth position.

Dégager. Raise the leg *à la demi-hauteur*. Place the *pointe* on the ground. Close.

Four of each, *en croix.*

Allow four beats for each complete movement.

925 EXERCISE PLIES AVEC DEMI-HAUTEUR

In profile at the barre, in fifth position.

The same exercise as in the preceding paragraph, with *plié* at the close and stretching for the *dégagé.*

926 EXERCISE 6. RONDS DE JAMBE

In profile at the barre, in fifth position.

Four *ronds de jambe en dehors.*

Four *ronds de jambe en dedans.*

Each *rond de jambe* is broken up as we explained in paragraph 857.

Two *ronds de jambe en dehors à la demi-hauteur.*

Two *ronds de jambe en dedans à la demi-hauteur.*

Each *rond de jambe* is broken up in the same manner.

The barre should be released during the pause in second *à la demi-hauteur* to control balance.

At the end of the last *rond de jambe,* instead of closing in first, place the *pointe* on the ground *en quatrième devant.* Raise the working arm *en couronne* and lean forward until touching the knee with the head, if possible, but keep the back quite straight and the arm in prolongation of the trunk. The inclination comes from the rotation of the hips—there must be no rounding of the back (§ 34). Straighten up. Raise the other arm *en couronne.* Balance.

927 EXERCISE 7. BATTEMENTS FRAPPES

In profile at the barre, in fifth position.

Dégager in second position. Raise the leg *à la demi-hauteur.* Bring the working foot in front of the supporting ankle in the position described in paragraph 883. Tighten again and do in this manner four *frappés* alternately in front and behind.

Four *frappés* with *plié* when the working foot is on the ankle of the other foot.

Finally, four *frappés,* rising *sur la demi-pointe* at the same time the leg is extended *à la demi-hauteur* and with *plié* at the closing on the ankle.

For the exercise to produce best results, the pupil must exert the same force to bend the working leg as to stretch it. He therefore must not cease to apply pressure, being content to check the fall, but actively contract his flexor muscles.

928 EXERCISE 8. KEEPING THE LEG A LA DEMI-HAUTEUR

In profile at the barre, in fifth position.

Dégager. Raise the leg *à la demi-hauteur.* Remain in this position. Place the *pointe* on the ground. Close. The entire movement takes eight *temps.*

En croix.

929 EXERCISE 9. PETITS BATTEMENTS SUR LE COU-DE-PIED

In profile at the barre, in fifth position.

Two *petits battements* backward-forward. *Pointer* in second. Twice in succession.

Six *petits battements* on the instep.

Raise the working leg *au raccourci. Relever sur la demi-pointe.* Place the heel of the supporting leg. *Plier,* the working leg being still *au raccourci. Relever* once again *sur la demi-pointe.* Balance *en raccourci sur la demi-pointe.*

930 EXERCISE 10. PREPARATION FOR PETITS RONDS DE JAMBE SOUTENUS

In profile at the barre, in fifth position.

Dégager in second position. Lift the leg in second *à la demi-hauteur. Plier* the leg *au raccourci.* Stretch. *Plier.* Place the *pointe* on the ground in second. Close.

Four times in succession.

The thigh must not move when the leg bends or is stretched.

931 EXERCISE 11. GRANDS BATTEMENTS

In profile at the barre, in fifth position.

Dégagé. Battement ending *sur la pointe.* Close.

Four of each kind, *en croix.*

932 EXERCISE 12. RELEVES

Face to the barre, in first position.

Plier. Relever sur les demi-pointes. Descend, feet *à plat.* Allow four *temps* for the whole movement.

Four times.

Dégagé to go into second position. Four *relevés* in second, as before.

933 EXERCISE 13. FOOT ON THE BARRE

In profile at the barre, *en quatrième croisée devant à la hauteur,* foot on the barre. The arm corresponding to this leg passes behind the trunk and the hand holds the barre from underneath; the other hand is placed normally on the barre.

Plier slowly four times.

A quarter-turn, facing the barre, both hands placed on it, the working leg in second *à la hauteur*, the foot on the barre.

Two *pliés*. A balancing.

Four times.

A quarter-turn to pass into *quatrième derrière*, the working foot being still at the same place on the barre.

Plier slowly four times.

Repeat the whole exercise from the other side.

934 EXERCISE 14. SUPPLENESS

Back to the barre, in standard position.

Lean forward until touching the knees with the head. Next do the movement described in paragraph 856.

Four times in succession.

In the Center of the Floor

935 PLIES WITH PORTS DE BRAS

In first position, arms in second.

Plier while bringing down the arms into the *position de départ*, rise while lifting the arms in first. *Relever sur les demi-pointes* while continuing to raise the arms until reaching fifth position. Descend, feet *à plat*, while opening the arms in second.

Two times.

The same exercise in second obtained by a *dégagé*, then in fifth obtained by closing of the *dégagé*, forward. One *dégagé* in second position with the anterior foot, closed to the rear, makes it possible to obtain the other fifth.

The movement of the arms must be continuous, very tightly connected, without jerks or sudden interruptions. Attention must be paid to good coordination of the arm and leg movements.

936 DEGAGES

In fifth position.

> *Dégager en croix* with each foot.

> Care should be taken that the hips are horizontal. The student has a tendency to raise the hip of the working leg.

937

In fifth position.

> *Dégager.* Place feet *à plat. Relever sur les demi-pointes.* Descend *à plat.* Close with *plié. Relever sur les demi-pointes* while stretching. Descend *à plat.*

> *En croix,* or according to the order explained in paragraph 897.

938

In fifth position.

> *Dégager.* Raise the leg *à la demi-hauteur. Pointer.* Close.

> Order of paragraph 897.

> When the children have acquired enough strength and control not to raise the hip or take faulty positions at the end of the exercise, it will be *en croix.*

939 BATTEMENTS SUR LE DOU-DE-PIED

In fifth position.

> Raise the anterior leg in fourth *à la demi-hauteur. Plier,* bringing the foot in front of the ankle (position described in § 884). Stretch. Close in fifth.

> Do the same exercise in second, bringing the working foot behind the supporting leg; then *en quatrième derrière.*

> *Relever* in fifth *sur les demi-pointes* with the arms *en couronne.*

> Repeat the whole exercise with the other leg.

940

RONDS DE JAMBE

In fifth position.

> One *rond de jambe en dehors* with each leg, broken up without pause in each position.

> One *rond de jambe en dehors* with each leg, broken up, while bending the supporting leg and stretching it again for the closing.

> One *rond de jambe en dehors* with each leg, *à la demi-hauteur,* with pause in each position.

One *rond de jambe en dehors* with each leg *à la demi-hauteur*, with pause in each position, while bending the supporting leg, which is stretched again at the closing.

941 PORTS DE BRAS

In fifth position, arms in *position de départ*.

Raise the arms in first, open them in second. *Relever sur les demi-pointes.* Descend *à plat* while lowering the arms.

Raise the arms in first, then in third. *Relever sur les demi-pointes.* Descend *à plat*, lowering the arms by way of second position.

The same exercise with the other third.

Raise the arms in first, then in fifth. Do a *dégagé* in second position with the anterior foot and close to the rear, while the arms descend in second, then in the *position de départ*.

Repeat the whole exercise from the other side.

942 PORTS DE BRAS MARCHES

A little later in the year, the small boys should do *ports de bras marchés*, which are a bit harder; one might, for example have them do the following:

In fifth, arms in *position de départ*.

Plier. Pass the anterior foot into fourth, while remaining *plié*. Stretch, raising the posterior foot *à la pointe*. The arms rise in first, then in third; reverse third; fifth. Place the foot *à plat*. *Plier*. The arms descend in first. Raise the anterior foot *à la pointe*. The arms open in second, rise in third, then in fifth. Lift the anterior leg *à la demi-hauteur*, do a *rond de jambe soutenu à la demi-hauteur en dehors*, with the arms in fifth. The leg goes as far as *arabesque croisée* and the arms take the corresponding position. Close in fifth. *Plier*. The arms descend in the *position de départ*. *Relever sur les demi-pointes* while stretching. The arms rise in first, then in fifth. Descend *à plat* while opening the arms in second, then lowering them to *position de départ*.

943 ADAGIO

In fifth, arms in second position.

Plier; the arms descend in the *position de départ*, then rise in front while the legs are stretched once again. *Relever sur les demi-pointes*. The arms continue to rise up to fifth. Descend *à plat* while opening the arms in second.

Lift the anterior leg *en quatrième devant à la demi-hauteur*. Close.
Lift the same leg in second *à la demi-hauteur*. Close to the rear.
Start the exercise afresh from the other side.

Raise the anterior leg *en quatrième devant à la demi-hauteur*, move it in second *à la demi-hauteur*, then *en quatrième derrière à la demi-hauteur*. Close. The dancer must remain in each *position à la demi-hauteur*—this is not a *rond de jambe soutenu à la demi-hauteur décomposé* (broken up).

The same thing from the other side.

944 PAS DE BOURREE

In fifth position.

Eight *pas de bourrée dessus*, observing a pause for each *temps*.

After a rest period during which the other students do the exercise:

Eight *pas de bourrée dessous*, executed in the same manner.

After a rest period:

Four times: first part of a *pas de bourrée dessus-dessous*. Raise the anterior foot *au raccourci* and close it *en cinquième derrière*.

After a rest period:

The same exercise with the second part of the *pas de bourrée dessus-dessous*.

Later in the year the student may execute the *pas de bourrée* without pause and the *pas de bourrée dessus-dessous*.

945 GLISSADES

Here is an exercise analogous to the one described in paragraph 907 for the little girls.

One might also do, for example: *glissade en quatrième croisée devant*, broken up like the other *glissades*.

946 GLISSADES COMPOSEES

In fifth position.

One *glissade en quatrième croisée*. Second part of a *pas de bourrée dessus-dessous*. Rise *sur la demi-pointe* while bringing the anterior leg *au raccourci*. Close *en cinquième devant*. Rise *sur la demi-pointe*, bringing the anterior leg *au raccourci*. *Close en cinquième derrière*.

Repeat the whole exercise from the other side.

947 PAS DE BASQUE

In fifth position.

Pas de basque en descendant, observing a pause in each position. One *relevé sur demi-pointes.*

Repeat four times in succession.

The student will subsequently learn, in the same manner, the *pas de basque en remontant.*

948 ASSEMBLEES

In fifth position.

Eight *assemblées en descendant,* broken up: *plier;* raise the leg in second *à la demi-hauteur;* leap; fall back in fifth *plié,* both feet right at the same time; stretch. One pause (*temps d'arrêt*) between two *assemblées.*

After a rest period, the same exercise with the *assemblées en remontant.*

949 SAUTS

In first position.

Four *soubresauts,* while remaining on the *plié* and taking off directly from this *plié* without any little redundant movements of stretching and bending. The last *soubresaut* falls back in second.

Four *soubresauts* in second executed in the same manner. The last one closes in fifth.

Eight *changements de pied* executed in the same fashion.

Care should be taken in this exercise that the movements are clean; the *plié* is free, without any sudden *sauts.* This is the essential condition to the acquisition of elevation.

950 SALUT

In standard first position, one hand on the hip, the other along the trunk.

The foot corresponding to the arm that is along the body does a *dégagé* in second position, while the arm executes a *port de bras en tournant,* passing in front of the body and arriving in fifth. The working foot passes first and is placed *à plat en quatrième derrière.* The arm is lowered in front while passing through first. The trunk is inclined slightly forward. The anterior foot rises *à la pointe,* while the trunk is made erect. The anterior foot comes to close in standard first position.

The arm whose hand was on the hip is stretched out along the body, the other hand is placed on the hip.

Repeat the whole exercise from the other side.

951

We saw in paragraph 919 that girls start from the beginning to work on style and expression. The same is true for boys. But the latter, of course, exercise in a different direction. They must acquire the manner of elegance and nobility, of broad and precise movement. Great care must be taken that they do not lapse into mannerisms when they lose their own natural awkwardness.

The reader may have noticed that boys, like girls, do not lift up the leg above *demi-hauteur*, whereas in times past the legs of young students were forced up *à la hauteur*. However, by the end of school, all students lift the leg very high, much higher than it was lifted fifty years ago. In fact, when the muscles are strained to excess, it causes little contractions which little by little make them lose their elasticity. In contrast, the very slow and gradual exercise of drawing them, which appears only in the *pliés* with the leg on the barre, allows the elasticity of the muscle to increase. When the muscle has the desired resistance, the leg may be raised higher and higher and can without difficulty be maintained at levels often forming a 135-degree angle with the supporting leg.

Furthermore, this exercise should avert the formation of over-developed calf muscles or of a sway-back due to incorrect exercise of the thigh muscles.

THE FIRST DANCE LESSONS

952

We saw in paragraph 877 how important it is that instruction in the dance be gradual. The essential purpose to be pursued is that the pupil not acquire any bad habits. The less advanced the pupil, the greater the risk of his acquiring them. The manner in which he is directed from the beginning is thus of primary importance. That is why we are now going to explain, according to the principles of Geneviève Guillot and Jacqueline Moreau, how the first part of a child's contact with the dance takes place.

In the past, the beginner was placed in a class with more advanced pupils. Usually he was placed at the barre, between two good pupils, and he was told to follow—which he proceeded to do, one way or another. He was left to his own devices until he began to imitate the movements. Only then did the dancing master start to correct his faults: "Place your foot *en dehors,* open your thigh," etc.

Today it is thought that the beginner should not be placed in contact with pupils who know how to dance. Either all beginners may be regrouped in a single class—something that is possible in the large schools such as that of the Opera, the municipal conservatories, the private schools with a great many pupils, etc. Or, if the school groups together only a restricted number of students or if the beginner enters school when the school year is already in progress, one may have recourse to private lessons.

The children should wear soft slippers. A leotard, which keeps the leg muscles warm, is recommended.

At the Barre

953

The teacher and the student find their place near the barre, each facing the other. The teacher takes first position with the arms in the *position de départ.* He says: "First position. My feet are *en dehors,* all my toes are resting firmly on the ground, my knees are completely taut."

A child who is naturally limber can spontaneously place himself *en dehors* in first position. The others should not be made to open the feet beyond the limit of the correct position.

When a child takes a position *en dehors* he has a tendency to lean his head and shoulders forward, to hollow the back and throw out the buttocks. The teacher explains the correct position to him, with the pelvis tilted, then tells him to tighten his shoulder-blades. The child then throws out his chest while pushing back his shoulder-blades. The teacher has the child place his hands on his shoulders without their moving, then gently brings the elbows down along the body. The correct position of the back is thus obtained. Have the child become aware of this, then have him lower the arms without moving the back. Afterward, to recall the child to the correct position, the teacher might say to him: "Straighten up, stretch your back, lower your shoulders, tuck in your abdomen."

Ask the child, now that he is in the correct position, to move the head so that he will immediately become aware of the independence of his movements and not become tense.

954

The barre, if possible, should be at the height of the child's hip. The teacher raises his arms in first, saying: "First position of the arms." He has the child observe that he is in first position of the feet and of the arms. The child makes the same movement. The teacher places his hand on the barre while explaining the position: elbow slightly bent (about 135 degrees), hand placed gently, he says: "We must not hang onto the barre; we shall release it from time to time when we do the exercises to be sure that we are in very good balance." The child must, in fact, become aware of this new balance which the positions of the dance impose upon his body. The working arm descends along the body, in *position de départ*. Tell the child to "press firmly on the legs while rising up." Then: "Now this is the way we will place ourselves each time we do an exercise at the barre."

The teacher next shows him the *port de bras*, first, second, of the working arm, and which precedes each exercise, by counting simply: "One, two. . . ."

For the following lesson the teacher shows the child each movement, commenting on it, then having the pupil do it.

955 PLIES

A small *demi-plié*. The teacher says: "*Demi-plié.*" He asks the child to "push the thighs very *en dehors*." He will deliberately speak of the thighs in order to show that the opening must start from the hip and not from the knee.

Straighten up. The teacher says: "Stretch as far as you can." Most of the time, a leg considered to be stretched does not have its extensor muscles completely contracted. The child must become aware of just what a totally extended leg is, and he can only do it after the *plié*. The notion of the "straightened leg" is not intuitive, contrary to what one might think.

Do a second *demi-plié*.

The exercise is done to a very slow rhythm, but the movement is continuous. The child must immediately acquire the sense of rhythm and flow of the dance.

The teacher will not require a deep *plié* because the child "would relax his back"—that is, he would not maintain the contraction of the intended muscles, but would hollow out his back, etc. At the end of no more than three or four lessons the pupil will learn to do the deep (*grand*) *plié* while releasing his heels. The teacher will explain that one must first do the *plié* with feet *à plat*, to the extent that this is possible, and not to raise the heels except when it is not possible to do otherwise. Never force the instep on a *grand plié*.

Open in second by way of a *dégagé*, but without stressing its name or its execution. Place the foot *à plat* and say: "Second position." All the children may place themselves *en dehors* in second position, but advise them to "press the toes firmly into the floor."

Two *demi-pliés*. Explain to the child that he must feel that he is pressing down very hard on his heel.

At the end of three or four lessons the pupil will learn the *grand plié* in second position. The teacher will then explain that in this *plié* the heels are never raised.

Have the pupil execute a *demi-tour,* explaining to him that he must always turn from the side of the barre. The same exercise on the other side. Because the *demi-pliés* are in first and second, it may seem pointless to do them from both sides, but it is good for the pupil to become accustomed from the very beginning to exercising this way.

956 DEGAGES

The teacher does a *dégagé en quatrième devant* and says: "*Dégagé.*" Then, joining gesture to word: "My leg is *en dehors*; if I turn it this way, it is *en dedans;* I am placing it back *en dehors.*" Have the pupil's foot stretched forward to the toe in normal position, then ask him to turn his leg *en dehors*. To make sure that the child has understood, the teacher asks him to show the position *en dedans* once again, then *en dehors*. Insist upon the importance of opening up the thigh. If the child has a tendency to raise the hip, the teacher will have him exercise while pressing the working hand on the hip during a few lessons.

The child has returned to first position. The teacher says to him: "*Dégagé*. Stretch the toe. Close in first. *Demi-plié*. Tighten." The teacher may make the movement at the same time he is speaking. Young students need to learn by imitation. They will find it an advantage to see the movement made by the teacher. For older beginners, imitation alone is no longer sufficient: further explanations will be necessary for them.

Have this exercise done twice in succession, very slowly.

The same exercise in second. The teacher will first make them aware of the position *en dehors* as above. He may use the expressions "turn the thigh, or the leg, *en dehors*" but it is better to avoid speaking of the heel because children are inclined to stretch the ankle incorrectly while "falling on the toe," or to twist their foot into a hooklike shape with the ankle turned inward.

In second position the child must, even more than in fourth, become aware of the correct position of the hip. It will almost always be necessary to have him place the working hand on top of it.

Demi-tour. The same exercises from the other side. Remind the pupil that the *demi-tour* is always done from the side of the barre.

957

It is only after three or four lessons that the child will start to do *dégagés en quatrième derrière.* The teacher will make him aware of the position of the leg *en dehors* as already indicated. In *quatrième derrière* we may speak of "lowering the heel." Very often the child will find it to his advantage to place the working hand on the hip to start out.

The *dégagés* are done in first up to the tenth lesson, in which the teacher will introduce the positions of *troisième cinquième croisée.* Because the child will ordinarily be unable to go into fifth position, the teacher will replace it either by a third or by a fifth that is only partially opened. Later, he will gradually progress in the direction of the crossing, in the case of the third, and toward the opening, in the other case. The child must not be made to do fifth positions in which the knees cannot stretch or in which the feet "fall on the toe." The teacher should wait the necessary time in order to obtain a fifth.

958 BATTEMENTS A LA DEMI-HAUTEUR

Two *battements à la demi-hauteur en quatrième devant* followed by two in second.

The teacher shows the movement while saying *battement.* He indicates that "the leg remains *en dehors* as we have learned for the *dégagés.*" Point out that *both* knees must be stretched.

959 RONDS DE JAMBE

The teacher says the name *rond de jambe en dehors* and executes it with *arrêt pointé* (pause, toe pointed) *en quatrième devant*, in second, and closing with feet *à plat* in first. Notice: the leg does not go into *quatrième derrière.* The teacher explains: "We begin now as for a *dégagé*, then we pass into second without changing the position of the leg, and we close in first."

Four *ronds de jambe en dehors.* A *demi-tour.* The same thing on the other side.

Demi-tour.

Four *ronds de jambe en dedans* starting with a *dégage* in second position and explanations. The same thing on the other side.

When the child has learned to do the *dégagés en quatrième derrière*, he will execute the *ronds de jambe*, complete but always *décomposés*.

960 BATTEMENTS FRAPPES

In first position. *Dégager* in second position, raise the leg *à la demi-hauteur*. Bend the working leg while bringing the foot behind the supporting leg. Remain one *temps* in this position. Place the working *pointe* in second. Close in first and remain there for two *temps*.

The teacher shows the exercise, demonstrating that the thigh does not move when the leg bends.

Start afresh four times.

At the end of three or four lessons the pupil will then perform the exercise four more times, doing a *plié* with the supporting leg at the moment of the *frappé* and stretching it again for the *pointé*.

Not until after about ten lessons will the teacher require the *frappé* to the front, showing the forward position described in paragraph 884 (Fig. 118). The *frappés* will then be done alternately to the front and to the rear.

After two or three lessons the pupil will conclude this exercise with a balancing with feet *à plat* in the position of the *frappé*.

961 DEMI-HAUTEUR

In first position. *Dégager en quatrième devant*. Raise the leg *à la demi-hauteur*. Remain there. Release the barre, grasp it again. Place the *pointe en quatrième devant*. Close.

The teacher asks the child who has a tendency to "sit down" to "straighten up" or to "grow tall" during the balancing.

The exercise is done twice *en quatrième devant* and twice in second.

Care should be taken that the trunk remains straight. The child will have a tendency to lean backward when he raises the leg forward. Remind him that throughout the whole exercise one must "tuck in the abdomen and lengthen the back."

The same thing on the other side.

When the child has learned the *quatrième derrière*, the exercise may also be done in this position and at that time the order of sequences indicated in paragraph 887 may be adopted.

962 PETITS BATTEMENTS SUR LE COU-DE-PIED

After the fifth lesson, the *petits battements* on the instep may be done at the barre. The pupil does a *dégagé in second*; *petit battement* forward-backward, then *pointé in second position*. The rhythm is very slow: count 1 for placing the foot forward, 2 for the back, 3 to *pointer,* and on 4 the pupil has come to a stop.

The exercise is done four times in succession, without closing in first, the *battements* on the instep being executed starting from the *pointe in second position.*

963 GRANDS BATTEMENTS

In first position.

Dégagé en quatrième devant. Battement ending on the *pointe.* Close in first.

Explain that the trunk must not move, that the leg must be fully extended. Above all, one should not tell the child to "raise his leg as high as possible" because with this aim in mind he would surely take up faulty positions. Simply say "raise the leg."

Four *battements en quatrième devant.*

The same thing on the other side.

Four *battements in second position,* done in the same manner.

The same thing on the other side.

When the child has learned *quatrième derrière,* the teacher will have him do these *battements* by placing himself facing the barre and changing feet after the first four *battements,* by way of a *dégagé in second.*

964 FOOT ON THE BARRE

After the fifth lesson, if the teacher determines that the child has a large enough spread (lit., opening), he will have him put the foot on the barre in second, facing the barre. The child will do four *demi-pliés*. A little later the child will learn the *ports de bras* explained in paragraph 891.

Care must be taken that the trunk remains straight, that the back is not hollowed, and that the leg does not turn inward.

965

For a first lesson, this barre exercise with the explanations takes about three-quarters of an hour. Under no circumstances must one try to go too fast. The teacher must be careful to use simple terms; not to confuse the pupil with too many explanations, but to make frequent use of the same words, which must be familiar by the end of this work at the barre: first position (of the feet and arms), second, *dehors, dedans, demi-plié, dégagé, battement, rond de jambe,* close, *demi-hauteur.* The expression *battement frappé* will be learned a bit later along with others such as *battements sur le cou-de-pied.* The child will also learn what it means to "hold in your abdomen," "lengthen your back," "lower your shoulders," "bear down on your toes," "open up your thigh," "stretch your knees," "lengthen your *pointe.*" It is not sufficient that he merely know the meaning of these words: it is necessary that hearing them be followed immediately by the adequate muscular reaction. The teacher must, in fact, bring about the appearance of actual conditioned reflexes.

In the Center of the Floor

966

The teacher gives the name and illustrates the five positions of the feet and arms. The pupil does the first, which he knows already, then the second, for which he learns the position of the arms.

Place the pupil back in first, arms in *position de départ.* Remind him of the correct position of the trunk, then tell him he is going to do a *port de bras.*

Raise the arms in first, open in second. Count 1 on the starting position, 2 on the first, 3 on the second, and on 4 the child does not move. When several *ports des bras* are strung together, the 1 corresponds to the descent of the arms in the *position de départ.*

Do the movement four times, very slowly, but without jerks. Show that the arms must remain supple, neither stretched nor *pliés.* Present the idea—even this soon—of a "pretty hand." Have the pupil follow the hand with his eye. The child must form the habit of never letting his glance be vague.

The first lesson will stop here.

967 DEGAGES

At the second lesson the pupil, in first, will perform the following, four times with the same foot: one *dégagé in second position* closed in first; *demi-plié*; stretch. Count 1 on the *dégagé*, 2 on the closing, 3 on the *demi-plié*, 4 on the stretching. The same thing with the other foot.

968   SAUTS

Toward the fourth lesson the *sauts* will be taught. After the *ports de bras* and the *dégagés* in the center of the floor, the pupil will return to the barre and assume first position.

Demi-plié. Soubresaut in first, falling back *plié.* Stretch.

Four times in succession.

The same thing in second.

Go back to first position. Four *échappés*, going from first to second.

In the following lesson the pupil will do the *sauts* in the center of the floor, taking care that the trunk remains erect in correct position, and that the feet leave or touch the floor at exactly the same time. Do not require a high *saut*. The whole idea of performance must be excluded from the first lessons. The central idea is that of always being in the correct position.

969   DEGAGE PLIE

When the pupil has learned the *positions croisée*—third or fifth—he will do the following exercise in the center of the floor:

Plier. Dégager while remaining *plié.* Stretch while closing.

The exercise may be done at first according to the order of paragraph 887, then later *en croix* (§ 811).

970   BOWS

Around the fifth lesson the pupil will learn to make the bow. It will be done starting from a first and will conclude in this position, because the *positions croisées* have not yet been learned. From there on, the bow will be made as indicated (§ 918 for the girls' *révérence*; § 950 for the boys' *salut*).

971

We have not specified whether these first lessons applied to a girl or to a boy, because they are in actual fact valid for both. The differences will only appear a little later.

Among the simple elements not yet studied are the *demi-pointes.* These will be introduced quite some time later, first in the form of *relevés* on both feet at the barre (§ 893), then as *relevés* on both feet in the center of the floor, as *piqués* on one foot in the center, as *relevés* on one foot at the barre, and finally as *relevés* on one foot in the center. This apprenticeship will be spread out over several months.

As for the *pointes,* we have reiterated that there can be no question of introducing them. Only the good teacher is able to judge the proper moment in terms of what is possible for his pupil. But even for talented pupils, one must allow at least two years of daily exercise before being able to take up *pointes.*

In regard to dance steps, the first one to be taught will be the *glissade.* The *pas de bourrée,* which used to be used as a beginning, should come later. For the *pas de basque*—much more complex—one must wait a few months, with children practising daily.

From among the *sauts,* after the *soubresauts* and *échappés,* the *assemblées* will be learned first because they can be broken up easily and they call forth precise elements which are familiar to the pupils.

These few examples show us how necessary it is to re-examine traditional habits in this regard. The order in which the steps will be taught depends only in part on their degree of difficulty. What matters first of all is their resolution into simple, familiar elements and the possibility of analyzing them. Take for example the *sissonne* and the *assemblée.* In the past it was customary to teach the *sissonne* first. Theoretically, as we have seen (§ 288), the two steps are the reverse of one another and call for the same elements, namely: *plié* in fifth, *plié* in second *à la demi-hauteur* (or *à la hauteur*), *saut.* But in the *assemblée,* the breaking up is easy: *plié* in fifth; lift the leg in second *à la demi-hauteur* while remaining *plié; saut,* alighting on both feet with the knees flexed; stretch. The child easily breaks up the step into four *temps,* utilizes only known positions, and familiarizes himself with the technique. For the *sissonne,* on the other hand, one must alight on the *plié* with the leg *à la demi-hauteur*; it is much harder to remain in this position after a *saut* and the breaking up proves more arduous than the step itself.

With beginners, even more than with seasoned dancers, the teacher must test very broad theoretical knowledge; he must give a great deal of thought to the courses, have a perfectly worked-out plan of exercise, and anticipate with rigorous logic the slow acquisition of techniques which complete one another and eventually adjust themselves like the pieces of a puzzle.

Need one be reminded that the child must never work or exercise except under the teacher's supervision and that a beginner must not have several different teachers?

Index

Abridgement (See *Raccourcissement*)
Acrobatics, 189-94, 284
  influence of classical dance on, 284
Acrobatie en couple, 284
Actéon, 237
Adagio (See also *Pas de deux*)
  69, 70, 71, 84, 86, 87, 88, 134, 167, 190,
    208, 219, 221, 225, 252-288, 230, 310,
    311, 353
  for beginning boys, 387-88
  for beginning girls, 375
  definition, 252
  exercise for men, 363
  final comments, 288
  further development, 283-84
  general statement, 252
  meaning as love song, 254-55
  movements in general, 275
  movements on the ground, 255
  pas à terre avec parcours, 277
  pliés, 277
  portés, 280, 281, 283-84
  poses, 255
  relationship between male and female
    dancer, 255
  sauts, 279-80
  tours, 278-79
  for two, 253-74
  "vertical development" of, 286
Adagio at the bar:
  correct body position, 343-44
  exercise for beginning girls, 370-71
  exercise for men, 361-62
Adagio composé, 347-48
'Adame Miroir, 232
Aesthetic moment, definition, 5
L'Age heureux, 103
Agenouillement, 88, 89, 90, 91, 166, 270,
  277
Aida, 89
Alexandre le Grand, 90
Allègement, 279
"American leap," 123
L'Amour, 233
Andreani, Xavier, 194
Angel's leap (See *Saut de l'ange*)
Animals:
  ballets grouping numerous, 239
  water, represented in dance, 239
  without wings, dance movements of, 237-40
Animaux Modèles, Les, 216, 236, 238, 239

Anklework:
  correct body positions, 319-20
  exercises, 319
  practices for men, 358
Ant, represented in dance, 238
L'Appel de la Montagne, 91, 232
Arabesque, 36, 37, 38, 40, 56, 69, 87, 98,
  102, 156, 159, 162, 165, 168, 169, 174,
  175, 178, 179, 181, 183, 208, 210, 211,
  224, 271, 276, 277, 279, 297, 305, 307,
  308, 343, 347, 348, 349, 360, 363, 364
  body position, 343
  definition, 33
  hand position, 241
  history of term, 37-38
Arabesque croisée, 35, 157, 347, 350, 387
  definition, 34
Arabesque croisée à bras ouvert, 34, 35
Arabesque étirée, definition, 37
Arabesque ouverte, 33, 35, 160, 302, 363
Arabesque ouverte à bras croisée, definition,
  33, 34, 35
Arabesque poussée, definition, 37
Arabesque sur la demi-pointe, 361
Arabesque sur la pointe, 356
Arcades, 104
Ashton, F., 176, 219, 227
Arm positions, 18-19, 195-250
  asymmetrical, definition, 198
  general statement, 196-97
  horizontal and to the rear, definition, 205
  intermediate, definition, 206
  lateral, vertical and horizontal positions,
    202-203, 205-209, 215
  low and forward positions, definition, 212
    214
  low and to the rear, definition, 205, 215
  low for intermediate positions, 205
  movements:
    in character ballets, 227-28
    involving one arm only, 228-29
  open and horizontal positions, 205, 206
  pliés, 198, 199, 216, 218
  "sustained," 194
  "symmetrical," definition, 198
  tendu, 198, 199, 200-201, 202, 206, 207
    208, 210, 211, 216, 218
Arms in a circle (See *Bras en couronne*)
Arrêt pointé, 394
Arrow movement (See *Temps de flèche*)
Assemblée, 86, 115, 116, 128, 181, 294, 300,

Assemblée, (con't.):
305, 349, 378, 399
for beginning boys, 389
for beginning girls, 376
without change of feet, 117
characterized by *devant* or *derrière*, 116
compared with *sissonne*, 115-16
definition, 115-16
Assemblée battu, as *entrechat de volée*, 139
Assemblée-changement de pied, 117
Assemblée derrière, 291, 297, 298, 305
with change of feet, definition, 117
Assemblée devant, 291, 296, 299
positions, 117, 118
Assemblée en descendant, 376, 389
Assemblée en raccourci, 118
Assemblée en remontant, 376, 389
Assemblée in second position, 116
Assemblée soutenu, definition, 181
Assiette à plat, 9
Assiette du pied, 8, 9
Assis sur le talon, 91
Attitude, 19, 38, 39, 40, 42, 61, 108, 115,
156, 157, 158, 159, 160, 161, 162, 165,
167, 168, 169, 174, 175, 176, 178, 179,
180, 183, 207, 279, 284, 292, 297, 302,
307, 340, 343, 344, 356, 360, 361
body position, 343-44
definition, 38, 115
Russian variation, 38, 39
variations of, 40
Attitude croisée, 347
definition, 38
Attitude devant (See *Raccourci en quatrieme
devant*)
Attitude étirée, 40
Attitude ouverte, definition, 38
Attitude pousée, 40
Auric, Georges, 61
Aveline, A., 22, 71, 72, 89, 91, 102, 103, 106,
111, 112, 158, 178, 179, 190, 206, 219,
229, 231, 233, 237, 239, 253, 291

Backward (See *Derrière*)
Backward fourth (See *Quatrième derrière*)
Backward somersault (See *Culbute en arrière*)
Backwards walk (See *Marche à reculons*)
Baiser de la Fée, Le, 234
Bal des Blanchisseuses, Le, 193
Balance, feats of, 192
Balanchine, G., 58, 90, 98, 123, 176, 177,
181, 225, 234, 238, 258, 260, 266, 269,
271
Balancing, exercise for men, 364
Balancing acts (See *Equilibrés*)
Ballets Russes, 128, 249, 254
Ballon, 381
Ballonné, 130, 131, 187, 299, 300
definition and various positions, 125
Ballonné pas de basque en descendant,
definition, 293
Ballotté, definition, 126

Bas (*See* Low)
Basic position, definition, 11
Battement, 28, 50, 51, 52, 53, 98, 117, 123,
124, 226, 311, 335, 336, 346, 360, 361,
396, 397
definition, 49
exercise for beginning girls, 371-72
exercise for men, 361
on the instep with *pliés*, exercise for beginning girls, 369-70
more an exercise than a dance step, 52
in relation to *relevé sur la pointe*, 69-70
starting from various basic positions, 51
Battement à la demi-hauteur, 345, 394
definition, 50
Battement à la hauteur, 50
Battement à la pointe, 371
Battement à la seconde, 4, 56, 338, 396
definition, 50
Battement à la seconde at *demi-hauteur*, 319
Battement arrondi, 52, 292, 348
Battement arrondi en dehors, 224, 307, 360
Battement arrondi, relevé sur la pointe, 70, 356
Battement d'ailes, definition, 236
Battement en cloche, 103, 168
essential moments, 51-52
exercise, 339
exercise for men, 363
Battement en croix, 331
Battement en quatrième à la hauteur, 54
Battement en quatrième derrière, 331, 338
definition, 50-51
Battement en quatrième derrière à la pointe,
372
Battement en quatrième devant, 123, 276,
331, 361, 396
definition, 50
Battement en quatrième devant à la hauteur,
157
Battement en quatrième devant à la pointe,
371
Battement en quatrième devant ouverte, 338
Battement frappé, 397
exercise for beginning boys, 383-84
exercise for beginning girls, 370
exercise for the child, 395
Battements on the instep (See *Battements
sur le cou-de-pied*)
Battement plié, 331
Battement pointe à terre, 338, 371
Battement relevé sur la demi-pointe, 337
Battement relevé sur la pointe, 337, 356
Battement sur le cou-de-pied, 397
for beginning boys, 386
correct body position, 330-32
definition, 52, 53
Battement tendu, 331, 337
Batterie, 118, 131, 137, 142, 294, 306, 349,
350
Batterie à croisements, 131-39, 298, 331, 337
Batterie de choc, 139-46
Bear, dance moments of, defined, 238

Beating of wings (See *Battement d'ailes*)
Beating steps (See *Batterie; Pas battu*)
Beatings (See *Battement*)
Beats with impact (See *Batterie de choc*)
Behind the body (See *Quatrième derrière*)
Bejart, M., 45, 85, 89, 91, 96, 125, 192, 206, 226, 237, 238, 242, 243, 249, 255, 268, 274
Bell (See *Cloche*)
Belle au Bois Dormant, La, 127, 138, 227, 235, 236, 238, 244, 279
Belle Hélène, La, 190
Bent (See *Plié; Plier*)
Billy-goat, represented in dance, 238
Bird tucking head under wing, 236
Bizet, Georges, 176
Blanche-Neige, 21, 237
Blasis, Carlo, 37, 38, 40
Body positions, 17-18
  facing forward (See *Corps de face*)
  leaning backwards (See *Corps penché en arrière*)
  leaning forward (See *Corps penché en avant*)
  leaning sideways (See *Corps penché de côté*)
  twisted forward (See *Corps épaulé penché en avant; Epaulé*)
Bogomolova, Ludmila, 243
Boléro, 64, 91, 216
Bolshoi Theatre of St. Petersburg (Russia), 235
Bourmeister, Wadimir, 102, 178, 192, 212, 216, 243, 280, 288
Bournonville, 108
Bourrée, 24
Bows (curtsies) (See also *Révérence*), 85
  for the child, 398
Bras au dos, 215
Bras croisés, 212
Bras d'arabesque, 224
Bras d'attitude, 19, 207
Bras en couronne, 19
Bridge (See *Pont*)
"Bring the leg forward" (See *Passer la jambe devant*)
Brisé, 186, 299, 306, 351, 364
  definition, 137-38
  as *glissade battue,* 139
Brisé de volée, 138
Brisé en tournant, definition, 178
Brisé Télémaque, definition, 306
Brisé volés de volée, 207
Broken back (See Les *Reins cassés*)
Broken down (See *Décomposé*)
Broken up (See *Décomposé*)
Brugnoli, Amalia, 10
Brushings (See *Frottement*)
But, 283

Cabriole, 140, 146, 296, 345
  with beating step, 350
  definition, 141

Cabriole (con't.):
  designation of, 146
  etymology of, 141
  principle of, 142
Cabriole à la hauteur, 143
Cabriole battue, 102
Cabriole battu double, 187
Cabriole devant, 98
Cabriole en quatrième derrière, 143
Cabriole en quatrième derrière non battue, 98
Cabriole en quatrième devant, 98, 143
  definition, 142
Cabriole in second position, definition, 143
Cabriole non battue, definition, 98
Cage, The, 238, 239, 242, 265
Calves not beaten together (See *Non battue*)
Cambré, definition, 22
Cancan, 191
Caprices de Cupidon, 233-34
Carmen, 263
Cartwheel (See *Roue*)
Casse-Noisette, 102, 106, 128, 130, 228, 244, 287
Castor and Pollux, 64, 224
Cat, dance movements of, 238
Center of balance, shifting of, 46
Center of the floor (See also *Milieu*)
  dance lesson for beginning boys, 385-390
  exercises for beginning girls, 373-80
  exercises for men, 363-66
Chained turns (See *Tours chaînés*)
Change of foot (See *Changement de pied*)
Changement de pied, 177, 306, 349, 350, 364, 376, 389
  as name for *entrechat 2,* 132
Changement de pieds sur les deux pointes, 356
Changement en demi-cinquième, 80
Characteristic moment, definition, 5
Charrat, Janine, 232, 237
Chassé, 127, 299, 365
  definition, 61-62
  start of, 62
Chassé croisé, 127
  definition, 62
Chassé en remontant, definition, 62
Chassé ouverte, 127
  definition, 62
Chassé sauté, 127
Chauvire, Yvette, 42
Chemin de Lumière, Le, 190
Chevalier Errant, Le, 81, 160, 215, 216, 233, 243
Chevalier et la Demoiselle, Le, 57, 69, 89, 90, 216, 237, 249
Chimaera, 214
Choc, 131, 140, 143, 146
Chopin, F., 61
Chute, definition, 47
Cigogneau, Le, 235
Cinquième derrière, 74, 112, 126, 165, 167, 170, 171, 223, 297, 298, 306, 307, 323, 335, 346, 348, 349, 364, 370, 375, 378, 380, 388

Cinquième devant, 74, 110, 170, 171, 293, 335, 336, 344, 349, 353, 361, 368, 372, 373, 388
Circle (See *Couronne*)
Circling series of turns (See *Manège*)
Clairière, 262
Clapping the hands (See *Claquement des mains*)
Claquements de doigts, 293
Claquements des mains, 243
Classical dance, grammar of (*See* individual terms)
Classical sequences (See also *Enchainement classique*)
  definition, 289-90
Clenched fist (See *Poing fermé*)
Closing (See *Fermeture*)
Clustine, Yvan, 81, 90, 98, 115, 125, 225, 228, 281, 299
Cocteau, Jean, 61
"Complex" arm positions, definition, 218
Complex poses, 32-46
Compound *port de bras* in third position, 223
Compound steps (See *Pas composés*)
Contretemps, definition, 127
Coppélia, 21, 40, 58, 76, 80, 98, 124, 130, 205, 206, 214, 219. 231, 243, 248, 253, 293
Coralli, J., 21, 63, 87, 105, 112, 126, 158, 159, 161, 178, 180, 202, 205, 206, 208, 212, 217, 219, 225, 244, 253, 280, 292, 294, 299
Corps de ballet, 154
  procession of, 219
Corps de face, 17
Corps épaulé penché en avant, 44
Corps penché de côté, 17
Corps penché en arrière, 17-18
Corps penché en avant, 17
Cou-de-pied, sur le, 159
Coup d'un pied, definition, 129, 130
Coup des deux pieds, definition, 129-30
Coupé, 68, 124, 131, 184, 296, 297, 304
  definition, 60
Coupé en tournant, definition, 183-84
Coupé fouetté, 299
  with *temps de pointe piqué en remontant,* 292
Coupé jeté, 180
Coupé jeté en tournant, 184, 290
Coupé non sauté, 378
Coupé sauté, 87, 183, 184
  definition, 126
Coupé tourné, 180
Couronne, 102, 122, 124, 151, 161, 162, 168, 180, 181, 182, 227, 230, 272, 276, 281, 287, 327, 329, 340, 343, 348, 358, 361, 362, 368, 370, 372, 378, 379, 382, 383, 386
Course, definition, 104
Couru, 41
Créatures de Prométhée, 23
Croisé, 191, 296

Croisé en quatrième derrière, 151
Croisement, 131
Croisement derrière, 131
Croisement devant, 131
Croix, 358, 359, 361, 364, 368, 371, 383, 384, 386. 398
  definition, 323
Cross (See *Croix*)
Crossed (See *Croisé*)
Crossed arms (See *Bras croisés*)
Crossing (See *Croisement)*
Crystal Palace, 98, 176, 177. 181, 225, 260, 271, 276
Culbute, 141
Culbute acrobatique, definition, 192-93
Culbute en arrière, definition, 192
Culbute en avant, definition, 192
Cullberg, Birgit, 238
Curtsy, as expression of *tête penchée en avant,* 21
Cygne, Le, 91
Cygne Noir, Le, 352

da Bologna, Giovanni, 40
Dame à la Licorne, La, 237
Damnation de Faust, La, 91, 96, 125
Dance, distinguished from movement, 3
Dancing lesson, 310-99
  advice for instruction of child, 391-92
  beginning boys, 381-90
  beginning girls, 366-81
  comments on bar exercise, 396-97
  concluding comments on beginner, 398-99
  daily program, 354-56
  exercise in center of floor, 397-99
  exercises at the bar, 391-97
  general comments, 390-91
  general sequence, 310-11
  program for one week on the variation from *Giselle,* 356
  responsibilities of teacher, 311
Dance steps:
  categories of, 45
  essential and secondary movements, 5
Danse classique, La, 35*fn*
Danse d'aujourd'hui, La, 284*fn,* 286*fn*
Danse du Marin, 232
Danse grecque antique, 154*fn,* 183*fn,* 235*fn*
Danse russe, 128
Danses de caractère, 9
Danses polovtsiennes du Prince Igor, 40, 128, 129. 170, 214, 229, 234, 254, 283
Daphnis et Chloé, 23, 84, 89, 92, 106, 186, 192, 205, 228, 232, 242, 244, 272
Darsonval, Lycette, 36, 176
Dauberval, 219
David triomphant, 233
de Mille, Agnes, 244
Death of the Swan (See *Mort du Cygne, La*)
Déboulé (See also Pirouette), 158, 183, 352
  definition, 154
  developments of, 155-56
  origins, 154

Déboulé (con't.):
  variation in technique, 155
Décomposé, 395
Dedans, 26, 40, 53, 54, 56, 57, 58, 84, 173,
    174, 178, 190, 291, 304, 335, 360, 393,
    397
  definition in terms of a movement, 52
Deuxième position, 80
  as movement, 44
Deep bend (See *Fondu*)
Deer, dance movements of, 237
Défilé du corps de ballet of the Opera, 202
Dégagé, 48, 49, 87, 164, 171, 208, 221, 224
    252, 284, 306, 307, 311, 319, 323, 324,
    336, 337, 345, 346, 358, 373, 378, 382,
    383, 385, 387, 389, 393, 395, 396, 397,
    398
  with *battements,* 345
  for beginning boys, 386
  for beginning girls, 374-75
  for the child, 397
  correct body positions, 322
  definition, 47
  exercise for beginning boys, 382
  exercise for beginning girls, 368
  exercise for the child, 393-94
  exercises for men, 359, 363
  general exercises, 322-24
  with *pliés,* 345
Dégagé à la seconde, 50, 74, 374
  definition, 47
Dégagé avec demi-hauteur:
  exercise for beginning boys, 382-83
  exercise for beginning girls, 368
Dégagé avec jambe libre pliée, 49
Dégagé en croix, 382, 386
Dégagé en descendant, 48, 345, 375
Dégagé en quatrième, 25
Dégagé en quatrième, croisée, 49
Dégagé en quatrième derrière, 49, 53, 210,
    372, 373, 374, 382, 394, 395
Dégagé en quatrième devant, 49, 53, 166, 346,
    364, 371, 374, 375, 393, 395, 396
Dégagé en quatrième devant croisée, 363
Dégagé en quatrième ouverte, 49
Dégagé en remontant, 345, 375
  definition, 48
Dégagé plié:
  for the child, 398
  exercise for beginning boys, 382
  exercise for beginning girls, 368
  exercise for men, 358
Dégagé pointe à terre, 336
Dehors, 15, 23, 25, 26, 53, 54, 56, 57, 58,
    74*fn,* 83, 84, 90, 105, 117, 130, 131,
    149, 173, 178, 273, 291, 304, 305,
    318, 323, 324, 326, 329, 330, 335,
    337, 340, 344, 360, 381, 391, 392,
    393, 394, 397
  definition, 10-11
  movement, definition, 44, 52
  used by Middle and Far Eastern dancers, 11
Demi-arabesque, 67, 266
  definition, 36

Demi-arabesque ouverte, 307
Demi-attitude, definition, 40
Demi-cinquième, 57, 75, 77, 78, 80, 150
  definition, 25-26
Demi-contretemps, 296
  definition, 127
Demi-hauteur, 28, 36, 69, 77, 79, 98, 102, 104,
    106, 112, 117, 122, 130, 137, 140, 152,
    156, 161, 171, 175, 178, 301, 304, 306,
    307, 319, 330, 334, 339, 340-41, 358,
    359, 360, 368, 369, 370, 375, 377, 378,
    379, 382, 383, 384, 386, 387, 388, 389,
    390, 395, 397, 399
  definition, 27
  exercise for the child, 395
Demi-hauteur en quatreième effacee, 128
Demi-normale, 149
Demi-plié, 63, 82, 340, 358, 368, 370, 373,
    377, 382, 392, 393, 396, 397, 398
Demi-pointe, 9, 10, 23, 45, 46, 58, 59, 61, 65,
    75, 80, 81, 82, 107, 126, 149, 150, 151,
    152, 154, 155, 156, 163, 164, 170, 171,
    173, 174, 269, 276, 326, 327, 330, 331,
    334, 337, 340, 342, 344, 346, 347, 356,
    357, 358, 360, 361, 362, 364, 370, 375,
    379, 382, 383, 386, 388, 398
Demi-pointe en cinquième derrière, 379
Demi-positions, definition, 23
Demi-première, 26
  definition, 23
Demi-quatrième, 49, 126, 348
  definition, 24
Demi-seconde, 47
  definition, 23
Demi-tour, 151, 154, 157, 162, 169, 179, 180,
    181, 182, 183, 185, 291, 356, 358, 367,
    370, 371, 382, 393, 394
Demi-tour relevé, definition, 153
Demi-troisième, definition, 23
Demoiselles de la Nuit, La, 238
Départ de détourné, 25
Déplacement, 92, 158, 208
Derivative positions (See also *Positions
    derivées*) 23-32
  à la hauteur, 56
  definition, 23
  fourth 28-32
  kinds of, 26
  second, 28
Descendant, 67, 301, 374
  definition, 48
Descombey, Michel, 21, 45, 91, 102, 191, 196,
    215, 226, 231, 242, 243, 245, 249, 253,
    257, 258, 262, 271, 274, 283
Dessus-dessous, 79
Détourné, 150-51, 152, 344, 349
  principle of, 150
Détourné à la hauteur, 348
  definition, 157
Détourné à terre, 151, 224, 347
  definition, 150-51
Détourné sur les deux pieds, 222
Détourné sur les deux pointes, 152
  definition, 151

Deuil en 24 Heures, 215
Deux Pigeons, 112, 229, 281
Deux pointes, 181
Développé, 28, 51, 54, 72, 82, 126, 157, 161,
    253, 284, 291, 302, 304, 305, 336, 344,
    351, 364
  correct body position, 333
  definition, 56
  essential moments, 56
  exercise for beginning girls, 371
  exercises, 332-34
  with *pliés,* exercises, 334
Développé à la demi-hauteur, 334
Développé à la hauteur, 334
Développé en arabesque ouverte, 347
Développé en quatrième croisée, 72
Développé en quatrième derrière, 162, 362
Développé en quatrième derrière à la
  hauteur, 335
Développé en quatrième devant, 56, 57, 115,
  361
Développé en quatrième devant à la demi-
  hauteur, 346, 371,
Développé en quatrième devant à la hauteur,
  325, 335, 337, 364
Développé en quatrième ouverte, 72
Développé relevé en quatrième ouverte devant,
  350
Développé in second à la hauteur, 290
Développé relevé, 71, 72
Diaghilev, Serge, 128, 249, 254
Dictionnaire d'Esthétique, 36
Disengaged (See *Degage*)
Divertissement, 97, 127, 158, 228
Divertissement, 291
Djali, 112
Dog, dance movements of, 238
Doigts interlacés, 244
Doigts tendus et écartés, 242
Doigts tendus serrés, 242
Don Quichote, 281
Dos rond, 342
Double acrobatics (See *Acrobatie en couple*)
Double fouetté, 176
Double sissonne, 296
Double sissonne en descendant, definition,
  296
Double sissonne en remontant, definition,
  296-97
Drawn-out arabesque (See *Arabesque étirée*)
Dung-bettle, represented in dance, 238

Ecarté à la seconde, definition, 42
Ecarté en arrière, 42, 103
Echappé, 84, 96, 118-23, 171, 186, 300, 306,
  340, 349, 378, 398, 399
  arm movements, 122
  for beginning girls, 376
  definition, 118
  executed with different types of *entrechats,*
  139
Echappé à plat, 122

Echappé battu, 351
  definition, 138-39
Echappé battu 3, 350, 364
  definition, 138
Echappé battu 4, definition, 139
Echappé battu 5, definition, 139
Echappé battu 6, definition, 139
Echappé battu en tournant, definition, 186
Echappé fermé, 120, 290, 350
Echappé in fourth position, definition and
  uses, 122, 123
Echappé in second position, definition, 119,
  121-22
Echappé in second *sur lex deux pointes,* 303
Echappé sauté, 164, 350, 351, 364
  definition, 119-20
Echappé sur les demi-pointes, 118, 378
Echappé sur les pointes, 118, 166, 349, 351
  definition, 119
Echappé sur les talons, 128
Ecole de Danse du Théâtre National de
  l'Opéra, 85, 154, 219, 222, 367, 381
Edux printanières, 243
El amor brujo, 64, 245
Elan, 68, 82
Elevation (See *Ballon*)
Elfes, Les, 235
Elssler, Fanny, 253
Elssler, Therese, 253
Elvire, 206
Emboîté, 68, 351
  definition, 61
Encased steps (See *Emboite*)
Enchaînement, 8, 23, 288-308
Endymion, 236, 237
Ensellé, definition, 18
Ensemble, 381
Entrechat, 5, 68, 131, 132, 134-37, 139, 140,
  141, 142, 161, 187, 230, 280, 292, 300,
  345
  as soubresaut battu, 139
Entrechat 0, 132
Entrechat 1, definition, 131-32
Entrechat 2, definition, 132
Entrechat 3, 135, 136, 138, 298, 299, 306,
  350, 351, 364
  compared to *entrechat 6,* 135
  definition, 132
Entrechat 3 vole, 298
Entrechat 4, 135, 136, 298, 299, 306, 351,
  364
  definition, 132
Entrechat 4 volé, 137, 298, 306
Entrechat 5, 135, 136, 138, 364
  definition, 132
Entrechat 5 de volée, 294
Entrechat 6, 135, 136, 292, 350, 364, 365
  compared to *entrechat 3,* 135
  definition, 132
Entrechat 7, 135, 136
  definition, 134
Entrechat 8, 135
  definition, 134
Entrechat 10, definition, 134

Entrechat de volée;
  as *assemblée battue,* 139
  definition, 136
Entrechat en tournant, 178, 186
Entrechat with demi-tour, 178
Entre Deux Rondes, 49, 85
Entrée, definition, 21
Enveloppé, 152-53, 155, 160, 180, 181, 349
Epaulé, 29, 33, 40, 42, 58, 64, 74, 79, 112,
  127, 155, 222, 224, 272, 348
  definition, 17
Epaulement, 30, 74, 113, 338, 353
Equilibré, 300
Etchevery, J.J., 130, 210, 228
Etudes, 83, 88, 96, 103, 143, 175, 176, 186,
  190, 226, 253
Eugene Onegin, 235
Extended position toward the back (See
  Ecarté en arrière)
Execution, 252-308
Exercises:
  in balance, 346-47
  at the bar, 314-45
    for beginning boys, 382-85
    general comments, 311, 314
    for men, 357-63
    purposes, 310
  in the center of the floor, 345-53
  for terminating lessons, 352-53

Face forward the front (See *Tête de face*)
Fallen *flic-flac* (See *Flic-flac tombé*)
Fall River Legend, 244
Falls (See *Chute*)
Farandole, 38
Failli, 159, 160, 180, 297, 356
Failli devant, definition, 128
Failli grand jeté, 231, 290
  definition, 180-81
Failli posé tour enveloppé, definition, 297
Fancy Free, 232
Faust, 22, 71, 103, 158, 229, 253
Fear, as expression of tête penchée en avant,
  21
Fermeture, 47
Festin de l'Araignée, Le, 72, 91, 231, 237,
  238, 239
Fifth position:
  of arms, definition, 19
  of body, 4, 15
Fille mal gardée, La, 219
Finale, 176*fn*
Final exercise, for men, 365
Fingers clasped (See *Doigts interlacés*)
Fingers extended and close together (See
  Doigts tendus serrés)
Fingers extended and spread apart (See *Doigts
  tendus et écartés*)
Fingersnapping (See *Claquements de doigts*)
Firebird, The (See *L'Oiseau de feu*)
First dance lessons, 390-99

First position, 50, 51, 52
  of arms, definition, 18
  definition, 11, 12
Fish (See also *Poisson*)
  represented in dance, 239
Fist (See also *Poing*), 242
Flames, as symbolic gesture, 245
Flat-footed stamping (See *Piétinement à plat*)
Flic-flac, 301
  definition, 56-57
Flic-flac tombé, definition, 57
Flip-flap *acrobatique,* definition, 193
Flying *entrechat* (See *Entrechat volé*)
Flying insects, dance movements of, 237
Fokine, 18, 21, 23, 40, 91, 107, 112, 129, 134,
  149, 170, 177, 190, 193, 205, 206, 214,
  216, 227, 229, 234, 238, 239, 241, 276,
  279, 283
Fond de jambe, 175
Fondu, 127, 208, 224, 262, 263, 269, 346,
  347
  definition, 87-89
Fondu croisé, 348
Foot, placement of the, 8-10
Foot in the hand (See also *Pied dans la main*)
  correct body position, 340
  exercise, 339-40
Foot on the bar:
  correct body position, 325-26
  exercise for beginning boys, 385
  exercise for beginning girls, 372
  exercise for the child, 396
  exercise for men, 362
  exercises, 325-29
  with no support, 329
Forains, Les, 193
Forward (See *Devant*)
Forward fourth (See *Quatrième devant*)
Forward leap on the hands (See *Saut en avant
  sur les mains*)
Forward somersault (See *Culbute en avant*)
Fouetté, 28, 51, 87, 167, 168, 176*fn,* 278,
  304, 305, 332, 352
  as abbreviation for *rond de jambe fouetté,*
    168
  background of, 175-76
  definition, 56
  essential movements, 56
  number performed, 176
Fouetté à la seconde, 56, 175
Fouetté détourné, 169, 210, 290
  definition, 168-69
Fouetté en quatrième derrière, 56
Fouetté en quatrième devant, 56
Fouetté relevé, 72
Fourberies, 164
Four Temperaments, The, 58, 258
Fourth *croisée,* definition, 29
Fourth position:
  à la demi-hauteur, 158
  of arms, definition, 19
  fundamental, 15
Foyer de la danse, 48*fn*

Franchetti, Raymond, 356
Frappé, 383, 395
  definition, 53
Frappé devant, 337
Free foot, definition, 27
Frottement, 57
Fundamental positions, 11-16

Gaining suppleness, exercise for, 344
Gargouillade, 87, 301
  definition, 110-11
Gestures:
  of animals, 235-40
  varieties of, 232-35
Gigue, definition, 57-58
Girls' dance lesson, exercises at the bar,
    368-73
Giselle, 21, 36, 63, 87, 97, 98, 102, 105, 112,
    126, 158, 159, 161, 167, 174, 178, 180,
    202, 205, 206, 208, 212, 217, 219, 225,
    233, 234, 235, 244, 248, 253, 279, 280,
    292, 294, 299, 356
Glide (See *Glisser; Glissade*)
Glisser, 47
Glissade, 71, 74, 98, 136, 142, 276, 277, 295,
    305, 399
  for beginning boys, 388
  for beginning girls, 376-77
  common first element of a sequence, 290
  definition, 62-64
Glissade-arabesque, definition, 291
Glissade-assemblée, 63, 117, 294, 377
  definition, 291
Glissade battue, as *brisé*, 139
Glissade cabriole, 98, 146
Glissade cabriole battue à la seconde, 290
Glissade composée:
  for beginning boys, 388
  for beginning girls, 377
Glissade derrière, 63
Glissade devant, 63
Glissade-developpé, definition, 290-91
Glissade en descendant, 143, 290, 291, 376,
    377
  definition, 63
Glissade en descendant battue, 137
Glissade en quatrième croisée, 388
Glissade en quatrième derrière, 64
Glissade en quatrième devant, 64
Glissade en remontant, 291, 305, 377
  definition, 63
Glissade en remontant battue, 306
Glissade-entrechat 5, definition, 294
Glissade in second position, variation on, 63
Glissade-jeté, 104, 377
  definition, 291
Glissade-rond de jambe, definition, 291
Glissade-tour piqué, definition, 292
Glissade-tour piqué en attitude, in second, 295
Gounod, Charles, 179, 291
Grand battement:
  correct body position, 338

Grand battement (con't.):
  exercise, 337-38
  exercise for beginning boys, 384
  exercise for the child, 396
Grand battement en quatrième devant, 337,
    338
*Grand battement pointe à terre en quatrième
    devant*, 337
Grand écart facial,
Grand écart, 258, 362
  definition, 190
Grand écart facial, definition, 190
Grand jeté, 108, 123, 131, 179, 180, 279, 280,
    280, 295, 296
  definition, 106-107
  distinguished from *petit jeté*, 107
Grand jeté en attitude, 297
Grand jeté enlevé, 284
Grand jeté en tournant, definition, 179-80
Grand jeté enveloppé, 180
Grand jeté-pas de bourrée enveloppé,
    definition, 293
Grand pas classique, 90
Grand pas de trois, 176, 176*fn*, 178
Grand plié, 392, 393
Grand rond de jambe, 28
  correct body position, 335
  exercise, 335
Grand rond de jambe à la hauteur, definition,
    53
Grand rond de jambe en dedans, 335
Grand rond de jambe-pas de bourrée détourné,
    definition, 292
Grand rond de jambe soutenu, 71, 305
  definition, 54-55
Grand rond de jambe soutenu à la demi-hauteur,
    304
*Grand rond de jambe soutenu à la demi-hauteur
    en dehors*, 346
Grand rond de jambe soutenu à la hauteur, 193
Grand rond de jambe soutenu à la hauteur, 347
*Grand rond de jambe soutenu à la hauteur en
    dehors*, 363
Grand saut, 280, 296, 349
Grande batterie, 135
Grande Jatte, La, 190, 233
Grandeur Nature, 102-103
Grisi, Carlotta, 280
Growing lighter (See *Allègement*)
Gsovsky, Tatiana, 90, 288
Guélis, Jean, 80, 232
Guerra, Nicholas, 64, 224
Guignol et Pandore, 21, 59, 97, 178, 179,
    205, 206, 241
Guillaume Tell, 178
Guillot, Geneviève, 311, 390

Half-bending (See *Demi-Plié*)
Half-fifth (See *Demi-cinquième*)
Half-height (See *Demi-hauteur*)
Half-positions (See Demi-positions)
Hand: (See also *Mains*) 240-45

Hand *(con't.)*:
    when arms are in second position, 240
    movements of particular significance, 244
    position in modern and character ballets,
        241
    representing a claw (See *Main en griffe*)
    as symbol of flames, 245
Hands on the back (See *Mains au dos*)
Hands with fingers extended and joined
        together (See *Mains aux doigts tendus
        accolés*)
Harmony, 2
Hauteur, 28, 53, 55, 69, 98, 117, 142, 143,
    152, 160, 167, 170, 171, 175, 178, 180,
    183, 190, 191, 252, 276, 277, 307, 329,
    333, 335, 337, 338, 344, 348, 360, 362,
    372, 385, 390, 399
    definition, 27
Head bent backward (See *Tête penchée en
        arrière*)
Head bent forward (See *Tête penchée en avant*)
Head bent sideways (See *Tête penchée de côté*)
Head in profile bent backwards (See *Tête de
        profil penchée en arrière*)
Head positions, 20-23
Helpmann, R., 18
Hens, dance movements of, 236
Hindu dance, 45
Hip movement (See *Temps de cuisse*)
Hoist up sail, definition, 232
Hops (See *Sautillement*)
"Horizontal" arm, definition, 198
Horse's step (See *Pas de cheval*)
Horses, dance movements of, 237
Humility, as expression of *tête penchée en
        avant,* 21
Hungarian Dance, 214

Icare, 68, 91, 205, 215, 235
Idylle, 57, 237
Impact (See *Choc*)
Impulse (See *Élan*)
L'Inconnue, 266
Indes galantes, 192, 238
"Indifferent position," definition, 322
"In the knee," (See *Jarret, dans le*)
Isolated *piqués* (See *Piqué isolé*)
Istar, 36, 210, 226, 234
Istomina, Avdotia, 10, 235
Ivanoff, 18, 70, 81, 90, 104, 110, 130, 158,
    160, 175, 200, 205, 221, 225, 243,
    244, 352

Jackson, Rowena, 176
Jarret, dans le, 159
Jeté, 74, 87, 104-11, 125, 180, 184, 292-93,
    304, 305, 306
    for beginning girls, 376
    definition, 104
    followed by a *petit rond de jambe sauté,*
        definition, 293

Jeté battu, 140-41, 186
Jeté en descendant, 293, 304
Jeté en remontant, 293
Jeté-pas de bourrée, not to be confused with
        pas de bourree-jete, 293
Jeté pointé, definition, 106
Jeté-rond de jambe, 293
Jeux d'Enfants, 102, 105-106
Jumping, exercises for, 349-50
Jumps that include beats (See *Saut battu*)
Jungle, 268, 273

Kalamatianos, 76
Kalioujny, A., 107, 170
Kelly, Gene, 37, 91, 243, 266
Khamma, 210
Kneeling (See *Agenouillement*)
Knees bent (See *Plié*)
Korrigane, La, 21, 253

Labis, Attilio, 96, 104, 193, 232
Lac des Cygnes (Bourmeister), 102, 177, 192,
    212, 216, 232, 243, 280, 288
Lac des Cygnes (Petipa and Ivanoff), 70, 71,
    81, 90, 91, 104, 110, 160, 200, 205, 206,
    221, 225, 233, 235, 236, 243, 254, 276
Lachâtre, Maurice, 141
Lady with the Unicorn, The (See *Dame à la
        Licorne, La*)
Lalo, Edouard, 176
Lander, Harald, 83, 88, 103, 143, 175, 176,
    186, 190, 226, 234, 253
Landing (See *Retombée*)
Lapaouri, Alexandre, 280
Lashing (See also *Fouettant*), 378
Lavrovski, 104, 283
Leap (See *Saut*)
Leap intercepted in the air (See *Saut bloqué
        en l'air*)
Leap of the carp (See *Saut de carpe*)
Leap of the fawn (See *Saut du faon*)
Leaping up (See *Sautant*)
Leaping turns (See *Tour Saut*)
Leg movement (See *Temps de cuisse*)
Leg outstretched behind the body (See
        Quatrième derrière)
Legnani, Pierina, 154, 175
Lesson:
    beginning girls, 366-67
    female dancers, 311-14, 353
    male dancers, 356-66
Levinson, André, 283, 284*fn,* 286, 286*fn*
Lifar, Serge, 22, 23, 36, 36*fn,* 37, 37*fn,* 42,
    45, 49, 57, 59, 61, 69, 80, 81, 84, 85,
    89, 90, 91, 92, 97, 102, 103, 105, 107,
    150, 158, 160, 164, 176, 178, 179, 181,
    190, 192, 194, 201, 205, 206, 210, 212,
    214, 215, 216, 219, 220, 225, 226, 227,
    228, 231, 232, 233, 234, 236, 237, 238,
    239, 241, 242, 243, 244, 245, 249, 254,
    255, 280, 281, 352

Lifts (See *Porté*)
Linchine, David, 90, 266
Lion, represented in dance, 238
Little Crippled Horse, The (See *Petit Cheval Bossu, Le*)
Little exercises, definition, 345
Livry, Emma, 235
Louis XIV, 136
Loup, Le, 238
"Low" arm, definition, 197-98
Lucifer, 92, 239

Maanerenen, 238
Machkowski, 280
Main classique féminine, definition, 240
Main classique masculine, definition, 240
Main en griffe, 244-45
Mains au dos, 205
Mains aux doigts tendus accolés, 244
Malheurs de Sophie, Les, 238, 239
Mandolins, 176fn
Manège, 156, 158, 160
    definition, 124, 351-52
Manège de piqués, 159, 356
Marche, 25, 41, 60, 61, 62, 64, 72, 75, 81, 89, 150, 210, 221, 246
    definition, 59
    relation to temps de pointe piques, 67
Marche à quatre pattes, 91, 92
Marche à reculons, definition, 59-60
Marche espagnole, definition, 81
Marche sur la demi-pointe, 276
Marche sur les mains, definition, 193-94
Marche couru sur pointe, 276
Marines, 263
Marquis de Cuevas, 253
Marteau:
    definition, 129
    in second position, definition, 129
Massacre des Amazones, Le, 237
Massine, Léonide, 91, 191, 192, 237, 239, 245
Mazurka, 130, 181, 214, 219, 293
Men's dance lesson, general remarks, 365-66
Mérante, Lucien, 21, 68, 91, 229, 233, 244, 253, 281, 283
Mercury, 40
Messerer, Assaf, 243
Meunier, Antoine, 35, 35fn
Mime, as distinguished from mimicry, 245-46
Mimicry:
    development and use of, 248-49
    distinguished from mime, 245-46
    general statement, 245
    gestures listed, 246-47
    gestures, symbolic, 247-48
    as used in classical dance, 245-49
Miracle in the Gorbals, 18
Mirages, 22, 91, 214, 226, 227, 228, 231, 234, 235, 236, 246, 249, 255
Moment of impulse (See *Temps d'élan*)
Moments, 45
    of movement, 4

Monsters, represented in dance, 239
Moreau, Jacqueline, 367, 390
Mort du Cygne, La, 61, 91, 235
Moulin enchanté, 90
Movement, 2, 45
Movements of the arms (See also *Port de bras*), 18, 197, 225-40
Moving from one place to another (See *Déplacement*)
Myrtil, 284

Namouna, 176
Nautéos, 239
Neck and head of swan, represented by the arm, 236
Nijinsky, 107, 208
Noces Fantastiques, Les, 80, 194, 201, 212, 213, 231, 232, 233, 239, 244
Non battu, 98
Nonjerky stamping (See *Piétinement non saccadé*)
Nonleaping coupe (See *Coupé non sauté*)
Nontraveling steps (See also *Pas à terre sans parcourir*) 47-59
    definition, 46
Nontraveling steps *à terre,* 49
Notre-Dame de Paris, 59, 89, 90, 96, 191, 203, 212, 226, 235, 237, 244

L'Oiseau bleu, 91, 97, 138
L'Oiseau de Feu, 91, 206, 235, 239
On the instep (See *Cou-de-pied*)
One arm lateral positions, 219
One arm low positions, 217
One arm forward positions, 208-11, 218-19
One arm *tendu* positions, 220-21
Open fourth (See *Quatrième ouverte*)
Opening of the feet, exercise for men, 362-63
Opening of the legs, exercise for men, 363
Opéra, 253
Outrepassés, 69
Outstretched (See *Tendu*)
Ouvert, 296
Overextended (See *Outrepassés*)

Panthers, represented in dance, 238
Papillon, Le, 235
Pas, 126, 196
Pas à terre, 46, 82, 139, 148, 275, 351
    definition, 45
Pas à terre sauté, 255
Pas battu, 131
Pas composé, 349
Pas de basque, 74, 126, 187, 300, 399
    definition, 72
    for beginning boys, 389
Pas de basque en descendant, 72, 229, 299, 365, 389

Pas de basque en descendant (con't.):
definition, 73-74
Pas de basque en remontant, 72, 389
definition, 74-75
Pas de batterie, 299
Pas de batterie à croisements, 139
Pas de bourrée, 86, 164, 169, 181, 183,
187, 276, 294, 300, 348, 349,
350, 363, 364, 365, 399
arm movement, 76
for beginning boys, 388
types of, 75-80
Pas de bourrée assemblée, 279, 290
definition, 183
Pas de bourrée assemblée battu,
definition, 187
Pas de bourrée bateau, 78, 302
Pas de bourrée cabriole, 146, 169,
183, 290
Pas de bourrée cabriole battu,
definition, 187
Pas de bourrée cabriole battu derrière,
290
Pas de bourrée cabriole en tournant,
102
Pas de bourrée couru, 143
misnamed, 80
Pas de bourrée dessous, 290, 301, 302,
388
definition, 77
Pas de bourrée dessus, 290, 301, 302,
388
definition, 77
Pas de bourrée dessus et dessous, 77-78,
388
Pas de bourrée détourné, 152, 153, 301, 349,
350, 363
definition, 151
Pas de bourrée double, definition, 79
Pas de bourrée double en descendant, 302
definition, 79
Pas de bourrée double en remontant, 302
definition, 79-80
Pas de bourrée en remontant, 77
Pas de bourrée entrechat, 290, 294
Pas de bourrée enveloppé, 159, 301
definition, 152-53
*Pas de bourrée enveloppé-pas de bourrée
détourné*, 153, 290
Pas de bourrée grand jeté en tournant, 290
definition, 181-83
Pas de bourrée jeté, 86, 182, 183, 202, 279,
281, 350, 352, 365
not to be confused with *jeté-pas de bourrée*,
293
Pas de bourrée relevé en arabesque, 365
Pas de bourrée relevé détourné, 290
definition, 169
Pas de bourrée simple, 78, 79, 302
definition, 75-77
Pas de cabriole non battu, 187
Pas de cheval, definition, 57
Pas de course, 143

Pas de deux (See also *Adagio*) 63, 115, 138,
165, 175, 280, 281, 351, 352, 366
cambres, 276
classical definition, 254
general statement of origin of, 253-54
movements on the ground, 270-75
poses on the ground, 274-75
plié, 258
poses, 256-57
poses of female dancer clinging to partner,
268-70
poses where female dancer does not touch
the ground, 260, 261, 262, 263, 265
poses where female dancer is supported,
262-70
positions balanced for a dancer alone, 258,
260
seated poses, 273-74
shifting of the axes, 257-58
Pas de Dieux, 37, 91, 243, 266
Pas d' élan, 135
Pas de gigue, definition, 80
Pas de liaison, 128
Pas de Patineurs, 176
Patineurs, Les, 227
Pas de polka piquée, definition, 81-82
Pas de trois, as step, 97
Pas de Trois, 90
Pas tombé, 131, 184, 185, 295, 297
definition, 126-27
*Pas tombé-cabriole en quatrième derrière
battue*, definition, 294
Pas tombé-coupé-jeté, 185, 352
definition, 297
Pas tombé en tournant, definition, 184-85
*Pas tombé-pas de bourrée sissonne-pas de
bourré*, 294
Pas tombé-posé-jeté, definition, 295-96
Pas tombé tourné, 180
Passage from one position to another,
definition, 46-47
Passé, 68, 98, 102, 131, 136, 142, 146, 296,
350
definition, 60, 126
Passé-assemblée, 365
Passé-assemblée en quatrième effacée, 117
Passé-assemblé-passé cabriole devant,
definition, 293-94
Passé-cabriole, 72, 210
definition, 98-99, 146
Passé-cabriole battue, 290
Passé cabriole devant, 146
Passé cabriole battue devant, 290
Passé cabriole battue double, definition, 146
Passé-cabriole en quatrième devant, 350, 351
Passé-cabriole en quatrième devant battu,
230
Passé-cabriole non battu, 146, 230, 290
Passé-entrechat 5, definition, 294
Passé relevé, 276, 290, 351
definition, 72
Passé relevé-arabesque, 349
Passé sur pointe, definition, 72

410

Passer la jambe devant, definition, 60
Pause (See *Temps d' arrêt*)
Pause, toe pointed (See *Arrêt pointé*)
Pear tree (See *Poirier*)
Penché, 327, 329, 332, 333
Penché de côté, definition, 326
Penché en arrière, 329
Penché en avant, 17, 36, 325, 329, 342
Père, Le, 280
Peretti, Serge, 91, 232
Péri, La, 275
Perrot, J., 21, 63, 87, 105, 112, 126, 158, 159, 161, 178, 180, 203, 205, 206, 208, 212, 217, 219, 225, 244, 253, 292, 294, 299
Petipa, Lucien, 280
Petipa, Marius, 18, 70, 81, 90, 91, 97, 102, 104, 106, 110, 127, 138, 160, 200, 205, 221, 225, 227, 236, 238, 243, 244, 253, 254, 279, 281, 287, 352
Petit, Roland, 45, 59, 89, 96, 191, 193, 203, 212, 215, 226, 235, 237, 238, 244, 263, 271
Petit Cheval Bossu, Le, 237
Petit battement, 337, 345, 352, 353, 356, 371, 396
  exercise for men, 361
Petit battement sur le cou-de-pied:
  correct body position, 337
  exercise, 336-37
  exercise for beginning boys, 384
  exercise for beginning girls, 371
  exercise for the child, 396
  use with *relevé sur la pointe,* 70
Petit coupé sauté, 102
Petit jeté, 104-106, 108, 126, 140, 351
  compared with *course,* 105
  definition, 104
Petit jeté à la seconde, 106
Petit jeté dessous, 106
  definition, 140
Petit jeté dessus, 106, 130
  definition, 140, 179
Petit jeté en descendant, 104, 106, 291, 299, 304, 306, 376
Petit jeté en remontant, 106, 291, 304, 306, 376
Petit jeté en tournant, 87, 179, 180, 290, 352
Petit pas de bourrée couru, 224
Petit plié, 381
Petit rond de jambe, 110-11, 305
Petit rond de jambe au raccourci en quatrième devant, 123
Petit rond de jambe en dedans, 152, 293
Petit rond de jambe en dehors, 293
Petit rond de jambe soutenu, 80, 305, 360
Petit rond de jambe soutenu à la hauteur, 360
Petit rond de jambe soutenu à la seconde, 291
  definition, 55-56
Petit rond de jambe soutenu en dedans
  in second position, 345

Petit rond de jambe soutenu en quatrième devant, definition, 56
Petit rond de jambe soutenu relevé, 71
Petit saut, 295
Petit série, definition, 306
Petit soubresaut, 351
Petit soubresaut en tournant, 191
Petit soubresaut sur une pointe, 356
Petit soubresaut tourné, definition, 177
  in derivative position, 173-74
Petite batterie, 135, 298, 351
Petite cabriole battue, 351
Petite glissade, 202
Petite sissonne, 351
Petite sissonne en descendant, 126
Petites variations, 352
Petrouchka, 18, 21, 128, 134, 149, 177, 190, 193, 205, 206, 214, 229, 234, 238, 239, 241
Phèdre, 61, 84, 91, 102, 105, 179
Phlegmatic, The, 58
Pied dans la main, definition, 191
Pied en serpette, definition, 333
Piège de Lumière, 237
Piétine, 150
  definition, 149
Piétine en tournant, 150
Piétine in fifth position, definition, 149-50
Piétine in first position, definition, 149
Piétine in second position, definition, 149
Piétinement, definition, 58-59
Piétinement à plat, 58
Piétinement en quatrième normale, 59
Piétinement espagnol, definition, 58
Piétinement non saccadé, definition, 58
Piqué, 68, 159, 161, 162, 349, 351, 352, 398
  for beginning girls, 379
  circle of, 4
  short for *pirouette piquée,* 158
  sur la pique, definition, 65
Piqué à la seconde, 292
  definition, 160
Piqué en arabesque, 160, 292
Piqué en attitude, definition, 159
Piqué derrière, 292
Piqué en cinquième derrière sur la pointe, 292
Piqué en quatrième derrière, 292
Piqué enveloppé, 161
  definition, 160
Piqué enveloppé dans le jarret, 161
Piqué enveloppé en manège, 161
Piqué enveloppé sur un cou-de-pied, 161
Piqué isolé, 67
Piqué sur la demi-pointe, 379
Piqué sur la pointe, 61, 291
  common second element of a sequence, 290
Piqué sur la pointe en arabesque, 356
Pique sur la pointe en attitude, 356
Piquer, definition, 65
Piquer sur la pointe, 67
Pirouette (See also Déboulé), 18, 154
  definition, 157

411

Pirouette (con't.):
  role of arms, 163
Pirouette à deux, 17
Pirouette en dedans, 158
Pirouette en dehors, 158
Pirouette piquée, 157
  definition, 158
Pirouette relevée, 157, 158
Pizzicati, 178, 233
Plat, 11, 15, 23, 24, 45, 57, 58, 60, 61, 63, 64,
  65, 67, 74, 75, 77, 78, 79, 83, 84, 87,
  102, 104, 107, 118, 149, 150, 151, 156,
  158, 159, 161, 162, 163, 167, 168, 169,
  170, 175, 181, 224, 256, 257, 290, 292,
  301, 304, 307, 314, 323, 324, 325, 326,
  329, 334, 336, 337, 344, 346, 347, 348,
  350, 353, 356, 358, 359, 361, 362, 363,
  364, 368, 370, 372, 374, 375, 377, 378,
  379, 380, 382, 384, 385, 386, 387, 392,
  393, 394, 395
Plat en quatrième derrierè, 353, 363, 365, 389
Plat en quatrième devant, 350
Plat en quatrième ouverte, 74
Plié, 36, 51, 69, 78, 82-88, 97, 119, 123, 132,
  134, 138, 139, 142, 148, 163, 167, 173,
  179, 186, 198, 211, 258, 277, 281, 297,
  322, 323, 325, 326, 327, 329, 332, 337,
  343, 346, 347, 353, 357, 358, 361, 381,
  382, 383, 385, 386, 387, 389, 390, 395,
  398, 399
  399
  basic definition, 82
  body position, 319
  in derivative positions, 85-86
  exercise for beginning boys, 382
  exercise for beginning girls, 368
  exercise for the child, 392-93
  exercises for men, 357-58
  lean to the side, 314, 318, 319
  with *port de bras,* for beginning boys, 385
  in various positions, 83-84
Plié à fond, 82
Plié à la demi-hauteur, 86, 87, 383
Plié à la hauteur, 86
Plié en demi-cinquième, 85
Plié en demi-positions, 84
Plié en raccourci, 87, 377
Plié pointe à terre, 84-85
  definition, 87
Plié relevé sur les pointes:
  correct body position, 341-42
  exercise, 340-42
Plissetskaia, Maia, 205, 243
Poing fermé, 243
Point de départ, 112, 113
Pointe, 9, 10, 23, 24, 25, 26, 37, 45, 57, 58, 59,
  60, 64, 65, 68, 74, 75, 77, 78, 79, 80, 81,
  84, 85, 97, 98, 102, 104, 106, 112, 114,
  115, 121, 122, 125, 149, 151, 152, 153,
  154, 155, 156, 158, 159, 162, 163, 164,
  167, 168, 169, 170, 174, 175, 179, 181,
  223, 224, 253, 256, 257, 278, 281, 283,
  290, 291, 292, 301, 302, 303, 307, 311,

Pointe (con't.):
  319, 321, 323, 324, 333, 340-42, 343,
  344, 348, 350, 353, 356, 357, 358, 359,
  361, 363, 365, 368, 373, 377, 379, 380,
  384, 387, 389, 396, 399
Pointe à terre en quatrieme devant, 346
Pointe classique, 9
Pointe en quatrième devant, 151, 160, 332,
  371, 395
Pointe en quatrième, très ouverte, 155
Pointe en raccourci, 260
Pointe in second position, 396
Pointe néo-classique, 9
Pointe oblique, 9
Poirier, definition, 192
Poisson, 167
  definition, 262
Polonaise, definition, 81
Pont, 192, 193
  definition, 191
Porte, 254, 255, 260, 261, 283, 366
  used in acrobatics, 284
  various positions, 286-88
Porté cambré, 208
Port de bras, 18, 87, 197, 201, 202, 207, 209,
  212, 221-25, 230, 277, 346, 347, 348,
  358, 360, 365, 368, 374, 375, 382, 392,
  396, 397, 398
  for beginning boys, 387
  for beginning girls, 373
  definition, 221
  general statements, 225-26
  in various positions, 221-23
Port de bras composé, 346
Port de bras marché:
  for beginning boys, 387
  for beginning girls, 373-74
Port de bras tournant, 223-24, 347, 365, 389
  with a forward progression, definition, 224
Port de bras en troisième croisée, definition,
  224
Pose, 45, 356
Pose d'attitude, 271
Position assise sur les talons, definition,
  89-90
Position croisée, 398
Position de départ, 46, 51, 52, 56, 95, 99, 124,
  154, 161, 199, 200, 202, 208, 221, 222,
  223, 224, 227, 230, 302, 304, 305, 307,
  347, 353, 357, 362, 368, 369, 370, 373,
  375, 376, 378, 380, 382, 385, 387, 391,
  392, 397
  of arms, definition, 18
  definition, 15
Position dérivée, definition, 23
Position effacée, 379
Position on all fours (See *Quatre pattes*)
Positions:
  definition, 11
  number and variety of, 44-45
Pouce seul écarté, 242-43
Pour Piccolo et Mandoline, 262
Praying mantis, represented in dance, 238

Prélude à l'Après-Midi d'un Faune, 91, 242
Prenant pointe fixe, 321
Preparations:
    for *coupé,* beginning girls, 377, 378
    for *fouetté,* exercise, 344
    for *petit rond de jambe soutenu,* beginning
      boys, 384
    for *tour,* beginning girls, 380
Prince Igor, 21, 128, 129, 170, 214, 229, 234,
    254, 283
Procession (See *Defile*)
Prodigal Son, The, 269
Profil:
    combined with *tête penchée en avant,* 22
    definition, 21
Progression (See also *Déplacement*) 95
Projected leaps (See *Saut porté*)
Prokofieff, S., 288
Prudhommeau, G., 154*fn*, 183*fn*, 235*fn*
"Pruning-knife foot" (See *Pied en serpette*)
"Pushed" arabesque (See *Arabesque poussée*)
Pushkin, A., 235
Pyrénées, Les, 94

Quatre pattes, 91
Quatrième, derivative position, 26
Quatrième croisée, 15, 87, 99, 123, 124, 224,
    269, 347, 351
    derivative position, 26
Quatrième croisée devant, 324
Quatrième croisée devant à la demi-hauteur,
    138
Quatrième croisée devant à la hauteur, 385
Quatrième derrière, 28, 30, 33, 36, 52, 56, 61,
    62, 64, 86, 87, 91, 102, 103, 104, 112,
    127, 146, 157, 160, 164, 165, 169, 175,
    182, 183, 187, 224, 323, 325, 326, 329,
    334, 335, 337, 346, 358, 359, 360, 361,
    370, 372, 374, 375, 385, 386, 394, 395,
    396
Quatrième derrière raccourci, 31-32
Quatrième derrière à la demi-hauteur, 138,
    186, 388
Quatrième derrière à la demi-hauteur ouverte,
    138
Quatrième derrière à la hauteur, 33, 51,
    99, 107, 112, 117, 142, 143, 146,
    174, 182, 185, 273, 329, 335, 360,
    362
Quatrième derrière à plat, 380
Quatrième derrière à la pointe, 162
Quatrième derrière croisée, 74
Quatrième derrière, derrière à la demi-
    hauteur, 127
Quatrième derrière ouverte, 51, 78
    definition, 30
Quatrième derrière ouverte à la hauteur,
    168
Quatrième derrière raccourci, 31-32
Quatrième derrière très croisée, 150
Quatrième devant, 28, 52, 56, 59, 60, 61,
    62, 65, 72, 73, 74, 81, 82, 86, 87,

Quatrième devant, (con't.):
    91, 102, 104, 107, 123, 125, 129,
    130, 136, 146, 151, 156, 157, 164,
    169, 171, 175, 179, 182, 246, 296,
    301, 323, 325, 327, 339, 340, 348,
    351, 358, 359, 360, 363, 370, 372,
    374, 375, 383, 395
Quatrième devant à la demi-hauteur,
    57, 67, 81, 158, 179, 186, 304,
    388
Quatrième devant à la hauteur, 51, 56, 60,
    103, 107, 112, 117, 123, 142, 185,
    257, 294, 329, 331, 335, 347, 360,
    361, 362
Quatrième devant à la hauteur, effacée,
    125
Quatrième devant à la hauteur sur une
    pointe, 276
Quatrième devant à la pointe, 362
Quatrième devant à peine ouverte, 158
Quatrième devant croisée, 223, 347
Quatrième devant croisée à la hauteur, 180
Quatrième devant ouverte à la hauteur, 99,
    113, 126, 296
Quatrième devant point à terre, 373
Quatrième devant raccourci, 31, 156
Quatrième effacée, definition, 30, 40
Quatrième effacée cambrée, definition, 41
Quatrième ouverte, 15, 30, 40, 57, 78, 85,
    112, 123, 127, 142, 269, 296, 351
    definition, 29
    derivative position, 26
Quatrième ouverte à la demi-hauteur, 78,
    113
Quatrième ouverte derrière, 126, 324
Quatrième ouverte derrière à la demi-
    hauteur, 126-27
Quatrième très ouverte, 154
Quinault, Robert, 238, 286

Raccourci, 44, 55, 56, 57, 60, 64, 87, 104,
    106, 108, 110, 115, 125, 126, 153,
    157, 158, 159, 160, 161, 162, 164,
    165, 166, 170, 173, 174, 175, 178,
    179, 256, 260, 276, 292, 296, 297, 301,
    304, 305, 307, 308, 320, 322, 335, 339,
    340, 341, 344, 347, 349, 352, 361, 362,
    370, 372, 379, 380, 384, 388
    correct body positions, 321
    definition, 21, 31
    exercise for beginning girls, 370
    exercises, 320-22
Raccourci à la seconde, 55, 343
Raccourci derrière, 126, 306
Raccourci devant, 126
Raccourci en quatrième derrière, 33, 38, 56,
    57, 64, 65, 67, 74, 140, 153, 191, 257,
    258
Raccourci en quatrième devant, 56, 58, 90,
    123, 125, 140, 160, 161, 179, 183, 191,
    271, 325, 332, 339, 344
Raccourci en quatrième devant très croisée,

Raccourci en quatrième (con't.):
  321
Raccourci sur la demi-pointe, 361, 384
Raccourcissement, 333
Race (See *Course*)
Raide, 241
Real and adapted gestures, character on
  horseback, 234-35
Reculbute, 193
Reindeer, dance movements of, 237-38
Reins cassés, 191
Relevé, 68, 71, 82, 84, 86, 166, 171, 210, 302,
  329, 340, 341, 349, 352, 379, 385, 398
  in derivative positions, 69
  exercise for beginning boys, 384-85
  exercise for beginning girls, 373, 378
Relevé en arabesque, 349, 365
Relevé en dehors, 348
Relevé en raccourci, definition, 69
Relevé en tournant, 301
Relevé plié, exercise for men, 360-61
Relevé sur demi-pointes, 69, 327, 329, 334,
  342, 344, 346, 347, 360, 370, 373,
  380, 384, 385, 386, 387, 389
Relevé sur la pointe, 72, 87, 291, 296, 297,
  304, 344, 351
  common second element of a sequence,
  290
Relevé sur la pointe en attitude, 115
Relevé sur les deux demi-pointes, 361, 378,
  definition, 68
Relevé sur les deux pointes, various uses of,
  69
Remontant, 67, 301, 374
  definition, 48
Renard, 96, 237, 238
Renault, Michel, 164
Rencontre, La, 266
Retombée, 121
Révérence, 85, 87, 207, 365, 398
  for beginning girls, 380
  definition, 353
Revolta, definition, 185, 186
Rhythm, 3
Rising half-turns (See *Demi-tour relevé*)
Rising on the toes (See *Relevé sur les deux
  pointes*)
Rising turns (See *Tour relevé*)
Rising turns performed on the ground on one
  foot (See *Tour à terre relevé sur un
  pied*)
Rising up (See *Pointe*)
Robbins, Jerome, 232, 238, 239, 242, 243,
  265
Roméo et Juliette (Aveline), 291
Roméo et Juliette (Béjart), 104, 111, 179,
  192, 217, 274
Roméo et Juliette (Gsovsky), 288
Roméo et Juliette, (Labis), 193, 232
Roméo et Juliette (Larrovski), 283
Rond de jambe, 52, 53, 55, 224, 305, 325,
  349, 395, 397

Rond de jambe (con't.):
  for beginning boys, 386-87
  definition, 53
  done with *relevé sur la pointe,* 71
  exercise for beginning boys, 383
  exercise for beginning girls, 369
  exercise for the child, 394-95
Rond de jambe à terre, 366, 160
  correct body position, 325
  definition, 53
  exercise, 324-25
  exercises for men, 359-60
Rond de jambe à terre en dedans, 224, 324,
  358
Rond de jambe à terre en dehors, 324, 358,
  359
Rond de jambe à terre plié:
  correct body position, 325
  definition, 53
  exercises, 325
Rond de jambe en dedans, 335, 336, 360,
  369, 373, 374, 383, 395
Rond de jambe en dedans à la demi-hauteur,
  383
Rond de jambe en dehors, 335, 336, 346,
  359, 360, 369, 374, 383, 386, 387,
  394
Rond de jambe en dehors à la demi-hauteur,
  383, 386
Rond de jambe en tournant, 305
Rond de jambe fouetté, definition, 175
Rond de jambe soutenu, 352
  definition, 54
  exercise for men, 360
  in second position, correct body position,
  336
*Rond de jambe soutenu à la demi-hauteur
  décomposé,* 388
*Rond de jambe soutenu à la demi-hauteur en
  dehors,* 387
Ronde, 102
  definition, 150
Rooster, dance movements of, 237
Rosen, H., 237
Roue, definition, 193
Rouleau, 3
  definition, 227
Round back (See *Dos rond*)
Round dance (See *Ronde*)
Rowe, Iris, 284
Royal, definition, 135-36
Rubbing the head against the feathers, 236
Running step (See *Couru*)
Russian dancing (See *Danse russe*)

Sacre de Printemps, Le, 85, 89, 90, 91, 96,
  206, 226, 243, 249, 255, 268, 274
Sailor, 80
Saint-Léon, 21, 40, 58, 76, 80, 98, 124, 130,
  205, 206, 214, 219, 243, 253, 293
St. Petersburg (Russia), 175

Salade, 103, 220
Salut (*See also* Bow) 398
   for beginning boys, 389-90
   definition, 365
Santons, 106
Sarabande, 96
Saut, 45, 82, 84, 86, 87, 98, 103, 106, 118,
   120, 126, 127, 128, 129, 131, 140, 141,
   142, 176, 181, 184, 185, 230, 252, 280,
   292, 295, 296, 311, 334, 351, 357, 367,
   381, 399
   for beginning boys, 389
   for beginning girls, 376
   for the child, 398
   classified according to logic of technique, 95
   common second element of a sequence, 290
   definition, 94, 95
   executed on both feet, 103
   exercise for men, 364
   temps simples, 95-130
Saut à pied joints (See also *Soubresaut*) 95,
   141
Saut battu, 131, 186
Saut bloqué en l'air, 280, 281
Saut de l'ange, definition, 97
Saut de basque, 187
   definition, 125-26
Saut de carpe, definition, 129
Saut de chat, 87, 110, 111, 131, 294, 299,
   301, 356
   definition, 108-109, 181
Saut de chat en tournant, 87
Saut du faon, definition, 123
Saut en avant sur les mains, definition, 193
Saut isolé, 123
Saut porté, 243
Saut simple, 131, 139
Sautant, as third method of rising on the toes,
   68
Sauté, 127, 185
Sautillements, 174, 175, 178
"Scissors leap," 123
Sea-horses, represented in dance, 239
Seated position on the heels (See also *Position
   assise sur les talons*) 89
Second position:
   of arms, definition, 19
   fundamental definition, 12-13
   derivative position, 26
   as *raccourci,* 31
Seconde à la demi-hauteur, 57, 292
Second à hauteur, 4, 53, 156, 174, 290,
   292
Seconde effacée (See *Quatrieme effacee*)
Semi-arabesque, 210
"Semi-horizontal" arm, definition, 198
"Semi-vertical" arm, definition, 198
Sequences (See also *Enchaînements*)
   composed of three elements, 295-97
   exercise for men, 365
   with four elements, 298-300
   formed of two elements, 290-95

Serial arrangement of poses (See also
   Enchaînement) 8
Series, 300-308
   assemblée, definition, 303-304
   balancing acts, definition, 302
   definition, 300
   échappé, definition, 303
   pas de bourée, definition, 301-302
   petit sissonne, definition, 303
   relevé, definition, 301
   rond de jambe, definition, 304-306
Series de tours en dedans, definition, 307-308
Series de tours prepared in fourth, definition,
   306-307
Series de tours taken directly, definition, 308
Serre, 314*fn,* 326
Set-back fourth (See *Quatrième effacée*)
Set-back fourth, arched (See *Quatrième
   effacée cambrée*)
Seventh position, definition, 15
Shame, as expression of *tête penchée
   en avant,* 21
Shéhérazade, 128
Shellfish, represented in dance, 239
Shortening (See *Raccourci*)
Shoulder twisted forward (See *Epaulé*)
Shouldering (See also *Epaulement*) 353
Siang-Sing, 90, 118, 244
Single *adagio,* 252-53
   à la hauteur, 256
   arabesque, 256
   attitude, 256
   écarté, 256
   effacée, 256
   fondu, 256
   port de bras, 256
   posé, 256
   quatrième derrière, 256
   quatrième devant, 256
   second position, 256
   training for poses, 256
Single movement (See *Temps*)
Sissonne, 86, 111-15, 146, 177, 279, 299,
   300, 349, 357, 399
   compared with *assemblée,* 115-16
   definition, 111
Sissonne avec un choc, 146
Sissonne double, 114
Sissonne en descendant, 111-12, 113, 181,
   296, 303
   variation, 112-13
Sissonne en raccourci, 111, 115, 118, 127,
   305
Sissonne en raccourci en quatrième derrière,
   115
Sissonne en raccourci en quatrième devant,
   definition, 115
Sissonne en remontant, definition, 113, 296,
   303
Sissonne en tournant, 177
   definition, 181
Sissonne in second position, definition,

Sissonne in second position *(con't.):*
113-14
Sissonne-posé-assemblée, 114
Sitting turns (See *Tour pose*)
Sixth position:
of arms, definition, 19
fundamental definition, 12
Skibine, Georges, 57, 84, 89, 92, 106, 186,
192, 205, 228, 232, 237, 242, 263, 272,
275
Slavenska, Mia, 176
Soir de Fête, 104, 180, 249
Solo, 68, 69
Solo adagio:
battement, 276
dégagé, 276
détourné, 277
developpé, 276
enveloppé, 277
fouetté, 276
grand rond de jambe soutenu, 276
pas à terre sans parcours, 276
pas à terre avec parcours, 276
pas de bourrée détourné, 277
pas de bourrée relevé détourné, 278
petit rond de jambe soutenu, 276
piétine in fifth sur la pointe, 277
plié, 277
relevé sur pointe or demi-pointe, 276
rond de jambe, 276
saut, 279
tours, 277-78
Somersault (See *Culbute*)
Soubresaut, 83, 104, 111, 129, 131, 141, 142,
168, 174, 177, 291, 293, 297, 303, 304,
306, 389, 398, 399
for beginning girls, 376
definition, 95
in various positions, 96-98
Soubresaut battu, as entrechat, 139
Soubresaut en quatrième derrière, 98
Soubresaut en quatrième devant, 103
Soubresaut en quatrième devant
à demi-hauteur, 97-98
Soubresaut en raccourci, 102
Soubresaut en raccourci en attitude, 102-103
Soubresaut en raccourci en quatrième
derrière, 102
Soubresaut en raccourci en quatrième devant,
102, 141
Soubresaut en raccourci in second position,
102
Soubresaut sur la pointe, 103, 356, 176
Soubresaut tourné, 86, 177
in derivative position, 178
substitute for *tour à l'Italienne*
Soubresaut tourné sur la pointe, 178-79
Spectre de la Rose, Le, 107
Spider, represented in dance, 238
Split-type separation (See *Ecart*)
Spotting, definition, 155
Springing steps (See *Pas d'élan*)

"Square" (See also *Carré*)
term used with sequences and music, 298
Staats, Leo, 90, 104, 118, 244, 249
Stampings (See *Piétinement*)
Star, The, 179
Steps, naming and classifying, 68
Stiff position (See *Raide*)
Street, The, 241
Striking (See *Choc*)
Stoutchkova, Raissa, 280
Sudden bounds or leaps (See *Soubresaut*)
Suite de Danses, 81, 90, 98, 115, 125, 225,
228, 281, 299
Suite en Blanc, 90, 103, 150, 158, 176, 178,
180, 181, 219, 225, 228, 252, 254, 280,
281
Suppleness:
correct body positions, 342-43
exercise for beginning boys, 385
exercise for beginning girls, 372
exercises for men, 359
Sursaut, 381
Sustained (See *Soutenu*)
Swan Lake, 18
Sylphide, La, 216, 235, 244
Sylphides, Les, 112, 206, 227, 276, 279
Sylvia, 21, 68, 91, 233, 244, 283
Symphonie Concertante, La, 21, 37, 91, 191,
196, 215, 226, 242, 243, 245, 249, 253,
257, 258, 260, 271, 274
Symphonie Fantastique, La, 91, 191, 192,
237, 239, 245
Symphonie pour un homme seul, 242
Symphony in C, 176

Tabby-Cat, The, 238
Taglioni, Marie, 10, 216, 235, 244
Talon, sur le, 149
Tarantella, 160
Taras, 237
Tears, as expression of *tête penchée en*
avant, 21
Temps, 74, 76, 77, 81, 112, 118, 125, 302,
303, 373, 374, 376, 382, 384, 395, 399
Temps d'arrêt, 304, 356, 376, 377, 389
Temps de bottes, definition, 130
Temps de bottes-pas de basque en
descendant, 293
Temps de cuisse, 307, 346, 348
definition, 51
Temps d'élan, 107
Temps de flèche, 4, 123-25, 131, 345
Temps de pointe, 171, 292, 293
also called *piqués,* 64, 65, 67, 68
on both feet, 292
Temps de pointe-coupé fouetté, 299
Temps de pointe détourné, 151
Temps de pointe en descendant, 67
definition, 65
Temps de pointe en remontant, 67, 299
definition, 64

Temps de pointe in second position, definition, 67
Temps de pointe piqué, 166, 276
  relationship with *marche*, 67
Temps de pointe piqué en descendant, 351, 356
Temps de pointe piqué en remontant, 351
Temps de pointe piqué en remontant-petit jeté en descendant, 292-93
Temps de pointe relevé, 165, 302, 350
Temps de valse, definition, 81
Temps relevé sur les pointes, 169
Temps sauté, 148, 169
Tendu, 51, 198, 206, 323, 326, 331
  classical definition, 199
Tendu en demi-arabesque, 281
Tendu lateral, definition, 207-208
Terre, 57, 140, 230, 338
Tête de face, definition, 20-21
Tête de profil penchée en arrière, definition, 23
Tête penchée de côté, definition, 21
Tête penchée en arrière, definition, 22
Tête penchée en avant, 21
Thaïs, 227
Théâtre Marie, 175
Théâtre National de l'Opéra, 48*fn*, 68
Theme and Variations, 123, 266
Third position:
  of arms, definition, 19
  fundamental definition, 13-14
Three-Cornered Hat, The, 64
Thumb alone held apart (See *Pouce seul écarté*)
Tiroirs (See also Drawers) 98
  definition, 98*fn*
Toe on the ground (See *Pointe à terre*)
Tolling of bell movement (See *Cloche*)
Tour, 45, 82, 84, 126, 128, 148-76, 181, 184, 203, 207, 212, 214, 230, 262, 284, 295, 297, 308, 311, 344, 348-49, 351, 356, 367
  for beginning girls, 380
  with change of feet, 290
  exercises for men, 364
  general comments, 148
  general methods of execution, 171-72
  momentum for, 163
  movement of the head, 155
  prepared for by a *temps de pointe relevé*, 290
  prepared in fifth, 290
  role of arms, 163
  in second position *en dedans relevé*, 364
Tour à l'Italienne, definition, 173-74
Tour à terre, 175, 176
  definition, 149
Tour à terre relevé, 156
Tour à terre relevé sur un pied, 162-76
Tour à terre sur deux pieds, 149-56
Tour à terre sur un pied, 156-62

Tour au raccourci, 171
Tour au raccourci en quatrième devant, 180
Tour chaîné (See *Pirouette* or *Deboule*) 154
Tour de force, 175, 286
Tour de promenade, definition, 156
  with change of position, definition, 157
Tour de soubresaut en raccourci en quatrième devant, 178
Tour de soubresaut en arabesque, 179
Tour en arabesque, 122, 160, 308, 363
Tour en attitude, 122, 356
  definition, 173
Tour en changeant de pied, definition, 170
Tour en dedans, 122, 165, 170, 224, 356
  definition, 163
  terminated by a *fondu*, 278
Tour en dehors, 122, 165, 170, 175, 350
  definition, 163
  terminated by a *fondu*, 278
Tour en dehors relevé, 364
Tour en demi-arabesque, 160
Tour en l'air, 68, 90, 97, 141, 292
  definition and types, 177
  exercise for men, 365
  simple, 297
Tour enveloppé piqué en attitude, definition, 161-62
Tour enveloppé piqué en raccourci en quatrième devant, definition, 161
Tour enveloppé relevé, 348
Tour fouetté détourné, 349
Tour fouetté enveloppé, 174, 295, 297, 349
  definition, 167
  position of trunk and head, 168
Tour in second position en dedans, definition, 171
Tour piqué, 164, 210, 295
Tour piqué en arabesque, definition, 160
Tour piqué en attitude, 356
Tour piqué en quatrième devant, definition, 160
Tour piqué-failli, 295
Tour piqué posé en attitude, 173
Tour posé, 350, 349
  definition, 162
Tour posé en attitude, definition, 162
Tour prepared in fourth position *en dehors*, definition, 164-65
Tour relevé, 84, 87, 178, 294
  categories of, 163
  definition, 162-63
Tour relevé en arabesque, 165
Tour relevé en arabesque en dedans, 363
Tour relevé en attitude, 163, 165
Tour relevé en attitude en dehors, 307, 308
Tour relevé en dedans, 307, 348, 356
  prepared for by a *temps de pointe relevé* on both feet, 167
Tour relevé en dehors, 306, 307, 308, 348, 349, 364
Tour relevé en dehors en cinquième derrière,

Tour relevé en dehors (con't.):
  363
Tour relevé en dehors prepared for by a
  temps de pointe relevé on both feet,
  definition, 165-66
Tour relevé en dehors prepared in fourth
  position-*tour fouetté enveloppé*, 295
Tour relevé in second position *en dehors,*
  definition, 170-71
Tour relevé in second position *sur un pied pris
  directement,* 174
Tour relevé in second prepared for by a
  dégagé, 290
Tour relevé prepared for in fourth by a
  pas de bourrée, 290
Tour relevé prepared in fourth *en dedans,*
  definition, 165
Tour relevé preparé sur deux pieds,
  definition, 164
Tour relevé sur un pied, various types,
  172-75
Tour ressauté, 179
Tour sauté, 86, 87, 176-87
Tour sur pointe, 90, 164
Traité de Danse académique, 36, 36*fn,* 42
Transition steps (See *Pas de liaison*)
Traveling steps (See also *Pas à terre avec
  parcours*) 59-82
  definition, 46
Trépak, 128, 130
Troisième cinquième croisée, 394
Troisième croisée, 224, 307
Tulipe de Harlem, La, 175
Turn in the air (See also *Tour en l'air*) 68

Turns performed on the ground on both
  feet (See *Tour à terre sur deux pieds*)
Tutu, 200, 202

Unequal *pliés,* definition, 85

Vainonen, V., 280, 287
Valse, definition, 81
Valse, La, 280
Van Dantzig, Rudi, 268, 273
Variation, definition, 167
Vaussard, Christiane, 381
Vertical (See *Haut*)
"Vertical" arm, definition, 198
Violon, Le, 271
Vronska, 284

Walk (See *Marche*)
West Side Story, 243
Whipping motion (See *Fouetté*)
Wigman, Mary, 241
Will, of the subject, 3
Wingless insects, represented in dance, 238
Wolf, represented in dance, 238

Young Stork, The (See *Le Cigogneau*)

Zadig, 107, 194
Zambelli, Carlotta, 154
Zucchi, Virginia, 154